WOMEN of the
New Testament

Also by Camille Fronk Olson

Women of the Old Testament
Mary, the Mother of Jesus
In the Hands of the Potter
Mary, Martha, and Me
Too Much to Carry Alone

WOMEN of the New Testament

CAMILLE FRONK OLSON

Paintings by ELSPETH YOUNG

AL R. YOUNG, AND ASHTON YOUNG

DESERET BOOK

SALT LAKE CITY, UTAH

Library of Congress Cataloging-in-Publication Data
Olson, Camille Fronk, author.
  Women of the New Testament / Camille Fronk Olson ; paintings by Elspeth Young, Al R. Young, and Ashton Young.
      pages cm
  Includes bibliographical references and index.
  ISBN 978-1-60907-918-5 (hardbound : alk. paper)
1. Bible. New Testament—Biography. 2. Women in the Bible—Biography. 3. Women in Christianity—History—Early church, ca. 30–600.
I. Young, Elspeth C., illustrator. II. Young, Al R., illustrator. III. Young, Ashton, illustrator. IV. Title.
  BS2445.O47 2014
  225.9'22082—dc23   2014006629

Printed in China
Global Interprint, Inc., Shenzhen, China

10   9   8   7   6   5   4   3   2   1

For Emily and Dave

CONTENTS

ACKNOWLEDGMENTS

I thank the many people who assisted and inspired me in the production of this book. It was the numerous classes of students in my Women in the Scriptures courses both at Brigham Young University and earlier at the Institute of Religion near the University of Utah that first assisted me to organize my thoughts and identify the questions associated with a study on biblical women. A BYU graduate, Letty Preston Goering, maintained an interest in the subject eight years after the class and volunteered to edit and organize the manuscript in a brilliant way that made me a better writer.

I am indebted to BYU colleagues who shared their expertise in ancient history, sources, language, and archaeology as well as insights into the stories and questions I posed. The generous assistance I received from Lincoln Blumell, Matt Grey, Shon Hopkin, Eric Huntsman, Kerry Muhlestein, Kelly Ogden, Don Parry, Stephen Robinson, Gaye Strathearn, Stephen Ricks, and Thom Wayment was invaluable and clearly led to a better manuscript. I am grateful to my former department chair, Dennis Largey; former and current deans, Terry Ball and Brent Top, respectively; and mentor, Robert Millet, for their long-time encouragement and support in making available resources to do the research necessary for the book. Student assistants at BYU—Matthew Merrill, Jenna King Cannon, Emma Watkins, Ben Berlin, Corbin Jacobs, Kindal McGill, Kimberly Sowards, Helena Steinacker, and Ashley Thompson—made their mark on this project by hours of source finding, source checking, and formatting. Jeanine Ehat, department secretary for Ancient Scripture, has served me well as an editor, assistant, and friend. Colleagues Kent P. Jackson, Richard Neitzel Holzapfel, David Whitchurch, and George Pierce freely contributed photographs and commissioned artwork that represent years of experience in the Holy Land.

An essential component of this book, as of its companion volume, *Women of the Old Testament,* is the original artwork that Al Young and his daughter Elspeth and son Ashton created. Tanner, the youngest of Al and Nancy's three children, created the maps for this book. Working with the Young family has been a constant blessing and inspiration for this project from its inception. Their devotion to the Savior and his gospel is recognized through their work.

Working with Deseret Book has again been a privilege. My deepest thanks to Sheri Dew and Jana Erickson, who believed in this project from the beginning and found ways to make it manageable; to Suzanne Brady, for her astute editing eye; and to designer Shauna Gibby and typographer Malina Grigg for making the final product visually engaging.

Without question, my greatest support and cheerleader is my husband, Paul, who read and critiqued the first drafts of each chapter and ate meager meals without complaint while I worked. I have dedicated this volume to his children ("our" children), Emily and Dave, for their exemplary, Christlike acceptance of me since I joined the family. They demonstrate what was vital in the early Christian church and is still essential today if we would "be one" with the Savior and our Father (John 17:21), regardless of how we finally come to the place of belief.

Sidon

SYRIA

Damascus

Tyre

THE HOLY LAND

GALILEE

Capernaum
Bethsaida
Magdala
Sea of Galilee
Cana
Sepphoris
Nazareth
Tiberias

DECAPOLIS

Caesarea

SAMARIA

Jordan River

Sychar

Mt. Gerizim ︿

Joppa

Lydda

Emmaus
Jericho
Jerusalem ✳
Bethany
Ein Kerem
Bethlehem

PEREA

The Dead Sea
Machaerus

JUDEA

IDUMEA

NABATEA

SCALE   20 miles

THE ROMAN EMPIRE

N

MACEDONIA

ACHAIA

Thyatira
Lydia

Athens

Corinth • • Cenchrea

Tiber River

Rome

ITALY

MACEDONIA

Philippi •
Thessalonica •

Troas •

ASIA

GALATIA

• Iconium
Lystra • • Derbe

Antioch •

SYRIA

Ephesus •

Chalcis •

Berytus •

ACHAIA

Tyre •

Jerusalem •

Alexandria

EGYPT

Nile River

200 miles

SCALE

INTRODUCTION

*M*ore than fifty specific women are introduced in the New Testament with multitudes of others numbered in the crowds. By examining clues in the scriptural text and hints from ancient primary sources, my intent is to provide historical and cultural context to illuminate these women's lives. I hope to create a fuller picture of what it would have been like to be a female disciple of Christ in the first century. In the process, my wish is to invite you, the reader, to know Christ better by exploring his example and teachings through the eyes of the women of the New Testament. This unique perspective writes women back into history. It provides a glimpse from a different angle into the ancient world, hopefully to inspire readers toward a deeper reverence for the gift of the Savior and a greater commitment to serve him.

The historical context for women of the New Testament comes from the first-century Roman empire in which they lived. Collectively, they represent many different ethnic, social, and economic backgrounds. Although many came from religious traditions of idol worshipping in Greco-Roman societies where Jews were a minority, most of these women first encountered Christianity as Jews. They made their homes in and around Jerusalem, Galilee, and among Gentiles in cities where a synagogue was established.

Female disciples of Jesus Christ are frequently described in the New Testament as devout believers who eagerly served and sacrificed to follow him. Some, like Phebe and Prisca, were co-workers with the apostle Paul in his efforts to proclaim truth and spread the gospel. Others were key witnesses to Jesus' role as the Son of God. Mary, Elisabeth, and Anna all bore powerful witness of him both before and after he was born. In John's record, the Savior first confirmed to an unnamed woman in Samaria that he was the Christ, and he declared that he was the resurrection and the life to another woman, Martha, shortly before he died on the cross. In a unique way, Martha's sister, Mary, accepted the Savior's need to give his life and so anointed him in preparation for his death while other disciples attempted to prevent it. And in the crowning moment of his ministry, the Redeemer showed himself as the firstfruits of the resurrection to Mary Magdalene before anyone else. In turn, each of these women then bore her witness of truth to men. Consistently, the New Testament portrays women as abundantly capable of understanding doctrine, receiving revelation through the Spirit, and nurturing testimony in others.

UNDERSTANDING CULTURAL CONTEXT

A vast cultural chasm separates us and the world of the past. True, God is the same, his plan of salvation is constant, and his gospel focus does not change; but the way ancient peoples thought—their social norms, values, and cultural structure—is remarkably alien to our way of life. Due to the diverse nature of opportunities for women at the time, background information describing the social and religious milieu is essential for understanding the role and status of New Testament women. To establish this cultural backdrop, introductory essays for sections in this book on Jewish (including Galilean), Samaritan, and Greco-Roman societies precede chapters on corresponding individual women of the New Testament. Where applicable, each essay provides a general description of the land, the people of that region, the social hierarchy, religious influence, women at home, women in the public sphere, and educational possibilities for women. Where corresponding detail is not provided in the scriptural stories of each woman, these panoramic views of society offer texture and cultural meaning to the story.

Cultural differences distinguished the myriad of peoples within the Roman empire, with the sharpest distinction being between Jewish society and the widespread Greco-Roman society with its strong Hellenistic influences. Also, expanded participation for women in the public sphere grew significantly during the first century, including within some Christian societies. Through the lens of these cultural dynamics, it becomes readily apparent that a knowledge of the various norms in antiquity is an essential element in the story of the birth and spread of Christianity.

In both Jewish and Greco-Roman societies anciently, opportunities for social mobility and pursuing one's talents for the betterment of society were strictly limited by family origins. Dynamics such as population density, degree of urbanization, level of technology, distribution of wealth, level of education and literacy, shared values, and acceptable roles for men and women created communities and perspectives that challenge our imaginations and sensibilities. Just as modern-day readers must confront dissonance between their world and the ancient world, so a similar disconnect often prevented Hellenists from understanding and appreciating Jewish attitudes and practices. The strictly distinct nature of Judaism and Israel's remarkable history kept the Jews decidedly apart from the rest of the empire as much at the end of the century as at the beginning. Notwithstanding, Jews and Jewish Christians were not impervious to the ubiquitous Hellenistic influences that surrounded them even in the Jewish territories.

Though public space and political and commercial functions were traditionally considered male domains while the domestic sphere and home life were considered female space, in a change that began in Rome and gradually spread eastward, women in the first century increasingly took part in public forums. This participation included being active preachers, patrons, and public servants. This trend of participation moving eastward from Rome coincided with the spread of Christianity westward from the Holy Land to facilitate Christian women's early contributions as witnesses, teachers, patronesses, and co-workers with the apostles.

CHRIST'S INFLUENCE ON WOMEN

A major purpose of this volume is to explore the influence of Jesus Christ and his gospel on women. Independent of their social or cultural background, women of the New Testament who encountered Jesus or his gospel witnessed behavior or heard teachings that communicated that they had intrinsic value. In the face of so many self-righteous leaders and in contrast to later-recorded rabbinic teachings about women, Jesus dared to defy cultural taboos against publicly associating with women, defending them, and proclaiming their virtues. At the same time, stories about these women convey their need for repentance and redemption made possible only through the righteousness of Christ. Finally, at times Jesus described himself in feminine terms that further aligned himself with women's experiences and roles.

Instead of restricting women to a certain role or defining them by their relationship to men—someone's daughter, wife, or mother—Jesus saw them first as individuals with agency to choose how they would use their God-given gifts. Notably, the scriptures record no statements by Jesus that articulate women's roles or status. Instead, the scriptural narrative shows that he valued women collectively and individually by the way he interacted with them.[1]

Jesus publicly drew attention to the sincere and faith-filled actions of women whose existence had previously been invisible in public. He conspicuously befriended women and men who were outcasts and sinners, and they gladly embraced his invitation to follow him. Without being patronizing or embarrassing, Jesus' efforts to bless and support the downtrodden unmistakably communicated that he preferred time spent with them over more prestigious encounters with the social elite.

Amid repressive traditions that so often marginalized and even silenced women outside the confines of home, the Savior communicated through his expanded ministry that women were needed as disciples and ministers. In contrast to rabbinic sayings that proclaimed, "The woman, says the law, is in all things inferior to the man" (*Apion* 2.201) and "Rather should the words of Torah be burned than entrusted to a woman" (*mSot* 3.4), Jesus invited women to "come, follow me," right along with the men (Luke 18:22). The profound differences between Christ's teachings and rabbinic traditions about women appear often in this volume. A dramatic example is revealed by contrasting their views on marriage and divorce. Perceiving women as chattel to be discarded at will, Jewish law allowed a man to divorce his wife for any reason. Jesus considered marriage to offer similar rights to men and women and placed equal responsibilities to preserve the sanctity of marriage on both husbands and wives (Matt. 19:3–10; 5:32; Mark 10:2–9).

Collectively New Testament women illustrate humankind's desperate need for redemption and the enabling power that is available only through the Redeemer. Regardless of circumstance, illness, poverty, sin, abandonment, or death of a family member, their lives signaled a need for the mercy and grace freely given from an all-powerful and loving God. Every woman in the New Testament who is reported to have interacted with Jesus went away changed. Although the same could be said for men who interacted with Jesus, I find it remarkable that the biblical narrative does not include a single instance in which a converted woman abandoned her faith. Instead, they turned their lives to Christ and never retreated. The same cannot be said for all of the men.

In a bold disregard for assumed male superiority, the Savior was not ashamed to describe himself by using feminine images. He is the mother hen yearning to protect his own under her ample wings if they will come to him in faith (Matt. 23:37; Luke 13:37), and the woman who searched her house until she found the lost coin (Luke 15:8–10). He invited all who were thirsty to come to him and drink from his *koilia* (John 7:37–38), an interesting but debated image. The term refers to a "hollow of the body" and is typically translated "belly" or "womb."[2]

READING TO ENHANCE OUR UNDERSTANDING

Modern readers who wish to enrich their understanding of the complex relationships and cultural influences experienced by women in the ancient world should understand four considerations in having a balanced learning experience. First, extant primary and secondary sources by no means convey a complete picture of first-century women. Second, we have a tendency to view the biblical world through modern-day lenses. Third, each of us brings to the text personal biases. Fourth, by accepting the unique contribution that a feminine perspective contributes, we can enhance our scriptural comprehension.

Ancient sources are limited by class and education, subject to the biases of the authors, and liable to loss or deterioration over time. Because histories of New Testament times were written by educated, aristocratic men, what they knew and experienced rarely included the life of the common people. Very little was recorded about the working class, slaves, and lower-class women. As a result, most scholars agree that women were leaders and teachers in the early church, but they disagree over the extent of women's authority. We wish we had modern-day acuity to accurately envision those who were often overshadowed, ignored, or forgotten. Insistence on forcing details that are not specifically given, however, generally leads to faulty conclusions. As in all studies in antiquity, a certain comfort with ambiguity is therefore wise.

Humans have a natural inclination to assume that their personal customs, attitudes, and morals also apply in other times and other places. We must avoid the tendency to see the biblical world through modern lenses. Readers most commonly default to their own experience to supply a plausible explanation in the absence of desired details, to explain a strange custom, or in an attempt to find personal relevance in a story. This practice more often twists the text to say what we want it to say rather than teaches us what the authors intended. For example, if we think of the early Christian church as a microcosm of the latter-day church, Paul's expectation that a woman pray with her head covered may seem an extreme rule of dress and decorum. We can fall prey to emphasizing outward appearance rather than focusing on the message of the worship service and miss completely that women were even *allowed* to pray in church. By our ignorance of traditions and attitudes that were commonplace or our resistance to acknowledging them, we can inadvertently diminish our appreciation for women's contributions to the early spread of Christianity.

Scripture study can be more meaningful to readers who acknowledge their own biases. The way each of us responds to these scriptural stories is conditioned by the cultural context of our own experiences, education, gender, and age. For example, I bring to my reading of the Bible a bias developed from being white, Latter-day Saint, born in the mid-1950s in a small community in Utah, first married in my forties, and with a PhD education. Individuals from different educational experiences and geographical origins would likely encounter the scriptural narrative quite differently. In addition to cultural differences, gender plays a role. Women often read scripture differently from men, seeing different details and asking different questions. Furthermore, among women, there are as many insights, interpretations, and challenges with the text as there are women. Acknowledging this myriad of perspectives will encourage us to be open to others' insights and questions to enlarge and inform our own understanding.

Critical readers appreciate that a feminine perspective contributes to biblical exegesis without denigrating centuries of remarkable insights from a masculine perspective. A feminine perspective on biblical truths inspired nineteenth-century pioneers for emancipation and women's rights to engage in public discourse. For example, through her New Testament study, Harriet Beecher Stowe became convinced of the equality of all who are grounded on the foundation of Christ. This conviction inspired her influential novel *Uncle Tom's Cabin* and her treatise *Women in Sacred History*, a tribute to women in the Bible.

Frances E. Willard, a duly elected delegate at a general conference of the Methodist Episcopal Church, was denied the privilege of speaking because of her sex. As a result, she observed two conflicting methods of biblical interpretation that men employed to determine the duties and privileges that God afforded women, "one of which strenuously insisted on a literal view, and the other played fast and loose with God's word according to personal predilection." Willard's study led her to conclude that "we need women commentators to bring out the women's side of the [Bible]. . . . I do not at all impugn the good intention of the good men who have been our exegetes, and I bow humbly in presence of their scholarship; but, while they turn linguistic telescopes on truth, I may be allowed to make a correction for the 'personal equation' in the results which they espy."[3]

Similarly, Sarah M. Grimké, a Quaker and a serious reader of the New Testament, wrote a letter to the president of the Boston Female Anti-Slavery Society in November of 1837 to share her arguments in support of equality for women. In the opening section of her lengthy communication, she observed that the Savior's admonitions to his followers did not differentiate expectations by any reference to sex or social standing. Grimké reasoned that his command to "'let your light so shine before men, that they may see your good works, and glorify your Father which is in Heaven'" therefore applies to men and women equally. She observed that men and women "are both moral and accountable beings, and whatever is *right* for man to do, is *right* for woman."[4]

Contrary to this Christian tenet, however, Grimké experienced efforts to make women's influence "private and unobtrusive; her light is not to shine before man like that of her brethren; but she is passively to let the lords of the creation, as they call themselves, put the bushel over it, lest peradventure it might appear that the world has been benefitted by the rays of *her* candle." She blamed the contradiction between the Lord's teachings and current application on "a misconception of the simple truths revealed in the Scriptures," in part created by ignoring a feminine perspective.[5]

HOW THIS VOLUME IS ORGANIZED

Women of the New Testament has six sections, each of which represents a specific group of New Testament women with whom Jesus interacted. We begin with the prophecy-fulfilling pedigree of Jesus Christ, including Mary, his mother, and the women of the Old Testament whom Matthew identifies in Christ's genealogy. The following sections discuss the other women mentioned in the New Testament, grouped by the societies in which they lived. Each section begins with an introductory essay that describes the land, people, and the cultural and religious practices in that society generally. Within each section, accounts of individual women include descriptions of her place of residence, her daily work, historical background to her story, her appearance in the New Testament narrative, and other possible connections to her (which I call Between the Lines). I conclude with reasons why these women of antiquity are worthy of our continued attention and study.

After the analysis of each woman is a section called Points to Ponder, which invite the reader to consider how that woman's example and circumstances apply to our lives today. These points are also intended as a starting place for group discussion and the sharing of personal insights among readers. The points are not intended to be comprehensive; teachers and facilitators should add to them as they feel inspired.

Mary, the mother of Jesus, is to the New Testament what Eve, the mother of us all, is to the Old Testament. Her faith and courage to act without knowing the consequences were foundational to God's plan and to the meaning of discipleship. The first section is therefore dedicated to her. A careful analysis of scriptural teachings about her in the Bible and the Book of Mormon is followed by myths and variant interpretations of her life that evolved in later centuries.

The second section considers progenitors of Jesus outlined in the opening chapter of the New Testament: Matthew 1. Beginning with Abraham, Matthew commences his testimony of Jesus as the promised King of kings by showing that He was born into the tribe of Judah and the royal line of David. Surprisingly, Matthew lists four women in the lineage. Various theories explaining why Matthew included these women are discussed, and the subsequent chapters in the section review and analyze each woman's unique story and the thread that binds them for Matthew's purposes.

The third section focuses on women in Jewish society, including many who knew and followed the Savior during his ministry. The fourth section considers Samaritan society and the woman at the well as a representative of that society. The fifth section looks at the Roman and Jewish aristocracy and its prestigious women whose responses to Jesus and his representatives provide a perspective that is significantly different from that of the other women in the New Testament. Due to their status and their response to Christian teachings, they have their own space in this book, which is perhaps fitting, given the privileges they greedily hoarded in mortality. The sixth section discusses women in Greco-Roman society, both those with Jewish backgrounds and those with Gentile origins.

Each woman's name is provided in a language in which she would have communicated—Aramaic or Greek. I also provide a suggestion for what her name meant, as names frequently communicated something about the woman's family, status, geographical origins, or religion. The practice of naming children after family members (in contrast to examples from the Old Testament in which individual names do not reflect a person's ancestry) was probably influenced by Hellenistic tradition, as clearly seen within royal families of Judea. Romans gave their daughters the name of a male progenitor but with a feminine ending: Octavius's daughter Octavia, Alexander's daughter Alexandra, and Claudius's daughter Claudia. The Jews often used the same pattern: Judah/Judith, Herod/Herodias, and Yohanan or John/Joanna. In addition, Jews in Greco-Roman Judea and Galilee used very little variation in selecting names for girls. Historians have documented only 122 known names for first-century Jewish women, the vast majority being given one of only a handful of popular names: Mariamne/Maria/Mary, Shlomzion/Salome, Martha, Shapira/Sapphira, and Joanna. It is not surprising that each of these names appears in the New Testament.

Among the final elements of this volume are the appendixes, whose purpose is to facilitate additional study. Appendix A includes an explanation for dating the year Jesus was born and gives a working chronology for the New Testament. Appendix B lists all the women mentioned in the New Testament, whether named or not.

Sources contains a description of ancient sources consulted and the abbreviations used for them, as well as a list of selected modern sources consulted. An index of subjects rounds out the volume.

According to Thy Word

by Elspeth Young

MARY, THE MOTHER OF JESUS

מרים   Μαρία

*A Greek form of the Hebrew Miriam; meaning uncertain
but perhaps related to Egyptian Maryē, "the beloved"*

ewer than ten days in the life of Mary, the mother of Jesus, are revealed in scripture, but every generation since her lifetime has been taught about her and has called her blessed. She was the mother of the Son of God—a loving mother in challenging times. And she was an exemplary disciple of Jesus Christ, an inspired witness of God's gracious favor, and a guardian of remarkable truths. Unique among women throughout all scripture, Mary, the mother of Jesus, is never portrayed in a negative light but is universally reverenced. Every mention of her signals purity, goodness, and discipleship.

The actual meaning of her name is uncertain, but the suggestion of "excellence" implied in a related Hebrew word meaning "height, exalted, or to give strength to" seems appropriate for the mother of the Lord.[1] Mary's name in Hebrew was probably the same as that of Moses' older sister Miriam, who was born in Egypt and whose name may rather have had origins in the Egyptian word *Maryē,* meaning "the beloved," and even "beloved of God."[2] Several royal daughters of the Hasmonean family were called Mariamne, another derivative of the name, which contributed to the fact that by the first century, the name Mary was arguably the name most often given to Jewish girls. It was the mother of Jesus, however, who gave the name Mary its later sense of awe.

In the twenty centuries since the young virgin gave birth to the Son of God, Mary's story has been told in multiple ways, giving rise to diverse traditions that have significantly influenced Christian worship among peoples all over the world. Some traditions encouraged a form of Mary veneration (or Mariology) that placed her on a level with her Son as co-Redeemer. As early as the second century, Christians began praising her as the woman who restored humankind from the "sin of Eve." Early church father Ireneaus (A.D. 120–202) claimed that as Eve "having become disobedient, was

MATTHEW 1–2; 12:46–50; 13:53–58
MARK 3:31–35; 6:3–4
LUKE 1–2; 3:23; 4:16–30; 8:19–21;
11:27–28
JOHN 2:1–12; 6:42; 19:25–27
ACTS 1:14

9

made the cause of death, both to herself and to the entire human race; so also did Mary . . . by yielding obedience, become the cause of salvation, both to herself and the whole human race" (*Haer* 1.309–567). For many early Christian writers, Mary became the model woman, described as docile, innocent, and unquestionably obedient to male authority.[3] She was also soon viewed not merely as one who had found the grace of God but as one who possessed the power to bestow such grace on others.

A lack of information enticed other early Christians to fabricate stories and hymns imagining what her life should have been like to qualify her as chosen of God. Primary among these extracanonical works is the second-century *Protevangelium of James,* which offers an imaginative view of Mary's birth and childhood. It commences with the myth that she was miraculously conceived by her mother, Anna, and reared at the temple, where she was "nurtured like a dove and received food from the hand of an angel" (*Prot Jas* 8.1).[4] Included in the care afforded her by the temple priests was their selection of Joseph, a widower, as the most appropriate Jewish man to wed her. Ultimately, the priests' plan was to ensure that the sinless Mary remain a virgin all her life; Joseph would be her husband in name only to care and provide for her after she left her temple abode.

As widely known as the name of Mary is throughout Christendom, the Bible and Book of Mormon are the only authoritative sources that actually tell us much about her. In areas where the accounts in Matthew and in Luke invite divergent interpretations or do not intersect, another witness of Jesus Christ— the Book of Mormon—validates, clarifies, and harmonizes the New Testament accounts. For example, the Book of Mormon tells us that Mary lived in Nazareth before Jesus was born (1 Ne. 11:13), she was a virgin (1 Ne. 11:20; Alma 7:10), and she was overshadowed and conceived the Son of God by "the power of the Holy Ghost" (Alma 7:10). The Book of Mormon also validates that Jesus was the literal son of Mary, after the manner of the flesh, and was the Son of God the Father, not the offspring of the Spirit or of a mortal man (1 Ne. 11:18, 21; Mosiah 3:8).

In seven important ways, however, the accounts of Matthew and Luke coincide and agree:[5]

1. Jesus was born in the time of Herod the Great (Matt. 2:1–3; Luke 1:5).

2. Mary and Joseph were legally married but not yet living together (Matt. 1:18; Luke 1:27, 34).

3. Joseph was of Davidic descent (Matt. 1:16, 20; Luke 1:27).

4. An angel announced the conception and coming birth of the Son of God (Matt. 1:20; Luke 1:28–35).

5. The angel revealed that the holy child's name would be Jesus (Matt. 1:21; Luke 1:31).

6. Jesus was born in Bethlehem (Matt. 2:1; Luke 2:4–7).

7. The family went to Nazareth where the child spent his childhood and much of his adult life (Matt. 2:22–23; Luke 2:39).

We need not venerate Mary to appreciate her contribution to God's work on earth. It is Mary's conviction of God's reality and power rather than fabricated stories of her moral perfection that deserves our admiration and emulation.

MARY'S PLACE OF RESIDENCE

The only domestic background we are given for Mary comes from Luke's Gospel. There we learn that she lived in Nazareth (Luke 1:26–27). Nazareth is situated about fifteen miles west of the Sea of Galilee and twenty miles from the Mediterranean Sea. At the beginning of the first century, the town likely covered less than sixty acres and sustained a population of under five hundred inhabitants.[6] Most likely, Mary's home with her parents in Nazareth would have been small and unassuming, much like the other homes in the vicinity.

Childhood of Jewish girls in the first century. Mary's life in little Nazareth of Galilee does not fit the portrayal of childhood for a well-born Jewish girl such as Philo described.[7] Living far from any urban center and families with elite social status, parents in Nazareth could not have afforded to keep their daughters in seclusion.[8] Their girls would more likely have been involved in assisting with the family's vocation, whether farming, raising livestock, creating stone masonry, pottery, or textiles, or selling such goods. Daughters would also have assisted their mothers in preparing food and caring for the home. Praising rural women in Italy, the Roman scholar Varro (116–27 B.C.) reported that their fortitude and usefulness put to shame the pampered women in the cities. Of Varro, one scholar noted, "He describes those women who look after the herdsmen watching the livestock in the mountains, claiming that the women are often not at all inferior to the men in working with the flocks. Not only can they look after the animals, but they can also cook food and keep the huts clean. And they do this all with nursing babies at their breast!"[9]

All children had the potential to contribute to a family's livelihood, and whomever a daughter attracted as a marriage partner could significantly affect the family's social prestige. A girl's status as unmarried may have been indicated by specific clothing. For example, she may have worn a distinctive veil, such as the one Rebekeh wore before she met Isaac (Gen. 24:65). The apocryphal story of Asenath, the bride of Joseph who was sold into Egypt, indicates that virgins wore a second sash, or girdle, to distinguish them from other women. All women wore the first sash around the waist, but virgins may have worn an additional sash under or over the breast.[10] When a daughter followed social norms, behaved modestly, and worked hard, she would be a source of pride for the family and would advance the family honor. The scant information we have about Mary in the New Testament indicates that she was a model daughter. After all, the angel told her that she was "highly favoured" by God (Luke 1:28).

Six centuries earlier, Nephi saw Mary in vision and described her as "most beautiful and fair above all other virgins" (1 Ne. 11:15). Because qualifications for beauty are often cultural and differ over time, we may wonder whether Nephi was noting Mary's physical characteristics or her purity, goodness, and diligence—or all of those attributes. That the vision first focused on Mary herself, before she gave birth to Jesus, indicates that she was important to God as a precious daughter, apart from her later role as the mother of his Son.

During her childhood, Mary would likely have been taught to work and in other ways to prepare for marriage and motherhood. Her mother would have been her most important teacher. Because no reputable ancient record preserves anything about her life or her family before the angel Gabriel appeared to her in Nazareth, we therefore assume Mary's was a typical life for a Jewish girl. We wonder, however, if while she worked in and around her family home, she received any premonition or other spiritual preparation for the God-given assignment that would be hers.

Jewish marriage customs in the first century. At Mary's introduction in the Gospel of Matthew, she was "espoused" to be married to Joseph (Matt. 1:18). The Greek used here to describe Joseph is more accurately translated "the betrothed of Mary," rather than "husband," as the King James Version renders it (Matt. 1:16).[11] The Jewish marriage procedure in Mary's day consisted of two ceremonies that usually took place a year or more apart, one before puberty and the other afterward. The first ceremony was one in which the legally binding contract of marriage was signed before witnesses (Mal. 2:14). The second ceremony preceded the consummation of the marriage and the relocation of the bride to live in the husband's home, as portrayed in the parable of the ten virgins (Matt. 25:1–13).

Artwork by Elspeth Young

The Mishnah indicates that Jewish girls reached marriageable age when they were about twelve years old. Mary was likely very young when Gabriel appeared to her.

According to the Mishnah, a girl was considered a child when she was younger than twelve years old, of age to marry between twelve and twelve and a half years old, and "past her girlhood" when she was older than twelve and a half years of age (*mKet,* 3.1.8; *mQidd,* 1.2). A young man was deemed "fit" for the "bride-chamber" at eighteen years of age (*mAboth* 5.21). Even though these Mishnaic passages postdate Mary by nearly two hundred years, they may well still reflect customs in the early first century. In part because of the youthfulness of a bride and groom, parents played a prominent role in selecting marriage partners for their children. The families were therefore often well acquainted before the marriage, and more often they were related. In fact, a marriage of relatives, such as between cousins or between an uncle and a niece, was often the safest way to ensure a socially appropriate spouse and also to protect property from being taken from the family. Further, love between a man and a woman was believed to be a natural result of a well-matched union rather than a preexisting condition to marriage.

The first formal step in the marriage procedure was to establish a legal agreement before witnesses in which the men of the bride's and groom's families formally consented to join their families through the marriage. This event was likely accompanied by a meal served at the bride's father's home (*mPes* 3.7). The Hebrew term for the consent phase is often translated as "betrothal" or "espousal," but it constituted a legal marriage in that the young woman was permanently bound to the young man. In other words, it was not simply an engagement in the way we use that term today. Any compromise of the groom's marital rights over the young woman made her legally liable to punishment for adultery. Although the bride continued to live in her father's home until the second part of the marriage procedure was accomplished, she was the "wife" of her betrothed. The Mishnah states that at the time of "betrothal," the bride "enters into the control of the husband" in place of her father, which includes "the right to set aside her vows" with a "bill of divorce" (*mKet* 4.4–5). Thus, Joseph would have had to obtain a divorce to be released from his marital obligation to Mary (Matt. 1:19).

The second stage of the marriage procedure occurred after the husband established a home for his wife and future family, usually in his parents' home. The formal relocation of the bride from her father's house to her husband's house was apparently ceremonial and therefore easy to recognize. According to rabbinic sources, the bride was carried in a litter (*mSot* 9.14; *tSot* 15.9). Matthew 25:1–13 describes this event, in which the virgin bride waits at her home for the bridegroom's formal arrival to take her to his home, where he will assume full responsibility for her support.

Before the temple was destroyed in A.D. 70, Jewish brides could wear a crown on their heads and leave their hair unbound, a hairstyle apparently unique to brides to indicate their virginity (*mKet* 2.1). Brides could also wear a veil that was "apparently the color of flame, a bright yellow or orange. After [relocating to her husband's home], the bride, now a matron, wore a *stola* (a sleeveless dress over her tunic) and a *palla,* a rectangular cloth that she wrapped around her shoulders and could pull up to cover her head" (*mKet* 4.4–5).

Now a member of her husband's family, the teenage wife would typically be instructed in her new role by her mother-in-law. The transition could be very difficult for the young bride, considering that despite the likelihood of their families' acquaintance and even relationship, her new surroundings were potentially strange and even hostile, and she was expected to quickly adapt to them.[12]

According to Matthew's account, Joseph and Mary had completed the first part of the marriage—the contract and vows—but the marriage procedure had not yet been completed (Matt. 1:18). We are not told whether Joseph also resided in Nazareth while the couple was espoused. It is possible that he did, if only because he was a descendant of David. Historical evidence shows that some Davidic families relocated to Galilee from their ancestral homes in Judea, likely to avoid attention from Hasmonean leaders who feared competition for the throne of the Judean kingdom.[13] Or Joseph may have lived in Bethlehem and gone to Nazareth only when it was time to take his espoused wife home. Considering how long the holy family remained in Bethlehem after Jesus was born gives further credence to this latter suggestion. Regardless of Joseph's residence, however, the couple were likely not well acquainted with each other before they began living together.

HISTORICAL CONTEXT

Prophecies concerning Mary. Without question, the primary purposes and main focus of revelation from ancient prophets were related to the coming of a Redeemer who would be the Son of God. The Savior's coming, however, could not be fully understood or appreciated without knowing about his mother. Ancient prophets spoke of Mary and of her calling as the mother of the Son of God long before she was born. These prophecies written by Isaiah and Book of Mormon prophets never confused the Savior's mother with deity: she would be a mortal from among the multitude of God's people. Notwithstanding, his mother was not just any woman; she was chosen and known by name centuries before her birth. Clearly, God intended us to know about her and her contribution to his plan of salvation.

Isaiah. Although he does not call her by name, the Old Testament prophet Isaiah delivered what may be the earliest prophecy of Mary. During a military siege of Jerusalem by the combined armies of Syria and the northern kingdom of Israel (734 B.C.), Isaiah gave King Ahaz of Judah a sign that Jerusalem would be spared. The words that came from "the Lord himself" were "Behold, a virgin shall conceive, and bear a son, and shall call his name Immanuel" (Isa. 7:14; 2 Ne. 17:14). Some scholars have discounted this as a reference to Mary because the Hebrew word translated as "virgin" can also mean young woman or girl. When Jewish scholars later translated the Hebrew text into Greek for the Septuagint, however, they chose the Greek word *parthenos* to describe the mother, which word specifically means "virgin" or a young wife. Isaiah's prophecy also applied to Isaiah's own day, perhaps to the birth of Hezekiah, who proved to be one of the "rare righteous kings of Judah, and in many ways he was an anticipation of Christ."[14] Two hundred years before Mary gave birth to Jesus, however, Jewish scholars believed that Isaiah had prophesied the miraculous virginal birth of "Immanuel," whose name means "God with us."[15]

Nephi. While receiving instruction about his father's dream of the tree of life six hundred years before Jesus' birth, Nephi saw Mary in vision in "the city of Nazareth." She was "beautiful and fair above all other virgins" (1 Ne. 11:13, 15). Nephi's next scene again described Mary as a virgin, but this time she was cradling in her arms her newborn son, who was the Son of God (1 Ne. 11:18–20). As Jesus was represented in Lehi's dream by the tree of life, so the Father worked through Mary to give life to all his children through her son.

King Benjamin. Some four centuries after Nephi's vision of Mary, an angel revealed to King Benjamin that "Jesus Christ, the Son of God, the Father of heaven and earth, the Creator of all things from the beginning" (Mosiah 3:8) would "come down from heaven . . . and shall dwell in a tabernacle of clay" (Mosiah 3:5). The angel then told King Benjamin that "his mother shall be called Mary" (Mosiah 3:8). Although the names of others have been specifically revealed in prophecy, such as Hannah's son, Samuel, and Elisabeth and Zacharias's son, John, Mary's is the only woman's name on the list. Furthermore, Mary's name was revealed more than one hundred years before her birth and to a prophet in a distant land, whereas John's and Samuel's names were revealed to their parents.

Alma. The prophet Alma taught the Nephites living in Gideon that Mary was "a virgin, a precious and chosen vessel," who would give birth to "the Son of God." He explained that this miracle would occur because she "shall be overshadowed and conceive by the power of the Holy Ghost, and bring forth a son, yea, even the Son of God" (Alma 7:10). Alma spoke of Mary's giving birth to Jesus "at Jerusalem," phraseology used by Nephite authors for the environs of a prominent city. Bethlehem was part of greater Jerusalem, being some five miles south of the holy city and it therefore easily fits the description "at Jerusalem."[16]

King Lamoni. The Book of Mormon provides another witness for the birth of Jesus Christ. After being in a comatose state for three days, King Lamoni awoke and exclaimed, "I have seen my Redeemer; and he shall . . . be born of a woman" (Alma 19:13). In learning of his Redeemer, King Lamoni must have been amazed to realize that Christ would be "born of a woman." In other words, the Savior would be born into this fallen and mortal world like the rest of us. After the Savior's mortal ministry, the apostle Paul used similar terminology when he spoke of the miraculous birth of Christ: "God sent forth his Son, made of a woman" (Gal. 4:4).

Mary's lineage. According to Jewish custom in that day, genealogy was traced through the father rather than the mother. That tradition is illustrated in both genealogies of Jesus found in the Gospels, which trace Joseph's lineage rather than Mary's, as though Jesus were Joseph's biological son (Matt. 1:16; Luke 3:23). Similarly, both Matthew and Luke identify Joseph as being of the tribe of Judah and a descendant of King David; they do not mention Mary's parentage (Matt. 1:20; Luke 2:4). But Matthew never records that Joseph begat Jesus, as the genealogical pattern would seem to anticipate; in an obviously awkward yet knowing way, he communicates that Jesus is both the literal Son of God and directly descended from the royal Davidic lineage.[17] The purpose of Luke's genealogy is to identify Jesus as God's Son, not as Joseph's son.

With equal certainty, we must conclude that Jesus was the son of Mary. He inherited mortal qualities from her that allowed him to feel hunger, thirst, pain, and even death. These attributes were essential to allow him to be "filled with mercy" and "know . . . how to succor his people according to their infirmities" (Alma 7:12). Through Mary, he became mortal so that he could lay down his life as a sacrifice for sin (Mosiah 15:5–8; Heb. 2:9, 17–18).

Certain verses of scripture validate the premise that Mary as well as her husband, Joseph, inherited royal blood. When Gabriel announced to her that she would conceive a child in her womb who would be given "the throne of his father David" (Luke 1:31–32), Mary did not protest that because she did not descend through that lineage, how could her son? Neither did she think about someone else who could supply that legacy for her son—the Davidic Joseph, for example. The only deterrent to her ability to bear a son with royal lineage was the existence of the requisite man in the equation. "How shall this be, seeing I know not a man?" (Luke 1:34). Her statement may argue that she could provide the Davidic lineage, regardless of who the man was.

The apostle Paul spoke of the Savior in terms that make it impossible to deny Mary's Davidic lineage. Speaking in past tense and thereby not by prophecy but by accomplished fact, Paul wrote "concerning [God's] Son Jesus Christ our Lord, which was made of the seed of David according to the flesh" (Rom. 1:3). The term "according to the flesh" indicates literal, not adoptive, lineage. In his final epistle, Paul again wrote of "Jesus Christ of the seed of David was raised from the dead" (2 Tim. 2:8).

Consideration of Mary's lineage must also take into account Luke's observation that she was a "cousin" to Elisabeth (Luke 1:36). What can we understand from indications that Mary had lineage through the royal line of Judah and was also related to Elisabeth, who was descended from Levi, the lineage of priesthood? Perhaps Mary's father was of Judah and her mother was of Levi. Mary's son could therefore possess a blood lineage to qualify as literally the King of kings as well as the great High Priest.

Just as Mary was chosen to be the mother of God's Son long before she was born, God also orchestrated her lineage. Her genealogy is not preserved in scripture, but the necessary lineal criteria for Mary may be found there. If indeed Jesus needed a biological connection to both the royal and priestly lineages, it is highly probable that Mary provided them. At various times Jesus was called Prophet, Priest, and King. Because of Mary's lineage, those titles were not merely legal but literal for her son. Because of the Father, those titles for the Savior are eternal.

MARY'S APPEARANCE IN THE NEW TESTAMENT STORY

The annunciation in Nazareth. When Gabriel, whom Joseph Smith identified as the Old Testament prophet Noah,[18] appeared to Mary, he calmed her "troubled," or startled, heart with "Fear not, Mary: for thou hast found favour with [or received grace from] God" (Luke 1:29–30). In responding to this glorious angel and the immortal Being he represented, the mortal Mary acknowledged great wonderment that the Lord knew her name and so favored her. Gabriel then proclaimed the holy words: "Thou shalt conceive in thy womb, and bring forth a son, and shalt call his name JESUS. He shall be great, and shall be called the Son of the Highest: and the Lord God shall give unto him the throne of his father David: and he shall reign over the house of Jacob for ever; and of his kingdom there shall be no end" (Luke 1:30–33).

Only two other accounts of an angel appearing to a woman are recorded in the Bible, and both times the visit was to announce that the woman would soon give birth to a son. The first of these recorded appearances was to Hagar, the mother of Ishmael (Gen. 16:7–11); the second was to the mother of Samson (Judg. 13:3). In other words, Jewish girls in Mary's day did not likely anticipate such angelic communications.

The announcement was to Mary alone, emphasized by the angel's use of the second person singular. In today's vernacular, Gabriel said, *You* will conceive . . . *you* will bear . . . and *you* will name . . . [19] Mary apparently showed no concern over how she could bear a child who could inherit the throne of David but only over how she could bear a child because she was a virgin (Luke 1:34). That Mary herself was a descendant of David would explain how her child could inherit the requisite lineage; her concern was, therefore, "How shall this be, seeing I know not a man?" (Luke 1:34). How could a virgin give birth?

One purpose of Gabriel's annunciation was to communicate how the seemingly impossible can indeed happen but only through the grace or gift of God. Similar to what the prophet Alma learned through revelation, the angel explained to Mary how she would conceive this chosen Son: "The Holy Ghost shall come upon thee, and the power of the Highest shall overshadow thee: therefore also that holy thing which shall be born of thee shall be called the Son of God" (Luke 1:35; see also Alma 7:10). Luke's Gospel uses some of the same Greek words translated as "the power of the Highest shall overshadow thee" to explain the phenomenon that occurred on the Mount of Transfiguration when Peter, James, and John were "overshadowed" (Luke 9:34) and when Peter's shadow healed the sick as he passed by them (Acts 5:15).

In Matthew's Gospel, the angel described the phenomenon to Joseph: "That which is conceived in her is of the Holy Ghost" (Matt. 1:20). We know that by the power of the Holy Ghost, Mary was enabled miraculously to conceive God's Son, "the Son of the Highest," in her womb (Luke 1:32). Latter-day scripture clarifies that no man or woman "can see the face of God, even the Father, and live" (D&C 84:22), for "without . . . the authority of the priesthood, the power of godliness is not manifest unto men in the flesh" (D&C 84:21). Without question, Mary experienced a miracle: "He that is mighty hath done to me great things; and holy is his name" (Luke 1:49), but we are not justified in speculating further.

As the only mortal participant in this unique miracle, Mary reported no other details, a fact that testifies of her reverence for the sacred event. Her foreordained mission, as important as it was, did not include a detailed account of the great condescension of God—how he, as Jesus, descended from his glorious state to live among mortals in a fallen world. Rather than through a testimonial of words, Mary proclaimed her faith in God through her actions in choosing to obey his will. Demonstrating true discipleship, she responded to the angel's announcement with the words, "Behold the handmaid of the Lord; be it unto me according to thy word" (Luke 1:38). The word translated here as "handmaid" is the feminine form of the Greek word meaning "servant," or possibly even "slave." She had not chosen this assignment but quickly accepted it, reverencing God's authority without question, even though at that moment she could not have completely understood all that was said and done nor the challenges that awaited her.

In classical Judaism, it was uncommon to refer to a man in terms of his mother, therefore Paul's writing "God sent forth his Son, made of a woman" communicated that something unusual had occurred:

Jesus was virgin-born (Gal. 4:4).[20] The description of Jesus as "the only begotten of the Father" suggests that "God the Father was uniquely Jesus' father to the exclusion of any man as his father."[21] God was literally his father, and Mary was literally his mother. Elder James E. Talmage of the Quorum of the Twelve Apostles observed of Gabriel's visit to Mary: "True, the event was unprecedented; true also it has never been paralleled; but that the virgin birth would be unique was as truly essential to the fulfillment of prophecy as that it should occur at all. That Child to be born of Mary was begotten of Elohim, the Eternal Father, not in violation of natural law but in accordance with a higher manifestation thereof."[22] Mary's expression "be it unto me" is in the form of a prayer, such as "may this occur to me as thou hast declared." Her desire to obey God was not merely mechanical or dutiful but almost enthusiastic. Committed and consecrated, Mary lived her faith in God.

Joseph's response. The scriptures do not tell us how Joseph learned that his betrothed was carrying a child. We know only that Joseph knew Mary was pregnant and that he was not the father of her child, because her pregnancy occurred "before they came together." He therefore planned to "put her away privily" (Matt. 1:18–19). Under the law of Moses, if a woman was found not to be a virgin at marriage, she could be stoned to death (Deut. 22:20–22). It is uncertain whether the Mosaic law was applied with sufficient strictness in Galilee in the first century to put Mary's life in danger, but at the very least, her reputation would have been damaged if her condition had been made public.[23]

Born into the tribe of Judah and a descendant of King David, Joseph is described as a "just," or upright, man (Matt. 1:19). But Joseph was more than upright. He was also merciful. His strict obedience to the law did not prevent him from showing compassion toward Mary and resisting an opportunity to expose her "sin" publicly.

Joseph's compassion, however, did not extend to completing the marriage contract and taking his pregnant bride into his home. His uprightness in the law precluded his seeing any option but divorce, even a private divorce. Because Jewish law in that day required a man who wished to put away his wife to denounce her before two or three witnesses in order to receive a legal writ of repudiation (Matt. 19:7), knowledge of the reason for the divorce could not have been kept completely secret. Moreover, in only a few months, Mary's pregnancy would have been impossible to hide and would likely have become the subject of small-town accusations and scorn. Most likely, the act of "put[ting] her away privily" (Matt. 1:19) meant Joseph would not bring criminal charges of adultery against Mary nor repudiate her publicly, thereby subjecting her to as little ugliness in the process as possible.[24]

Such was Joseph's intent as "he thought on these things" (Matt. 1:20), perhaps hoping for another option, when his pondering gave rise to a vision in which an angel appeared to him with a message from God. That Joseph was sufficiently in tune with the Spirit to receive such a revelation is again evidence of his obedience to God's word and of his merciful regard toward Mary. He was steadfastly prepared to obey what he understood to be God's will. Then the angel announced, "Joseph, thou son of David, fear not to take unto thee Mary thy wife: for that which is conceived in her is of the Holy Ghost. And she shall bring forth a son, and thou shalt call his name Jesus: for he shall save his people from their sins" (Matt. 1:20–21).

It is significant that Mary did not reveal to Joseph the sacred truth of the origin of her unborn child, which could easily have been justified in her precarious situation. She was not commissioned to proclaim the paternity of her child. Even though she did not understand all the ramifications of God's work through her, she "kept all these sayings in her heart" (Luke 2:51). She kept sacred things sacred, even when, as far as she could tell, her reputation and future were clearly in jeopardy. It took the visit of an angel to Joseph in a dream to vindicate Mary's character and give him God's directive to complete his marriage to Mary by taking her to live with him in his house. Furthermore, in the vision Joseph learned that the child's name would be Jesus, a Hellenized form of the Hebrew *Yeshua* (Joshua), meaning "Jehovah helps," or as the angel observed, "Jehovah saves."

In his Gospel, Matthew cites Isaiah's extraordinary prophecy concerning Mary: "Behold, a virgin shall conceive, and bear a son, and shall call his name Immanuel" (Isa. 7:14). This prophecy shed further light on the identity of the baby. Not only did the name of Mary's unborn child declare that Jehovah saves, but in her womb she carried that very Jehovah, even Immanuel, or "God with us" (Matt. 1:23). Through Mary, the Son of God—he whom the Israelites knew as Jehovah—would be born to live among mortals in a fallen world. Thus the angel declared to Nephi in a vision of the Savior's birth, "Behold the condescension of God!" (1 Ne. 11:26).

Mary's visit to Elisabeth. Before the angel Gabriel departed from Mary in Nazareth, he gave her a sign that certainly must have bolstered her faith and given her comfort after his life-changing announce-

ment. Six months previously, her relative Elisabeth, who lived in Judea, had also conceived a son, even though "in her old age . . . [she] was called barren" (Luke 1:36). Because Elisabeth hid herself away during her pregnancy, probably out of modesty, few if any besides Zacharias would have been aware of her good news (Luke 1:24). The text of Luke suggests that soon after the annunciation and conception, Mary left home to visit Elisabeth "in those days" and went "with haste" to the city in Judea where Elisabeth lived with Zacharias (Luke 1:39). Her prompt

Mary traveling to visit Elisabeth, Church of Visitation in Ein Kerem, Israel.

departure reveals her complete commitment to God's plan rather than fear of what others may say or do should her secret be known.

Likely no one else was aware that Mary was pregnant when she set off for the Judean hill country. Although the scriptural text is silent concerning traveling partners, Mary would have made the journey in the company of others. A traditional location of Elisabeth and Zacharias's home is Ein Kerem, a town about five miles west of Jerusalem. If Mary's journey commenced in Nazareth, as Luke chronicles, she traveled close to one hundred miles, a journey of approximately five days.[25]

Visualizing Mary and Elisabeth together illustrates the unique parallels and stark contrasts in their personal experiences. The Bible rarely preserves dialogue between two women, and in this case, no one else was around. No other event, conversation, or experience anywhere else in the world at that moment was as important as this one. Heaven's spotlight was focused squarely on two women, one elderly and the other very young, who were carrying within them "the hopes and fears of all the years."[26]

The central focus of this event is Mary and Elisabeth's double witness of the divinity of Mary's unborn Son. Considering other biblical stories that feature two women, we might anticipate potential competition, jealousy, or conflict, as is reported between Sarah and Hagar, Leah and Rachel, Hannah and Penninah, and the New Testament sisters Mary and Martha. Nevertheless, like Ruth and Naomi, Mary and Elisabeth epitomized mutual respect, cooperation, and an understanding and reverence for the grace of God that surrounded them.

Nothing suggests that Elisabeth was expecting a visit from Mary, let alone that Elisabeth guessed anything amazing had happened to Mary in Nazareth. But as soon as she saw Mary enter her home and heard her greeting, Elisabeth knew all the essential truths. "When Elisabeth heard the salutation of Mary, the babe [John the Baptist] leaped in her womb; and Elisabeth was filled with the Holy Ghost" (Luke 1:41). In a dramatic and personal manner, God revealed to this priestly woman the secret of the ages.

Notice that Mary did not utter these truths—all was communicated through the Spirit to Elisabeth, who then gave it voice. "For, lo," Elisabeth exclaimed to Mary, "as soon as the voice of thy salutation sounded in mine ears, the babe leaped in my womb for joy" (Luke 1:44). God gave each of these women a clear revelation of what he had done for the other; neither could have known of the other's condition without God's communication.

Although Mary would not yet have been showing any visible signs of pregnancy, Elisabeth knew immediately that she was carrying a child. More importantly, where Elisabeth's natural response to that information alone might be to feel shame or at least embarrassment for Mary, instead, Elisabeth praised her! In words that have been called a hymn, or canticle, Elisabeth testified, "Blessed art thou among women, and blessed is the fruit of thy womb. And whence is this to me, that the mother of my Lord should come to me?" (Luke 1:42–43).

Elisabeth was surely in awe of her own miraculous pregnancy, especially in comparison with all the younger mothers-to-be around her, yet she was clearly aware that the fruit of Mary's womb was infinitely greater even than her own. Furthermore, she was ecstatic to confess it aloud. As miraculous as Elisabeth's pregnancy was after years of barrenness, Mary had conceived a child without "knowing" a man, a phenomenon that was exponentially more astonishing. Mary's child was "totally God's work—a new creation."[27] And in that instant, Elisabeth realized it. She knew that Mary would give birth to him who had the power to save her as she declared Mary's child not as merely *the* Lord but "*my* Lord" (Luke 1:43).

Elisabeth praised Mary: "Blessed art thou among women." This was not a prayer to Mary but the recognition of a blessing God had already bestowed upon her. Concerning Elisabeth's comparison of Mary "among women," biblical scholar Raymond Brown explained, "This phrase has a comparative (but not an absolutely superlative) value both in Greek and in Hebrew. It means that Mary has been specially blessed by God, but not necessarily that she is the most blessed woman."[28] Yes, God blessed Mary in a unique way—but he did not love and bless Mary more than he loves and blesses any other woman. In truth, the accounts of both Mary and Elisabeth show us that God bestows his gifts on each of us individually.

With striking humility, considering her own private miracle, Elisabeth sincerely wondered, "Who am I to receive a visit from the mother of my Savior?" Through the Spirit and in an instant she knew that God had engaged Mary in his plan of salvation. In that sacred setting, Mary then burst into her own praise for God in a canticle known in Latin as the Magnificat "([my soul] magnifies," the words that begin her song). Many scholars today think that the Magnificat did not originate with Mary, claiming that the words fit Elisabeth's position better than Mary's or that the hymn was already widely known at the time and Luke simply attributed it to Mary in his narrative.[29] Whatever the true origin, however, the words of the Magnificat can be seen to resonate with Mary's state at that moment of greeting Elisabeth. Even if she was not the first to utter the lines, she linked them to her life and thereby offered to them the application so meaningful to us.

MARY'S MAGNIFICAT

Each line of the Magnificat underscores how God's goodness and power are magnified through the experiences of Mary and Elisabeth.

My soul doth magnify the Lord
And my spirit hath rejoiced in God my Saviour.
For he hath regarded the low estate of his handmaiden:
For, behold, from henceforth all generations shall call me blessed.
For he that is mighty hath done to me great things;
And holy is his name.

And his mercy is on them that fear him

From generation to generation.

He hath [shown] strength with his arm;

He hath scattered the proud in the imagination of their hearts.

He hath put down the mighty from their seats,

And exalted them of low degree.

He hath filled the hungry with good things;

And the rich he hath sent empty away.

He hath holpen his servant Israel,

In remembrance of his mercy;

And he spake to our fathers,

To Abraham, and to his seed for ever (Luke 1:46–55).

The first two lines portray three sets of parallels: "soul" and "spirit" are used identically; "magnify" is echoed in "rejoiced;" and "the Lord" is identified as "God my Saviour." Through Mary's jubilant spirit, the greatness of the Lord God is magnified. She will forever stand as a witness of God's miraculous goodness and power.

God noticed the "low estate" of his "handmaiden." Reproach and low estate reflect the Jewish perception of wives who were barren. Elisabeth's childlessness and consequent "reproach among men" for so many years are also reflected here (Luke 1:25). The phrase may additionally point to the potential for scandal surrounding Mary's pregnancy, putting her in a "low estate." But Mary may have intended something simpler. She was part of a minority society within the Roman empire. In her own Jewish culture, women were viewed as being less than men. Yet within that same Jewish society, she was singled out for a glorious mission by her "Saviour." Only one woman in the history of the world would receive such a call, and God had chosen and graced Mary. Her deep humility was not lessened by her astounding realization that "all generations will call me blessed." She was blessed not because of her willing obedience but because of God's abundant gift.

The remainder of the hymn celebrates the power of God given to all those who hunger and thirst after righteousness. Through his might, the Lord accomplishes miracles and showers "mercy," or unmerited loving kindness, upon those who "fear him," or honor, revere, and feel intense awe for him. Certainly, "Holy is his name."

Considering that "hath shewed strength" is translated literally as "hath made strength," it is apparent that God *makes* those who fear him strong enough to surmount whatever he requires.[30] By contrast, those who fear not God, "the proud," are left to flounder, being guided only by their imaginations.

With his infinite wisdom and power, God pulls down the earthly "mighty," the princes of this world, and elevates the good people of no social or political status. Like Mary and Elisabeth, good women everywhere are "exalted" from the "low degree" in which the world sees them, not through the efforts of the so-called mighty but through the power of the one and only Almighty.

In a parallel comparison to the preceding verse, Luke 1:53 states that through God's almighty power and mercy, the wicked wealthy will find themselves impoverished, or "empty." On the other hand, those who are "hungry" for righteousness will be filled with an abundance of "good things."

The Greek word here translated "holpen" means more than merely "helped." The verb implies "taking hold in order to support."[31] Mary's canticle reminds Israel that God has taken Abraham's descendants by the hand, as manifest by his constant gift of mercy. The great extent of God's "help" is identified in the next verse. Included in the Abrahamic covenant are God's vow to speak to Abraham, Isaac, and Jacob forever through direct revelation and his promise that their descendants will receive his gospel and have the opportunity to spread it to all the families of the earth (Abr. 2:9–11).

As does Hannah's psalm in 1 Samuel 2:1–10, Mary's canticle recognizes the wonder of God, who works reversals in our lives. Moved by the Holy Spirit, she bears witness of truths that have not yet occurred as though they were an accomplished fact. When we consider her exchange with Elisabeth, we marvel even more at the depth of Mary's faith, courage, and maturity at such a young age.

Luke tells us that Mary remained with Elisabeth for the final three months of the latter's pregnancy before returning to "her own house" in Nazareth; in other words, she had not yet moved into Joseph's house (Luke 1:56). No doubt, then, she was with Elisabeth for the birth of John before she returned. In his narrative, Luke completes his account of Mary's actions in this segment with verse 55 before bringing to its conclusion the story of Zacharias and Elisabeth in verses 56–80, and so his narrative should not be viewed as strictly chronological. In addition to helping Elisabeth at John's birth, the time Mary spent with Elisabeth would have been most educational in preparing for her own delivery. No mention is ever made of Mary's own mother, but we may surmise from this scene that Elisabeth was a mother-figure in Mary's life.

The Savior's birth in Bethlehem. Luke recorded that everyone went "into his own city" to be taxed, according to a government decree some time before Mary was to give birth (Luke 2:1–3). From verse 4 of Luke's account, we know that Joseph's own city was Bethlehem, "because he was of the house and lineage of David," and Bethlehem was David's city. This census was specifically linked to ancestry because recording people by families made the count more accurate. Later, Luke observes that Joseph *and* Mary's "own city" was Nazareth (Luke 2:39). The earlier use of "own city" must refer to place of ancestral origin, whereas the second instance refers to place of current residence.

The Judean town of Bethlehem is about five miles south of Jerusalem. Because the time of Passover was also at hand, the city of Jerusalem and its environs would have been crowded with the Jewish faithful who had come to worship at the temple, as required by the law of Moses. This picture of an overcrowded Jerusalem spilling into nearby villages such as Bethlehem makes clear Luke's observation that "there was no room for them in the inns" (JST, Luke 2:7). Public inns of the time were a type of caravansary called a *katalyma* in Greek, in which parties of travelers were lodged under a single roof, often on the second floor,

Journey to Bethlehem. Joseph went "out of the city of Nazareth, into Judaea, unto the city of David, which is called Bethlehem . . . to be taxed with Mary his espoused wife, being great with child" (Luke 2:4–5).

while their animals slept beneath them on the first floor or in an open, central courtyard. The term could also refer to a simple guest room.[32]

We know that Mary did not give birth in one of these caravansaries because there was no room for her and Joseph "in the inns," as we have said, but the shelter in which Jesus was born is not specified in the scriptures. Later Christian records assert that Mary gave birth to Jesus in a cave near Bethlehem. Justin Martyr (A.D. 110–165) wrote, "But when the child was born in Bethlehem, since Joseph could not find a lodging in that village, he took up his quarters in a certain cave near the village; and while they were there Mary brought forth the Christ and placed Him in a manger, and here the magi who came from Arabia found Him" (*Dial* 78). Origen (A.D. 185–254) reported, "With respect to the birth of Jesus in Bethlehem, if any one desires . . . to have additional evidence from other sources, let him know that, in conformity with the narrative in the Gospel regarding his birth, there is shown at Bethlehem the cave where He was born, and the manger in the cave where He was wrapped in swaddling-clothes" (*Cels* 1.51).

Although the scriptures do not specifically state where Jesus was born, they do report that Mary "laid him in a manger" because of the lack of room in the inns (Luke 2:7). A manger (Greek, *phatnē*) most often refers to a trough, placed on the ground or created from a cavity in a rock, from which animals eat. The Greek Septuagint translation of Isaiah uses the same word for "manger" in the passage "The ox knows his owner, and the ass his master's crib [manger]: but Israel does not know me, and the people has not regarded me" (LXX Isa. 1:3). Christmas tradition adds animals to the scene, but the scriptures do not mention that Mary shared Jesus' birthplace with sheep and donkeys. Nevertheless, we sense the humble surroundings in which young Mary gave birth to God's Only Begotten Son. President Brigham Young observed, "Others may have been born in as low a state as this, but it is hard to find anybody, among the civilized portions of mankind, that gets any lower."[33]

Photo by Kent P. Jackson

According to Luke's account of the birth of Jesus, Mary placed her newborn baby in a "manger," a stone trough like this one used to hold feed for animals.

Without a word about a midwife or Joseph's role in attending the birth of Jesus, Luke focuses completely on Mary: "She brought forth her firstborn son, and wrapped him in swaddling clothes, and laid him in a manger" (Luke 2:7). We are drawn to her efforts to care for her newborn child the best she could in the rude circumstances. Swaddling clothes were strips of cloth used to wrap around newborns to keep them warm, dry, and protected from skin infections. The baby was typically first rubbed with oil before the strips of cloth were applied. Medical professionals of the day recommended swaddling a newborn, including bandaging the fingers so they would not become twisted, tying arms at the wrists and elbows, then the legs and head. Babies were to remain in this restricted position for two months.[34] Some doctors wrote of their displeasure over women of the lower classes bathing their newborn babies too often, rocking them when they fussed, failing to keep them swaddled, and nursing them to calm them.[35]

Meanwhile "in the same country," or in the open fields surrounding Bethlehem, shepherds were taking turns watching over their sheep through the night. In the Roman empire, the night was divided into four watches lasting from sundown to sunup.[36] Shepherds, who were among those often considered to be the lowest among the low in the Jews' social order, were invited to witness that the King of kings had come. The scriptures do not specify why these men were chosen to be witnesses of such "good tidings of great joy," but their love of God and reverence for his word are clearly indicated by their action (Luke 2:10). When an angel from the Lord appeared to these shepherds in the silence of the night, like Mary they "were sore afraid" at first (Luke 2:9). Through direct revelation from God, the angel announced to them, "For unto you is born this day in the city of David a Saviour, which is Christ the Lord. And this shall be a sign unto you; ye shall find the babe wrapped in swaddling clothes, lying in a manger" (Luke 2:11–12).

A choir of heavenly angels echoed the announcement of the first angel with praise of God: "Glory to

God in the highest, and on earth peace, good will toward men" (Luke 2:13–14). Whether the choir was made up of spirits who had once lived on earth or those waiting to be born or both, the emotion in their announcement would have been profound. They deeply understood and celebrated what few people on earth realized: "The hopes and fears of all the years are met in [the little town of Bethlehem] tonight."[37]

In reverent obedience to God, the shepherds left "with haste" to find Mary, Joseph, and the baby in the manger (Luke 2:16). Their immediate actions and clear direction also indicate their understanding that Bethlehem was "the city of David" (Luke 2:11). That very night they were privileged to behold their Savior soon after he came to earth in the flesh. Afterwards, the shepherds glorified and praised "God for all the things that they had heard and seen" (Luke 2:20). In return, Mary and Joseph received the added comfort and strength that came with additional witnesses to their wondrous miracle.

While shepherds "made known abroad the saying which was told them concerning this child," Mary "kept all these things, and pondered them in her heart" (Luke 2:17, 19). Reviewing *all* the miraculous support, protection, and direction God had already afforded her in her young life, she could discern his care and that he had a plan for her and the child. But how could she understand what lay before her? Rather than speak of sacred things that she did not fully comprehend or was unable to interpret correctly, she pondered what was happening to her and spoke nothing publicly of this miracle. Declaring her Son as the Anointed One of the Jews and the Savior of the world was not the errand God had assigned to Mary. In addition to mothering the Son of God, her mission and testimony were evidenced through her obedience to God's directions, allowing the Spirit to appropriately communicate to others the truth of his identity as the Son of God.

The law of Moses and childbirth. Four times in Luke 2 we are told that Mary and Joseph did "according to the law of Moses" (v. 22), or the "law of the Lord" (vv. 23–24, 39), underscoring that they were humble followers of the law, including the ordinances pertaining to childbirth. Luke indicates that Mary and Joseph observed the rites of circumcision, purification, and redemption of the firstborn.

The law of circumcision. God established "a covenant of circumcision" (Acts 7:8) with Abraham and his male descendants when they were eight days old (Gen. 17:12) "that thou mayest know forever that children are not accountable before me until they are eight years old" (JST, Gen. 17:11). In obedience to this law, Mary and Joseph took eight-day-old Jesus to be circumcised and at the same time to officially give him the name Jesus, as the angel had instructed Mary "before he was conceived in the womb" (Luke 2:21) and as the angel had rehearsed to Joseph before Mary went to live in his house (Matt. 1:21).

The law of purification for mothers. Mary needed to be ritually purified after giving birth (Luke 2:22–24). According to the law of Moses, birth, not conception, rendered a woman ritually unclean for seven days before a son was circumcised and thirty-three days afterwards, for a total of forty days (Lev. 12:2–8). After giving birth to a daughter, the days a mother was "unclean" doubles to eighty (Lev. 12:5). No explanation for this difference is provided in scripture.

During her days of ritual impurity, a new mother was not allowed to visit the temple, or sanctuary (Lev. 12:4). "When the days of her purifying are fulfilled, for a son, or for a daughter," she was commanded to take to the "door of the tabernacle," or temple, a young lamb for a burnt offering and either "a young pigeon, or a turtledove, for a sin offering" (Lev. 12:6). If a mother was "not able to bring a lamb, then she shall bring two turtle[dove]s, or two young pigeons; the one for the burnt offering, and the other for a sin offering: and the priest shall make an atonement for her, and she shall be clean" (Lev. 12:8). Luke does not record what Mary took to sacrifice for her purification, only that she fulfilled the law. For Herod's Temple, which was the temple in use during this time, the door she would have approached is presumed to have been the gate on the west side of the Court of Women, which leads into the Court of the Israelites and the Court of Priests. This was the farthest point an Israelite woman could enter into the temple complex.

Two doves on a rock at Masada. The law of Moses required the sacrifice of two turtledoves or two young pigeons after the birth of a son (Luke 2:23–24).

The law of redemption for the firstborn. In declaring Jesus the "firstborn son" of Mary (Luke 2:7), Luke was not implying that Mary would give birth to additional sons, or that Jesus was the eldest, or first, of many. Rather, the Greek indicates more simply that Mary had not given birth to a child before Jesus.[38] As the first to open the womb (Luke 2:23), Jesus had the blessings and responsibilities of the firstborn, according to Mosaic law (Ex. 13: 1–2; Num. 3:11–13; 18:15–16).

The birth of the firstborn also mandated special sacrifices under Jewish law. Originally, the firstborn was seen as belonging to God to serve him throughout his life; eventually, however, the tribe of Levi as a whole was assigned to bear this lifelong responsibility (Num. 18:6). In exchange for "five shekels," the firstborn could be bought back, or redeemed, from the service of the Lord (Num. 18:16). Parents of the firstborn were commanded to pay the price of redemption at the temple. Perhaps Luke did not mention payment for Jesus because he considered that Jesus also had Levite lineage and would therefore remain in God's service throughout his life.[39]

Simeon, a man previously unknown to them, stopped Mary and Joseph while they were at the temple to offer this sacrifice. Luke does not call Simeon a priest or give him any other position of special status to qualify him for the revelation he received at that moment. He was qualified because he was "just and devout, waiting for the consolation of Israel [the Messiah]: and the Holy Ghost was upon him" (Luke 2:25). That same Spirit had already promised Simeon he would not die "before he had seen the Lord's Christ"

(Luke 2:26). On any given day, parents would be seen bringing their young children to the temple to offer the requisite devotions, but the Spirit led Simeon to the temple on the day Mary and Joseph brought the child Jesus there and led him to immediately recognize the baby as the Messiah (Luke 2:27–29).

Taking Mary's child into his arms, Simeon offered his own hymn, or canticle, called in Latin the Nunc Dimittis ("Now you dismiss," the opening words of the song). This canticle contained two blessings—the first to God for preserving him until that moment (Luke 2:28–29) and the second for Mary and her child (Luke 2:34–35). Upon beholding the holy infant, Simeon praised God for "eyes [to see] thy salvation." He also bore witness that this Savior would be a light to the Gentiles as well as to Israel, literally to "all people" (Luke 2:30–32). Who else in Israel at this time could affirm that great truth? Understandably Joseph and Mary "marveled" at that which Simeon testified (Luke 2:33). Their reaction here echoes the responses of others to related miraculous events (Luke 1:21, 63; 2:18).

In his blessing on the family, Simeon prophesied that Jesus was "set for the fall and rising again of many in Israel" (Luke 2:34). This child would be seen as the cause for division among the Jews. The Greek verb translated here as "set" reflects imagery associated with building stones, suggesting that through the mission of Jesus Christ, Israel would experience destruction and yet rise again, like a building of stones, perhaps a foreshadowing of resurrection.[40] Truly the Savior's mission would have expansive effects on the world, yet most would speak evil against him, Simeon forewarned, and would work to stop his efforts.

Simeon then turned to Mary. She too would undergo a further challenging test of true discipleship. Simeon prophesied, "(Yea, a sword shall pierce through thy own soul also,) that the thoughts of many hearts may be revealed" (Luke 2:35). As presented in the King James Version of the Bible, this phrase about Mary's suffering is parenthetical, suggesting that the thoughts of those who reject Christ would be revealed, whereas her own suffering would be private.[41] Some have suggested that a sword figuratively pierced Mary's heart as a sword literally pierced her Son when he was crucified. Although it is John and not Luke who records the scene of Mary at the crucifixion (John 19:25), Joseph Smith's translation of these words reinforces Simeon's meaning as figurative: "Yea, a spear shall pierce through him to the wounding of thine own soul also; that the thoughts of many hearts may be revealed" (JST, Luke 2:35). Others have suggested that Mary suffered each time Jesus was rejected. She could have felt the symbolic sword through her soul whenever she was maligned by people charging Jesus with being illegitimate or a fraud.

But Luke does not mention any of these meanings. Perhaps Mary experienced a broken heart, as we often do, while learning to accept and keep the word of God even when covenants supersede and transcend loyalty to our family. We cannot become perfect without suffering (JST, Heb. 11:40). After all, a sword is double-edged and symbolically both punishes and saves. Later in his Gospel, Luke portrays Mary as one who exemplifies commitment to covenant, even amid suffering and heartache (Luke 8:21; Acts 1:14).

While the holy family was yet in the temple, an elderly woman named Anna came "in that instant" to them (Luke 2:38). Like Simeon she also recognized the Christ child and gave thanks to God for the blessing. Although the narrative does not specifically note how she received her revelation, she was called a "prophetess" (Luke 2:36). Like Miriam, Deborah, and Huldah before her, Anna had the "spirit of prophecy," which is a testimony of Jesus (Rev. 19:10). Her title of prophetess indicates her openness to the Spirit for such revelation. This devout widow, one of perhaps a lower degree in the social order, was known and chosen by God to greet his Son and proclaim a reason to hope for all "that looked for redemption in Jerusalem" (Luke 2:37–38).

Mary worshipped God through her adherence to the sacrifices and other ordinances prescribed under the law of Moses. While doing what she and all other Jewish women were commanded to do, God blessed her. There at the temple, Mary encountered two additional witnesses, one male and one female, who bolstered her commitment to motherhood and served as a reminder of God's watchful eye. She would never be completely alone in the daunting assignment to rear the Son of God. We wonder how often she might have thought back on that day at the temple to remember that with God, nothing is impossible.

The escape to Egypt. Matthew's testimony alone reports that "wise men," or magi, visited the Holy Child and his mother. The identity, number, and geographical point of origin of these wise men are not given in scripture. We know only that they came "from the east" (Matt. 2:1). Various traditions portray them coming from Persia or Babylon, where there was still a significant Jewish presence, but the earliest attested view claimed they came from Arabia.[42]

These magi did not coincidentally wander into Jerusalem soon after the Savior was born. They came purposefully, knowing of the Messiah's birth and having a desire to worship him. Only a few others in Judea had this knowledge—and that only through divine revelation. These men were no different. The wise men saw "his star in the east," where it rose, and knowing its significance through prophecy or perhaps by direct revelation, traveled to the land of the Jews "to worship him" (Matt. 2:2; JST, Matt. 3:2). Their recognition of the star's importance may indicate that these men were prophets or recipients of God's word similar to Simeon, Anna, Zacharias, Elisabeth, Joseph, or the shepherds. Supporting the premise that they were prophets is the fact that as remarkable as this star appears to have been, there is no record of anyone else taking notice, let alone perceiving its stunning significance. Further, the wise men were later warned by God through a dream (Matt. 2:12).

Because the wise men did not know precisely where to locate the Messiah upon their arrival in Jerusalem, they inquired of Herod, the nominal king of the Jews, for more information (Matt. 2:2–8). Going directly to Herod indicates their lack of awareness of Jerusalem's political situation and reveals Herod's pathological insecurity. Herod was "troubled" ("startled" in the Greek) upon learning that the Jews' rightful king had recently been born (Matt. 2:3). That was not what he had expected. History shows how paranoid he had become over his own sons who schemed to overthrow him. Now he would have to consider a greater threat from someone outside his own family.

With the help of chief priests and scribes, Herod learned from Jewish scripture that the Christ would come out of Bethlehem (Micah 5:2), but he learned nothing more. Feigning an interest in adoring the young "King of the Jews," Herod sent the wise men "to Bethlehem, and said, Go and search diligently for the young child; and when ye have found him, bring me word again, that I may come and worship him" (Matt. 2:2–8).

In the testimonies of these wise men that the Messiah was born, we may see God's intent to alert all members of the Jewish population that the hope of their salvation was at hand. The working class could be told of his birth by the shepherds, the priestly and highly educated by the chief priests and scribes, the dutiful temple worshippers by Anna and Simeon, and the royal and aristocratic elite by Herod. "With this, we begin to see God's orchestrated scheme to reveal the presence of his Son among his people a full generation before his Son began ministering to others as Jesus of Nazareth."[43]

The scene of Mary and her Son that met the wise men was significantly different from that which the shepherds encountered. Whereas the shepherds found a newborn wrapped in swaddling clothes and lying in a manger, suggesting an area prepared for animals, the wise men found the family in a "*house*," and Jesus was described not as an infant but as a "*young child*" (Matt. 2:11; emphasis added; compare Luke 2:11–12). The temple in Jerusalem was still being built at this time. With Joseph's carpentry skills (Matt. 13:55), or perhaps more accurately translated, his "construction" skills, the family might have remained in the area because of the income a good carpenter or stonemason could earn working on the temple.

Divine directives came to both Joseph and the wise men to warn them of Herod's design to "seek the young child to destroy him" (Matt. 2:13). In his rage and extreme paranoia, Herod ordered the death of "all the children . . . from two years old and under" in Bethlehem and its environs (Matt. 2:16). More specific in the Greek, the word *pais* used in this passage refers to male children, in contrast to *teknon,* which means children generally, both male and female. Thus the text itself indicates that Herod's orders focused on young boys in Bethlehem. Concerning the number that would have been subject to the ruler's infamous edict, biblical scholar Raymond Brown noted, "Because of the high infant mortality rate, we are told that if the total population was one thousand [in Bethlehem], with an annual birthrate of thirty, the male children under two years of age would scarcely have numbered more than twenty."[44] Though this estimate of casualties is fewer than most have previously imagined, the slaughter of twenty infant boys is nonetheless heinous by any account.

In 7 B.C., not long before Herod carried out his massacre of the innocents, he ordered the death of his two favorite sons, Alexander and Aristobulus, who he believed were plotting to avenge his murder of their mother. Herod's reaction to the news of a Jewish Messiah is thus not surprising. Just five days before his own death, Herod executed his eldest son, Antipater (*Ant* 16.1–11; 17.8.1). Herod's infamous brutality toward family members reportedly inspired the emperor Augustus to quip, "It is better to be Herod's pig [*hys*] than his son [*huios*]."[45] In other words, while Jews would never slaughter pigs, which were unclean, Herod did not hesitate to slaughter his own sons.

Having been warned by God through dreams of Herod's intent to destroy young Jesus, the wise men "departed into their own country another way," rather than returning to report to Herod as they had initially agreed, and Joseph "took the young child and his mother by night and departed into Egypt" (Matt. 2:12–14). Because of its proximity, Egypt offered the family a sanctuary, as it had for many of God's people in times past.[46] God later sent an angel to Joseph in a dream to "take the young child and his mother, and go into the land of Israel: for they are dead which sought the young child's life" (Matt. 2:19–20; compare Ex. 4:19).

After Herod's death in about 4 B.C., his son Archelaus ruled Judea in his stead. Although the Jews hoped for better treatment under the son, Archelaus proved even more brutal than his father (*Ant* 17.11.2). Matthew indicates that the family's intent had

Caesar Augustus, Corinth Museum, Greece.

been to return to the Bethlehem area in Judea to take up residence until Joseph was warned yet again through a vision. Changing course, the young family continued northward into Galilee until they arrived at Nazareth, where they would live throughout the Savior's childhood and into his adulthood (Matt. 2:21–23; JST, Matt. 3:24–26).

Herod Antipas, another of Herod's sons, was given jurisdiction over Galilee and Perea after his father's death. Whereas Archelaus was soon removed from power in Judea and replaced by a series of Roman governors, Herod Antipas was still in power when Jesus began his ministry and remained the tetrarch of these regions during the Savior's ministry, trials, and death.

Although little about Mary's life during the first years after she gave birth to Jesus is recounted in scripture, we wonder if she might have been surprised at some events involving her son. We wonder how often the family changed residences, including the temporary move to a foreign land, which naturally disrupted their domestic order.

Mothering the child Jesus. The scriptural record is virtually silent about Mary and her family during the next several years. Luke summarizes these years with a description of the young Jesus: "And the child grew, and waxed strong in spirit, filled with wisdom: and the grace of God was upon him" (Luke 2:40). Watching her child grow from a helpless infant into a spiritually strong and exceptionally wise young man must have given Mary daily cause to marvel. She would have watched his physical growth much as other parents do, considering it occurred at a normal pace. But his spiritual and intellectual growth must have been astounding, quickly exceeding what she could teach him. The Joseph Smith Translation indicates that "he spake not as other men, neither could he be taught" (JST, Matt. 3:25). Mary must have often felt inadequate, humbled, and also profoundly blessed to be this gifted child's mother. No doubt her own commitment to diligence in God's service was enhanced through her observations of her completely and strikingly diligent Son.

President Joseph Fielding Smith suggested various ways young Jesus could have been tutored during his primary years. "Evidently, before he was 12 years old, [Jesus] had learned a great deal about his Father's business. This knowledge could come to him by revelation, by visitation of angels, or in some other way. But his knowledge, so far as this life was concerned, had to come line upon line and precept upon precept."[47]

One specific incident is recorded in scripture of the Savior's later childhood. Joseph and Mary had traveled to Jerusalem for the feast of the Passover, as was their custom. Whether they took Jesus with them the previous years is not known, but in the year when Jesus was twelve years old, the age at which Jewish boys were considered to have become men, he did accompany them (Luke 2:41–42).

Under the law of Moses, adult males were specifically required to appear at the temple, or sanctuary, three times a year: the law names Passover, or the Feast of Unleavened Bread; Pentecost, or the Feast of Weeks; and Succoth, or the Feast of Tabernacles (Deut. 16:16; Ex. 34:23). Many Jews lived far from Jerusalem and even from Israel in the early first century, so it is likely that a great number would have made the pilgrimage only once a year or perhaps even once in a lifetime. The law does not mention any requirement for women and children in this regard, and the Mishnah notably exempts women from such travel (*mHag* 1.1). That Mary made the trek annually underscores her spiritual nature and active faith (Luke 2:41).

After completing the duties associated with the feast, Mary and Joseph began making their way back north to Nazareth in the company of "their kinsfolk and acquaintance," people who likely were returning to the same area (Luke 2:44). Supposing that the twelve-year-old Jesus was somewhere in the traveling party, "Joseph and his mother" did not notice until the end of the first day of travel that he must have remained in Jerusalem. Returning the approximately twenty miles the next day, they searched the city on the third day and finally found him at the temple "after three days" (Luke 2:43, 46). They came upon him "sitting in the midst of the doctors [teachers], and they were hearing him, and asking him questions" (JST, Luke 2:46).

The Jewish teachers in the temple reacted to the boy's wisdom with the same awe and wonder as had those who heard the shepherds' report (Luke 2:18) and as Mary and Joseph had responded to Simeon's canticle (Luke 2:33). According to Luke, the scene caused Mary and Joseph again to be "amazed" (Luke 2:48). Because Mary and Joseph had received revelations about Jesus' divine identity and observed his remarkable spiritual growth to which they alone had been privy, it may seem surprising at first that Mary and Joseph could be awed by the scene at the temple. Therefore this scene puts new light on the rapidity with which Jesus learned and the depth of wisdom he had achieved, all while looking like a normal boy of twelve.

Joseph Smith taught that Jesus progressed intellectually and spiritually more dramatically than he did physically, as shown by his superior understanding before the Jewish intellectuals at the temple that day. "When still a boy He had all the intelligence necessary to enable Him to rule and govern the kingdom of the Jews, and could reason with the wisest and most profound doctors of law and divinity, and make their theories and practice to appear like folly compared with the wisdom He possessed; but He was a boy only, and lacked physical strength even to defend His own person; and was subject to cold, to hunger, and to death."[48] Most likely Mary experienced surprise and increased awe in her daily interactions with young Jesus.

At the temple in Jerusalem, Mary's first words rang with what seems to be a tone of reproach but probably more deeply reflected the fear and anguish that had built inside her over the past two days: "Son, why hast thou thus dealt with us? behold, thy father and I have sought thee sorrowing" (Luke 2:48). Her words are understandable to parents who have felt the terror of not knowing where their child is. Similarly, Jesus' response should not be seen as criticism for their anguish and worry but as sadness that they knew him so little. They should have guessed immediately that he would be at his Father's house. "How is it that ye sought me?" he asked them. "[Did ye not know] that I must be about my Father's business?" (Luke 2:49). But Mary and Joseph did not comprehend the full import of what this twelve-year-old boy was saying (Luke 2:50). Again, the contrast in understanding between Jesus and all others, including Mary, his mother, is marked.

Throughout this exchange at the temple and the many teachings in the years that followed, Jesus shows us the power and wisdom that come from giving first priority to our relationship with the Father. Because Jesus' commitment to his Father in heaven transcended mortal family ties, he was able to bless Mary and all of humankind. Nothing—not even his love for his mother—could distract him from his foreordained mission. He was not yet prepared to commence his official ministry, however. Apparently that preparation included additional lessons to be learned within the family, lessons that would be learned back home in Nazareth.

Leaving the temple, Jesus returned to Nazareth with Mary and Joseph "and was subject unto them" (Luke 2:51). Although by this young age he already knew that he was God's Son and that he excelled in wisdom over everyone around him, he meekly obeyed his mortal parents. The unavoidable tie between willing obedience and wisdom is illustrated again. Might this exchange at the temple and Jesus' subsequent submission to Mary have intensified both her confusion and her reverence for her Son when they returned to Nazareth? As Jesus continued to increase "in wisdom and stature, and in favour with God and man," his mother was the one most likely to notice (Luke 2:52). Wisely, she still "kept all these sayings in her heart" (Luke 2:51). Instinctively, she seemed to recognize that the answers to her questions would not come by broadcasting her observations to those around her or by complaining of her unique challenges to her neighbors. Instead, she pondered what she had been given and prepared herself to gain additional insight that would eventually lead her to understanding. Like her Son, she was gaining that understanding line upon line, grace by grace, albeit at a much slower pace than she might have wished.

During the Savior's mortal ministry. Little is communicated in the scriptures about Mary's life and character once the Savior began his ministry. The implication of the four Gospels is that she was more often at home with her family, as was customary for Jewish women of that day, than accompanying Jesus in his travels. Jesus was known by his neighbors in Nazareth simply as "the carpenter's son" (Matt. 13:55), suggesting the ordinariness of Jesus' birth and childhood. Apparently the villagers were unaware of his royal lineage, his miraculous escape from Herod's heinous edict in Judea, or his being visited by mysterious magi from the East. All of this again indicates the maturity, wisdom, and restraint exercised by Mary throughout her Son's mortal life.

An incident in Nazareth after Jesus had become known for his miracles in other parts of Galilee further illustrates Mary's success in giving Jesus a normal childhood. Jesus went to the synagogue on the Sabbath day "as his custom was" and was invited to participate in the weekly Torah reading. After reading a passage from Isaiah that speaks messianically and in the first person, Jesus offered the following commentary: "This day is this scripture fulfilled in your ears" (Luke 4:16–21).

The townspeople of Nazareth, Mary's neighbors and friends, who had watched Jesus grow up before their eyes, "wondered at the gracious words which proceeded out of his mouth. And they said, Is not this Joseph's son?" (Luke 4:22). In Mark's account of the event, the people in the synagogue asked, "Is not this the carpenter, the son of Mary, the brother of James, and Joses, and of Juda, and Simon? And are not his sisters here with us?" (Mark 6:3). They spoke of Mary's family with familiarity: "Is not this Jesus, the son of Joseph, whose father and mother we know?" (John 6:42). To these Galileans, Jesus was merely the son of people they knew well, so how could he be the powerful and wise figure he had declared himself to be?

Even their expectations of seeing the kind of healing Jesus had performed in nearby Capernaum, however, did not prepare them for the spiritual outpouring that accompanied his teaching in their synagogue. They must have mused, "This certainly could not be the one whom the Spirit identified as the Anointed One," for there was nothing unusual about Jesus' childhood. "This is Joseph's son, not God's Son," they apparently thought. When Jesus pointed out their stubbornness to accept the truth set before them, adding examples from the Old Testament of Gentiles who responded more readily to the Spirit than they, the villagers became angry enough to try to kill him (Luke 4:24–30). The reaction of the villagers of Nazareth to Jesus during his ministry indirectly points to Mary's having so well deflected attention away from the divinity of her Son that he was allowed to grow up without unnecessary opposition.

We see Mary again early in Jesus' ministry when they both attended a wedding feast at Cana, a Galilean village less than ten miles north of Nazareth. During the wedding feast, probably the night the groom took his bride to his home, the host of the feast had unexpectedly run out of wine, a social embarrassment (John 2:1–3). The six large stone water pots that held "two or three firkins apiece" could have held more than one hundred gallons of wine.[49] Upon discovering this oversight, Mary instinctively turned to her Son, fully believing that he could somehow resolve the problem. By this time, she had complete confidence and faith in his abilities, knowing what Peter would later discover: there was no one else to go to for help (John 6:68). Recognizing her faith in him, Jesus responded to her request for help not only by miraculously pro-

Each of these ancient limestone pots from the first century A.D. held large quantities of liquid. They are similar to those that would have been used at the wedding feast at Cana (John 2).

ducing more wine but by producing better wine than had been previously served, much to the amazement of the guest of honor.

To his mother alone, however, Jesus offered the significant comment, "Mine hour is not yet come" (John 2:4), foreshadowing Gethsemane (John 13:1; 17:1; Mark 14:41). The miracle at Cana was not his hour, but it could help Mary understand that hour when it came. When it did, Jesus, the "true vine" (John 15:1, 5), went into Gethsemane, the garden of "the oil press" and shed his blood (*Gethsemane* means "oil press" in Aramaic). Then and there, Jesus gave humankind the wine of the Atonement, the very best wine, of which the Saints symbolically drink when they partake of the sacrament (Luke 22:19–20, 44).

> *There was no other good enough*
> *To pay the price of sin.*
> *He only could unlock the gate*
> *Of heav'n and let us in.*[50]

The Son of Mary was the *only* one whose atoning blood was enough to satisfy the demands of justice. Furthermore, his gift of wine for the wedding guests anticipated the great gift of salvation he would give to all of God's children.

At the wedding feast, Jesus addressed his mother as "Woman" (John 2:4). Although not impolite or disrespectful in any way at the time, this was an unusual manner for a Jewish son to address his mother. Perhaps by calling his mother "Woman," he directs us to remember scripture's first mention of her. In the Eden narrative, our Redeemer was described simply as the "seed" of "the woman" (Gen. 3:15). Mary was *the* one and only woman to give birth to a son who had no mortal father: Jesus was the seed of Adam's female descendant, the woman, but not of mortal man.

By calling his mother "Woman," Jesus may also have reminded Mary that he put a higher priority on his Father's work than on his mortal family. Was he telling her that she could not assume he would continue to be at her beck and call simply because she was his mother? Through the Atonement, Mary, like the rest of humankind, would become *his* daughter (Mosiah 5:7).

Jesus would later teach that sincerely loving God should take a higher priority in our hearts than love for others, including family (Matt. 22:36–40; 10:37). The commandment not to put any other gods ahead of the Lord God preceded the command to honor father and mother (Ex. 20:3, 12). Our ability to love others, including family members, will always be enhanced and informed when God comes first in our lives.

At the same time, the verbal exchange during the wedding feast at Cana shows the Savior's sensitivity to his mother. Unlike so many of his later miracles, when Jesus turned water to wine in Cana the phenomenon was not accompanied with the exclamations of astounded bystanders. The miracle was for his mother alone, an affirmation of her strength and support through years of pondering so many things in her heart. When the celebration concluded, Jesus and his disciples accompanied Mary and his brothers to Capernaum for a few days before departing from his family to continue his ministry (John 2:12).

Because Joseph is not present in any scene after his discovery of the boy Jesus at the temple in Luke 2:41–51, most scholars assume that Mary was widowed before the Savior's ministry began. James, Jesus' younger half-brother and author of the epistle in the New Testament, defined "pure religion and undefiled before God and the Father" as "to visit the fatherless and widows in their affliction" (James 1:27). If indeed Joseph did die early in the Savior's and James's lives, the widowed Mary and her fatherless children may have first experienced pure religion through selfless acts of kindness they received.

Mary in the Passion narrative. Other than during the wedding feast in Cana (John 2:1–5), John speaks of Mary only one other time: at the scene of the crucifixion, where she stood near the cross (John 19:27). Here again John refers to Mary not by name but by her role as Jesus' mother, again emphasizing Jesus' mortality by reminding the reader of his mortal mother (John 19:26).

None of Mary's words are recorded in John's depiction of the crucifixion; her only action is standing by the cross. To see Mary standing, however, does not suggest that she was passively waiting or even paralyzed with grief. Because thinking, reflecting, and analyzing are valuable attributes that are often lacking in eras of constant distraction and immediate gratification, we may fail to consider that with her meditative qualities, Mary could learn while the world spun around her. Standing by Jesus in what others perceived as a shameful predicament, Mary also communicated that her fear of God was greater than her fear of man. Whatever accusation a bystander could fling at her, Mary's quiet stance communicates that unlike others of his disciples, she would not deny her association with Jesus. Furthermore, even more telling than remaining loyal to a son, Mary was a stalwart disciple of her Redeemer.

In this poignant scene, filled with overwhelming pain, grief, and foreboding loneliness, it was Jesus who spoke first. And just as he did in Cana, Jesus addressed his mother as "Woman." "When Jesus therefore saw his mother, and the disciple standing by, whom he loved, he saith unto his mother, Woman, behold thy son! Then saith he to the disciple, Behold thy mother! And from that hour that disciple took her unto his own home" (John 19:26–27). Even in his excruciating pain, Jesus expressed compassion for individuals and taught the importance of service. The assumption that arises when he assigned the care of his mother to a beloved disciple, presumably the author of the Gospel of John, is that James and the other biological brothers of Jesus were not yet Christians. Many interpret from this scene the Savior's emotional, passion-filled expression of love for his mother in his final moments of mortality. Yet Jesus did not give a charge only to the beloved disciple; Mary also received a commission. He was not merely divesting himself of his family obligations as the eldest son; he was assigning Mary another son to mother in his place. "Inasmuch as ye have [shown compassion to one another], ye have done it unto me" (Matt. 25:40). In the Savior's final moments in mortality, we see his mother and other disciples acutely aware of their need for him. He alone performed the atoning sacrifice, died, and after three days rose again to depart eventually in glory (Acts 1:9–11).

God's offer of salvation to the world came not only *through* Mary but also *for* her. Mary and the other disciples remained on earth as witnesses of their Redeemer. They remind us that no family connection or ecclesiastical position of authority supersedes the dependence we all have on Jesus Christ for hope and salvation.

BETWEEN THE LINES

Mary's other sons. In the years after Jesus' birth, Mary and Joseph apparently had children, beginning with a son they named James (Matt. 13:55; Mark 6:3).[51] Because Mary's later children are not mentioned in the scriptural narrative until the Savior's ministry, we do not know the age difference between Jesus and James. Considering responses of modern-day mothers to children of differing sensitivities, we might imagine that Mary understood the joys and immense challenges associated with mothering multiple children who differed from each other in many ways.

Despite being reared in the exemplary home of Mary and Joseph (Luke 2:51; JST, Matt. 3:24–26), Jesus appears to have experienced significant rejection by his brothers (Mark 3:21). They tried to keep him away from home (John 7:3–5), which may have included keeping him away from his mother, and in so doing restricted his influence in the community. Restrictions such as these may have encouraged Jesus to teach that spiritual bonds were of greater import than bonds of blood (Matt. 12:46–50; Mark 3:31–35; Luke 8:19–21; 11:27–28). In so doing, Jesus dared to attack familial restrictions whose victims were primarily women.[52]

The suggestion that Mary was not often alone with Jesus does not mean she independently chose to remain at home and away from him. In the absence of the father in Jewish homes, the eldest son typically ruled the family. Since Jesus was away from home more often than not, that responsibility would fall on the next oldest, or James. If James did not agree with Jesus' message and mission and Jesus was absent leaving James in charge, Mary would not have had the freedom to support Jesus as she desired.

Hints about Jesus' half-brothers in the scriptures imply their resistance to the Savior's work during his mortality. During the Savior's ministry, James and his younger brothers not only did not believe in Jesus' divinity but seem to have been embarrassed by his behavior and notoriety. For example, Mark reports that Jesus observed, "A prophet is not without honour, but . . . in his own house," or stated another way, a prophet has honor except in his own home (Mark 6:4). The same Gospel teaches that his family (in Greek, "those near to him or those of his own," which scholars conclude means "his family" rather than the KJV translation "his friends") said Jesus was "beside himself," or crazy (Mark 3:21).[53] Moreover, after Jews in Galilee rejected Jesus because of his Bread of Life sermon and Jews in Jerusalem sought his life because of miracles and condemnatory teachings, Jesus' brothers encouraged him to depart from them in Galilee and return to Jerusalem, "for neither did his brethren believe in him" (John 7:5). Despite Mary's own beliefs and religious desires, her actions would have been restricted by the family's presiding male. At the very least, Mary would have known the heartache that plagues a part-member family or a parent of nonbelieving children.

At least once Mary went with the brothers of Jesus to where Jesus was teaching (Mark 3:31; Matt. 12:46; Luke 8:19). Jewish scribes from Jerusalem had come to Galilee to stir up opposition against him (Mark 3:22–30). In the middle of Jesus' teachings, the crowd alerted him to his family's presence. Jesus asked, "Who is my mother, or my brethren?" Then, gesturing to the multitude, he added, "Behold my mother and my brethren! For whosoever shall do the will of God, the same is my brother, and my sister, and mother" (Mark 3:32–35; Matt. 12:47–50; Luke 8:20–21).

From the context, it seems Jesus was teaching the people about discipleship when his mother and brothers approached. With their arrival and the attention brought to them by someone in the crowd—"Behold, thy mother and thy brethren without seek for thee" (Mark 3:32)—he found an opportunity to illustrate the principle that those who follow his teachings are his family. Blood relationship is not a substitute for discipleship. In a similar exchange with a woman from the crowd who expressed her appreciation for him by blessing his mother, or "the womb that bare thee, and the paps which thou hast sucked," Jesus responded, "Yea rather, blessed are they that hear the word of God, and keep it" (Luke 11:27–28).

Although James and his younger brothers did not "believe in [Jesus]" (John 7:5), nowhere does scripture indicate that Mary was a nonbeliever. Faith includes remaining steadfastly loyal to the Savior, and Mary possessed such faith, from her initial call by Gabriel to be the mother of God's Son to the excruciating pain she knew at the cross and all the heartache in between. The Savior's inclusion of the multitude with his family did not diminish his love for his mother or his reverence for motherhood. Rather, his teachings on these topics underscore that it is not the act of giving birth—even to the Son of God—that qualifies a person to receive God's greatest blessings. The requisite qualifications are obedience and sacrifice, which every person is capable of making. Anyone who hears, receives, and willingly follows his gospel is blessed. Mary's blessed state grew out of her reverence for God's word, not because she gave birth to his Son.

One other incident hints that ugly rumors may have cast a shadow over Mary during her Son's life. As some of the Jewish leaders were seeking reasons to fault him, Jesus spoke of Abraham's children as those who "do the works of Abraham" (John 8:39). According to Jesus, because these Jewish leaders sought to kill him, they could be considered not Abraham's children but rather children of the devil who sanctions such heinous deeds. The Jewish leaders spat back at Jesus, "*We* be not born of fornication," suggesting that Jesus was shamefully born (John 8:41; emphasis added). They appear to have been calling Jesus illegitimate, thereby implying that his mother was guilty of fornication, and thus he could be disqualified as a legitimate religious authority (Deut. 23:2). Elder McConkie saw in the Jews' remark "We be not born of fornication" not a reference to inherited mortal lineage but a reference to spiritual lineage. He explained the passage by paraphrasing what they said as "The devil is not our father; we are not spiritually illegitimate; we are the children of Abraham and have the true religion, and hence God is our Father."[54]

No evidence survives to suggest how Mary responded to embarrassment created by false conclusions about her or her firstborn Son. Nor are we told of her reactions to divisions among her own family. She may have replied in the same way she did after the annunciation—pondering and praying for understanding. Most importantly, the scripture narrative indicates that she did not have an easy life and that answers to her prayers did not come quickly. Mary knew the reality of an imperfect world, made more intense by her early encounter with the divine.

After the Resurrection. Mary's commitment to God was evident from the time of Gabriel's annunciation that she was "highly favored" of God (Luke 1:28). She showed remarkable faith in accepting her mission to become the mother of the Son of God. More unexpected occurrences caused her to ponder in her heart what was happening around her and what the divine truths she was told really meant. She kept all those things in her heart, rather than spread them abroad, allowing herself gradually to gain a greater witness and understanding of her Son's unique mission.

Luke gives us our final glimpse of Mary. After the Savior's forty-day post-Resurrection ministry, she joined her surviving children and other disciples to pray and worship together (Acts 1:14). Unexpectedly, we read that the brothers of Jesus were at this time numbered with the believers. They must have experienced a mighty change of heart in the weeks after Jesus died. The apostle Paul gives one hint to explain this conversion, observing that the resurrected Lord appeared to his half-brother James, presumably during the forty-day ministry (1 Cor. 15:7). James eventually became a key Christian leader in Jerusalem after the death of James, brother of John (Acts 15:13–20; 21:17–19); he and another half-brother, Jude/Judas, each wrote an epistle that became a part of the New Testament canon. The record is silent concerning Mary's response to this newfound religious harmony in her family, but any believing parent who has witnessed a doubting child repent and embrace the gospel could empathize with Mary as she experienced unified worship as a family.

Mary would likely not yet have been fifty years old at the time of Jesus' resurrection, but the scriptures do not tell us anything about her health or her later years. Naturally, legends abound, but reliable information about her ends with the passage in Acts 1:14. From Luke's portrait of her with the Christians after the Resurrection, Mary's prayer, "Behold the handmaiden of the Lord; be it unto me according to thy word" (Luke 1:38), was answered, and she remained loyal to God's word throughout her life.

Scripture most often employs Mary to further portray Jesus Christ, such as her proclamation in the Magnificat: "My soul doth magnify the Lord" (Luke 1:46). Through her experiences, Mary invites us to see our Savior more clearly. Her example as a mother and a disciple heightens our perspective as we grow in awe of God's almighty goodness and power in our daily walk with each other.

POINTS TO PONDER

1. Considering Mary's example of pondering rather than proclaiming, what spiritual truths are best left for the Holy Ghost to teach?

2. How does God's choice of Mary before she was born illustrate his trust in assigning important missions to his daughters?

3. What does young Mary's response to her calling suggest about a young woman's capacity to respond to challenges with integrity and maturity?

4. How does Mary teach us to reverence the opportunities of motherhood? How does her example give us hope in the face of family divisions?

5. What is the equivalent today of standing by and enduring the shame of the cross of Jesus, such as Mary experienced?

EARLIER WOMEN IN THE LINEAGE OF JESUS

*W*ith Matthew's account of Christ's genealogy, the New Testament canon introduces the reader to Jesus. Biblical scholar Raymond E. Brown wrote: "Genealogy is not a record of man's biological productivity but a demonstration of God's providence. . . . A genealogy . . . reflects the working out of God's plan of creation in a history of salvation."[1] Certainly the Savior's pedigree reflects the Father's plan of salvation centuries before his Son was born. The first chapter of Matthew declares the royal line of Israel to which Jesus belonged and demonstrates that he was God's anointed representative: a son of Abraham, through whom God promised to bless all families of the earth; a son of David, through Judah's royal line; and the Messiah, the long-awaited Savior of God's people.

Matthew's source or sources for the genealogy of Jesus are not known. In the time of Jesus, most families of pure Israelite ancestry kept a record of their pedigree for at least their immediate ancestors and knew to which of the twelve tribes they belonged. The early Christian historian Eusebius suggests that the family of Jesus kept an ancestral record that facilitated the emperor Domitian's efforts to locate two grandsons of Judas, "called the brother of our Lord, according to the flesh," and to determine that they were descendants of David (*Eccl Hist* 3.12; 3.19; 3.32).[2] Proof of lineage was required not only for priests before they took office but also for women who married priests. Those of the tribe of Judah are mentioned more often than other tribes in Israel's historical records, largely because Israel's messianic hope rested on a Deliverer from the Davidic line.

Because the Savior's pedigree in the Gospel of Matthew includes names that are not provided in the Old Testament record (Matt. 1:13–15) and excludes some generations that are noted earlier in the Bible, questions arise over its completeness and whether it is a direct father-to-son lineage. It obviously differs from Jesus' genealogy recorded in Luke's Gospel. For example, Luke lists seventy-seven generations from Jesus back to "Adam, which was the son of God" (Luke 3:38), whereas Matthew reports forty-two generations starting from Abraham rather than Adam. Furthermore, Luke's genealogy names fifty-six generations in the same time period covered by Matthew's forty-two names.

Blessed Is She That Believed

BY ELSPETH YOUNG

Matthew's selection of names was likely influenced by the significance he found by arranging the generations in three groups of fourteen. The Jewish people appear to have been fond of presenting information in patterns and symmetries, which lends further credence to the belief that Matthew was writing to a Jewish audience.[3] He counted fourteen generations from Abraham to David (ca. 1750–1000 B.C.), another fourteen from David to the Babylonian captivity (ca. 1000–600 B.C.), and still another fourteen from the captivity to Jesus (ca. 600–5 B.C.) (Matt. 1:17). Clearly, the years spanning the time of Abraham to Jesus exceeded forty-two generations, as shown by the years represented in each of the three sections in Matthew's genealogy: from Abraham to David was approximately 750 years; from David to the Babylonian captivity, about 400 years; and from the captivity to Jesus, some 600 years. In addition to Luke's fifty-six generations, this is further evidence of an incomplete count in Matthew of the actual generations from Abraham to Jesus.

Omissions in genealogies were not considered problematic among the Israelites, as attested in early rabbinic records in which grandchildren are listed as children.[4] Because biblical genealogies often functioned more to summarize history than meticulously trace ancestry, by omitting some generations, Matthew likely intended to communicate something more to his audience by his three groups of fourteen than a complete father-to-son lineage would show. Another logical explanation for the significance of three groups of fourteen is found in ancient Hebrew alphabet numerology, or gematria. In Hebrew, David's name consists of three letters (*dwd*) which, read as numbers instead of letters (4 + 6 + 4), give the value of fourteen. The 3 x 14 formula may have underscored to Matthew's Jewish audience that even in symbolic numerology Jesus was *the* son of David whom the prophets had foretold. This conclusion is strengthened by the fact that Matthew counted Jechonias's generation twice (Matt. 1:11–12) to arrive at three groups of fourteen each. Fourteen has also been considered as the combination of four and ten: the four represents completeness—as in the tetragrammaton, or divine name of Yahweh/Jehovah—and the ten represents God's will, as shown in the tithe and the Decalogue.[5]

Matthew's genealogy contains other internal surprises. Delineating progenitors down to Joseph, the ultimate intent of the genealogy is to introduce Jesus, perhaps through his mother, who was espoused to Joseph. Since Jesus was actually the Son of God, for Matthew, Jesus' genealogy *must* include Mary to establish the biological link to David. To show biological parentage, Matthew alters his pattern of "A begat B; B begat C" (such as is found in Ruth 4:18–22 and 1 Chr. 2:10–15) when he gets to Joseph. There the pattern changes to "A begat B, and of B's wife was begotten C," or "And Jacob begat Joseph the husband of Mary, of whom was born Jesus, who is called Christ" (Matt. 1:16). The variation reflects the truth that Joseph was *not* the father of Jesus and prepares the reader for an extraordinary revelation: Mary would conceive Jesus through the power of the Holy Ghost and not by sexual union with Joseph (Matt. 1:18–25). Since Jewish law made no distinction between the rights of natural sons and those of adopted sons, Jesus is not only Abraham's covenant son and David's royal son through Joseph but he is also Immanuel, the Son of God, through Mary.

Perhaps the most surprising addition to Matthew's account of Jesus' lineage, however, is the inclusion in Jesus' pedigree of four women other than Mary. Jewish genealogies did not customarily identify women in the list of descendants. We therefore ask why does Matthew's Gospel, the most Jewish of the synoptic Gospels, include women in the Savior's lineage, and why these four women in particular? Did their lives illuminate the Savior's future ministry in some way, or did Matthew see parallels between them and the fifth woman, Mary? Because personal traits were believed by Jews to reappear at times in one's descendants,[6] perhaps Matthew, by including these four women, was preparing his audience to recognize something about Mary revealed in Jesus' messianic lineage.

Among the forty-two male names in Matthew's genealogy are the names of five women:

1. Thamar (Matt. 1:3; or Tamar, in Gen. 38)
2. Rachab (Matt. 1:5; or Rahab, in Joshua 2; 6)
3. Ruth (Matt. 1:5; Ruth 1–4)
4. "Her that had been the wife of Uriah" (Matt. 1:6; or Bathsheba, in 2 Sam. 11–12)
5. Mary (Matt. 1:16)

We may wonder why Matthew did not mention the more highly regarded mothers of Israel in the Savior's genealogy—Sarah, Rebekah, or Leah—alongside the listing of their prestigious husbands, Abraham, Isaac, and Jacob. What different message would the inclusion of those women have sent to Matthew's first-century Jewish audience?

Several intriguing theories have attempted to explain Matthew's inclusion of Tamar, Rahab, Ruth, and Bathsheba in the Savior's genealogy. Four of the many suggestions are discussed here. Although each one has potential merit, two of the four are problematic with respect to Matthew's intent. That intent depends largely on whether the Gospel writer posited a connection between the four women and Jesus' ministry, or between the four women and Mary.

Theory 1: These women were obvious sinners in need of redemption. This theory is first attributed to Jerome in the fourth century when he wrote, "In the Savior's genealogy it is remarkable that there is no mention of *holy* women, but only those whom Scripture *reprehends,* so that [we can understand that] he who had come for the sake of sinners, since he was born from sinful women, blots out the sins of everyone" (*Comm Matt* 1.3).[7] The women were mentioned, according to this suggestion, to illustrate that Christ's compassion and sacrifice was for the most sinful as well as the most righteous.

This theory has problems. First, Matthew's genealogy already contains the names of a multiplicity of men who could demonstrate the same truth about the Savior's mercy for the immoral and unrighteous. Matthew did not need to break from the customary all-male genealogical pattern just to show that

Jesus' lineage contained sinners. For example, Ahaz and Manasseh (Matt. 1:9–10) were notoriously wicked kings, not to mention the sinful acts recorded of Judah, David, and Solomon. Second, the Old Testament does *not* declare these women to be sinners. In fact, later Jewish tradition honors each of them for preserving Judah's messianic lineage. Finally, if Matthew is believed to have included these "sinful" women in Christ's lineage to introduce Mary, her connection to the category fails. Neither Matthew nor any other Christian writer portrays Mary as "a sinner."

Theory 2: These women were not Israelites. According to this theory, the four women were important to the Gospel story because they were initially alien to the people of God but later united with the Israelites and contributed to their new nation's greatness. This proposal is first attributed to Martin Luther in the sixteenth century. Luther intended to show that the Jewish Messiah could claim kinship to both Israel and non-Israel. Including these other four women in Matthew's genealogy communicates that the Savior's sacrifice was intended for both Jew and Gentile from the beginning. But if this had been Matthew's intent, why does he begin the genealogy with Abraham, thus excluding the Gentiles, while Luke, the Gentile evangelist, begins his genealogy with Adam, thus including all humanity? True, Rahab was clearly a Canaanite and Ruth was a Moabitess, and although it cannot be proved, Tamar could have been a Canaanite, having been married to Judah's half-Canaanite son. Neither can Bathsheba's ethnic background be positively identified, but her name is Hebrew for "daughter of Sheba or covenant." She was married to a Hittite named Uriah, which may suggest she was also a Hittite.

So, did Matthew include these women to bear witness of the Savior's promise of salvation for foreigners, or Gentiles, along with the children of Abraham? Truly, Christ's Atonement does cover all who embrace the gospel of Abraham—and the biblical narrative implies that all four of these women feared the God of Abraham, Isaac, and Jacob. Because they may have already been daughters of Israel or eventually converts or proselytes to Judaism, however, none of the four was considered a foreigner in postexilic Jewish literature and perhaps not in Matthew's day either. If we assume these four women were mentioned to highlight the universality of Jesus' mission only and not to inform the reader about Mary in any way, this theory may have merit. On the other hand, if Matthew's intent had any connection to Mary, the only other woman in his genealogy, then this theory falls short. Nothing in scripture or tradition allows for Mary, the mother of Jesus, to be considered a Gentile or foreigner under any definition.

Theory 3: These women were accused of bearing illegitimate children. It is theorized that the four women were named to support Mary against claims that Jesus was illegitimately born.[8] The Old Testament evidence, however, does not support such a theory. Bathsheba clearly gave birth to an illegitimate child, but that child died at birth; Solomon was legitimately born. Although Tamar may have been perceived by some to have illegitimately conceived twin sons, the children were deemed to be legitimate because of her rights under the levirate law, as will be discussed in the chapter about her. Also, Ruth and Boaz were unquestionably married before they conceived a child, and although Rahab is described as a "harlot," details of her giving birth are completely absent. Interestingly, there is evidence of an early Jewish polemic over questions of the legitimacy of Jesus' birth (*GNic* 2:3; *Cels* 32; *GThom* 105).[9]

By a twist of the first theory discussed above, some have even argued that Jesus was the illegitimate son of Mary but was subsequently chosen and empowered by God. By extension, according to this theory, other women besides Mary who give birth out of wedlock should not be judged harshly or shamed.[10] From this perspective, the four women in Matthew's Gospel may have conceived through rape or even by willing participation in a scandalous tryst but were thereafter forgiven by God. So also, the theory goes, Mary's unspoken indiscretion was excused by simply explaining that "she was found with child of the Holy Ghost" (Matt. 1:18). This theory tries too hard to exonerate the guilty by misunderstanding or ignoring the miraculous and divine plan in Mary's sacred story.

Theory 4: These women were originally considered to have behaved scandalously but were later recognized for their wisdom in preserving the Messiah's lineage. This last theory has attracted considerable acceptance in modern scholarship. "It does not go beyond the biblical evidence and . . . it gives the women something in common with Mary as she will be described in Matt. 1:18–25."[11] More specifically, it combines two elements found in the four Old Testament women which help to portray them as types of Mary. First, all four women experienced irregular histories or marital unions that could be misjudged as scandalous by outside observers. Second, in each story, the woman showed initiative in carrying out God's plan and thereby continuing the chosen lineage of the Son of God. Moreover, God's approval of her actions and his miraculous intervention in her challenges are not altogether obvious.[12] Bathsheba has been cited as the exception, significantly weakening the theory because she showed no evidence of initiative when David summoned her to his palace.[13] However, it was Bathsheba who later orchestrated the plan for her son Solomon to inherit David's throne, thus demonstrating her self-will and initiative (1 Kgs. 1–2). Mary's conception of Jesus, which appeared shameful at first, even to Joseph, was foreshadowed by similar scandals involving the four women listed earlier in Matthew's genealogy. Together these five women in Jesus' lineage illustrate that from the beginning God had a specific plan, foreshadowed in the scriptures, to bring his Son and our Redeemer into the world. As some scholars have observed, "A genealogy is a striking way of bringing before us the continuity of God's purpose through the ages."[14]

When considered collectively, the parallel circumstances of these five women witness of God's foreknowledge, planning, and ultimate rescue of his Son's mortal lineage. Matthew's selected genealogy communicates that the chosen Abrahamic-Davidic line survived through the centuries in part because of the courage of these four women. "These women were held up as examples of how God uses the unexpected to triumph over human obstacles and intervenes on behalf of His planned Messiah. It is the combination of the scandalous or irregular union and of divine intervention through the woman that explains best Matthew's choice in the genealogy."[15] The fact that all the women except Mary were *possibly* Gentiles can also be seen as an added message of their inclusion. Taken together, these complementary theories indicate Matthew's foreshadowing both the role of the Savior *and* that of his mother.

Subscribing to this fourth view, we will examine the story of each of these women in Matthew's genealogy of Jesus. Their stories could easily fall into the two-dimensional treatment that women in scripture often receive—they are either totally righteous or totally wicked. Ruth is often viewed as an ideal role model, without a single flaw. Rahab is often transformed by commentators into an innkeeper rather than a harlot. Tamar is labeled a conniving and selfish amateur prostitute, and for many Bathsheba was an adulteress at best and a seducer and destroyer of men at worst. Yet, Matthew calls our attention to all four of them before he introduces us to Mary and her divine Son. Certainly he intended by this that his audience see much more than black and white—or even gray—but the full colors of their lives and stories.

Interestingly, of the twenty-two women in the Hebrew Bible identified in the Jewish *Midrashim* (rabbinic traditions) as "women of valor," three are also listed in the Savior's genealogy: Rahab, Ruth, and Bathsheba.[16] That is additional evidence of the high regard later Jews had for these women who were earlier so easily misunderstood. Our study of women of the New Testament therefore requires us to give attention to these four women, their unique challenges, and their ultimate victories. Such an exploration will add clarity to our understanding of Mary's foreordained mission as well as that of Jesus. Hopefully, their stories will encourage our own discipleship with the Lord.

By the Wayside

BY ASHTON YOUNG

TAMAR

תָּמָר

"Palm Tree" (Hebrew)

andwiched between the stories of young Joseph being sold by his jealous brothers to a band of Ishmaelites (Gen. 37) and his later courageous escape from the sexual advances of Potiphar's wife (Gen. 39) is the unseemly story of Tamar and Judah (Gen. 38). Often viewed as an interruption of the tale of virtuous Joseph's rise to power, Tamar's moment on the biblical stage is hardly ever mentioned. Deemed inappropriate for Sunday School, the story of Tamar remains largely unknown and unappreciated. After all, finding any redeeming application from a story about a widow who plays the harlot in order to have a child can be a challenge at best. But Tamar's story is a necessary part of the patriarchal narrative. In the first book of the Old Testament, she is inseparably connected to the family of Jacob and Judah, and in the first chapter of the New Testament, she is highlighted by Matthew as an ancestress of Jesus Christ (Matt. 1:3).

In addition to being listed by Matthew as one of five women in the messianic line, the biblical text communicates three other hints about Tamar that may indicate we are missing important elements of the story if we simply write it off as dealing with deception, immorality, or revenge.

First, when one of Tamar's descendants, the honorable Boaz, married Ruth, the community leaders in their day pronounced a blessing upon them: "Let thy house be like the house of Pharez, whom Tamar bare unto Judah" (Ruth 4:12). Obviously, neither Tamar nor her sons were an embarrassment to the tribe of Judah during the period of the judges.

Second, one of King David's daughters and one of his granddaughters were named Tamar (2 Sam. 13:1; 14:27). Again, this would indicate that within the royal tribe of Judah, leaders during the Israelite monarchy were not ashamed of their ancestress Tamar. At the very least, the name carried no taint of shame or impropriety in David's day.

GENESIS 38

RUTH 4:12

1 CHRONICLES 2:4

MATTHEW 1:3

49

Third, after Tamar was found pregnant with Judah's child, he publicly pronounced that "she hath been more righteous than I" (Gen. 38:26). Although some within Judah's clan may at first have found it shameful, details surrounding the story show that Tamar did not break any moral law. Tamar could have rightfully expected additional privileges and respect as the wife of the birthright son. In Canaanite practice, the levirate law declared that a woman was only truly a widow when her husband and father-in-law were both dead and she had no son. The same law declared that her marital obligation to her husband's family continued for as long as her husband's brother or her father-in-law lived (*Middle Assyrian Law* #33; *Hittite Law* #193).[1] Since a woman's security in old age depended upon her sons, the law stated that a widow of child-bearing age was entitled to bear children through a male "in-law" acting as proxy for her dead husband. Under the levirate law, then, Judah was a legal proxy for Tamar's deceased husband.

Considering the story in its historical context, Tamar's actions can be viewed as appropriate within the laws of her day and in the eyes of God.[2] Seen through this lens, Tamar's proactive choices gave a restorative influence to Judah and his posterity.

HISTORICAL CONTEXT

In approximately the eighteenth century B.C., Jacob (or Israel, as he was renamed by the Lord) settled in the area of Hebron with his twelve sons, daughters, servants, and numerous flocks (Gen. 37:1). Jacob loved Joseph, his eleventh son and the firstborn of his deceased wife, Rachel, better than all his other sons, as illustrated by his making only Joseph a special coat, or covering. Not only did Joseph's older brothers covet that unique coat but they "hated" and "envied" Joseph (Gen. 37:3–11). When they were feeding their father's flocks in Shechem (about fifty miles from Hebron), Jacob sent Joseph to meet them and report on them and their flocks. When Joseph finally found his siblings, they were in Dothan. Recognizing their teenage brother coming from a distance, the older sons schemed to kill him and leave his body in a pit to be rid of him forever (Gen. 37:17–20). Reuben, the eldest of Jacob's sons and the firstborn of Leah, recoiled at this plan, suggesting instead that they merely drop him in a pit without harming him, making it possible for Reuben to rescue Joseph later and return him to their father. The brothers did as Reuben advised (Gen. 37:21–24).

But while Reuben was inexplicably away, "a company of Ishmeelites came from Gilead with their camels bearing spicery and balm and myrrh, going to carry it down to Egypt" (Gen. 37:25). In Reuben's absence, Judah took over as leader of the brothers, even though he was not the next oldest. Judah, the fourth son of Jacob and Leah, is first mentioned individually apart from his brothers in this incident. Judah saw a way to eliminate his brother and to make a profit from him at the same time (Gen. 37:26–28). His brothers agreed with his plan, and Joseph was long gone before Reuben returned. Rending or tearing his clothes, Reuben showed his profound remorse for the loss of Joseph, crying, "The child is not; and I, whither shall I go?" (Gen. 37:29–30).

Having kept Joseph's unique coat, Judah and his brothers dipped it in goat's blood and returned it to their father with the deceptive report that Jacob's young son must have been attacked and devoured by "an evil beast" (Gen. 37:31–34). This coat, or covering, may represent the "goodly raiment" that Rebekah requested that her son Jacob wear to receive the birthright blessing and priesthood leadership from his father, Isaac (Gen. 27:15). Jewish Midrashim claim that various coverings typify the animal-skin coats with which the Lord covered Adam and Eve.[3] The legend states that this garment was passed down (at least emblematically) through the generations of patriarchs, and its symbolic power and authority were often coveted or counterfeited.

The Jewish legends invite deeper insight into how Joseph's special covering typified the Atonement of Jesus Christ, as implied by the Hebrew word for "atonement," *kaphar,* meaning "to cover" or "a covering."[4] The imagery here is rich. The grace of God *covered* Joseph throughout his dramatic trials in Egypt, just as his special garment had been intended to cover him. However, our subject here is not Joseph, Jacob's virtuous son, who was saved by the grace of God, but rather Judah, Jacob's immoral and mercenary son. Eventually, Judah would also be covered by the Atonement of Christ, and, arguably, he was awakened to that fact through the mediating influence of Tamar.

Upon closer examination, we can see that Genesis presents stories about Joseph and Judah that give us points of comparison to consider. First, Judah's standard of virtue is juxtaposed with that of Joseph. Joseph showed his moral fortitude in refusing the sexual advances of Potiphar's wife, even when it meant paying for his standards by going to prison. In contrast, Judah solicited a woman he believed to be a harlot but was actually his daughter-in-law, Tamar. These stories reveal that Judah was the antithesis of Joseph— licentiousness versus impeccable character.

Second, a comparison of Judah's character before the events in Genesis 38 with his portrayal in later chapters is revealing. It was Judah who concocted the plan with his brothers to sell their father's chosen heir to the Ishmaelites, because "what profit is it if we slay our brother, and conceal his blood?" (Gen. 37:26–33). A significant change of heart is evident in the contrast between Judah's jealous, mercenary attitude and his mature character years later when he believed that Benjamin was in mortal danger. Judah offered himself as a slave in place of Benjamin, who had replaced the betrayed Joseph in Jacob's heart (Gen. 44:18–34). Judah, the betrayer, offered his own life to redeem his victim's successor. In a striking parallel, it was the apostle Judah (Judas) and the people of Judah who sold God's beloved Son to the Romans. And just as Joseph was unrecognized by Judah when they were later reunited, so the beloved Son will at first be unrecognized by Judah and his brothers when he returns to save them (D&C 45:51–52).

Certainly Judah was a changed man. How is his changed heart to be explained? What did Judah experience to awaken him to the patriarchal covenant and his responsibilities before God? The answers are found in Genesis 38. The story of his encounter with Tamar is essential for understanding Judah's return to God and appreciating the Savior's being born into his lineage.

TAMAR'S PLACE OF RESIDENCE

Living among the Canaanites. Geographically reflecting what had happened to him spiritually, Judah left Hebron and traveled west to the lower elevation of Adullam.[5] Jewish tradition suggests that Judah departed from his father's land to live among the Canaanites because his brothers were afterwards ashamed of his plan to sell Joseph and therefore "excluded him from their fellowship, and he had to seek his fortune alone."[6] Shortly after establishing himself in Adullam (about three miles southwest of Bethlehem), Judah made a friend named Hirah and married a Canaanite woman whose father was named Shuah. His Canaanite wife soon bore Judah three sons, whom they named Er, Onan, and Shelah (Gen. 38:1–5).

Because Abraham came from the Mesopotamian area of Aram (later called Syria), his descendants were distinguished ethnically from Canaanites by being called Aramaeans before they were known as Israelites (see Deut. 26:5*a*). The few biblical clues to Judah's life away from his family suggest that Judah was influenced more by the customs of his Canaanite friends and wife than by his own religious upbringing.

When his eldest son, Er, reached marriageable age, Judah selected a wife for him. We are told only that her name was Tamar. Was she a Canaanite like the others in the community in which Judah lived or was she an Aramaean, like Judah, who had somehow joined their society? The Bible is silent on this detail, but both possibilities have been argued. Among the Old Testament Pseudepigrapha are passages that read, "Judah took a wife for Er, his firstborn, from the daughters of Aram, and her name was Tamar" (*Jub* 41:1),[7] and "Er brought from Mesopotamia Tamar, daughter of Aram" (*T Jud* 10:1).[8] Early Hebrew traditions state that Tamar was not a Canaanite but "a daughter of Aram, the son of Shem."[9] This tradition further posits that Judah's wife rejected Tamar because she was *not* a Canaanite and therefore found ways to alienate her from her sons.

Salient evidence also supports claims that Tamar was a Canaanite. By the time Judah chose Tamar to marry his son, he was living among the Canaanites, married to a Canaanite, and looked to a Canaanite as his best friend and confidant. Why would Judah require that his half-Canaanite sons marry from among his people when he himself had not done so? Had Tamar been part of Nahor and Milcah's clan or the daughter of one of Judah's brothers, we might expect Genesis to report it. Furthermore, the scriptural narrative provides a series of facts that collectively hint that because of the lack of background about Tamar, we cannot know whether she was a Canaanite or whether she worshipped Abraham's God before her marriage to Judah's son. Evidence on both sides of these questions can be persuasive.

Consequences of the levirate law. Tamar's opportunities in life were severely restricted by the ramifications of an ancient custom of marriage for childless widows called the levirate law. In the ancient world, a woman belonged to her father as a child, to her husband as an adult, and to her son as a widow. Therefore, a woman did not simply marry a man; she married his entire family. The levirate law was applicable if the woman became a childless widow. The suggestion is that Tamar did not do anything to displease the Lord but that her husband did. The narrative implies that however financially, politically, or culturally beneficial the marriage appeared to Judah initially, it did not benefit Tamar. Because the marriage did not produce an heir, a law that was widely observed in the Near East applied to Tamar and her in-laws.

Before the levirate law was formalized in the law of Moses, it was legally observed for generations in the ancient Near East as a way to continue a family line and provide lifelong sustenance for the widow without adoption (Deut. 25:5–10). If a woman's husband died before she bore a son, she was to return to her father's household, unless her dead husband's family kept her with them under the law of the *levir* (Hebrew, *yabam*; Latin, *levir,* means "brother-in-law"). More specifically, the widow's brother-in-law or other male in-law was given to her "to raise up seed" so that the lineage of the dead man would continue and the widow would have security in her old age.

According to Middle Assyrian law, the widow's father-in-law was obliged to arrange a levirate marriage for her. The daughter-in-law had the right to demand one of her husband's brothers as a levirate husband. The men in the family could refuse, but they would be shamed in a public ritual probably similar to that described in the law of Moses in which the widow removes his shoe and spits in his face (Deut. 25:9). The same law also stipulated that if a father-in-law had no other son over the age of ten years, he could himself be the levir for a widowed daughter-in-law (*Middle Assyrian Law,* #43).[10]

When Er died, Onan was expected to perform the role of levir for his sister-in-law Tamar. As the eldest son, Er is assumed to have held the birthright, which would normally be passed to his son. Er's inheritance from his father would be twice that of his two brothers, or half of all that his father, Judah, possessed. By contrast, Er's brother Onan could anticipate only a fourth of his father's wealth if Er had an heir. Apparently, Onan considered the economics of his situation and decided not to impregnate Tamar. Therefore, he married Tamar publicly but privately refused to honor his role as levir. In a primitive attempt at birth control, "he spilled [his seed] on the ground" (Gen. 38:9), further degrading Tamar by using her for his pleasure while thinking to deny her a child.

Jewish tradition blames Judah's Canaanite wife for inciting her son's "care not to beget any children with [Tamar]," as well as forbidding Judah to give Tamar to his youngest son, Shelah.[11] These Midrashim explain the death of Judah's wife in Genesis 38:12 as evidence of God's anger against her. The biblical text, however, indicts Er, who "was wicked in the sight of the Lord; and the Lord slew him" (Gen. 38:7) and Onan, whose actions "displeased the Lord; wherefore he slew him also" (Gen. 38:10).

Genesis records that Judah feared that Shelah would die as his brothers had if he married Tamar (Gen.

38:11). Tamar had done all that she was asked but was once again in the vulnerable position of being without legal tie to family support and honor. Judah instructed her to "remain a widow" until Shelah grew up (Gen. 38:11). Her only other option was to risk death if she illegally went outside Judah's family to obtain the security that only a son could provide her.

TAMAR'S APPEARANCE IN THE BIBLICAL STORY

Judah remains the focus of the chapter until his intention to ignore his daughter-in-law's right to marry Shelah becomes apparent. At that point, Tamar takes center stage, and the reader follows her activities to create a life for herself rather than await an awakening of Judah's sense of duty. The narrator of Genesis invites the reader to know what is happening before Judah figures it out. The result is a delightful story of a woman's ingenuity that saved a lineage and awakened Judah to return to his God.

Tamar becomes proactive. The length of time that Tamar remained in her dead-end circumstance is not noted, only that after a "process of time" she learned of Judah's whereabouts (Gen. 38:12). Tradition claims that she "remained a widow in her father's house for two years" before the "holy spirit" revealed the need to confront her father-in-law,[12] and so Tamar prepared to leave the protection of her family in order to see him.

Tamar knew that Shelah had reached marriageable age by then and that Judah was not going to keep the levirate obligation. When she heard where her father-in-law would be traveling to shear sheep, she made plans to intercept him on his way to Timnath (Gen. 38:13).

Removing any indication of her widowhood, Tamar covered herself with a veil so as not to be recognized (Gen. 38:14). Wearing a veil did not in and of itself signify that a woman was a prostitute. On the

MIDDLE ASSYRIAN LAW FOR WEARING A VEIL

"Neither wives of seigniors nor [widows] nor [Assyrian women], who go out on the street [may have] their heads [uncovered]. The daughters of a seignior . . . whether it is a shawl or a robe or [a mantle], must veil themselves; [they must not have] their heads [uncovered]. . . . When they go out on the street alone, they must veil themselves. A concubine who goes out on the street with her mistress must veil herself. A sacred prostitute whom a man married must veil herself on the street, but one whom a man did not marry must have her head uncovered on the street; she must not veil herself. A harlot must not veil herself; her head must be uncovered; he who has seen a harlot veiled must arrest her, produce witnesses, (and) bring her to the palace tribunal; they shall not take her jewelry away, (but) the one who arrested her may take her clothing; they shall flog her fifty (times) with staves (and) pour pitch on her head. However, if a seignior has seen a harlot veiled and has let (her) go without bringing her to the palace tribunal, they shall flog that seignior fifty (times) with staves" (*Middle Assyrian Law* #40).[13]

contrary, veils usually indicated respectability. Rebekah donned a veil before meeting Isaac (Gen. 24:65). Leah was probably veiled for her wedding to Jacob to disguise the fact that she was not Rachel (Gen. 29:23–25). By contrast, wanton women fully disclosed their faces to clearly communicate who and what they were. In fact, Assyrian law prohibited prostitutes from wearing veils at all.

Not all scholars agree concerning Tamar's original intent: was her initial plan to trick Judah into thinking she was a harlot, or did that idea occur to her when he mistook her for a harlot? Considering the cultural and legal background of the story, one scholar proposed that "Tamar's wearing of the veil was not to make Judah think she was a prostitute. Rather, it was intended to prevent him from recognizing her. It is not the veil but Tamar's positioning herself [alone on an open road] that made her appear to be a prostitute."[14] More importantly, the text does not call Tamar a harlot; Judah did (Gen. 38:15). She simply set the scene in which Judah would be the main actor; she sat and waited for him by the road to let

Sketches by Ashton Young

Judah left his signet with Tamar as a pledge that he would send payment. He also left his staff with her, suggesting it had unique markings that would identify its owner.

him reach his own conclusions and carry out his own intentions. Perhaps, like Nephi in "not knowing beforehand" what he would do (1 Ne. 4:6), Tamar was receptive to the Spirit for guidance that can only come from God.

Judah's pledge for payment. Knowing that the levirate law permitted her father-in-law to be the proxy for his family, Tamar must have been relieved with Judah's indecent intent. But she was also aware that he would refuse to do his duty by her if he recognized her. Keeping her identity a secret, she accepted his proposition, and being aware that he did not have the requisite remuneration in his possession, Tamar required some collateral until payment delivered. According to the law, such a pledge was kept by the creditor until the debt was satisfied.[15] Tamar wanted something that would clearly prove that the man who had slept with her was Judah. Thus she requested as security "thy signet, and thy bracelets, and thy staff which is in thine hand" (Gen. 38:18). The Hebrew for "signet" and "bracelets" is better translated "signet ring with its cord." A signet ring of stone or metal was worn on a cord around the neck. Engravings on this ring allowed a man to endorse documents when it was pressed into a soft clay seal.

When Tamar returned to her father's house and resumed wearing her widow's garments (Gen. 38:19), everything was as it had been before—except that she was pregnant. Judah sent his Canaanite friend Hirah the Adullamite to deliver a kid-goat to "the harlot" for his payment (Gen. 38:21). Interestingly, Hirah did not ask the whereabouts of the *zona* (Hebrew for "harlot"), the term Judah used for the woman he approached on the roadway. Rather, Hirah asked for the *qedesh* (Hebrew for a "public woman" or "temple prostitute"), a more respectable occupation in the ancient world.[16]

After Hirah's attempts proved futile, Judah asked him to desist his search, saying, "Let her take it to her, lest we be shamed" (Gen. 38:23), or in other words, "Let her keep the things, or we shall become a laughingstock."[17] Failing to pay the "harlot," Judah decided to forfeit his pledge and avoid public ridicule, and he let the matter rest.

Judah's response to Tamar. Three months after his encounter with "the harlot," Judah was informed that his daughter-in-law had "played the harlot" because she was pregnant (Gen. 38:24).[18] Knowing that Shelah had not been near her, Judah assumed that Tamar had been immoral. As head of Er's clan, Judah held the power of life and death over its members, and he sentenced Tamar to be burned.[19] More than three hundred years later, under the law of Moses, the penalty for extramarital sex remained the same: the guilty were sentenced to be burned (Lev. 20:14; 21:9).

After being falsely accused, Tamar did not produce Judah's pledge until, as the Hebrew says, she was being led to her death (Gen. 38:25). Then, at that moment, she simply and publicly announced, "By the man, whose these are, am I with child. . . . Discern, I pray thee" (Gen. 38:25). Jewish tradition offers a twist to the story, claiming that Tamar was willing to die rather than shame him publicly. Trusting in Judah's sense of honor, she said: "By the man whose these are am I with child, but though I perish in the flames, I will not betray him. I hope in the Lord of the world, that He will turn the heart of the man, so that he will make confession thereof."[20]

Upon realizing his role in Tamar's pregnancy, Judah owned up to his fault and declared, "She hath been more righteous than I" (Gen. 38:26). Her dramatic example humbled him and helped awaken him to the need to repent. Judah's involvement in Tamar's successful pregnancy would also have erased the "Black Widow" stigma that he and others may have placed on her after Er and Onan died.

One rabbinic account portrays Judah's complete change of heart at the moment the truth about Tamar was publicly revealed. In his lengthy speech, according to this legend, Judah confessed both his sin against Tamar in withholding a levir and his previous crimes against his brother Joseph: "I make it known that with what measure a man metes, it shall be measured unto him, be it for good or for evil, but happy the man that acknowledgeth his sins. Because I took the coat of Joseph, and colored it with the blood of a kid, and then laid it at the feet of my father . . . I now confess . . . [I] unto whom belongeth this signet, this mantle, and this staff. But it is better that I be put to shame in this world than I should be put to shame in the other world. . . . Now, then, I acknowledge that Tamar is innocent. By me is she with child, not because she indulged in illicit passion, but because I held back her marriage with my son Shelah."[21]

Although the authority of the legend is uncertain, the lesson this one teaches is significant. Judah's change of heart was brought about by a greater concern for what God thought of him than for what his neighbors thought of him. Awakened to his covenant with God through Tamar's patient, wise, and courageous example, Judah learned that to act shamefully before the Lord brings heartache in return. He had lost a wife and two sons and risked losing his Israelite posterity. Only by Tamar's proactive righteousness was the latter ultimately preserved. The Genesis narrative of Judah's future encounters with his family, including Joseph, indicates that his change of heart was profound and permanent (Gen. 43:8–9; 44:18–34).

Because Judah was a legal levir, he was not guilty of adultery. The scriptures report that he did not sleep with Tamar again (Gen. 38:26), thereby respecting the law that the levir fulfilled his responsibility when the woman conceived.

Tamar's legacy. Tamar bore Judah twin sons, Pharez and Zarah (Gen. 38:27–30). In a sense, one could say these infants replaced Judah's two sons who had died. These boys secured their mother's place in Judah's family and support for her in her old age. But, more importantly

WORD STUDY: *RIGHTEOUS*, OR ṢADEQ

The Hebrew word ṣadeq, translated "righteous," suggests a person's standing in a moral or legal sense. If someone is righteous, he is just and law abiding or she has a just cause or is in the right. In Genesis 38:26, Judah proclaimed Tamar ṣadeq in a trial concerning her observance of the levirate law. In another biblical passage, Abraham wondered how many ṣadeq could be found in Sodom and Gomorrah to protect the cities from destruction (Gen. 18:23–28).[22]

for religious history, they provided a righteous maternal link in Judah's lineage to prepare for the Savior's birth. Matthew recognized the magnitude of these events when he noted them in the Savior's genealogy, "And Judas begat Phares and Zara of Thamar" (Matt. 1:3).

The birth of Pharez and Zarah echoed that of their grandfather Jacob. Zarah's hand appeared first, whereupon the midwife tied a "scarlet thread" to mark him as firstborn. "And it came to pass, as he drew back his hand, that, behold, his brother [Pharez] came out" (Gen. 38:29). Even though Zarah had been marked as the firstborn, it was Pharez who was actually born first and whose descendants inherited the birthright. Similarly, Esau ("the red one") was born first, his twin brother, Jacob, at his heel, though Jacob ultimately received the birthright (Gen. 25:25–26). Twin brothers, scarlet markings, and reversal in the expected birthright recipient seem to have been important hallmarks in the lineage of the Messiah (Rom. 9:10–12).

Tamar's sons are listed among Judah's descendants who journeyed to Egypt with Jacob's family after their reconciliation with Joseph (Gen. 46:12). Interestingly, Shelah was also numbered among the family of Judah who went to Egypt, and his descendants were listed with the Israelites who left Egypt generations later under Moses (Num. 26:20). Through Tamar's inspired actions, God saved the birthright lineage from Judah to Er to Pharez and likely allowed Shelah the blessing of life within a God-fearing community.

By Matthew's day, Tamar was viewed as a heroine in the history of Israel. Philo of Alexandria portrayed her as Veiled Virtue (*Prelim Stud* 23.124–26). Early rabbis saw her as chosen by the Lord to be a mother of a royal lineage.[23] Had Tamar remained subservient to Judah's orders and quietly waited in her father's home for good fortune to come her way, her story would likely not have been included in holy writ. Only when she became assertive and unconventional did her actions punctuate the biblical story. In order to derive a solution to her family crisis, a solution that was likewise acceptable to God, Tamar also became the unexpected deliverer for Judah and his patriarchal lineage. Exercising remarkable initiative and profound faith, Tamar boldly challenged unrighteous dominion and emerged the victor. No wonder Matthew elected to remember her in his account of the Savior's progenitors.

POINTS TO PONDER

1. Considering that when God first created woman, he made her a "help" (*ezer*) for man, how was Tamar an *ezer* for Judah and his line?

2. How did Judah's experience of losing two sons and then discovering that God "restored" them to him through the birth of Tamar's sons mirror Jacob's experience with Judah and Joseph?

3. How does continually hiding a mistake or sin through self-deception alter our relationships with family,

the Church, and God? Should our sin become public (as Judah's did), how could such embarrassment actually become a blessing in our lives?

4. Have you ever been taught by a Christlike example in someone you had previously deemed "less righteous" than you? What new insight about yourself and others did this experience teach you?

5. What qualities in Tamar do you admire?

6. Where can you find a testimony or type of Christ in the story?

Waiting for the Promise
BY ELSPETH YOUNG

RAHAB

רָחָב

"To Be Wide, Enlarge" (Hebrew)

Although the Bible usually portrays men as the political, military, and community leaders in ancient society, sacred history often depicts women as their rescuers. Though without position of power or prestige, Rahab, like Tamar before her, became such a deliverer. Without violence or threats, these women obtained victory by allowing men in power to assume they were weak and incapable. Such was Rahab, whose wisdom and courage secured her a place of great honor in Jewish history. According to Jewish tradition, she is one of a "quartet of the most beautiful women in history," the other three being Sarah, Abigail, and Esther.[1] Rahab is also one of twenty-two women named in Jewish Midrashim as "women of valor."[2]

A resident of the city of Jericho, Rahab was a Canaanite, a harlot, the proprietor of her own business, and a responsible provider for her family. She entered the biblical saga when she risked everything to preserve the lives of two Israelite spies in Jericho prior to the conquest of the promised land. Furthermore, motivated by her belief in Jehovah, Israel's God, she was subsequently numbered among the Israelites and became an ancestress of Jesus Christ. Rahab's checkered background tempts us to ignore some of it in order to paint her with hues acceptable to us. However, her unsavory origins combine to create a unique and memorable heroine who was perfectly prepared and placed to be an instrument in the hands of Jehovah.

RAHAB'S PLACE OF RESIDENCE

Old Testament Jericho. Rahab lived in the walled Canaanite city of Jericho. Fed by significant springs, the city of Jericho is in one of the richest agricultural areas of Canaan, located about five miles west of the Jordan River at the point where the Israelites must have crossed.

JOSHUA 2
JOSHUA 6:16–25
MATTHEW 1:5
HEBREWS 11:31
JAMES 2:25

61

The size of the partially excavated mound identified as Old Testament Jericho indicates that the city was home to fewer than two thousand residents when Rahab lived there.

Isolated from other Canaanite communities, Jericho was a lush oasis surrounded by a rugged and parched landscape.[3]

The well-defined mound upon which the Old Testament city of Jericho was built is relatively small, some nine to twelve acres in size, suggesting it to have been more of a town than a city. It is estimated that one thousand to two thousand inhabitants lived there in Rahab's day. Given the city's size, marching around Jericho's wall would have taken the Israelite army less than one hour. In other words, the Israelites could probably have overthrown Jericho by superior numbers alone. Their miraculous victory, however, came in a manner that showed them they were Jehovah's people and that it was by his power they were made strong, rather than by their numbers or their collective might.

From the archaeological remains, it would appear that Jericho was destroyed centuries before Joshua's arrival and uninhabited when the Israelites entered the land. Because elsewhere in Late Bronze Age Canaan defenses of cities were repaired using Middle Bronze Age fortifications, Rahab's Jericho may have been built with reused materials of an earlier town. Suggesting still another possibility, scholars have opined that the remains of Rahab's Jericho could have been washed away over time due to natural erosion. Although there were no Late Bronze Age remains to discover, archaeologists found one juglet lying by a small clay oven and a small amount of Late Bronze Age pottery beneath a floor. These evidences suggest the area could have been occupied at the time that Rahab lived in Jericho. An early date of thirteenth century B.C. for the Israelite conquest has therefore been suggested.[4]

Rahab's house in Jericho. The biblical narrative gives specific clues about the location and features of Rahab's house in Jericho. It was situated "upon the town wall, and she dwelt upon the wall" (Josh. 2:15). The Hebrew reading of this description suggests her house was within a double wall surrounding the town, or "in the wall of the wall." Called a casemate wall by archaeologists, the two walls ran parallel, with the outer wall thicker than the inner wall to provide extra protection against attack. With a sloping rampart, called a glacis, on the lower face of the outer wall, casemate walls could reach a height of thirty feet. Attackers could therefore neither undermine the loose glacis nor get close enough to the walls to use scaling ladders.

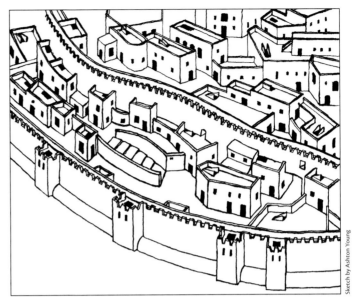

Rahab's home was built between the two walls that surrounded Jericho to provide added protection for the city.

The outer wall was about twelve feet wide, and the inner wall about half as thick, or six feet wide. The space between the walls was typically twelve to fifteen feet and was filled with rubble for added strength, used for storage, or divided into residential cubicles.

Rahab's house had a flat roof that was standard for houses in that day (Josh. 2:6). The roof area was an extension of the family's living quarters and could be used for storage, extra sleeping room, or work space. In Rahab's case, it provided a view outside the wall and perhaps overlooked the town as well.

RAHAB'S DAILY WORK

For more than one reason, Rahab was an "outsider" to Israel. As a Canaanite, she was a Gentile, with whom the Israelites were forbidden to mix. As a harlot and the owner of a public house, she pursued professions that were an abomination to Israel, and she was likely marginalized by other women in Jericho. On the other hand, her family looked to Rahab for support and protection. Such an arrangement was unusual in typical kinship relationships, in which women usually lived within their husband's or father's clan. Rahab's family depended on *her* for their living—and later for their very lives.

Ancient Near Eastern legal codes suggest that businesswomen were acceptable in their societies only under certain conditions. Rahab was the proprietor of a public house where people visited to eat and lodge. Ale wives, as they were often called, did not belong to traditional family units. They owned their own public houses, taverns, or saloons where they offered alcoholic beverages, meals, lodging, and often themselves. Laws concerning women who ran public houses were very strict; the edict proclaimed by

Ammisaduqa, a ruler of Babylon (1646–1626 B.C.), required the death of anyone who cheated a customer by serving less than what the customer actually purchased. Although part of the law is missing, its intended meaning is clear: "A taverness or a merchant who [. . .] dishonest *weight* shall die" (*Edict of Ammisaduqa* #18).[5]

That Rahab is clearly labeled a "harlot" in scripture has presented problems for some readers and critics. Josephus avoided any reference to her as such and instead called her the "keeper of an inn," adding that, after successfully reconnoitering the whole city, the Israelite spies stopped by Rahab's inn to "eat their supper" (*Ant* 5.1.2). Likewise, the early rabbis were uncomfortable about a harlot with a heart of gold, so they insisted that she changed her heart and her lifestyle *before* the spies came to Jericho.[6] Another tradition asserts that Rahab "had been leading an immoral life for forty years, but at the approach of Israel, she paid homage to the true God, [and] lived the life of a pious convert."[7]

Significantly, the New Testament specifies that Rahab was a harlot whose conversion to the God of Abraham provided early Christians with an example of sincere faith in the Lord (Heb. 11:31) and repentant action flowing from that faith (James 2:25). Rahab's earlier lifestyle in Jericho is not only important to acknowledge but essential to appreciate the message of scripture: Jesus Christ is Savior and Redeemer of *all* who will come to him.

In addition to being a harlot, Rahab was an industrious businesswoman with deep devotion to her family. She worked with flax, as evidenced by the flax stalks on her roof and possibly by the "scarlet thread" that she hung out her window to mark her house. She could have been a weaver, dyer, or a basket and rope maker in addition to keeping a public house. Typically women were the weavers in society (Prov. 31:13, 19) and used threads from flax to make linen fabrics (Lev. 13:47–48). Colorful dyes were derived from plants, minerals, and animals.

Flax was a valuable crop in antiquity because it could be processed into linen thread, which could in turn be made into either fabric or rope. Jericho, with its sufficient water and sunshine, was an ideal location for raising flax. Rahab laid out on her roof stacks of wet flax, which could have hidden the Israelite spies.

The Israelite conquest of Jericho occurred in the springtime, when flax is harvested (Josh. 3:15). As soon as flax is mature and ready to process into linen thread, fabric, or rope, it is pulled up from the roots and cut in three- to four-foot lengths. To produce "fine twined linen," flax stems were steeped in running water to break down the woody parts and separate the fibers. Flax stems were then soaked in water to separate the fibers and left to dry in the sun. The objective was to retain fibers at the greatest possible length. To make strong rope or cord for basketry, flax stems were made brittle and stiff by retting, or soaking, them in dew rather than in running water. Rahab laid out the wet flax on her roof where there would be plenty of sun and the stacks of flax would be high enough to hide the spies. When the fibers were dry, she could comb through the dry fibers and then twist them and spin them into a continuous thread.

The meaning of Rahab's name is also indicative of this message. Translated as "wide or broad" in Hebrew, her name may be a shortened version of "God has enlarged,"[8] foreshadowing the essential inclusion of Gentiles, public sinners, and outsiders of every kind into the gospel net. How "broad" is the door to God's love, protection, and covenant? He is the Rock "as broad as eternity" (Moses 7:53). Because of the Atonement of Christ, there is no division between the converted despite their various backgrounds (Eph. 2:12–22). If the infinite Atonement of Jesus Christ includes the repentant harlot, how can we exclude her? Rahab is a reminder that God is no respecter of persons and that his covenant extends to all who would believe and participate in the gospel of Abraham.

HISTORICAL CONTEXT

Rahab entered the biblical stage as Abraham's descendants returned to his land of inheritance after being in Egypt for centuries and wandering in the wilderness for forty years. Rahab and the Israelite conquest of Jericho introduce Joshua's campaign to overthrow the central part of Canaan. According to the narrative in the book of Joshua, Israel targeted the city of Jericho soon after the tribes walked into the promised land on dry ground after the Jordan River miraculously parted for them (Josh. 3–6). That part of the river that is nearest to Jericho is also near the place where the Jordan empties into the Dead Sea. Before modern pipelines diverted much of the Jordan for irrigation, the river in that area was approximately ninety to one hundred feet across and nearly twelve feet deep. The Bible narrative suggests that the Israelites crossed over the Jordan in the springtime, identified with "the first month" of the year, or at the end of the rainy season when the "Jordan overfloweth all his banks" (Josh. 4:19; 3:15). This area is also known for landslides due to flooding, which some have suggested as a viable explanation for the river completely stopping long enough for the Israelites to cross. In 1927, for example, the flow of the Jordan River was blocked for twenty-one hours because of a landslide.[9]

Canaan was the land west of the Jordan River, which God had promised to Abraham centuries earlier but which was inhabited by a variety of Semitic peoples when Joshua arrived (see Ex. 13:5). The Canaanites

Canaanites were master architects, as seen in their structures that survive today and in their ornate work in ivory, which they carved to adorn their buildings.

were similar in race and language to the Israelites. Some Canaanites settled along the Jordan River Valley; the Sidonians lived on the northern coast of Phoenicia; the Anakites, called "giants," lived along the southern coastal area; the Hivites, Jebusites, and Hittites inhabited the central hill country, and the Amalekites settled to the south of the hill country. In the Bible, these various peoples are often collectively called Canaanites.

Most of the Canaanite populace was subjected to taxes and other political controls determined by a central government (see 1 Sam. 8:11–18). Their society "was pyramidal, with numerically small but powerful and socially privileged elite. In most cases, the elite were first established militarily, but would rapidly acquire commercial control as well."[10] In the decades before Rahab lived, Egypt controlled the area through an appointed "king" in each city or community who regularly collected tribute from his city-state for the Egyptians, diminishing any hope of independent political power in Canaan. As Egypt withdrew its control over this area, probably about the same time that the Israelites entered, its patchwork of small city-states remained disorganized and vulnerable to invasion by another people. Rahab's community of Jericho was one of these fragmented city-states or mini-kingdoms that dotted the land of Canaan. The "king of Jericho" is mentioned in Rahab's story but is not named (Josh. 2:2).

Canaanites were masters in architecture, as evidenced by the construction of their city walls and buildings. Their skills in this area exceeded those of the Israelites, as shown by the few remains of Israelite fortifications while much of the result of the Canaanites' construction ingenuity survives. They built ornate palaces with intricate carvings in ivory, alabaster, and gold, of which many samples exist today.

Farming was the Canaanites' primary livelihood. Canaanites were also traders, exporting and importing goods especially from the coastal areas. They excelled in ceramic arts, music, and making musical instruments. One example of their linear alphabet survives in the Ugaritic clay tablets (dated between 1500 and 1400 B.C.) found in a "library" between two Canaanite temples in northern Syria. Considering Hebrew and Canaanite inscriptions from the Late Bronze Age and Iron Age, the written Hebrew language was likely adapted from a Canaanite dialect.[11]

Canaanite religious beliefs and practices, though related, differed from

Hebrew worship in some key aspects that made compromise impossible. A basic understanding of Canaanite religion is particularly meaningful when considering Rahab's background and dramatic conversion to Jehovah. Canaanite religion included fertility cults that the people believed invited their gods and goddesses into their agricultural and pastoral life cycles. These rituals were essential in the Canaanites' minds if they were to ensure abundant harvests and healthy herds. For example,

The Canaanite god Ba'al and his consort Astarte were believed to influence fertility in crops, animals, and humans.

Sketch by Ashton Young; Photo in public domain

they viewed the cyclical seasons of planting and harvesting to be the result of the death and resurrection of their god Ba'al. Their goddesses, the consorts of Ba'al, were depicted as provocative courtesans who were perpetually conceiving and bearing. At the same time, these maternal figures were bloodthirsty warriors. Canaanite religion focused on rituals that reenacted the wildly sexual behavior of their gods and thus invited more fertile harvests, successful travel, and fruitful families. Naturally, the Israelites' Jehovah decried these rituals as abominations because of the sexual promiscuity and decadence they encouraged and therefore forbade the men of Israel to marry Canaanite women. Because Canaanite wives might bring such perverse practices into an Israelite clan, Israelite worship would thereby be polluted and their unique relationship with Jehovah seriously threatened.

RAHAB'S APPEARANCE IN THE BIBLICAL STORY

Before attacking a city, Joshua would send spies to reconnoiter and assess the strength of the people (see Josh. 7:2). This was the case in the story of Rahab when Joshua sent two men "to spy secretly, saying, Go view the land, even Jericho" (Josh. 2:1). Moses had similarly assigned Joshua and twelve others to "spy out the land of Canaan" nearly forty years before (Num. 13:1–20), when only he and Caleb returned with correct intelligence concerning a proposed attack on Canaan (Num. 13:26–33). Now Joshua selected two men to explore Jericho before the Israelites mounted an assault. Perhaps the spies were to look for a vulnerable area of the wall or a weak place where their troops could enter the city. Josephus reported that Joshua assigned them "to discover what forces [the people of Jericho] had, and what were their intentions" (*Ant* 5.1.1).

Rahab meets the Israelite spies. Interestingly, the names of the two men are not given in scripture, whereas the name of Rahab the harlot is frequently mentioned. Rabbinic tradition identifies the men as Perez and Zerah, the twin sons of Tamar,[12] an impossible suggestion considering that some three or four generations separate them from the time of Joshua, or, according to the apostle Paul, close to four hundred years (Gal. 3:17). Another tradition claims the spies were Caleb and Phineas,[13] and still another rabbinic opinion was that they were two sons of Caleb, Kenaz and Seenamias, whom Joshua counseled to "do like unto their father" and give a good report of the land.[14]

Although the people of Jericho must have known about the massive invasion of people camped on the other side of the Jordan and had heard about Israel's victories in the wilderness, the Israelite spies were able initially to enter the city without arousing curiosity or suspicion. The fact that they infiltrated at least to Rahab's house with time to gain her trust and protection indicates that their appearance alone did not communicate alarm to the people. Jewish traditions report a variety of explanations for the spies' ability to go undetected. One claims that they posed as carpenters, another that they came selling pottery, and still another that they pretended to be deaf and dumb—apparently assuming that their dialects were different enough to arouse suspicion.[15]

It is not known why the spies went to a harlot's house or if they explored other areas of the city first. Scripture reports only that "they went, and came into an harlot's house, named Rahab, and lodged there" (Josh. 2:1). It is easy to surmise that a saloon or bordello might be the best place to gather information about the city and its inhabitants without being detected and where personal identification or credentials would not be required. It is also possible that the spies selected Rahab's house because it was built into the surrounding city wall, thereby providing both an overall view of the city and a clandestine escape route if necessary.

We are simply told that some of the townspeople learned that Israelite spies were in their city and reported to the "king of Jericho . . . there came men in hither to night of the children of Israel to search out the country" (Josh. 2:2). Because the gate of the city closed at nightfall, "to night" in this reference probably meant afternoon or late afternoon.[16]

A hiding place amid stalks of flax. The king's informants must have also known where the spies were lodging because he sent word to Rahab to "bring forth the men . . . which are entered into thine house" (Josh. 2:3). At this point, Rahab apparently set herself against her own people in order to save the men on "the roof of the house, and hid them with the stalks of flax, which she had laid in order upon the roof" (Josh. 2:4–6).

The ancient custom of hospitality included an expectation of protection.[17] Rahab thus went beyond ensuring the spies were cared for properly. Ancient laws of surrounding peoples indicate that Rahab risked her life when she agreed to harbor the Israelites without reporting them to the king. The Code of Hammurabi, a set of Babylonian laws dated from about 1700 B.C., declares, "If outlaws have congregated in the establishment of a woman wine seller and she has not arrested those outlaws and did not take them to the palace, that wine seller shall be put to death" (#108–109).[18]

Rather than denying any knowledge of the Israelite spies, Rahab was evasive, telling the king's men, "There came men unto me, but I [know] not whence they were." Furthermore, she explained that the men left her house as it was getting dark, just before the gate closed, and "whither the men went I [know]

RAHAB'S TESTIMONY OF JEHOVAH

I know that the Lord hath given you the land,

and that your terror is fallen upon us,

and that all the inhabitants of the land faint because of you.

For we have heard how the Lord dried up the water of the Red sea for you,

when ye came out of Egypt;

and what ye did unto the two kings of the Amorites,

that were on the other side Jordan, Sihon and Og,

whom ye utterly destroyed.

And as soon as we had heard these things,

our hearts did melt,

neither did there remain any more courage in any man, because of you:

for the Lord your God, he is God in heaven above, and in earth beneath (Josh. 2:9–11).

Several important points emerge from Rahab's testimony of Jehovah. First, she used the words "I know" (from the Hebrew *yadah*), suggesting not merely a cognitive understanding but a spiritual witness. Parallel examples of this word use in scripture include Jethro, father-in-law to Moses, after hearing of Israel's deliverance from Egypt (Ex. 18:10–11); Naaman, the Syrian captain, after being healed of leprosy (2 Kgs. 5:15); and Sariah, wife of Lehi, after seeing her sons safely return from Jerusalem (1 Ne. 5:8).

Second, Rahab was prophetic in her testimony; she stated future events as though they had already occurred. "I know that the Lord hath given you the land" (Josh. 2:9). The biblical Hebrew perfect tense allows one to speak of future events as established facts. Biblical scholars E. Kautsch and A. E. Cowley explained that this tense is sometimes used to "express facts which are undoubtedly imminent, and, therefore, in the imagination of the speaker, already accomplished," called in Latin the *perfectum confidentiae*, or for a prophet to speak of a "future event as if it had been already seen or heard by him," called the *perfectum propheticum*, or the prophetic perfect.[19] Rahab spoke as though Israel already occupied the land of Canaan. Her words reflect faith—the assurance of things hoped for (or feared, in Rahab's case), even when the evidence of such is unseen (see JST, Heb. 11:1).

Third, she was acquainted with stories of the Israelite exodus from Egypt through the Red Sea and their triumphs in the wilderness over the regional kings Sihon and Og, who had refused to let them pass through their Amorite lands (Num. 21:21–35).

Fourth, Rahab referred to God as "Jehovah" (rendered Lord in the King James Version) and recognized him as the only God in heaven above or earth below. Her words echo a sermon that Moses preached in the wilderness when he testified, "Know therefore this day, and consider it in thine heart, that the Lord he is God in heaven above, and upon the earth beneath: there is none else" (see Deut. 4:39). Remembering that Canaanite religion had a pantheon of gods underscores the dramatic conclusion that Rahab reached and of which she testified.

Having communicated her belief that Jehovah was God and would overcome all, she convinced the spies that her loyalty rested with Israel, and she proposed a deal or covenant: "Now therefore, I pray you, swear unto me by the Lord, since I have shewed you kindness, that ye will also shew kindness unto my father's house, and give me a true token: And that ye will save alive my father, and my mother, and my brethren, and my sisters, and all that they have, and deliver our lives from death" (Josh. 2:12–13). She would secure the spies' safe escape from Jericho if they would preserve her and her family alive when the Israelite army came to destroy the city. Rahab's two-way promise reflected that trust existed between the two parties because of reciprocal "kindness" or dealing "kindly and truly" with each other (Josh. 2:12, 14). The Hebrew word (*ḥesed*) translated here as "kindness" suggests mutual benevolence and mercy, much like that which Abraham and Abimelech swore to each other (see Gen. 21:23–24).

not: pursue after them quickly; for ye shall overtake them" (Josh. 2:4–5). Indicative of a quick and wise mind, Rahab's response resembles that of the midwives Shiphrah and Puah, who saved the lives of Hebrew babies rather than obey Pharaoh (Ex. 1:15–21). In both cases, women communicated what chauvinist men might expect from a woman, and the king's men immediately set off in other directions (Josh. 2:7).

Rahab's testimony of Jehovah. Before the spies were even settled under or behind the flax stalks, Rahab had already misdirected the king's men and joined the Israelites on her roof (Josh. 2:8). She was now ready to discuss religion, and more specifically, to reveal her confession of Jehovah as the only true God. Her own words are recorded in scripture, a testament to the power they had in influencing more lives than those of the two spies.

The spies' escape from Jericho. Rahab helped the spies escape through her window on the city wall by letting down "a cord" or "line of scarlet thread" (probably a rope; Josh. 2:15, 18). She instructed them to travel away from the camp of Israel in the direction of "the mountain, lest the pursuers meet you; and hide yourselves there three days, until the pursuers be returned: and afterward may ye go your way" (Josh.

2:16). Rahab referred to the mountains west of Jericho, a desolate area where centuries later Jesus would prepare for his ministry in fasting and prayer for forty days (Matt. 4:1–11).

When the spies finally returned to their Israelite camp and reported to Joshua, Rahab's testimony and faith fueled their confidence in God. "Truly the Lord hath delivered into our hands all the land," they told Joshua, citing Rahab, "for even all the inhabitants of the country do faint because of us" (Josh. 2:24). The declaration of a Canaanite woman bolstered their belief in the power of their God and in the demoralized state of the Canaanites.

The Israelite attack on Jericho. With their use of spies, advanced reports of their victories, and prolonged noisemaking, the Israelites applied psychological warfare in their attack on Jericho.[20] Conquering the walled city was more than a military event, however. It was a spiritual test. The Israelites did not deserve or earn a promised land—it was a gift from Jehovah, and *he* would deliver it to them. As the Israelite troops solemnly marched toward the city, following behind the ark of the covenant, the unspoken declaration of God's power created great fear among the inhabitants of Jericho as they watched from within their fortified city (Josh. 6:8–14).

The number seven, symbolic of wholeness, completeness, and perfection, appears fourteen times in describing the battle in Joshua 6. After the seven priests blew seven *shofars* on the seventh tour of the city on the seventh day, God finally gave them the victory (Josh. 6:15–20). Israelites typically sounded the *shofar,* or ram's horn, to signal the commencement of holy days or to rally troops (Judg. 3:27; 6:34), halt fighting (2 Sam. 2:28; 18:16; 20:22), or to signal victory (1 Sam. 13:3). In the case of the attack on Jericho, *shofars* were sounded to begin the battle (Josh. 6:4). The *shofar* reminded Israel that God had provided a ram in the thicket for Abraham to sacrifice in place of his covenant son, Isaac (Gen. 22:12–13). The horn of a ram therefore became symbolic to the Israelites of God's power.

"So the people shouted when the priests blew with the trumpets: and it came to pass, when the people heard the sound of the trumpet, and the people shouted with a great shout, that the

WORD STUDY: *COVENANTAL KINDNESS* (ḤESED)

The Hebrew word *ḥesed* appears 240 times in the Old Testament but is translated with various English words in the King James Version, most frequently "mercy," "kindness," or "loving kindness." The word implies a combination of strength, love, and steadfastness or permanence in a covenantal relationship that exceeds the demands of the law. In many cases, it is associated with life- or posterity saving.[21] *Ḥesed* is a fundamental characteristic of Jehovah, as shown when he redeems us from our trials or our sins. Mortals may also experience this divine quality between them, especially in caring for the vulnerable. God's *ḥesed*, however, is always deeper and more enduring and abundant than ours.

Naomi recognized the Lord's *ḥesed* for them when Ruth returned home after working in Boaz's field (Ruth 2:20), and Boaz viewed the quality in Ruth because of her treatment of others (Ruth 3:10). Rahab and the Israelite spies trusted each other when the covenant they established between them was built on *ḥesed* (Josh. 2:12, 14).[22]

Sketch by Ashton Young

Israelites sounded the shofar, or ram's horn, to signal the commencement of holy days, to rally troops, or to begin a battle. The shofar reminded Israel that God had provided a ram in the thicket for Abraham to sacrifice in place of his covenant son Isaac. The horn of a ram therefore became symbolic to the Israelites of God's power.

wall fell down flat, so that the people went up into the city, every man straight before him, and they took the city" (Josh. 6:20).

The ḥerem ("complete destruction"). Joshua gave command that Jericho be "accursed, even it, and all that are therein, to the Lord" (Josh. 6:17). Falling upon the now defenseless city, the Israelites "utterly destroyed all that was in the city, both man and woman, young and old, and ox, and sheep, and ass, with the edge of the sword" (Josh. 6:21). They also "burnt the city with fire, and all that was therein: only the silver, and the gold, and the vessels of brass and of iron, they put into the treasury of the house of the Lord" (Josh. 6:24). The complete annihilation of the enemy, called the *ḥerem* in Hebrew, appears fourteen times in the book of Joshua alone, usually translated "utterly destroyed" (see, for example, Josh. 2:10; 6:21; 8:26).

Archaeologist Carol Meyers convincingly argues that the reason for the *ḥerem* was to prevent contamination from foreign societies, which had frequently been the cause of devastating plagues.[23] Death from disease was more prevalent than from physical combat.

The greater inconsistency of the Lord's *ḥerem* at Jericho was sparing the life of Rahab and of her family. The scriptural record reports that "the young men that were spies went in [to Rahab's house], and brought out Rahab, and her father, and her mother, and her brethren, and all that she had; and they brought out all her kindred, and left them without the camp of Israel" (Josh. 6:23). How could the Israelite spies be justified in making a covenant with Rahab in the face of Jehovah's command to utterly destroy every inhabitant of every Canaanite city as they entered the promised land (see Deut. 20:10–20)?

The Bible records one explanation for this exception to God's command at Jericho. Joshua declared that Rahab and her family should live "because she hid the messengers that we sent" (Josh. 6:17). James wrote that God vindicated or justified Rahab when she "received the messengers, and had sent them out another way" (James 2:25). God had already forgiven her and declared her righteous before Jericho was attacked. Like Abraham, she was reckoned righteous because of her actions of faith (Gen. 15:6). Rather than resisting the Israelites and their religion, Rahab embraced Israel's God and was saved. Destruction was not a foregone conclusion for Canaanites who elected to join with the Israelites, as Rahab and other Old Testament examples illustrate.[24]

The Book of Mormon also provides insight concerning the conquest of Canaan and possibly the reason Rahab and her family were saved. The Canaanites were destroyed, Nephi explained, because they "had rejected every word of God, and they were ripe in iniquity; . . . yea [the Lord God] did curse [the land] against them unto their destruction" (1 Ne. 17:32–35). One must first be exposed to a message before one can reject it. Nephi later observed that "as one generation hath been destroyed among the Jews because of iniquity, even so have they been destroyed from generation to generation according to their iniquities; and *never hath any of them been destroyed save it were foretold them by the prophets of the Lord*" (2 Ne. 25:9; emphasis added). Nephi's commentary suggests that Canaanites were taught the gospel of Abraham before the children of Israel entered the land but "rejected" it and were therefore "ripe for destruction." As the biblical account reports that Jericho was "straitly shut up," or tightly shut against Israel, so their hearts shut out the truth about God (Josh. 6:1). Rahab the harlot confessed her loyalty to Jehovah and was saved from destruction.

Joining the camp of Israel. True to their covenant with Rahab, the Israelites ensured that she and her family escaped the destruction to eventually live among the Israelites. Before she and her family entered the camp of Israel, however, they were required to remain outside the camp for a time (Josh. 6:23, 25), similar to being ritually purified as was required of all "unclean" things (Num. 5:2–3; 19). They may also have been quarantined for several days to eradicate foreign germs so the camp would not be contaminated. Similarly, any Israelite man who killed anyone in battle or touched any who were slain was kept outside the camp for seven days. Furthermore, his clothing had to be washed from the impurities of death and destruction before he could reenter the camp. Inspired by the Lord, these laws directed the Israelites toward an appropriate fear of communicable diseases even when most likely they had no understanding of the inherent threat from biological contamination.

The biblical account of Rahab's story concludes with the narrator's report: "And Joshua saved Rahab the harlot alive, and her father's household, and all that she had; and she dwelleth in Israel even unto this day; because she hid the messengers, which Joshua sent to spy out Jericho" (Josh. 6:25). The wording of this passage suggests that the author of Joshua wrote this account long after the events occurred, so that no longer was it Rahab but her descendants who were still numbered among the Israelites. In subsequent centuries, Jews extrapolated from this verse additional events in Rahab's life. For example, the first-century historian Josephus reported that Joshua "gave her certain lands immediately, and had her in great esteem ever afterwards" (*Ant* 5.1.7).

A "common midrashic desire" was to connect women deemed heroic in the Bible to a husband, for certainly, it was assumed, a noble woman could not remain so without such a connection. Additionally, the rabbis concluded that such women "must . . . have married illustrious men who themselves appear in the biblical history."[25] Therefore, in one account, Joshua himself married Rahab, and she "became the ancestress of eight prophets and of the prophetess Huldah."[26] Another Jewish tradition claims that

Joshua was criticized by his people for marrying Rahab, perhaps because she was not an Israelite.[27] According to Matthew's genealogy of Jesus, Rahab's husband was Salmon (Matt. 1:5), whose name appears as Salma in the Old Testament (1 Chr. 2:11). Traditions aside, the New Testament preserves the most reliable and meaningful commentary about Rahab: she became an exemplar to the Israelites of faith (Heb. 11:31) and faith-inspired works (James 2:25) and was a notable progenitor of the Savior (Matt. 1:5).

BETWEEN THE LINES

The symbol of Rahab's salvation was the "scarlet thread" that was extended from her window on the wall to assist the spies' escape and to distinguish her house from others when the city was destroyed (Josh. 2:18). Translated "thread" in the King James Bible, the Hebrew word comes from the Hebrew root word meaning "to sew," so the thread could have been a braided or "sewn" rope or cord. With a deeply meaningful play on words, the Hebrew word in Joshua 2:21, translated there as "line," is used elsewhere in the Bible to mean "hope" (Ruth 1:12; Prov. 19:18; Jer. 31:17).[28] As we contemplate the story, we may recognize Jehovah as our only true source of hope even as Rahab viewed the scarlet line as her hope for rescue.

The color scarlet or crimson is not insignificant. Scarlet is the color of blood. The spies' reference to its protection for those within Rahab's doors is reminiscent of the first Passover when the crimson blood of a male lamb without blemish was spread on the doorposts and kept the angel of death from that home. All under the red sign receive salvation. The blood of the Redeemer likewise saves humankind from eternal death (Ex. 12:7, 13).

No other person in Jericho, regardless of wealth, title, or fame received the protection and promise that Rahab received. She lived at a violent time in one of the more dangerous areas of the city—on the outer wall—but she was covered by the mercy and grace of Jehovah. What she was, therefore, was not as important as what she became. As a "new creature" (2 Cor. 5:17), she prospered because of her willingness to join with the people of Jehovah and her ability to wisely act in innovative and unexpected ways. Despite irregular or scandalous circumstances in her life, Rahab was in fact righteous. She became a savior to the Israelite spies and was never forgotten. Like her descendant Mary, Rahab had a pure heart towards God beyond anything her neighbors would have observed or surmised. God was aware of her and saved her in spite of outward appearances. Her presence among the ancestors of the eternal Savior is therefore worthy of celebration.

POINTS TO PONDER

1. What difference does it make to the story that Rahab was a Canaanite and not a literal daughter of Abraham?

2. What evidence can you find to suggest that even though a harlot, Rahab was responsible and compassionate?

3. What hope did Jesus express for harlots? (see Matt. 21:31–32).

4. What did Rahab risk by saving the spies from discovery? What motivated her to hide them anyway?

5. How could Rahab contribute to continued success and prosperity among the Israelites after she joined them?

6. What does Rahab's story teach you about the Atonement of Jesus Christ?

7. What principles of the gospel are exemplified in Rahab's story?

Under Whose Wings Thou Art Come to Trust

BY AL R. YOUNG

RUTH

רוּת

"Friend; Companion" or "Satiation; Refreshment" (Hebrew)

The book of Ruth is a tale of loss, death, and grief that develops into a story of restoration, life, and joy. At the beginning of the story, Ruth appears to have not a hope in the world. Her husband has died and she is childless. By the end of her four chapters in the Bible, she is married and gives birth to the grandfather of King David. Yet Ruth's story is not a romance. It is a powerful witness of God's intricate providence toward those who love and trust him. A poignant reminder that redemption comes only through the mercy and grace of God, the book of Ruth shows that it is often through the loving kindness (Hebrew, *ḥesed)* of others that God's mercy and grace are experienced.

The worldview throughout this entire book is clearly female, and the storyteller is quite adept at selecting some details and omitting others while beautifully employing layers of symbolic imagery. The narrator empathizes with the women in antiquity while subtly interweaving God's awareness of the daily details in their lives. Together with the other women of Bethlehem, Ruth and Naomi illustrate a strong sisterhood found among women in small agricultural communities. "Hardly any other book of the Bible manages to express the 'female-voice' as authentically as Ruth does."[1] Such unique perspectives have even persuaded some modern scholars that the author may have been a woman.[2]

The story of Ruth, like that of Tamar, demonstrates how family heritage and the hope of ages were preserved by a woman. Moreover, the book of Ruth is not an account of national or religious leaders but a Bible story of everyday people in an unremarkable community at an undisclosed period of time. Ruth was not a queen or the daughter of a prophet but a Moabite widow of an Israelite farmer. Josephus perceived this fact and therefore expressed his "desire" to relate the history of Ruth "because I had a mind to demonstrate the power of God, who, without difficulty, can raise those that are of ordinary parentage to dignity and splendor" (*Ant* 5.9.4).

The primary characters in the narrative of Ruth have names, which may have been a literary device by the

THE BOOK OF RUTH 1–4

MATTHEW 1:5

NAMES AND MEANINGS

Naomi	Pleasant; My Sweet
Elimelech	My God Is the King
Mahlon	Sickness, Disease
Chilion	Destruction, Failing, Weak
Boaz	[He Goes] in Strength
Ruth	Friend; Companion
Orpah	Back of the Neck; Neck
Obed	Servant

author and can be seen to offer symbolic meaning concerning the person and the larger story.[3] These names may be an invitation to look beyond what we expect to see in that person.

HISTORICAL CONTEXT

The story of Ruth took place during a time of famine in Bethlehem "when the judges ruled" (Ruth 1:1). Scholars generally place the era of the judges between the thirteenth to the eleventh centuries B.C. The Old Testament book of Judges portrays the era as a time of unrest, of perpetual battles and disunity during which the Israelites "went a whoring after other gods, and bowed themselves unto them: they turned quickly out of the way which their fathers walked in, obeying the commandments of the Lord; but they did not so" (Judg. 2:17) and in which "every man did that which was right in his own eyes" (Judg. 21:25). In contrast to the circumstances of the times, the story of Ruth seems to describe Bethlehem in terms of relative social harmony.

As to when the story was actually written, most scholars suggest that the author lived generations after the events occurred, most likely during the United Monarchy (ca. 1020–920 B.C.). One reason for this dating is that the chronicler seems fully aware that a descendant of Ruth and Boaz would "be famous in Bethlehem" (Ruth 4:11). This could easily describe King David.[4] Furthermore, the book's opening, "Now it came to pass in the days when the judges ruled" (Ruth 1:1), indicates the author wrote after the era of the judges had ended.

RUTH'S PLACES OF RESIDENCE

Among family in Moab. Ruth began her life in Moab, close to Israel geographically but far away culturally and religiously. A large nation located south and east of the Dead Sea, Moab was probably best reached from Bethlehem by way of Jericho and then across the Jordan River into northern Moab, a distance of between fifty to seventy-five miles.[5]

Although the Moabites were not descended from Israel, they were a Semitic people related to the Israelites through Abraham's nephew Lot (Gen. 19:30–38). Despised by the Israelites for much of their history, the Moabites enticed the people of Israel into idolatry through their lascivious daughters (Num. 25:1–2) and were excluded from the Israelite congregation due to their hostility when Israel lived in the wilderness (Deut. 23:3–6). Despite the animosity between these two nations, when a famine devastated Bethlehem in Judah, Elimelech and his wife, Naomi, moved to Moab (Gen. 35:16, 19; 48:7).

The religious customs of Israel and Moab differed dramatically. Israelites reverenced one God and observed the law of Moses. Elimelech's name may even underscore the Israelite belief that Jehovah was the ultimate king over humankind and therefore Israel was the greatest nation. By contrast, the Moabites recognized multiple gods and were called "the people of Chemosh," who was their supreme deity. Various place names in Moab suggest shrines to several different gods from Egypt to Syria.[6] Solomon established a "high place" in Jerusalem for his Moabite wives to worship Chemosh, "the abomination of Moab," and a Moabite king once sacrificed his son to Chemosh in an attempt to garner the deity's favor against Israel (1 Kgs. 11:7; 2 Kgs. 3:26–27). Tablets dating back to between 2600 and 2250 B.C. in ancient Ebla refer to a god named Chemosh, perhaps the same deity that the Moabites adopted for their national god.

The Moabite Stone, discovered in 1868, is a monument commemorating the victory of the Moabites over the Israelites in ca. 860 B.C. In the inscription, King Mesha of Moab credits the victory to their god Chemosh.

Ruth's decision to leave Moab. Naomi and her family moved to Moab when her sons were of marriageable age. Not surprisingly, Mahlon and Chilion married Moabite women. Although the law of Moses forbade the intermarriage with Canaanites, it did not specifically prohibit marriage to Moabites (Deut. 7:3). Sparing details, the narrator simply reports that Mahlon and Chilion married Ruth and Orpah, Moabite women, and that neither woman bore children. And then, with no further explanation, Elimelech, Chilion, and Mahlon were dead. Rabbinic literature creates prestigious origins for Naomi's two daughters-in-law. In the Midrashim, they are sisters and daughters of the Moabite king Eglon,[7] although scripture makes no such claim. The Bible does clearly communicate, however, that Naomi's family structure changed dramatically in Moab, leaving no males and three new widows, two of them not Israelites (Ruth 1:1–5). It is noteworthy that the absence of the men provides the reason for the entire story.[8]

Hearing that "the Lord visited his people [in Bethlehem] in giving them bread" (in Hebrew *Bethlehem* means "house of bread"), Naomi prepared to return there alone (Ruth 1:6). Her daughters-in-law, Ruth and Orpah, expected to go with her, but Naomi would not have it. Arriving in Bethlehem with no male family and two Moabite daughters-in-law would have been awkward for many reasons. She told them, "Go, return each to her mother's house" (Ruth 1:8). One expects instead to read "return to her father's house," reflecting the androcentric culture at the time. Naomi's instructions to return to their "mother's house" may underscore the reality that these women had no men in their lives.

Naomi then pronounced upon her daughters-in-law a blessing: "The Lord deal kindly with [show *ḥesed* to] you, as ye have dealt with the dead, and with me. The Lord grant you that ye may find rest, each of you

Photo by David M. Whitchurch

in the house of her husband." And then they wept (Ruth 1:8–9). With rare exception in the ancient world, marriage was the source of "rest" or livelihood for a woman. Naomi here expresses her hope that Orpah and Ruth would find new husbands in Moab. Note that Naomi called not on the Moabite god Chemosh to show them *ḥesed* or grant them rest but on Jehovah, the God of Israel. Her plea to Jehovah illustrates her belief in the efficacy of his power both in Israel and outside Israel as well.

After Orpah and Ruth again expressed their desire to remain with their mother-in-law, Naomi spelled out the dismal facts should they follow her. Not only would she be the only one to care for them but she was too old to bear additional sons for them to marry. Her circumstances as an elderly widow represented total powerlessness within Israel's patriarchal culture. Therefore, Naomi explained, "My daughters; go your way, for I am too old to have an husband. If I should say, I have hope, if I should have an husband also to night, and should also bear sons; would ye tarry for them till they were grown? would ye stay for them from having husbands? nay, my daughters; for it grieveth me much for your sakes that the hand of the Lord is gone out against me" (Ruth 1:12–13). She believed their best hope for remarriage was in Moab.

Eventually the issue was settled. Orpah made the practical choice to turn back and remain in Moab. Ruth impractically chose an uncertain future by remaining with Naomi. Orpah has often been maligned for remaining in her homeland. Because Orpah's name means "back of neck" or "neck,"[9] she has been characterized as one who turned her back. In Jewish Midrash, Orpah is described as the mother of Goliath, the giant warrior who faced Ruth's great-grandson David and lost his life, suggesting that she relocated to Philistia.[10] But the scriptural text does not describe Orpah as the opposite of Ruth. On the contrary, her fine character serves to highlight the unusually remarkable character of Ruth.[11]

Moving to Bethlehem required cultural and social changes for Ruth in addition to a change in residence. Her expression of faith to Naomi is poetically and spiritually poignant: "Entreat me not to leave thee, or to return from following after thee: for whither thou goest, I will go; and where thou lodgest, I will lodge: thy people shall be my people, and thy God my God: where thou diest, will I die, and there will I be buried: the Lord do so to me, and more also, if ought but death part thee and me" (Ruth 1:16–17). Her faith, though perhaps not yet mature, was nonetheless steadfast.

When Ruth said "so" in "the Lord do *so* to me," she may have performed "some action, like drawing a hand across her throat, that symbolizes what God will do if she breaks the oath."[12] Ruth was pledging "covenant fidelity" that echoed Israel's covenant with Jehovah.[13] Clearly, she was determined that nothing, not even death, would separate her from her mother-in-law. When Naomi could see that Ruth was "steadfastly minded to go with her, then she left speaking unto her" (Ruth 1:18), meaning she ceased trying to dissuade Ruth from accompanying her.

A foreigner in Bethlehem. When the two women entered Bethlehem, Naomi's old neighbors immediately recognized her, asking, "Is this Naomi?" (Ruth 1:19). If Bethlehem was similar to other Judean villages during the early Iron Age (ca. 1200–1000 b.c.), the population was probably around four hundred to five hundred inhabitants, certainly small enough for villagers to be acquainted with each other. The Hebrew verb form attached to their greeting is feminine, which clarifies that a group of *women* greeted the newcomers and not a crowd that included men.[14] Edward Campbell estimated that Naomi would have been in her mid-forties and Ruth in her late twenties when this story occurred;[15] however, Ruth may have been even younger, considering that she is referred to in the text as a "damsel" and is included with the "maidens" (Ruth 2:5, 6, 8, 23).

Although again in her hometown, Naomi still felt abandoned by the Lord. She told the women of Bethlehem, "Call me not Naomi [which means "pleasant" or "my sweet one"], call me Mara [which means "bitter"]: for the Almighty hath dealt very bitterly with me. I went out full, and the Lord hath brought me home again empty: why then call ye me Naomi, seeing the Lord hath testified against me, and the Almighty hath afflicted me" (Ruth 1:20–21). The Greek Septuagint version of the Old Testament (LXX) changes the phrase "the Lord hath testified against me" to "the Lord has humbled me." She may have been comparing her current circumstances with the security of other women. Clearly, Naomi was poignantly aware of the dramatic changes in her life since she had left Bethlehem a decade before.

Neither Naomi nor the other women mentioned Ruth. As a Moabite, Ruth might have been "invisible" to Israelites. Unaware of their good fortune ahead, however, Naomi and Ruth had arrived in Bethlehem in time for the barley harvest, probably in the early spring—a harbinger of new life.

RUTH'S DAILY WORK

As widows without close male family members to take care of them, Naomi and Ruth had few options for survival when they reached Bethlehem. Most likely, food was accessible to them only by gleaning in Bethlehem's fields. According to the law of Moses, the poor had the right to harvest the corners of the field where the reapers were forbidden by law to reap (Lev. 19:9–10; 23:22; Deut. 24:19–21). "When reaping with a scythe, the swinging-arm movement naturally created a circular motion which would leave the square corners of fields untouched."[16] A remarkable exercise in compassion, diligence, and gratitude, this law taught the landowners, or the "haves," selflessness and consideration for others while at the same time teaching the "have nots" industry and self-respect.

The threshing floor was a circular parcel of ground anywhere from 50 to 320 feet in diameter. Generally one threshing floor was prepared for an entire village, and farmers took turns using it. As in the time when Deborah judged in Israel, the threshing floor was also used for determining legal outcomes (Judg. 4:5). This custom may have influenced Naomi's idea to send Ruth to the threshing floor to petition Boaz for marriage.[17] The farmer or his servants typically spent nights on the threshing floor to guard against thieves.

Today, the book of Ruth is read annually in Jewish congregations in conjunction with the festival of

Sketch by Ashton Young

Grain production in antiquity. Cereal grains constituted the most vital crops in the ancient Near East. Of these grains, wheat and barley produced the highest yields in Israel and surrounding areas. The Gezer Calendar, found on a broken limestone tablet that is believed to have been recorded as a "school boy exercise" in the tenth century B.C., outlines an annual farming schedule that is thought also to have been followed in the preceding centuries.[18] According to this calendar, grain harvest in the region lasted for two or three weeks, beginning as early as April or as late as early June, with the barley harvest occurring about a month before the wheat harvest.

The Gezer Calendar outlines on a limestone tablet an annual farming schedule that is thought to have also been followed in the later era of the Judges.

Photo by Kent P. Jackson

Photo by Kent P. Jackson

Above: A threshing floor in Shiloh. In antiquity, farmers often spent nights on the threshing floor to guard against intruders and prevent theft of the grain.

Left: Tools used by Israelite farmers to separate the grain from the chaff.

Pentecost (also known as the Feast of Weeks) in celebration of the spring grain harvest, much as the book of Esther is read during the festival of Purim.

RUTH'S APPEARANCE IN THE BIBLICAL STORY

Although among the most marginalized and poor of Bethlehem society, Ruth the Moabitess used her few options and resources to restore a family to prosperity and unite a community in recognition of Jehovah's vast power. The narrator of the story of Ruth features the strength of women working together to bring about mighty change for good. Ruth's ability to accomplish so much with so little, however, is not evident until the final scenes.

Gleaning in Boaz's field. The biblical narrative suggests that Ruth gleaned in other fields before she happened by chance upon Boaz's fields: "her hap was to light on a part of the field belonging unto Boaz" (Ruth 2:3). No indication is given that Ruth anticipated different treatment in this field than in others.

The Septuagint (LXX) introduces the reader to Boaz as "a friend [or] an acquaintance" of Naomi's husband before Ruth went to his field to glean. Moreover, the Armenian tradition adds to the text: "and he gave Naomi a widow's house in which to live," thus explaining why shelter was not a concern after her return.[19] At the first mention of Boaz in the LXX narrative, he is called "a mighty man of the kindred of Elimelech" (Ruth 2:1). The Hebrew word translated "mighty" here is otherwise translated a person "of substance" or "a worthy" individual. In the King James translation of the verse, he is called "a mighty man of wealth." Later, Boaz used the same Hebrew word to describe Ruth when he told her that "all the city of my people doth know that thou art a virtuous woman" (Ruth 3:11).

On Ruth's first day of gleaning in Boaz's field, he recognized that she had not been there before. Boaz therefore spoke to his servant who managed the harvest for him, asking, "Whose damsel is this?" The servant told Boaz, "It is the Moabitish damsel that came back with Naomi out of the country of Moab" (Ruth 2:5–6). The servant then reported to Boaz that Ruth "came and stood . . . and rested not even a little in the field" (LXX Ruth 2:7). In other words, she had been gleaning all day in the field without a break.

Boaz's response shows no prejudice or animosity toward a Moabite gleaner.[20] He personally advised Ruth not to glean in other fields but to "abide here fast by my maidens" who regularly gleaned there (Ruth 2:8). Furthermore, he told his workers, "Let her glean even among the sheaves, and reproach her not" (Ruth 2:15). He also forbade his reapers to "touch" her, using a word that is better translated as not to "molest" her.[21] Positioning himself as a protector for Ruth, Boaz gave instructions to allow her to drink from the workers' supply of water and to glean alongside the reapers without fear of harassment. Drinking from the workers' water was a luxury for Ruth because of the time it would save her from drawing water for herself. Likewise, in allowing Ruth to glean among the stacked sheaves, Boaz generously exceeded what the law required of him in caring for the poor.

Ruth responded to her benefactor's kind actions by humbly bowing her face to the ground and saying, "Why have I found grace in thine eyes, that thou shouldest take knowledge of me, seeing I am a stranger" (Ruth 2:10). She recognized that Boaz was behaving exceptionally, especially toward a stranger or foreigner.

Although he might not have recognized Ruth by sight, Boaz knew of her by reputation. He told her, "It hath fully been shewed me, all that thou hast done unto thy mother in law since the death of thine husband: and how thou hast left thy father and thy mother, and the land of thy nativity, and art come unto a people which thou knewest not heretofore" (Ruth 2:11). Rather than focus on her appearance, youth, or potential for enhancing his prestige, Boaz noted Ruth's loyalty and charity. He blessed her that "the Lord recompense thy work, and a full reward be given thee of the Lord God of Israel, under whose wings thou art come to trust" (Ruth 2:12). Boaz further directed his workers to secretly drop clusters of grain for her and not deter her (Ruth 2:15–16). After the reapers received Boaz's instructions, Ruth gleaned among the sheaves and easily collected a considerable quantity of grain. Boaz showed *ḥesed* to Ruth by offering to feed her along with his workers. "She did eat, and was sufficed, and left [some of the food she was given]" (Ruth 2:14), taking the remainder home to Naomi (Ruth 2:18).

That day Ruth collected and "beat out" an ephah, a "measure" or "bushel" of grain, or about a two-week supply for one person.[22] When Naomi first beheld Ruth's bounty, she exclaimed, "Where hast thou gleaned today? And where wroughtest thou?" or, in other words, "Where did you find such success?" Upon learning that Boaz was her benefactor, Naomi broke out in praise, "Blessed be he of the Lord who hath not left off his kindness [*ḥesed*] to the living and to the dead" (Ruth 2:19–20). She recognized far more in Boaz's gesture than physical sustenance; Naomi was envisioning redemption for herself and Ruth. Through Boaz the Lord would pour out his covenant faithfulness to "the living and to the dead" (Ruth 2:20).[23] Boaz was "one of our next kinsmen," she explained to Ruth. In other words, Boaz was a relative who could act as their redeemer, but he was not the only one.

Naomi then advised Ruth to avoid going to other fields during the remainder of the barley and wheat harvest. With Ruth's continued receipt of generosity in Boaz's field, she could gather enough grain to sustain them until the next year's harvest. She could also come to harm if she gleaned in other fields, so Naomi warned, "It is good, my daughter, that thou go out with his maidens, that they [masculine plural in Greek] meet thee not in any other field" (Ruth 2:22–23). The implication is that without a protector like Boaz, she might encounter hostility or molestation from the men in the fields.[24]

Despite her previous condition, Naomi began to return to life when she heard about Ruth's remarkable day. She would devise a plan for Ruth to further attract Boaz's attention. Interestingly, in the entire narrative, Naomi never speaks directly to Boaz, only through Ruth. In partnership with the Almighty, however, the two women would accomplish far more than either could do alone. Finally, Naomi knew "it is good" (Ruth 2:22).

Near kinsman or redeemer (go'el). Israelites believed that all their land belonged to Jehovah. Under the law of Moses, each Israelite family was assigned a land inheritance within a tribal allotment and were expected to protect and use the land wisely, leaving it to their descendants after them in perpetuity (Lev. 25:23; Josh. 13–19). This sacred inheritance served as a constant reminder of the ancestors who had farmed and honored that very land before them.

Because of severe hardship, however, a family could be forced to sell their land. In such cases, they were commanded to seek means to buy back the land as soon as possible, including securing a *go'el* to redeem it if needed. The word for "redeem" in Hebrew is *ga'al*. A redeemer, or "one who has the right to buy back," is a *go'el*; the word is translated as "near kinsman" in the King James Bible. A *go'el* was a "covenant-brother" in the Mosaic covenant whose relationship to one in need did not necessitate a close blood relationship but rather a willingness to assist, rescue, or protect.[25] The law of Moses listed ways a *go'el* could succor his needy relatives, including buying back family land sold in a time of indigence (Lev. 25:25–28) or redeeming a family member from servitude (Lev. 25:47–49). If the man who had lost his land had no *go'el,* then the land would revert to his estate, or his inheritance, in the fiftieth or Jubilee year (Lev. 25:28). Therefore, any land sales were, in effect, merely leases that expired at the next Jubilee, when the original owners would reclaim their property.

Through the covenant, the *go'el* sought to redeem the unfortunate and vulnerable who had lost their freedom or restore their property and former status. A true *go'el* would see, for example, that a widow was properly cared for without taking advantage of her distress. In this way, a *go'el* played a role in the Mosaic law that typified the mission of Christ. Recognizing our impossible plight in mortality, *the* Redeemer volunteered to pay our debts and restore us to the Father.

Because of his extraordinary qualities, Boaz can easily be viewed as a type of Christ. Even his name connotes the idea of "strength," an echo of "the mighty One of Israel" (Isa. 1:24). Although not substitutes for the Savior, such types help us better recognize the qualities of the One who is ultimately unlike any other.

Naomi's plan and Ruth's ingenuity. After hearing how Boaz looked out for Ruth when she gleaned in his field, Naomi devised a plan that would lead Ruth into a closer relationship with him (Ruth 3:1–5).[26] In Moab, Naomi looked to Jehovah to provide the needed "rest" for her daughters-in-law. Now she recognized that she could be a participant in securing such rest. "My

BOAZ AS A TYPE OF CHRIST

1. Redeemer
2. Savior of the poor
3. A "mighty one" in Israel who recognizes inner worth
4. Shows reverence for the law
5. Protector of the vulnerable
6. Lord of the harvest providing the bread of life
7. Bridegroom
8. Restores the rights of the dead
9. Mediator
10. Gives more than is required

Winnowing grain in Shiloh.

daughter," she asked Ruth, "shall I not seek rest for thee, that it may be well with thee?" (Ruth 3:1). With the barley harvest nearly over, Naomi knew the men would be winnowing the grain. More specifically, she knew that Boaz would be sleeping at the threshing floor that night to guard his harvest (Ruth 3:2).

Consequently, Naomi instructed Ruth, "Wash thyself therefore, and anoint thee, and put thy raiment upon thee, and get thee down to the [threshing] floor; but make not thyself known unto the man, until he shall have done eating and drinking" (Ruth 3:3). She wanted Ruth to make herself as presentable as possible—washed, perfumed, and dressed well. As for putting on her "raiment," Ruth would probably not have owned a dress for finery but likely had an apron or scarf to put over her dress. In the Septuagint translation, Boaz put grain in the "apron" that Ruth wore (LXX Ruth 3:15), perhaps a reference to this same "raiment." Naomi may also have suggested a scarf or wrap to keep Ruth from being recognized by others.[27] Finally, Naomi told her to stay out of sight until after Boaz had finished his meal and fallen asleep. She was to note where he lay down and then, when all was quiet, Naomi told her to "uncover his feet, and lay thee down; and he will tell thee what thou shalt do" (Ruth 3:4).

Trusting her mother-in-law, Ruth responded simply, "All that thou sayest unto me I will do" (Ruth 3:5). Unlike her earlier encounter with Boaz at his field, Ruth now met him in private and at night. She found him sleeping behind a heap of grain, away from the rest of the men. She approached him "softly" (or "secretly" in the LXX), then "uncovered his feet, and laid her[self] down" (Ruth 3:7).

Upon Boaz's awakening at midnight and noticing a woman near him, he was startled (or "amazed and troubled," according to the LXX). At that point Ruth made Naomi's plan her own, revealing her ingenuity and showing some initiative. After identifying herself, she said, "Spread therefore thy skirt over thine handmaid; for thou art a near kinsman" (Ruth 3:9). The request was an idiom meaning "Take me under your wing" or, even more directly, "Will you marry me?"[28] A Jewish tradition cites Ruth as explaining to Boaz on this occasion, "Thou art . . . thyself an honorable man, and a kinsman of my dead husband. As for me, who am in the flower of my years, since I left the home of my parents where homage is rendered unto idols, I have been constantly menaced by the dissolute young men around. So I have come hither that thou, who art the redeemer, mayest spread out thy skirt over me."[29] Considering the few options Ruth had at her disposal, her request was not inappropriate. The fact that she made her offer to Boaz in private rather than public allowed her to avoid public scorn should he choose to reject her offer.

This scene, however, is where the author of the book of Ruth creates the greatest tension by what is merely implied. The sexual overtones of their encounter are obvious, even though the extent of their possible intimacy is left ambiguous. Much has been written about what Ruth actually may have done when she "uncovered [Boaz's] feet." In Hebrew, the word "feet" could mean any part of the lower body. At one extreme, some have argued that Ruth simply uncovered Boaz's feet with the intention that he would become chilled and consequently awaken. Others have argued the opposite extreme, suggesting that Ruth and Boaz had sexual intercourse.[30] Considering that Boaz instructed Ruth to "tarry this night" and that Ruth "lay at his feet until the morning: and she rose up before one could know another," or while it was still dark outside (Ruth 3:13–14), further electrifies the scene. The narrative does not exclude possible sexual intimacy and purposely invites the reader to consider it but stops short of saying that anything inappropriate actually occurred.

Furthermore, Ruth's request to Boaz to "spread thy skirt over me" is a phrase used in a later Old Testament passage in which Jehovah covers Jerusalem's "nakedness" with his covenant (Ezek. 16:8). Although the intent of Ruth's request is marriage, this idiom easily communicates a request for sexual intimacy; she was asking him to take her *intimately* under his blanket and his protection. In his lengthy commentary on the book of Ruth, Campbell observed, "It is simply incomprehensible to me that a Hebrew story-teller could use the words 'uncover,' 'wing', and a noun for 'legs' [or feet] which is a cognate with a standard euphemism for the sexual organs, all in the same context, and not suggest to his audience that a provocative set of circumstances confronts them."[31] In short, Naomi's plan was to put Boaz in a situation where Ruth would be hard to resist and trust that, because he was an honorable man, he would not take advantage of her but would officially marry her.[32]

If we can unjustifiably assume that Boaz and Ruth engaged in sexual intimacy, what might Ruth's contemporaries have concluded? If someone discovered that Ruth had spent the night next to Boaz on the threshing floor, what natural assumption might the villagers have made? Improper use of this information would have destroyed Ruth's reputation. Admirable motives and actions could have been made to appear shameful.

Although tipsy with drink, Boaz remarkably took the most honorable course—he accepted Ruth's proposal without acting on the sexual temptation. A scandal occurred on the threshing floor that night but without any wrongdoing. That, however, is precisely the point that Matthew wants to emphasize by including Ruth among the ancestors of Mary. Like Naomi, Boaz called Ruth his "daughter" (Ruth 3:1, 10), implying an age difference of a generation. He praised her for showing "more kindness [*ḥesed*] in the latter end than at the beginning, inasmuch as thou followedst not young men, whether poor or rich"

(Ruth 3:10). Rather than merely seeking a husband—rich or poor—Ruth wanted to follow the correct protocols and seek a *go'el* who could redeem the whole family. Boaz then acknowledged that "all the city of my people doth know that thou art a virtuous woman" (Ruth 3:11). As noted previously, the Hebrew word here translated "virtuous" is also used to describe Boaz as "a mighty man of wealth" in Ruth 2:1. The word's meaning focuses less on economic success as the source of strength than on integrity and decency as the greater power. There on the threshing floor, in the middle of the night, a moral and upright woman met an equally moral and upright man to create a covenant that would enable God's redemption.

Although vowing to honor Ruth's petition for marriage (Ruth 3:11), Boaz recognized a possible snag that could prevent him from carrying out his promised intent. He knew a man who was more closely related to Elimelech and his sons than he himself was. A popular Jewish tradition asserts that Boaz was a nephew of Elimelech but that a brother to Elimelech still lived; that brother would have been a closer relative to Naomi than was Boaz.[33] Legally, that "nearer kinsman" must have the opportunity of first refusal before Boaz could act. Boaz would settle the matter with the man the following morning. If the man elected not to redeem Naomi and Ruth, Boaz would gladly do so (Ruth 3:12).

Before sending her home, Boaz filled Ruth's wrap with "six measures of barley" (Ruth 3:15). The amount of barley in "six measures" has been estimated to be as small as six omers, or about three-fifths the amount Ruth took home the first day (probably too little) or as much as six ephahs, or over two hundred pounds (certainly too much for her to carry).[34] The only consensus in the estimates is that Boaz's gift of grain to Ruth was again exceptionally generous.

Upon her return to Naomi, Ruth relayed all that had happened, including Boaz's wish for her not to go "empty unto thy mother in law" (Ruth 3:17). The abundant gift of grain may have been a signal from Boaz to Naomi that he recognized her authorship in the plan and that he was a willing participant. She now also knew that the final step was up to Boaz. She told Ruth, "Sit still, my daughter, until thou know how the matter will fall" (Ruth 3:18). Naomi's ability to now sit back and wait for Boaz to act indicated her confidence that he was trustworthy, most likely because of past acquaintance with him. Ruth, on the other

WORD STUDY: *VIRTUOUS (AYIL)*

The Hebrew word *ayil* has been variously translated in terms of an army: wealth, valor, strength, power, might, efficiency, virtue, and worthiness. The word carries the idea of moral worth or integrity in a variety of capacities, such as wealth in character as well as in substance, or strength in the power of God or in a military context.

Interestingly, the word is translated as "virtuous" or "virtuously" only four times in the Bible, and every one of those four instances describes a woman or women: "Who can find a virtuous woman? for her price is far above rubies" (Prov. 31:10); "Many daughters have done virtuously" (Prov. 31:29); "A virtuous woman is a crown to her husband" (Prov. 12:4): and Boaz's description of Ruth, "for all . . . know that thou art a virtuous woman" (Ruth 3:11). Considering the broader meaning of *ayil*, all knew that Ruth was a woman of great strength, power, valor, and integrity.

hand, trusted Boaz because of her faith in Naomi.

Redemption for Ruth and Naomi. The text portrays a scene at the city gate where "ten men of the elders of the city" acted as witnesses to Elimelech's case as mediated by Boaz. The Hebrew word translated "elder" refers to any man with a beard, so ten mature males heard the case.[35] During times of peace, the city gate was customarily the community center, where merchants and farmers peddled their goods and where the "elders" discussed and settled legal matters in transparent surroundings.

City gate. The remains of this gate area in Bethsaida near the Sea of Galilee date to the Iron Age, near the time of Ruth, and show the space available for a legal council as described in Ruth 4.

The name of the nearer kinsman is not given, but he is simply called in today's vernacular "So-and-So," or as the King James Version translates it, "such a one" (Ruth 4:1).[36] Not only was the name unimportant to the narrator but anonymity may have been a kindness to protect his family honor after his response to Boaz's proposition. In the presence of the witnesses, Boaz informed So-and-So that "our brother Elimelech" had some land that his widow needed to sell and inquired whether or not he would like to exercise his familial right as "redeemer" and purchase it. If not, Boaz would do so. Seeing no disadvantage in securing more land, So-and-So replied, "I will redeem it" (Ruth 4:3–4).

At this point in the negotiations, Boaz revealed an added responsibility that would accompany the purchase of the land: "Thou must buy it also of Ruth the Moabitess, the wife of the dead, to raise up the name of the dead upon his inheritance" (Ruth 4:5). Redeeming Elimelech's land for his widow, Naomi, could easily fit into a *go'el's* expected duties, but caring for Ruth, a young woman who could potentially still bear an heir to inherit that land, was another matter. As Josephus paraphrased Boaz's words to the nearer kinsman: "Thou must not remember the laws by halves" (*Ant* 5. 9. 4).

Although the traditional explanation for the second half of Boaz's business proposition is levirate marriage, described in the chapter on Tamar, a growing number of scholars argue against such a conclusion.[37] They see irregularities in the story of Ruth, such as the fact that Boaz was not a son of Elimelech or a member of his immediate family, the ceremony did not include Ruth's spitting in So-and So's face for refusing to marry her, So-and-So did not incur disgrace for declining to do his part, and the son born

The Trial of Faith

BY ELSPETH YOUNG

to Ruth was known as the son of Boaz rather than as the son of Ruth's deceased husband, Mahlon. They therefore caution against calling either Boaz or the nearer kinsman a levir.[38] A *go'el,* one who buys back land, is not a levir, that is, one who marries his brother's widow to beget a son who will perpetuate the family name and property.

Because of the difference in meanings between *go'el* and *levir,* biblical scholar D. Beattie argues for an alternative reading of Ruth 4:5 that does not require the one who purchases the family property to also marry Ruth and sire an heir.[39] He prefers the translation, "I have acquired or bought" rather than "you have acquired or bought," implying that Boaz revealed his plans to marry Ruth after So-and-So agreed to redeem the land, leaving So-and-So to suddenly anticipate the loss of the property should Ruth produce an heir.[40] "Thus, when Boaz stated his intention to claim the field on behalf of the children of his marriage to Ruth, the redeemer suddenly saw the redemption of the field as a profitless exercise,"[41] whether or not redemption of the land included marriage to the young widow. When Boaz added Ruth to the deal, So-and-So was no longer interested in the purchase, concluding that such an arrangement would "mar" his own inheritance (Ruth 4:6). As a result of this transaction, the text suggests something else about Boaz's character: he was not bound to marry Ruth because he purchased her deceased husband's land; he did so willingly to redeem her and her husband's family.

At the time when Ruth lived in Bethlehem, the nearest kinsman renounced his right to redeem land by removing his sandal and giving it to the one who would assume his obligation as "redeemer" (Ruth 4:7–8). The equivalent today might be a handshake in the presence of witnesses. The custom communicates that only the owner has the right to set his foot on the land. Similarly, God promised Joshua that he would possess the land upon which he walked (see Josh. 1:3; 14:9; Deut. 11:24). The ritual could also reflect a word play: the Hebrew word for shoe is *na'al,* and the word for inheritance is *nahal.*[42]

BETWEEN THE LINES

Blessings in abundance. "All the people that were in the gate, and the elders, said, We are witnesses" (Ruth 4:11). In a marvelous show of community support and unity, they then pronounced a threefold blessing on the engaged couple. First, they blessed Ruth that the Lord would make her "like Rachel and like Leah," who together "built the house of Israel."

The townspeople stated the next blessing in poetic-parallel fashion, perhaps to the couple jointly:

> *Do* thou *worthily* in Ephratah
> And *be famous* in Beth-lehem
> (Ruth 4:11)

Ephratah is an alternate name for Bethlehem in this parallel couplet, and "be famous" is the parallel for "do worthily." Of note, the adverb here translated "worthily" comes from the same Hebrew root that is translated as "wealth" in connection with Boaz and "virtue" in connection with Ruth earlier in the story. The people blessed them to receive renown by living with integrity.

The final blessing pronounced by the villagers was for Boaz. It recalls another outsider who, like Ruth, succeeded in saving the lineage of David and eventually the Son of David: "And let thy house be like the house of Pharez, whom Tamar bare unto Judah, of the seed which the Lord shall give thee of this young woman" (Ruth 4:12; see also 1 Chr. 2:5–12). Tamar had not been forgotten over the centuries and was now viewed in Israel as a role model for Ruth and succeeding generations. In referencing great women in Israelite history in these blessings, the villagers anchored Ruth the foreigner to Jehovah's people.

Ruth and Naomi were both childless when they left Moab, but in the end, they shared the blessing of new life and motherhood.[43] The text reads that the women of the village named the baby Obed, meaning "servant," in the sense that he would be a caregiver to his mother and grandmother in their later years (Ruth 4:17). Josephus identified Naomi as the one who named the baby "by the advice of the women" (*Ant* 5. 9. 4). More important, the baby represented for Ruth and Naomi God's compensation for their faith in him throughout years of adversity and uncertainty. The women blessed Naomi, "[This baby] shall be unto thee a restorer of thy life, and a nourisher of thine old age" (4:15).

Although the book is named for Ruth, the record begins and ends with Naomi, whose faith in the Almighty was strengthened and restored because of Ruth. On acount of one young woman, a foreigner without status or wealth, Naomi's neighbors could witness to her, "Blessed be the Lord, which hath not left thee this day without a kinsman, that his name may be famous in Israel" (Ruth 4:14). Of note, in the LXX, the women tell Naomi, "Even to make *thy* name famous in Israel" (LXX Ruth 4:14; emphasis added). In truth, Naomi is generally remembered more today than her grandson Obed.

As Naomi held the babe close, acknowledging him as her child, too, the women of Bethlehem cried out, "There is a son born to Naomi" (Ruth 4:17). Much like Hannah, who sang in her prayer, "The barren hath borne seven" (1 Sam. 2:5), the women praised Ruth as being better to Naomi than had she borne seven sons (Ruth 4:15). Their exclamation is all the more striking in a culture that valued sons more highly than daughters. This chorus of women was a witness of God's *ḥesed,* meted out to Naomi though Ruth's love and service.

Promoting unity among generations and peoples. Ruth became the catalyst to restore a family to a hopeful life. From that perspective, Ruth was also a *go'el;* she voluntarily sacrificed all that she had to show kindness beyond what anyone would expect or require. Void of material possessions, Ruth gave of who she was—unselfish, proactive, virtuous, respectful of others regardless of age or position, and loyal. In many ways, Ruth exemplifies Christlike attributes.

The birth of Obed to Ruth and Boaz created a reunification of Abraham's family. Boaz was a descendant of Judah, the fourth son of Jacob. Ruth was descended from Abraham's nephew Lot. "A genealogy is a striking way of bringing before us the continuity of God's purpose through the ages."[44] The genealogy at the end of the book of Ruth reveals how Obed is a grandfather of King David, thus making Ruth David's great-grandmother, a likely reason for preserving this remarkable story in holy writ. Considering his heritage from David's point of view is also instructive. As one who claimed the right of kingship over many peoples in the land, David was born through the lineage of Judah, which was promised the right to "the sceptre" until "Shiloh come" (Gen. 49:10). Because of Ruth and Rahab, however, David could also claim a blood lineage from the Moabites and the Canaanites.

Ruth's place in the lineage of Judah persisted in New Testament times, as noted in Matthew's Gospel. She can legitimately be called a child of Israel and a daughter of the covenant not because of blood lineage, royal standing, or religious position but because she followed God's law. Rather than looking through the direct lens of the temple or the prophets, as one biblical scholar observed, "The striking thing about the theology of the Ruth book . . . is that it brings the lofty concept of covenant into vital contact with day-to-day life."[45] As a result, Ruth's example continues to inspire greater faith and merciful kindness for others.

POINTS TO PONDER

1. What lessons do you think the author of the story of Ruth hopes that readers would recognize and apply?

2. Everyone feels at times "different" or like an outsider when their lives do not reflect the ideal. What does Ruth teach us about seeing opportunities and God's blessings in paths that are less traveled?

3. What can Ruth teach us about staying true to our covenant with God when we experience loneliness in a new location, death of a loved one, or sudden depletion of our financial resources?

4. How might Orpah have been following God's plan for her when she remained in her homeland? On the other hand, how may she have missed the door God was opening to her? How do we know? It is often easy to judge another's decision to "stay" or "go," but is such judgment helpful to you or the other person?

5. Considering how Ruth's choices blessed not only herself and Naomi but also her descendants, how might current decisions and dedication to your faith affect your family and future generations?

6. How is Jesus Christ a "kinsman" or Redeemer in your life?

Many Sorrows

BY ELSPETH YOUNG

BATHSHEBA

בַּת־שֶׁבַע

"Daughter of Oath/Seven" or "Daughter of Sheba" (Hebrew)

The story of Bathsheba's encounter with King David is well known for marking David's fall from grace and the scandal his sin cast on the Israelite empire and monarchy. On the other hand, Bathsheba's character and her feelings about the tryst are ambiguous at best. The Bible conveys no clues about her motives or emotions when she was summoned to the king's palace, was invited to his bed, learned of her subsequent pregnancy, was notified of her husband's death, and finally was taken by the king in marriage. She is rarely called by name in these chapters but is often referred to as "the woman" or "the wife of Uriah." Bathsheba is almost a nonperson in the way the text portrays her and therefore could be seen as "not an equal party to the adultery, but only the means whereby it was achieved."[1]

The story reveals David's weakness and sins before God while leaving many questions about the woman who was involved in his adultery unanswered. David, Bathsheba, and a few servants would have known when she was brought to the palace at the king's behest. Most likely only David and Joab, the military captain, knew the motive for the death of Bathsheba's husband, Uriah. The story is a powerful reminder, however, that God knew the true reason.

Rabbinic literature portrays Bathsheba in a positive light, even including her in a list of twenty-two "women of valor."[2] Josephus identified her as an "Israelitish woman" who was given to Uriah the Hittite in return for his aid in unfastening the armor of the prostrate Goliath" after he fell to David's lethal sling.[3] Scripture itself, however, does not indicate whether Bathsheba was an Israelite or from one of the numerous surrounding peoples who had assimilated with the Israelites over time. Her name is a compound Hebrew word meaning

2 SAMUEL 11

2 SAMUEL 12

1 KINGS 1:11–31

1 KINGS 2:13–19

1 CHRONICLES 3:5

PSALM 51:2

MATTHEW 1:6

DOCTRINE & COVENANTS 132:39

"Daughter (bath) of an Oath or Seven (sheba)." It could also mean simply "Daughter of Sheba," in reference to the country.

Uriah was a Hittite, a people who inhabited northern Syria and eastern Turkey in the centuries before there was a nation of Israel. By David's time, however, many Hittites had long resided in Canaan alongside the Israelites. Intermarriage between Israel and its neighbors was commonplace from the time of the Israelites' occupation, as described in the book of Judges: "The children of Israel dwelt among the Canaanites, Hittites, and Amorites, and Perizzites, and Hivites, and Jebusites: and they took their daughters to be their wives, and gave their daughters to their sons" (Judges 3:5–6). The text does not indicate when Uriah or his family joined with the Israelites.

Because Matthew included "her that had been the wife of Urias [the Greek spelling of Uriah]" in the lineage of Jesus (Matt. 1:6), we are encouraged to appreciate Bathsheba. Latter-day scripture also supplies evidence of redemption and eternal glory for this often maligned and misunderstood ancestress of the Savior.

HISTORICAL CONTEXT

Although little is known about most of David's wives, collectively these women represent David's connections to men of power and influence in different regions of the land of Canaan. This observation argues compellingly that his marriages were politically motivated to bolster his rise to power in Israel.[4]

With at least seven wives, King David saw a beautiful woman and desired to know who she was or perhaps *whose* she was. The King James Version reads, "And David sent and inquired after the woman. And *one* said Is not this Bathsheba, the daughter of Eliam, the wife of Uriah the Hittite?" (2 Sam. 11:3). Removing the italicized word *one,* which was added by King James translators, the text implies that David recognized Bathsheba as the wife of one of his military captains and simply asked his servants for verification. The narrative would thus read: "And David sent and enquired after the woman. And [he] said, Is not this Bathsheba, the daughter of Eliam, the wife of Uriah the Hittite?" (2 Sam. 11:3). In this case, David already knew who Bathsheba was before he summoned her. She was the daughter of Eliam, one of the king's elite force of thirty "mighty men" or military captains (2 Sam. 23:22–39). These mighty men were bodyguards to the king, trusted warriors, and fearless defenders of the kingdom. Eliam was not only Bathsheba's father but also the son of Ahithophel the Gilonite (2 Sam. 23:34), David's trusted counselor (2 Sam. 15:12). Rabbinic literature underscores the significance of Eliam and Ahithophel being Bathsheba's father and grandfather respectively.[5] In short, when David asked his clarifying question, he was well aware of the woman's family and political connections.

DAVID'S WIVES AND THEIR TIES TO GEOPOLITICAL POWER (1 CHR. 3:1–9)

Name of Wife	Political Connection	Known Children	Additional Evidence
1) Michal	Daughter of King Saul	None	1 Sam. 18:17–28; 19:11–17; 25:44; 2 Sam. 3:13–15
2) Ahinoam	Possible wife of King Saul	Amnon	1 Sam. 14:50; 25:43
3) Abigail	Wife of Nabal, chieftain near Hebron	Clileab/Daniel	1 Sam. 25
4) Maachah	Daughter of king of Geshur	Absalom; Tamar	2 Sam. 3:3–5
5) Haggith		Adonijah	2 Sam. 3:3–5
6) Abital		Shephatiah	2 Sam. 3:3–5
7) Eglah		Ithream	2 Sam. 3:3–5
8) Bathsheba	Wife of Uriah the Hittite and granddaughter of Ahithophel, David's chief counselor	Son who died soon after birth, Solomon, Nathan, Shobab, Shimea	2 Sam. 11–12
9) Abishag	From Shunem in Issachar territory	None	1 Kgs. 1:1–4

BATHSHEBA'S DAILY LIFE

When David inquired about the woman he could see from his rooftop, he learned something more about Bathsheba than the identity of her father and grandfather. He also learned she was a married woman—married to another of his mighty men (2 Sam. 23:39). She was the "wife of Uriah the Hittite" with whom David was also very well acquainted (2 Sam. 11:3). He knew that Uriah was not at home but with the Israelite army entrenched in a siege of Rabbah to enlarge David's empire. Uriah's name in Hebrew means "My light is Jehovah." Biblical scholar Kyle McCarter suggests that the title "Uriah the Hittite" does not necessarily dictate that he was a mercenary or a foreigner in David's army but that he was "probably born in Israel and [was] ethnically Aramean, [therefore] he is called 'the Hittite.'"[6] Certainly, his name would indicate that his parents followed Jehovah rather than the gods of the Hittites.

Considering the status rewards provided by David's previous marriages, biblical scholar Randall C. Bailey notes that David's marriage to Bathsheba may be more a story of "political intrigue" than a sordid tale of "sexual lust gone awry."[7]

BATHSHEBA'S PLACE OF RESIDENCE

Before the temple was built, David's palace was the highest structure in the City of David, the name for Jerusalem at the time, and had an excellent view of the rest of the city. The home of Bathsheba and Uriah was likely farther down the hill and within sight of the palace. Towards evening, David arose and

Photo by Kent P. Jackson

David's palace was on the upper hillside of the City of David, from which he would have had a clear view of the homes below.

"walked upon the roof of the king's house" and spied a woman bathing—a *beautiful* woman bathing (2 Sam. 11:2).

We do not know why David was not with the army he had sent to besiege Rabbah, the capital of the Ammonite nation (2 Sam. 11:1). The consequences for Israel should he be killed in battle could have outweighed respect for protocol. Furthermore, other affairs of the kingdom might have needed his specific attention while his generals ably managed the conflict. David's prestige could then be augmented when he entered the battlefield after the fighting had determined Israel was the victor and he ceremonially accepted the submission of the conquered kings. On the other hand, perhaps David was getting too old to fight effectively, having once become "faint" in battle (2 Sam. 21:15). During a later battle, his men begged him to cease fighting in person, saying, "Thou shalt go no more out with us to battle, that thou quench not the light of Israel" (2 Sam. 21:17).

It is against this backdrop of war (2 Sam. 10; 12:26–31) that David's encounter with Bathsheba occurred. Uriah the Hittite was fighting in Ammon. His wife, Bathsheba, remained in Jerusalem, where her home was visible from the royal palace. Whatever David's reasons for remaining in Jerusalem, David's downfall occurred not because he was not with the army but because of what he chose to do at home while his troops were away.

BATHSHEBA'S APPEARANCE IN THE BIBLICAL STORY

Co-conspirator or victim? Many readers conclude that Bathsheba must have been posturing in the hope that the king would find her irresistible if he espied her that afternoon. That, however, is not a conclusion that is necessarily justified by the text. Under the law of Moses, all Israelite women were required to perform a monthly purification rite of immersion. The law specified that women were ritually unclean seven days each month during their menstrual cycle and were required to bathe and offer sacrifice on the eighth day to become clean from blood. According to the law, moreover, any man who "lies with" a woman during those seven days is "unclean" for seven days because of his contact with blood, and he was also required to "bathe himself in water" (Lev. 15:19–30). The purpose of the author of 2 Samuel in reporting that Bathsheba was "washing herself" when David discovered her may be to show that the king knew the woman was ritually clean, or safe for sexual relations with little chance of conception. This theory is supported by the verse which can be read: "[David] lay with her; *[because]* she was purified from her uncleanness" (2 Sam. 11:4).

David was arguably more concerned over the ritual correctness of Bathsheba's purification than God's commandments, "Thou shalt not commit adultery;" "thou shalt not steal;" "and thou shalt not covet thy neighbor's wife" (Ex. 20:14, 15, 17). After his popularity and dazzling military successes had brought him to power, he had begun to see himself as being above the law. Although David must have known that coveting another man's wife was an abomination to God (Ex. 20:17; see also Jacob 2:24), he may have justified his actions for political reasons. Other rulers in neighboring kingdoms had large harems. Bruce and Marie Hafen observed: "King David . . . somehow developed too much confidence in his own ability to handle temptation. He was tragically willing to flirt with evil, and it destroyed him."[8] He could excuse his misdeeds by believing that since God was with him, whatever he did was beyond the reach of the Mosaic law.[9]

Adultery and murder laced with ambiguity. Though plainly comprehending Bathsheba's

Under the law of Moses, Israelite women were required to perform a monthly purification rite of immersion in a pool called a mikveh. This mikveh, discovered in Jericho, shows the traditional design of steps descending into the limestone-lined basin that would have been filled with water.

Photo by Kent P. Jackson

identity and connections, David "sent messengers, and took her: and she came in unto him, and he lay with her; for she was purified from her uncleanness: and she returned unto her house" (2 Sam. 11:4). Artfully ambiguous in reporting the facts, the text avoids any mention of emotions as the events occur.[10] Because David "took her," we can possibly assume that Bathsheba had no choice in the matter. As one of the king's subjects, how could Bathsheba refuse to comply when summoned? We are simply informed that an immoral act occurred between the king and Bathsheba and that afterwards she returned home.

Legal codes of the Hittites, Assyrians, and Babylonians from before the time of Bathsheba and David coincided with Israelite law on cases of adultery. All of these ancient laws declared that adultery was a capital crime (*Middle Assyrian Law* 13; *Hittite Law* 197–198).[11] Unlike neighboring codes, however, Israelite law viewed adultery as a sin against God rather than a crime against a husband (Ex. 20:14; Lev. 18:20; Deut. 5:18). Under the law of Moses, the offender did not owe recompense to the husband, nor was the husband required to forgive the guilty parties, who faced the penalty of the law and not of the husband. Whether it was rape or seduction, the law of Moses stated that the man involved was guilty of adultery and received the same punishment as an adulterous woman (Lev. 20:10; Deut. 22:22). Even so, the historian Josephus saw only Bathsheba as the sinner in the case of David's adultery (*Ant* 7.1.131).

By emphasizing Bathsheba's purification at this point in the story, "and he lay with her; for she was purified from her uncleanness" (2 Sam. 11:4), the reader knows that should she become pregnant, David would unquestionably be responsible for the pregnancy. Some scholars have speculated that David and Bathsheba may have concocted a scheme that would allow him to increase the power of his realm and permit her to become the queen whose son would inherit his father's throne.[12] That, however, is unlikely. The scriptures offer no support that such a plan was premeditated, and the timing of the affair argues against an intentional pregnancy. As will be discussed later, we simply know that by the time the king's death was nigh, Bathsheba, Nathan the prophet, and David intended that Bathsheba's son Solomon should be appointed the next king of Israel (1 Kgs. 1:17, 30).

The death of Bathsheba's husband. Without hinting at her emotions or motives, the scriptural text records that Bathsheba sent word to David of her pregnancy. The king's response to the news was an attempt to cover up his sin, which action further discredits the suggestion of a premeditated plan. David directed Joab to send Uriah home from the war. Uriah responded immediately by returning to Jerusalem and reporting to the king. Interestingly, we do not question Uriah's obedience in appearing when the king summoned him, so why do we question Bathsheba's motives when she similarly complied with David's summons? Assuming one expectation for a soldier who is summoned by the king and another for a woman in his kingdom who is summoned by the king indicates a double standard.

After Uriah briefed the king on "how the war prospered," David told him, "Go down to thy house, and wash thy feet" (2 Sam. 11:7–8). Reference to "the feet" in a context laced with sexual innuendo (see Ruth 3:4, 7; Ezek. 16:25) is likely a euphemism for sexual intercourse.[13] In other words, the king encouraged Uriah to spend time with his wife to forestall any question of paternity when Bathsheba's pregnancy became known. David sweetened the suggestion by sending a feast to Uriah's home (2 Sam. 11:8).

Uriah did not go home, however. Instead, he publicly remained with the king's guards and "slept at the door of the king's house with all the servants of his lord, and went not down to his house" (2 Sam. 11:9). When David learned of Uriah's actions, he confronted Uriah and reprimanded him. Uriah responded by explaining the inappropriateness of going "into mine house, to eat, and to drink, and to lie with my wife" while the ark of the covenant and the troops of Israel encamped in tents on the battlefield (2 Sam. 11:11). Uriah pointed out that his duty was with his regiment in Rabbah, not in relaxing at home with his wife. Hearing such commitment to principle must have been uncomfortable for David.

After his second attempt to induce Uriah to go home also failed (2 Sam. 11:12–13), the king sent a letter to Joab, instructing him to set Uriah "in the forefront of the hottest battle, and retire ye from him" so that he would be killed in the conflict (2 Sam. 11:14–15). Furthermore, David charged Uriah to carry the letter to Joab; thus Uriah, in effect, delivered his own death warrant.

How did Joab carry out his orders? Josephus says he "gave [Uriah] for his partners some of the best soldiers in the army; and said that he would also come to their assistance with the whole army, that if possible they might break down part of the wall, and enter the city" (*Ant* 7.1.137). Whatever it was, the plan worked. Uriah was killed by arrows shot from the wall surrounding Rabbah (2 Sam. 11:16–25). When word of Uriah's death reached the king, David sent a reassuring message back to Joab, "Let not this thing displease thee, for the sword devoureth one as well as another" (2 Sam. 11:25).

The first emotion attributed to Bathsheba in the scriptural story is when she received word of her husband's death: "The wife of Uriah . . . mourned for her husband" (2 Sam. 11:26). The customary length of time for mourning in the biblical era was seven days (Gen. 50:10; 1 Sam. 31:13). David honored this custom before again sending for Bathsheba, this time to fetch her for his wife (2 Sam. 11:27). The reader is given the impression that David now felt he had tied up all the loose ends and could proceed with his life, but "the thing that David had done displeased the Lord" (2 Sam. 11:27). The Lord therefore sent his prophet Nathan to awaken the king to an awareness of his grievous sins (2 Sam. 12:1).

To send with authority. It has been argued that the frequent use of the verb *to send* in 2 Samuel 11 is indicative of the power that one individual wielded over another.[14] In each of these instances, the one who *sends* has authority over the one being sent for, and in every case the one sent for does what the authority figure commands. In other words, the use of the verb illustrates David's authority over his subjects, including Bathsheba.

In rabbinic tradition, David is shown as modest, humble, and always worthy of praise—even in the case of Bathsheba and her husband Uriah. For instance, one legend reads: "[David] is one of the few pious men over whom the evil inclination had no power. . . . God Himself brought him to his crime [of passion with Bathsheba], that He may say to other sinners: 'Go to David and learn how to repent.'"[15] Furthermore,

Jewish tradition claims that David could not be charged with adultery or murder because soldiers customarily gave their wives a bill of divorcement before going to battle so the women would be free to marry again if their husbands were killed in battle. Because Uriah in fact was killed, the rabbis argued that David was legally free to marry Bathsheba. Such traditions even go so far as to claim that Uriah deserved the death penalty by refusing to heed the king's order to go home and sleep with his wife. Assuming that destiny excuses any misdeed, these interpretations conclude with "Bathsheba had been destined by God for David," who "had to undergo bitter trials before he won her."[16]

Notwithstanding their dramatic appeal, these apologies written a thousand years after the events have little historical value. By contrast, in a psalm attributed to David as a plea for forgiveness after his affair with Bathsheba, he acknowledged the sin was his. "Have mercy on me, O God. . . . Wash me thoroughly from mine iniquity, and cleanse me from my sin. For I acknowledge my transgressions: and my sin is ever before me" (Ps. 51: 1–3).

Nathan's parable. Acknowledging the seriousness of David's flagrant sins, the Lord sent Nathan the prophet to chastise him. Nathan concocted a case that presumably required David's counsel but which actually highlighted David's own sins.

The story awakened the king's sense of justice and made him recoil at the hard-heartedness of the selfish man. "And David's anger was greatly kindled against the man; and he said to Nathan, As the Lord liveth, the man that hath done this thing shall surely die: And he shall restore the lamb fourfold, because he did this thing, and because he had no pity" (2 Sam. 12:5–6).

NATHAN'S PARABLE

There were two men in one city; the one rich, and the other poor.

The rich man had exceeding many flocks and herds:

But the poor man had nothing, save one little ewe lamb, which he had bought and nourished up: and it grew up together with him, and with his children; it did eat of his own meat, and drank of his own cup, and lay in his bosom, and was unto him as a daughter.

And there came a traveller unto the rich man, and he spared to take of his own flock and of his own herd, to dress for the wayfaring man that was come unto him; but took the poor man's lamb, and dressed it for the man that was come to him (2 Sam. 12:1–4).

With four words, Nathan brought the message home to David: "Thou art the man" (2 Sam. 12:7). Suddenly the king realized that he was the rich man with such insatiable greed.

Nathan reminded David of all that the Lord had given him and done for him in order that he could lead a united Israel. Specifically, he mentioned that God gave him "thy master's house, and thy master's wives into thy bosom" (2 Sam. 12:8), potentially a reference to Saul's daughter Michal (2 Sam. 3:13) and his wife Ahinoam (1 Sam. 14:50), both of whom became David's wives. Was all this not enough for David? If not, God declared, "I would moreover have given unto thee such and such things" (2 Sam. 12:8).

Consequences of the affair. If they were

equally guilty, one would expect God's anger to be turned on both David and Bathsheba for their offense against him. Yet never a word of chastisement is directed against Bathsheba. David alone is the focus of God's angry gaze, and his entire family suffered because he "despised the commandment of the Lord" (2 Sam. 12:9). As David had declared the offender in Nathan's parable worthy of death, so Nathan pronounced a similar fate for David: "The sword shall never depart from thine house; because thou hast despised me, and hast *taken* the wife of Uriah the Hittite to be thy wife" (2 Sam. 12:10; emphasis added). This punishment implies that David was guilty of abusing his power not only to send for but also to take Bathsheba. Now David would experience the pain of being taken from. He was told, "I will *take* thy wives before thine eyes, and give them unto thy neighbour, and he shall lie with thy wives in the sight of the sun" (2 Sam. 12:11; emphasis added). David's "house," or family, would collectively be publicly humiliated because of the sins that David tried to hide from God.

In a fulfillment of Nathan's prophecy, David soon witnessed violence and murder among his sons and daughters, culminating in Absalom's attempt to overthrow his father (2 Sam. 13-15). Absalom seized Jerusalem and David's wives, making a public spectacle of his conquest with David's ten wives and concubines who had been left behind when David escaped the city (2 Sam. 16:21-22). When the revolt collapsed, Ahithophel committed suicide (2 Sam. 17:23), and David's military captain, Joab, killed Absalom (2 Sam. 18:9–17). Death and heartache, vengeance and betrayal occurred again and again to horrify and devastate David's family. These events were not caused by God; rather, they were tragic consequences of David's actions that wrought havoc within his family.

Latter-day revelation further describes David's losses. To the Prophet Joseph Smith, the Lord revealed, "David's wives and concubines were given unto him of me, by the hand of Nathan, my servant, and others of the prophets who had the keys of this power; and in none of these things did he sin against me save in the case of Uriah and his wife; and, therefore he hath fallen from his exaltation, and received his portion; and he shall not inherit them out of the world, for I gave them unto another, saith the Lord" (D&C 132:39).

This revelation is significant for a number of reasons. First, it informs us that Nathan held "keys" of the sealing power of God and therefore must have held the Melchizedek Priesthood. Second, it indicates that David had previously received higher priesthood authority and with his wives had been worthy to receive the sealing ordinances. He would therefore have been under special covenant with God before he commanded Uriah's death. Third, God approved David's other marriages, which removes some of the sting of some scholars' observations that David married women purely for political gain, but declared that David had "sin[ned] against [him] in the case of Uriah and his wife." Fourth, David fell from exaltation and will not be blessed with marriage in the hereafter. Notwithstanding those losses, however, God did not abandon him. David knew that although he would go to hell, "[God] wilt not leave my soul in hell," that is, he would eventually be redeemed from death and hell (Ps. 16:10; Acts 2:25–27). And finally, David's wives will be married to others in the hereafter—suggesting that all of his wives, including Bathsheba, will receive exaltation. In the genealogy of Christ, Matthew referred to Bathsheba as "her that had been the wife of Urias" (Matt. 1:6). Perhaps in God's eyes, too, Bathsheba was not the wife of David but forever the wife of Uriah.

The mother of Solomon. After the death of her first son, Bathsheba conceived another child by David. David named him Solomon, meaning "peace." Nathan the prophet called him Jedidiah, meaning "the beloved of Jehovah," signifying that this son of David was born for the Lord's sake or because of the Lord.

Not surprisingly, the scriptures are silent about Bathsheba's emotions about becoming a mother. According to Jewish tradition, however, when her son became king, Bathsheba told Solomon, "Whenever thy father's wives were pregnant, they offered vows and prayed that a son worthy to reign might be born unto them. But my prayer was for a learned son worthy of the gift of prophecy."[17] The rabbis clearly viewed Bathsheba in a favorable light compared to David's other wives.

Bathsheba secures the throne for Solomon. When "king David was old and stricken in years," perhaps about seventy years of age, the narrative again returns to Bathsheba (1 Kgs. 1:1). She would have been close to fifty years old at this time. With David hampered by family tragedies and the crimes of his own children, two rival parties had developed in Jerusalem, one favoring Adonijah, David's oldest surviving son, and the other favoring Solomon, Bathsheba's son. In these scenes, Bathsheba is no longer portrayed as passive. With her help, Nathan the prophet outwitted Adonijah and assisted Solomon in taking the throne.

The aged king David married yet again, but this time, he chose a very young woman to warm his bed. Her name was Abishag. She came from the Galilean village of Shunem in the territory of Issachar (1 Kgs. 1:2–3). Perhaps her presence in the palace reminded Bathsheba that her own beauty had declined since David first lusted for her from his rooftop. Josephus justified David's choice of a much younger wife with a comment that the physicians at the time agreed that a "damsel [girl] would communicate heat to him, and be a remedy against his numbness" (*Ant* 7. 14. 3). Others have argued that David's doctors prescribed a young bed partner to ward off complications from hardening of the arteries.[18] Everyone wants to make excuses for poor David—everyone, that is, except the Lord.

Adonijah was David's fourth son, but his three older brothers (Amnon, Chileab or Daniel, and Absalom) were already dead, so he naturally assumed that he would inherit the throne. Born in Hebron to Haggith when David was king of Judah (1 Chr. 3:1–3), Adonijah would have been in his mid-thirties when he openly declared his presumptive position while his father still lived. Furthermore, apparently King David had done nothing to indicate any objection to his behaving as though he were already king (1 Kgs. 1:6). Adonijah therefore rallied two of his father's closest allies, Joab the military captain and Abiathar the priest, to his support (1 Kgs. 1:7).

Deducing Adonijah's intent, Nathan sought audience with Bathsheba to devise a plan to counter the would-be king (1 Kgs. 1:11–14). No explanation is given for the prophet's insistence that Solomon should be the next king and not Adonijah. This is the first mention of Nathan in scripture since his poignant censure of David in 2 Sam. 12. Reminding her that she and her son would likely die if Adonijah succeeded, Nathan asked Bathsheba to speak to David of his promise that her son would be the next king (1 Kgs. 1:12–13). Nowhere in the Bible is such a vow to Bathsheba previously disclosed, but a rabbinic legend claims that after the death of their first son, David promised Bathsheba that he would name their next son his successor.[19]

The plan outlined that Bathsheba should first approach King David to remind him of his promise about Solomon, and then Nathan would enter "while [she] yet talkest there with the king" and "confirm [her] words" (1 Kgs. 1:13–14). The text specifies that Abishag "ministered" to the king when Bathsheba entered, thereby becoming an additional witness to the events that would transpire (1 Kgs. 1:15). The formality associated with deference to the king is described in the scene. When she approached David, Bathsheba "bowed, and did obeisance unto the king" but did not speak until he addressed her: "What wouldest thou?" (1 Kgs. 1:16).

Bathsheba told the aged and perhaps senile David of the uproar Adonijah was creating and how she and Solomon were endangered if Adonijah should have his way. She pleaded with him, "Thou, my lord, O king, the eyes of all Israel are upon thee, that thou shouldest tell them who shall sit on the throne of my lord the king after him" (1 Kgs. 1:17–20). Then Nathan entered and waited to be announced to the king. He also bowed before David "with his face to the ground" (1 Kgs. 1:22–23). It appears Bathsheba departed when Nathan commenced his address. He asked David if he had named Adonijah his successor and described celebration happening at that very moment with Adonijah's key supporters—"all the king's sons, and the captains of the host [Joab], and Abiathar the priest"—who were chanting, "God save king Adonijah" (1 Kgs. 1:24–26). Clearly, David was no longer in control of his kingdom and completely unaware that Adonijah was making him irrelevant (1 Kgs. 1:18).

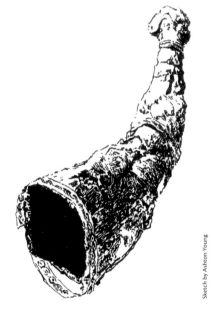

Calling Bathsheba back into the room, David made an oath to her, saying, "Solomon thy son . . . shall sit upon my throne in my stead" (1 Kgs. 1:28–30). In response, "Bathsheba bowed with her face to the earth, and did reverence to the king, and said, Let my lord king David live for ever" (1 Kgs. 1:31). Right away, the king gave orders for Solomon to be taken on the king's mule to the Gihon Spring to be publicly anointed as ruler of united Israel. "The anointing of Solomon served the purpose of counteracting Adonijah's claim to the throne."[20]

Shortly before his death and at Bathsheba's request, David gave orders for Solomon to be taken on the king's mule to the Gihon Spring to be publicly anointed as ruler of united Israel (1 Kgs. 1:32–34). Oil for the anointing was carried in a horn like this one.

Knowing his death was imminent, David counseled Solomon to follow the laws of God (1 Kgs. 2:1–4) and expressed confidence in his ability to deal with dissenters (1 Kgs. 2:5–9). So David died and "was buried in the city of David," having reigned seven years over Judah and thirty-three additional years over both Judah and Israel (1 Kgs. 2:10–11). Solomon, son of Bathsheba and David, reigned in his stead.

BETWEEN THE LINES

Bathsheba and Adonijah. The rivalry between Adonijah and Solomon did not end with David's death. Early in Solomon's reign, Adonijah sought favor by inquiring through Bathsheba, the mother of the king. Prefacing his request with, "Thou knowest that the kingdom was mine, and that all Israel set their faces on me, that I should reign" (1 Kgs. 2:15), he petitioned her to ask Solomon for permission for him to marry Abishag (1 Kgs. 2:16–17). Adonijah knew that his rightful claim to the throne would be significantly strengthened by marrying a wife of the former king.

Without explaining her reaction to the loaded request, the text reports that Bathsheba agreed to ask Solomon for permission for Adonijah to marry Abishag. Perhaps she was motivated by the thought that if Adonijah married Abishag, Solomon would not marry her.[21] But in any case, she certainly knew how to use her leverage as mother of the king to protect her son's position.

When Bathsheba carried Adonijah's message to Solomon, the young king showed respect and love for his mother. The text reads, "The king rose up to meet her, and bowed himself unto her, . . . and caused a seat to be set for the king's mother; and she sat on his right hand" (1 Kgs. 2:19). When she said, "I desire one small petition of thee," Solomon responded, "Ask on, my mother: for I will not say thee nay" (1 Kgs. 2:20). Again we are struck by the position of power and reverence Bathsheba held in Solomon's court.

But the "small petition" took Solomon by surprise; he immediately suspected Adonijah of treason, declaring in essence that he might as well be asking for the kingdom" and ordered his death that very day (1 Kgs. 2:21–25). Solomon then removed Abiathar from his priestly duties and demanded Joab's death (1 Kgs. 2:26–34). One scholar quipped of Adonijah's lack of judgment in making such a request: "If Adonijah did seek Abishag's hand in marriage, and if he did approach Bathsheba to entreat Solomon on his behalf, he deserved his speedy execution—for stupidity."[22] Bathsheba and her son had firmly established Israel's leadership and the direction of the royal lineage. The Savior would be a descendant of Bathsheba.

Ancestress of Mary. An irregular marital union, questions over paternity, and mothering a future king—these circumstances can describe both Bathsheba and Mary, the mother of Jesus. The rabbis called Bathsheba a "woman of valor." Joseph Smith taught that she will enjoy marriage in the eternities. Even though enmeshed in scandal and intrigue, Bathsheba emerged as someone a prophet could trust to assist him in his work. Of all David's sons from all his wives, Nathan anointed Bathsheba's son to be Israel's next king. God neither condemned her nor restricted her from influencing the affairs of the kingdom. David was condemned; Bathsheba was not. Matthew specifically listed her as an ancestress of Jesus.

Despite the sins and schemes of those who held worldly power, Israel survived because of Jehovah's mercy. "This presses us to conceive God's providence as both more *hidden* from direct human perception and vastly more *intimate* to the details of real human experience than theologians ordinarily think."[23]

The larger story of Bathsheba reinforces the fact that there is only one true King—he who never stoops to insatiable covetousness or dishonesty. It is Jehovah who promised David an enduring "house" to rule Israel (2 Sam. 7:16). And the events surrounding the life of Bathsheba with David underscore that it is Jehovah who preserves and enables that "house" to prepare for his coming. Like Bathsheba, we are similarly called to prepare the way for the Lord—despite the disappointments, tragedies, and surprises that life may throw our way. Like Mary and Bathsheba, our inspired decisions and actions may be misjudged as immoral, but the God of all knows our motives and offers his strength to overcome.

POINTS TO PONDER

1. How does an appreciation for Bathsheba's eternal promises give hope to someone who has made a serious mistake or been victimized?

2. How does the story of Bathsheba and David increase your faith in Jesus Christ and his omniscience?

3. How can Bathsheba's experiences encourage you to be less judgmental of others?

4. Do you think a double standard exists in our society when it comes to excusing men for promiscuity while condemning women for similar sins?

5. How does the story of David and Bathsheba underscore the blessings that come from fidelity and integrity in marriage?

6. What evidence can you identify in your own life for God's power to bring "beauty for ashes" (Isa. 61:3) or compensatory blessings in the aftermath of tragedy?

Go Forth to Meet the Bridegroom

BY ELSPETH YOUNG

WOMEN IN JEWISH SOCIETY

$\mathcal{A}$lthough only a small part of the greater Greco-Roman world, the Jews who remained in the Holy Land retained a distinct identity and society. They received a special dispensation from the Romans to continue their peculiar religious practices and enjoyed a sense of autonomy, especially in Jerusalem. As in the rest of the empire, most Jews were at the bottom of the social hierarchy, with women perceived as strictly second class and rabbinic law concerning them holding sway. The priestly leadership had high social standing, and religious teachers often wielded their influence to keep women out of sight and committed to serving men's needs. Meanwhile, Roman and Hellenistic customs increasingly prompted greater latitude of expression for both men and women.

The Savior's ministry among the Jews, including his inclusive treatment of women and perspective about them, encouraged early Christian women to make significant contributions. With little, if any, education, Christian women in the heart of Judaism found ways to spread the gospel of Jesus Christ without leaving their homeland.

THE LAND OF ISRAEL

In the Roman empire at the time of Christ, most Jews lived outside the Jewish territories and in Jewish communities within the cosmopolitan cities of the empire; only about 500,000 to 600,000 Jews lived in the land of Israel.[1] But Jerusalem was the religious center for all Jews, whether they lived in Judea, Galilee, Perea, or other parts of the Roman empire. With a resident population that had grown to almost 60,000 inhabitants at the time of Christ, the city's numbers swelled significantly during major religious festivals when Jewish pilgrims traveled to Jerusalem from all parts of the empire (Acts 2:5–11).[2]

There were over two hundred small villages and only a few cities in the Galilean region in New Testament times. It was less densely populated and more culturally isolated than Judea to the south. Although the description of life for Jewish women in Judea applies as well to Jewish women in Galilee, the women in rural areas were likely not held to the same strict rabbinic standards as were those in Jerusalem.

Although the Romans allowed the Jewish governing body, the Sanhedrin, to rule the Holy City, about six hundred Roman soldiers were stationed in the city, their presence a daily reminder of foreign occupation. Herod the Great built a spectacular temple for the Jews as a reconstruction of the one built in 516 B.C. when Cyrus permitted the return of Jews to their homeland. Herod's Temple was in construction from 19 B.C. to A.D. 64. It was destroyed only six years later, in A.D. 70, during the Roman suppression of a lengthy Jewish rebellion.

The land known as Israel in the Old Testament was called Palestine by the Romans in the second century. In New Testament times, the entire land was referred to as "the land of Israel" (Matt. 2:20–21). It covered some 7,500 square miles, being about 150 miles long from north to south with an average width of 50 miles, and was approximately the size of New Jersey in the United States. These Jewish territories were called Judea, Galilee, and Perea; the Romans also considered Samaria to be a Jewish territory.

The inhabitants of the land were called *Jews*, the Greek version of *Judeans*. They were the principal inhabitants of the territories of Judea, Galilee, and Perea, with the occasional Greco-Roman city or fortress inhabited by Gentiles. In Galilee, the Hellenistic city of Sepphoris was the largest city; its Greco-Roman population was about the size of the Jewish population of Jerusalem. Less than four miles from Sepphoris was the village of Nazareth. It had fewer than five hundred residents, similar to the size of other Jewish villages in Galilee.[3] Sepphoris was destroyed in 4 B.C. by the Romans in putting down a revolt that erupted after the death of Herod the Great. This city was rebuilt during the childhood and youth of Jesus, leading to the possibility that Jesus, with his carpentry skills and the proximity of Nazareth to Sepphoris, could have worked in the reconstruction of the city.

THE PEOPLE IN THE JEWISH TERRITORIES

The people of New Testament Israel retained a distinctive culture and religion within the Roman empire, even though they were increasingly influenced by Greek values and dominated by Roman law, military, and ideas of status and class (*Ant* 20.11.2).[4] The Holy Land was also a colonial society within the Roman empire after 63 B.C. As they did in many of their acquired territories, Roman emperors ruled Palestine through a client king, commencing with Herod, who was king when Jesus was born.

Greco-Roman politics in the Eastern Mediterranean world introduced a greater Gentile presence and civic practices, including taxation, and Greek was the language widely used in both writing and speech (*2 Macc* 4.10–15; *Ant* 12.5.1). In Judea and Syria, areas important in the spread of Christianity in the New Testament era, Greek was the language of provincial and city governments, social and business elites, and myriads of Hellenized immigrants. As many as fifteen thousand Jews in Jerusalem spoke Greek in the first century: one-third of the inscriptions on the ossuaries of the time are written only in Greek, and considerably more are written in both Hebrew and Greek.[5] The large number of Greek-speaking Jews who journeyed to Jerusalem from all over the Roman empire for the religious holy days would have

The Cardo in Sepphoris, Galilee. At the time of Jesus, Sepphoris was a growing Roman city in Galilee. Because Nazareth was close by, it is possible that the young Jesus visited or even worked in Sepphoris while it was being rebuilt.

added considerably to local residents' exposure to the Greek language. That Herod's Temple was built to accommodate a court of the Gentiles indicates the presence of more than a few God-fearing non-Jews in the land. Aramaic, however, was the language of the villagers, and we have little indication of how much Greek they would speak or understand, let alone read or write. One Roman soldier seemed surprised at how well Paul, a Jew, could speak Greek (Acts 21:37).

Various Jewish groups reacted differently to these outside influences. Many of the Jewish aristocracy, including the high priest and other Sadducees, willingly cooperated with the Romans to retain control in Jerusalem, partly from greed and partly for self-preservation. In return, Rome granted citizenship to many of the Jewish upper class, recognized the Jewish religion, and allowed Jews to apply their annual tax to Rome to build and support the Jewish temple. Most of the ruling Jewish class were likely to be more relaxed in their Jewish dietary regulations and often had diets similar to those residents of Athens or Rome, much to the chagrin of the strict Pharisees. Political control over the Jewish priesthood was exercised by Herod the Great and his successors, who appointed the Jewish high priests during their reigns (*Ant* 17.4.2; 17.6.4; 20.1.3). Some lower class Jews became tax collectors for the Romans because of the potential for financial gain.

Other Jewish groups resisted Greco-Roman influence in the Jewish territories. The Pharisees intensified obedience to expanded requirements of the law of Moses to protect themselves from foreign defilement (Matt. 9:10–11; 22:15-22; *Ant* 13.10.6). Zealot groups were willing to terrorize and murder in their efforts to liberate Jewish communities from the Romans and their influence (*Ant* 18.1.6). As for the lower classes residing in the villages away from Jerusalem, Hellenistic culture was only a thin veneer. Villagers retained their own language, culture, and religion, as did the common people in other parts of the empire, whereas it was mostly the upper classes that adopted Roman customs and values.

After the Resurrection of Christ, Jewish Christians who spoke Aramaic did not initially embrace Greek-speaking Jewish Christians from outside the Holy Land. This schism among early Christians became apparent as the church grew explosively and Greek-speaking widows were neglected in church-sponsored support (Acts 6:1–7). That Jesus and the Twelve were all "Hebrews" and not "Grecians" may have led some of the earliest followers of Christ to assume superiority over their fellow believers from outside their homeland. Even after Peter received the revelation that God is no respecter of persons and that people from all nations and cultures may be included in the gospel net through faith in Jesus Christ, repentance, baptism, and receipt of the Holy Spirit, many Jewish Christians in Jerusalem remained "zealous of the law" (Acts 21:20). Consequently, they resisted fellowship with those who were culturally and linguistically different from themselves. More than once, church policies reflected a need to coddle such Jewish Christians while expecting Gentile Christians to stretch themselves to better understand Judaism as the forerunner of Christianity (Acts 15; Gal. 2).

SOCIAL HIERARCHY IN JEWISH SOCIETY

Increasingly, Jewish society developed socioeconomic divisions similar to those in Greco-Roman society, and fragmentation and polarization within Jewish communities increased. The elites made up 10 percent of the population, with the governing class at the top being 1 percent and the affluent merchants, the upper echelon of priests, and the retainers who served the governing class making up the remaining 9 percent. The top 10 percent received more than 70 percent of total income within the Holy Land. Accumulating their wealth from villagers through taxation and rent for land, the upper classes of Jews did not represent the populace; they exploited them.

Because there was no middle class in the Jewish territories, villagers made up 90 percent of the population. Called the *'am ha-'arets* or "people of the land," they were marginalized and oppressed in Jewish society. The lower classes were impoverished not only economically but also socially and politically. Their attention to the law of Moses took a backseat to their efforts to survive on the edges of a society in which taxes took away any hope of ever getting ahead. These were peasants who spent most of their days eking out a living as farmers or fishermen and who rarely had the resources to pay a tithe or the half-shekel tax for the temple. Keeping the prohibitions of the weekly Sabbath was a luxury few could afford, and they were more often than not ritually impure. They were characteristically considered nonobservant, unclean, and "ignorant of the law."[6]

Included in the peasant class were owners of small land holdings, fishermen, sharecroppers, day laborers, and finally at the very bottom were the expendables—outcasts on account of dishonest or immoral occupations, diseases, and rejection of Torah observance. A few years with lean harvests could cost landowners their land, and they would be left to work at a craft, such as carpentry or sculpture. Galilean villages and towns were populated by those with very small farms or businesses; they are more accurately called peasants than merchants because there was no way for them to increase their landholdings or income.

Jewish society was fastidiously attached to distinctions in purity, separating the impure and nonobservant from the "righteous." The impure and shameful included publicans, prostitutes, thieves, the chronically ill, the maimed, and the Samaritans. Because of the value placed on ritual cleanliness embedded into their social system, the expectation to wash hands and utensils was not a trivial Jewish custom but a politically important one.

With the exception of Jerusalem, Jesus stayed mainly in the smaller villages and rural areas during his ministry. Most of those who followed him were from the peasant class, including most of the women we encounter in the New Testament. The Savior's parables also reflect this rural landscape and the daily challenge to survive. His primary social conflict was with the elites. Practices of worship instituted by Jesus and carried out by Christians were perceived as a threat to societal divisions between the classes and the sexes. For example, the ordinance of the sacrament invited people to eat together without regard to social boundaries, openly challenging accepted mores that reinforced social stratifications between honor and shame, patron and client, free and slave, rich and poor, Jew and Gentile, and men and women.

RELIGIOUS INFLUENCE ON JEWISH WOMEN

The culture of Jerusalem was grounded in religion with the temple and scriptures, especially the Torah, providing the foundation and canopy for their entire society. Despite the differing ideologies among the various

HOMES OF THE JEWISH POPULACE

New Testament Capernaum on the northern shore of the Sea of Galilee contains evidence of small houses, one- and two-room structures clustered close together and built into an enclosure wall surrounding a central courtyard. Floors were made of basalt stones common to the area or of beaten earthen clay. Some homes had sunken ovens for baking in the courtyard and a cistern for collecting water. Fire not only cooked food but was the only source of heat for a home. Because the ventilation in the home was poor, cooking was done outside whenever the weather permitted.

Most of the homes were small, single-story buildings with flat roofs. Stairs connected the ground floor with the roof to create a second floor which was used for cooler sleeping conditions in warmer weather. The roof top was sometimes framed with wood beams and smaller cross beams. Small branches and straw covered by clay created a roof to top off this second story on the house. Often extended families shared a home, with each couple and their children having their own room within the house. The poorest homeowners owned only a few kitchen

Photo by Paul F. Olson

On the northern shore of the Sea of Galilee, foundations and partial walls of houses of the common people are visible today. Small one- and two-room structures were clustered close together and built into an enclosure wall surrounding a central courtyard.

utensils and slept on simple reed mats with their cloak for bedding. Considering that this traditional way of life for peasants may not have changed much in the past two thousand years, Arab peasant families today are accustomed to sleeping together in one room to stay warm during cold nights.[7]

Separate quarters for women were viewed by practicing Jews as a necessity, primarily to prevent the blood of menstruation from rendering ritually unclean parts of the house occupied by others. Whatever a woman touched during her monthly cycle was believed to be contaminated, including surfaces on which she sat. From archaeological and ethnographic studies of dwellings in Capernaum, isolated areas within the houses are thought to have been women's quarters. On the other hand, the separate area of a house just for women may have been located on the second floor, none of which have survived in the remains in Capernaum.[8] Among the very poorest Jews, the luxury of a separate area for the women would not have been feasible.

CLOTHING

In first-century Israel, women adorned themselves as sumptuously as their social class allowed but within the expectation set by religious leaders that they should not draw undue attention to themselves. Pious men considered women immodest and inappropriate who attracted attention with their dress and adornments because the sight of them encouraged impure thoughts.

Common men and women wore the same basic articles of clothing, distinguished by color and other details. A long, tight-fitting tunic made of two lengths of cloth sewn together at the shoulders and sides was worn next to the skin, the simplest type being sleeveless. More expensive tunics were seamless, as was the one worn by the Savior when he was scourged; it was considered of value by the Roman soldiers (John 19:23). The tunic that Jesus wore may have been provided by one of the women who gave him financial support during his ministry (Luke 8:3). Josephus reported that the Jewish high priest also wore a seamless tunic (*Ant* 3.7.4). Undertunics were made of linen, wool, or leather.

In warm weather, the poor often wore only a tunic. Others draped a rectangular piece of cloth around their bodies over the tunic. A belt or sash around the waist of men or the hips of women was used especially during travel to control a loose tunic while one was walking, and it provided folds in which to secure money or small bundles. Jewish men and women wore sandals similar to those the Romans made; the sandals had leather, felt, cloth, or wooden soles. After washing their feet, Jewish people often left their feet bare while they dined.

Sketch by Elspeth Young

Head Coverings for Jewish Women and Men

A woman's unbound or uncovered hair in public indicated to some rabbis that she had compromised her modesty (*bKet.* 72a). Female disciples of Jesus probably wore a veil or scarf on their heads whenever they were out in public. One Jewess attributed the fact that all seven of her sons were called to officiate in the high priesthood to her practice of covering her head even inside her own home (*bYoma* 47a). How far these teachings were applied by Jewish women in general is difficult to ascertain because no images in art of Jewish women have survived from the New Testament period.

Most Jewish men wore a beard and their hair long. The exceptions would have been aristocrats who desired to stay in favor with the Romans and observant Jews who had taken a vow (Acts 18:18; 21:24). The average height of Jewish men at the time was between five foot five and five foot ten.[9]

Jewish sects at the time, they were united in their acceptance of these pillars of their society. The controversies arose from differences in opinion about how to interpret and apply temple rituals and the Torah.

Although Herod or another agent for Caesar selected the high priest from one of a few elite Jewish families, operating the temple afforded economic support and benefits to the larger community. In addition to the high priest, the temple personnel included chief priests, priests, Levites, musicians, gatekeepers, servants, scribes, temple prefect, and "police."[10] Certain families were commissioned to make ritual breads; provide ritually pure oil, flour, wine, and wood; make incense; and keep herds of animals for sacrifice. Innkeepers, shopkeepers, and food vendors catered to pilgrims. Scribes provided for sale copies of sacred writings.[11] When the temple was finally completed in A.D. 62, some eighteen thousand artisans, such as stonemasons, carpenters, and metal smiths, were put out of work (*Ant* 20.9.7).

Israel's religion could also be easily exploited to enrich a few. At the time of Christ, Jewish men throughout the Roman empire were expected to pay an annual temple tax, two drachmas or two denarii (half a shekel), to support the continual offering of sacrifices at the temple.[12] Financial stress on Jewish villagers who carried the primary burden of the temple tribute payment for the temple, in addition to costs associated with travel to and from the temple three times a year, changing Roman currency to temple currency, and taxes to Rome were daunting. Jesus called the money changers at the temple a den of thieves (Matt. 21:13; Mark 11:17) and denounced temple scribes who devoured the houses of widows (Mark 12:40).

Originally the temple of Israel was constructed to differentiate profane space from holy space, the secular world from the sacred, and to commemorate the substitutionary sacrifice of the Redeemer (symbolized by a ram) in the place of Abraham's son Isaac. By the time of Christ, however, the temple in Jerusalem had also become akin to a bank and a warehouse that stored donations from the poor and then redistributed goods and services, raw materials, crops, animals and the like into the hands of the powerful and rich (*TMos.*7.3–9). When Titus destroyed the temple and uncovered this storehouse, he exclaimed to the conquered Jews: "[We] Romans . . . have preserved the laws of your forefathers to you [and] . . . given you leave to gather up that tribute which is paid to God [rather than send it to Rome], . . . till at length you became richer than we ourselves, even when you were our enemies; and you made

Artwork by Balage Balogh

A priestly home, such as those inhabited by the chief priests in the upper city of Jerusalem overlooking the temple.

preparations for war against us with our own money" (*War* 6.6.2).

Women's obligation to religious law. First-century rabbis did not expect women to keep all the Jewish commandments as men were expected to do. One rabbi taught men to express gratitude for the same three blessings every day: "Praised [be Thou, O Lord] who did not make me a gentile; . . . who did not make me a boor; . . . who did not make me a woman. . . . [because] a boor does not fear sin [and] . . . women are not obligated [to

At the time of Christ, Jewish men throughout the Roman empire were expected to pay an annual temple tax of two drachmas or two denarii (half a shekel), to support the continual offering of sacrifices at the temple.

perform all] the commandments" (*tBer* 6.18). In truth, however, Jewish women were not excluded from obedience to all commandments, only from those connected to ritual and liturgy.[13] They were not required to observe laws that could interfere with their responsibilities at home, such as caring for children and protecting their husbands from work that would prohibit them from strictly following the law. In other words, women incurred ritual impurity so that men could avoid doing so.

The Christian comparative. Jesus viewed women differently from the way many men in his culture saw them. The scriptures indicate that some women bought into their role and often defined each other this way. When a woman attempted to compliment Jesus by praising his mother, "Blessed is the womb that bare thee, and the [breasts] which thou hast sucked," Jesus redirected the woman's focus by proclaiming that what makes a woman truly praiseworthy is how she chooses to think and live: "Yea, rather, blessed are they that hear the word of God, and keep it" (Luke 11:27–28). Again, Jesus did not limit women to their unique ability to bear children but reinforced God's gift of agency to all of God's children—male and female—and their individual opportunities to employ their hearts and minds to follow righteousness.

JEWISH WOMEN AT HOME

Ideally, in Jewish society women remained concealed at home so as not to reveal their beauty in public and tempt men to sin. Consequently a man was not to sit next to a woman or share a drink with a woman in public or even speak to a woman in public (*TReub* 6:3). How much of this ideal translated into historical reality is uncertain. One Jewish legend depicts a wise Jewish woman who encountered a Galilean rabbi on the road. He asked her, "Which road does one take to go to Lydda?" According to the legend, she replied, "Foolish Galilean! Did not the Sages say this: Engage not in much talk with women? You should have asked: By which to Lydda?" (*bErub.*53b). The woman's response exposes how impractical and remote the rabbinic legislation probably was to the ordinary Jew and also the contempt with which some Jewish women likely viewed such laws.[14]

The desirable wife. Rabbinic literature admonishes men to marry and to wisely choose a virtuous wife. For example, the first of seven failures that would ban a man from heaven was "a man who has no wife" (*bPes.* 113b). "He who has no wife dwells without good, without help, without joy, without blessing, and without atonement" (*GenRab* 17.2). Such success assumed that the woman matched the rabbis' definition of a "good" wife: "Well is he that dwelleth with a wife of understanding/ intelligence" (*Ben Sira* 25.8); "A silent and loving woman is a gift of the Lord" (*Ben Sira* 26:14); "As the golden pillars are upon the sockets of silver; so are the fair feet with a constant heart" (*Ben Sira* 26:18); "the beauty of a woman cheereth the countenance, and a man loveth nothing better (*Ben Sira* 36:22). In other words, a "good" wife was smart, docile, faithful and obedient to her husband, and beautiful.

The undesirable wife. Jewish men were warned to avoid marrying a bad wife: "I [would] rather dwell with a lion and a dragon, than to keep house with a wicked woman" (*Ben Sira* 25.16). "A wicked woman abateth the courage, maketh an heavy countenance and a wounded heart: a woman that will not comfort her husband in distress maketh weak hands and feeble knees" (*Ben Sira* 25.23). "Being cursed by one's wife in his presence . . . [will] bring man to poverty" (*bShab* 62b). In the event a man found himself married to a "bad" wife, it was "his duty" to divorce her (*bErub* 41b).

Divorce. In contrast to Roman law, which granted equal rights to women to initiate divorce, Jewish law allowed only men the right and responsibility to divorce: "A woman is put away/divorced with her consent or without it, but a husband can put away his wife only with his own consent" (*mYeb* 14.1). Josephus concurred: "For with us it is lawful for a husband to [initiate divorce]; but a wife, if she departs from her husband, cannot of herself be married to another unless her former husband put her away" (*Ant* 15.7.10).

Rabbinic teachings reveal divergent schools of thought concerning justification for divorce; all are based on the Mosaic law that a man could divorce his wife if "she find no favour in his eyes, because he hath found some uncleanness in her" (Deut. 24:1). Rabbi Shammai took a stance similar to the Savior's teachings about divorce in Matthew 5:31 and Matthew 19:9: "A man may not divorce his wife unless he has found unchastity in her" (*mGitt* 9.10). By contrast, Rabbi Hillel interpreted the law to allow divorce "if [the wife] spoiled a dish for him" (*mGitt* 9.10). By focusing on the first phrase in the law, Rabbi Akiva concluded that man could divorce his wife "if he found another fairer than she, for it is written, 'And it shall be if she find no favor in his eyes '" (*mGitt* 9.10). In other words, a man needed no evidence of fault in his wife to divorce her, nor did he need an ethical justification to divorce his wife and immediately marry another woman.

Despite all these rabbinic teachings on divorce, there are few documented cases of divorce in this era, and in many of those, the original couple later remarried.[15] One reason for the small number of cases of divorces was likely the economic burden of paying a former wife her *ketubbah,* the prenuptially agreed-upon amount that the man must pay his wife if he divorced her, which only the wealthy could afford.

Housework. Occupations and work were viewed as appropriate for women in Jewish society when they could be performed at home. By contrast, men's work occurred in the fields and the marketplace. Women were responsible for cooking, baking, spinning, weaving, and laundry, or "works which the wife must perform for her husband," as the rabbis described women's work (*mKet* 5.5). Jesus reflected the custom of women working at home in such parables as the one of the two women sitting together and grinding meal (Matt. 24:41; Luke 17:35); the woman who hid three measures of leaven in some flour, which he likened to the kingdom of heaven (Matt. 13:33–34; Luke 13:20–21); and the woman who scoured her house looking for a lost coin (Luke 15:8–9).

A reconstructed kitchen such as might have been seen in a first-century Jewish home.

Children. Child care was at the center of women's work. Jewish law allowed a mother greater latitude in compliance to its rules because of the unavoidable expediencies inherent in child rearing. For example, on the Sabbath, she could "pull her child along" without infraction because she was responsible for the children on the other days of the week (*mShab* 18.2). Similarly, a mother was permitted to wash one hand on Yom Kippur to properly feed her child because feeding children was among her routine duties (*bHull* 107b). Women were expected to care for sons and daughters when they were young, but fathers were "bound" by their commanded obligation to circumcise their sons, teach them Torah, train them for a trade, and find wives for them (*bQidd* 29a).

JEWISH WOMEN IN PUBLIC LIFE

Despite religious teachings to the contrary, it was not unusual for women to work in crafts or trades in the public arena. Women often had special training or knowledge that augmented the family's income. Even work performed at home could be turned into an income-producing occupation. The Mishnah tells of a woman who prepared dough at home that was then sold in the public market (*mHal* 2.7; *tHal* 1.8). Women also sold clothing they made from Judean wool or Galilean linen (*mBQ* 10.9). One rabbi taught that it was permissible to purchase olives from housewives "for sometimes a man is ashamed to be seen selling things at the door of his store, so he gives them to his wife, and she sells them" (*tBQ* 11.7; *bBQ* 119a). With a little creativity, homebound women could even rent space in their homes, thereby providing a semblance of hotel service without risking the disreputable label of innkeeper (*tDem* 4.32).[16]

A very few occupations outside the home were deemed appropriate for Jewish women. A midwife or "wise woman" held a respected, valued profession. In legal decisions involving childbirth, the sages trusted midwives and even women generally to identify the best action since women knew the laws related to childbirth better than the rabbis did (*yShab* 18.3, 16c). Women who were trained as midwives could often also work as physicians. They were acquainted with anatomy and the medicinal uses of plants and herbs and were already trusted advisors for mothers whom they had assisted in childbirth.

Women were not only allowed into professions to bring children into the world but also were hired to accompany the dead to their graves. Written ancient sources agree that professional mourners were women as the term describing them always appears in the feminine form.[17] These sources describe aspects of the mourners' service: "The women may sing dirges . . . they that are near to the bier may clap their hands. . . . After the corpse has been buried they . . . all sing together . . . [and wail]" (*mMQ* 3.8–9). They used a musical instrument, translated as "clappers" (*mKel* 16.7). Women often prepared the dead for burial, as Martha and Mary likely did for their brother, Lazarus, by wrapping his body in burial clothes (John 11:44) and as women of Galilee prepared to do for the body of Jesus after the Sabbath observance concluded (Mark 16:1; Luke 23:55–56; 24:1).

LITERACY AND EDUCATION OF WOMEN

Literacy was not considered essential for most people in the first century A.D. It has been estimated that as many as 95 percent of the people were illiterate.[18] Different from today, when we distrust oral works in favor of written ones, the ancients relied on oral tradition and were suspicious of written words. Religious participation did not require literacy, and beliefs were spread primarily by word of mouth. New Testament scripture, however, suggests that Jesus could read and possibly write (Luke 4:16–17; John 8:6–8). Some Jewish leaders appeared surprised that a commoner like Jesus was at least somewhat literate: "How does this man know letters, not having studied?" (John 7:14–15).

Educating children would have been a tremendous sacrifice for the poor because it required time away from other work or money that they did not have to pay a teacher. The apostle Paul received a superior education that eventually brought him to Jerusalem to study with a highly respected teacher named Gamaliel (Acts 5:34; 22:3). It is hard to imagine a young woman receiving even a fraction of such tutelage.

Later Jewish law interpreted Mosaic law to exclude women from studying God's words. Therefore "ye shall teach [the Law to] your children" (Deut. 11:19) was understood to mean to "thy sons, but not thy daughters" (*bQidd* 30a). Rabbis taught, "If any man gives his daughter a knowledge of the Law [Torah] it is as though he taught her lechery" (*mSot* 3.4). Women were probably expected to learn only that part of Torah that gave instructions for keeping a proper Jewish household (*Apion* 2.20). Contrariwise, in an unrelated context, the Mishnah implies that fathers could teach scripture to their daughters: "If a man is forbidden by vow to have any benefit from his fellow, . . . he may not teach him Scripture, though he may teach Scripture to his sons and to his daughters" (*mNed* 4.2–3), though some texts omit "and to his daughters." Israeli historian Tal Ilan surmised that the women who were taught scripture would most likely have focused on Genesis, that part of the Torah which is "relatively simple."[19]

Rabbinic literature does not relay to what extent women could read or write, even if they were allowed to study God's word. Some writings, however, assume a woman's ability to write. For example, "all are qualified to write a bill of divorce . . . a woman may write her own bill of divorce" (*mGitt* 2.5); and "a scroll of the Law [Torah], tefillin and a mezuzah written by a . . . woman . . . are invalid" (*bMen* 42b). Another law assumes that, theoretically, women could be skilled to teach their husbands to write (*tKet* 4.6–7).

Most likely, Jewish girls learned domestic duties rather than reading and writing. In poorer families, children began to work as soon as they were strong enough. For girls, that would have meant helping their mothers in food preparation, cleaning, and creating and maintaining clothing. Women were also responsible for hosting (1 Tim. 5:10), a considerable expectation considering the high value placed on hospitality in all cultures of the Roman empire. Paul taught that elderly women should teach younger women to be lovers of husbands and children, good housekeepers, and examples of virtue (Titus 2:3–5). Because no formal schooling for girls was available, if a Jewish woman achieved any level of literacy, her education would have occurred at home from either her mother or other female relative with skills to teach reading and writing, which likely was very rare.

WOMEN OF JUDEA IN THE NEW TESTAMENT

Many New Testament stories involving women in and around Jerusalem reflect evidence of Hellenistic influences that allowed women a greater voice and participation in society than they had previously enjoyed. The manner in which Jesus interacted with women underscores the value he placed on their understanding his teachings and contributions to spreading the gospel. Their stories illustrate how the Savior championed the inclusion of women as equal participants in his gospel and challenged cultural assumptions of their second-class status. Scripture also reports that Christian Jewish women were persecuted for their beliefs. When faced with willingly suffering rather than abandoning their new faith, women were arrested along with many men during the Jewish high priest's attempts to stop the spread of Christianity (Acts 9:1–2). In growing numbers, women who lived in and around Jerusalem embraced opportunities to edify the larger community through their words and actions. At the same time, their stories also reflect restrictions holding sway from their traditional surroundings.[20]

The next chapters explore the lives and lessons that can be learned from women of the New Testament who lived in the territories of Judea, Perea, and Galilee. They were among those who first experienced the confluence of strict, rabbinic directives with the influx of new freedoms for women championed by Jesus and the larger, Hellenistic society.

Nothing Shall Be Impossible

BY ELSPETH YOUNG

ELISABETH

אלישבע

"My God Is an Oath/Favor/Treasure" (Greek form of the Hebrew Elisheba)

*L*uke launches his testimony of Jesus Christ not with the birth of the Savior but with the story that introduces his forerunner, John. Furthermore, the third Gospel begins with female characters in leading roles, inviting readers to trust in the witness of women. Specifically, Luke relates the story of John's birth with the testimony of John's mother rather than that of his father. His introduction of the mother of John is unparalleled in scripture for its detail about one woman's family and social background.

First, John's mother is identified by her name, Elisabeth (the Greek form) and not merely as the wife of Zacharias the priest.

Second, we are told that she was born into the priestly lineage, meaning she was a "daughter of Aaron" (Luke 1:5), referring to the brother of Moses, to whom was given stewardship over the Levitical Priesthood. This fact also indicates that Elisabeth was the daughter of a priest. Moreover, her name is the same as that of Aaron's wife, Elisheba (Hebrew; Ex. 6:23), which means "my God is my oath/treasure," signifying "the one by whom I swear."[1]

Third, Elisabeth is shown in the Luke account to be a person of goodness equal to that of her priestly husband: "They were both righteous before God" (Luke 1:6). The only other woman described in the Bible as "righteous" is Tamar (Gen. 38:26). Many men are called righteous in the New Testament, including Joseph (Matt. 1:19), John the Baptist (Mark 6:20), Simeon (Luke 2:25), Joseph of Arimathea (Luke 23:50), Cornelius (Acts 10:22), Abel (Heb. 11:4; 1 John 3:12), and Lot (2 Pet. 2:7). A Roman centurion recognized Jesus as "righteous" when the Savior died on the cross (Luke 23:47). Luke defined the term *righteous* as "walking in all the commandments and ordinances of the Lord blameless" (Luke 1:6). Under Jewish law, men were expected to be "righteous," whereas women were often exempt from many requirements of the law because of women's many family and household duties that precluded their focusing singularly

LUKE 1:5–80

123

on righteous thought and obedience to the Mosaic law. But Elisabeth is recognized in scripture as showing exceptional devotion to God's commands, beyond what was expected of women in her society. She and her husband represented all that was good in Judaism.

Finally, we are informed that Elisabeth was aged, or "well stricken in years," and also "barren" (Luke 1:7). In the New Testament era, Jewish men could legally marry a second wife to secure offspring, as did Elkanah, who married Penninah while already married to the childless Hannah (1 Sam. 1). By contrast, polygamy was outlawed for Romans, but childless Roman women were likely not shamed as were their Jewish counterparts.[2] Rather than take a second wife, however, Zacharias petitioned God for another solution (Luke 1:13).

As Elisabeth's example of piety and righteousness makes clear, her childlessness was not God's punishment for sin. Still, she anticipated that her social shame would be removed only if she bore a child (Luke 1:25). Her miraculous conception and birth of a son did much more than remove her "reproach among men." By the time John was publicly presented, Elisabeth would be recognized with Sarah (Gen. 17–18; 21:1–7), Rebekah (Gen. 25:21), Rachel (Gen. 29:31–30:24), the mother of Samson (Judg. 13), and Hannah (1 Sam. 1–2:10), whom God had likewise miraculously blessed after years of infertility. She was like the great mothers of Israel who were foreordained to fulfill God's purposes.

In contrast to Elisabeth, however, Luke depicts Zacharias as fearful and doubtful. He was consequently silenced while Elisabeth accepted God's grace and proclaimed divine truths. Zacharias's role in fathering John is assumed; the focus of the story is therefore on Elisabeth. Zacharias becomes important again only when their neighbors object to her selection of a name, and then only to verify that Elisabeth is right. In fact, the voice of Elisabeth's husband is literally silenced as she becomes the one to profess faith and truth.

ELISABETH'S PLACE OF RESIDENCE

The traditional location of Elisabeth and Zacharias's home is Ein Kerem ("spring of the vineyard"), a town about five miles west of Jerusalem. Although Jewish priests, such as Elisabeth's husband, were paid a standard sum from the tithes and other special taxes collected at the temple, this payment was not sufficient income to support a family. Therefore, throughout their off-months, priests did other work to earn an income. For example, King Herod hired a thousand priests who were carpenters and stone masons to work on the temple in Jerusalem because only priests were permitted to enter the sanctuary (*Ant* 15.11.2). Other evidence indicates that some priests were butchers, scribes, oil merchants, and cattle breeders.[3] Zacharias's home on the outskirts of the city would have afforded nearby opportunities to earn a living to supplement the pay he received from performing his priesthood duties.

ELISABETH'S DAILY WORK

Jewish priests were restricted in their choice of a wife as not all Jewish women were deemed worthy to be married to a priest. A priest was naturally obliged to investigate his wife's lineage with great care before agreeing to the marriage. The law of Moses specified that a priest must choose a wife who was not a harlot, a defiled woman, or divorced (Lev. 21:7–8). Josephus indicated that priests were allowed to marry only a virgin or widow of Israelite descent (*Apion* 1.7.31). The stipulation for the high priest was even stricter; the woman he married must be an Israelite virgin (Lev. 21:13–15). According to the Mishnah, if a girl was known to be the daughter of a priest or a member of the Sanhedrin, there was no need to examine her background further; she qualified to marry into the priesthood (*mQidd* 4.5).

The principal aspect of Elisabeth's daily work would have been to support her husband's ability to accomplish his priestly assignment for two weeks every year. Zacharias was one of approximately 7,200 priests living in the land of Israel at any given time in the New Testament era, far more than could officiate at one time. They were therefore divided into twenty-four courses with about 300 priests assigned to each; the twenty-four courses were a restoration of the number of courses that existed before the Babylonian captivity (1 Chr. 24:7–19; *Ant* 7.14.7; *Life* 2).[4] Each course was made up of four to nine priestly families who performed service at the temple for a week at a time, two weeks a year, Sabbath to Sabbath (*Ant* 7.14.7; *Apion* 2.8).[5] Zacharias was of the course named Abia/Abijah (Luke 1:5), which was the eighth of the twenty-four courses (1 Chr. 24:10).

Each morning when ordinary service was rendered at the temple, twenty priests were chosen by lot from approximately 1,500 priests in that week's course to determine who would prepare and offer the daily sacrifice of the incense offering, the burnt offering of a lamb, and a food offering (*Ant* 7.14.7; *Apion* 2.8).[6] Assisting the priests during their week-long rotation at the temple were more than 400 Levites. Such a number indicates that some 9,600 Levites lived in the Jewish territories at the time, making at least 18,000 priesthood bearers in all.[7] Levites had less societal power and prestige than did the priests, who were descendants of Aaron, but they supported the priests by serving as gatekeepers, garbage collectors, economic functionaries, and witnesses for the sacrifices. Josephus tells us that 200 Levites were needed to close the temple doors each evening at sunset (*Apion* 2.10).

A document from the first or second century b.c. preserves a firsthand witness of priestly service on the Temple Mount in Jerusalem. "The ministering of the priests was absolutely unsurpassable in its vigor and the arrangement of its well-ordered silence." With over seven hundred priests engaged in a myriad of strenuous activities, their "service was unremitting" and all was done with "unerring accuracy. . . . A general silence reigns," while "everything is carried out with reverence and in a manner befitting supreme divinity. . . . I emphatically assert that every man who comes near the spectacle of what I have described will experience astonishment and amazement without words, his very being transformed by the hallowed arrangement of every single detail."[8]

Artwork by Balage Balogh

The Temple Mount in Herod's day is depicted from the west, where many of the chief priests resided. Herod began his massive expansion of the Temple Mount in Jerusalem in 17 B.C. His total reconstruction of the temple complex was finally completed in A.D. 64. Only six years later it was destroyed in the First Jewish Revolt.

Because priests were assigned to temple service for two weeks during the year, they were required to attend the three annual holy feasts in Jerusalem, and time was needed to travel between their permanent residence and Jerusalem for each visit, they lived at home during ten to eleven months of the year. Elisabeth's work at home would not have differed from that of other Jewish women, which may have included work that augmented the family income.

HISTORICAL CONTEXT

Luke tells us that while the elderly Zacharias was officiating at the temple with his course of priesthood bearers, he was the one priest of 300 chosen by lot "to burn incense when he went into the temple of the Lord" (Luke 1:8–9). It was, as biblical scholar F. F. Bruce described this moment for Zacharias, "the redletter day of his whole priestly career."[9] At the same time, "the whole multitude of people were praying without" (Luke 1:10), perhaps at the time of the morning sacrifice or at the "hour of prayer" in the later afternoon (Acts 3:1).[10] The table of incense was located at the far end of the first of two chambers within the temple. The table of incense stood before the veil of the temple, which separated the holy place from the most holy place, where only the high priest was allowed to go one day a year on Yom Kippur ("Day of Atonement").

When Zacharias was alone inside the sanctuary, "there appeared unto him an angel of the Lord standing on the right side of the altar of incense"; Zacharias became "troubled, and fear fell upon him" (Luke 1:11–12). The angel, later identified as Gabriel, the same who would appear to Mary a few months later (Luke 1:19, 26–28), told him, "Fear not," that God had heard his prayers and as a result Elisabeth would bear him a son, whom they shall call John (Luke 1:13). Gabriel further revealed to Zacharias that John had been chosen before he was born to be an Elias, a servant of God called to "make ready a people prepared for the Lord," being "filled with the Holy Ghost, even from his mother's womb" (Luke 1:14–17; D&C

Jewish men taking their animals to the priests to be sacrificed at the temple in Jerusalem.

84:27–28). The angel's words also suggest that John was to be consecrated to the Lord for his entire life, including refraining from drinking wine or strong drink (Luke 1:15), as did those who took the Nazarite vow.

Surprisingly, Zacharias—the righteous priest and recipient of an angel's visit and revelation within the holy temple—doubted Gabriel's words and requested some sign of assurance. "Whereby shall I know this? for I am an old man, and my wife well stricken in years" (Luke 1:18). Gabriel replied that Zacharias would "be dumb, and not able to speak, until the day that these things shall be performed, because thou believest not my words, which shall be fulfilled in their season" (Luke 1:20). While their exchange was occurring inside the temple, some 750 other priests and Levites were waiting outside the sanctuary, wondering why "he tarried so long." They concluded he must have "seen a vision in the temple" when he emerged speechless (Luke 1:21–22).

Joseph Smith added insight to explain how the multitude could assume a vision from God when such had been virtually unknown for centuries among the Jews. "The priesthood was given to Aaron and his posterity throughout all generations. We can trace the lineage down to Zacharias, he being the only lawful administrator in his day. And the Jews knew it well, for they always acknowledged the priesthood. Zacharias, having no children, knew that the promise of God must fail. Consequently, he went into the temple to wrestle with God, according to the order of the priesthood, to obtain the promise of a son.

Artwork by Balage Balogh

THE NAZARITE VOW

The Nazarite vow could be taken for a limited time or for a lifetime (Num. 6:2–6). The Hebrew word *nazir* means to consecrate, vow, or set apart. Hannah made such a vow when she pleaded with the Lord for a child (1 Sam. 1:11), as did the mother of Samson (Judg. 13:3–5). The vow-taker promised to observe three specific rules for the duration of the vow:

1. Diet: abstaining from strong drink and all products of grapes.
2. Appearance: refraining from cutting one's hair; therefore, the length of a man's hair indicated the length of time he had been under his vow.
3. Association: avoiding any contact with bodies of the dead.

And when the angel told him that his promise was granted, he, because of unbelief, was struck dumb."[11] Thus we learn that Zacharias was the rightful high priest and that observant Jews would have recognized that fact. Furthermore, we learn that Zacharias was prepared to petition God for a son when he entered the temple to burn incense that day.

As the "only lawful administrator" of the preparatory priesthood, Zacharias would have been keenly aware of his responsibility to produce an heir and preserve the priesthood's mission until the Savior's coming. Therefore, not only his prayers but Elisabeth's prayers for a son must have been intense and focused throughout their long marriage. When God sent a messenger to signal that their prayers would soon be answered, however, this righteous man reasoned it could not be: Elisabeth was past the age of child bearing. He was consequently rendered mute.

ELISABETH'S APPEARANCE IN THE NEW TESTAMENT STORY

Elisabeth's credentials are as impressive as those of her husband, whose Aaronic priesthood role was highly revered. But unlike Zacharias, she showed no sign of unbelief or skepticism but only of deep gratitude. Despite the onus of responsibility that was hers for failing to bear a child, she recognized that God was not humiliating or punishing her but had always had a plan for her. We are not told how or even if she learned the specifics of the angel's revelation to her husband before she discovered her pregnancy. Luke only reports that she "hid herself" and pondered how "the Lord dealt with me in the days wherein he looked on me, to take away my reproach among men" (Luke 1:24–25). She recognized what God has done "for me" rather than what he did for Zacharias the priest; she believed God was as aware of her and as gracious to her as he was to her husband. Furthermore, she knew that her suffering and humiliation in her childlessness were not willed by God but were a product of living in a fallen world. God was not the cause of her suffering but her deliverer from public disgrace.

Elisabeth was in seclusion for five to six months (see Luke 1:24–26), as was culturally appropriate for a woman in her condition. Like Mary, she also kept in her heart all that was happening to her. Although it would have been tempting, she did not race out to tell the world of her miracle in order to vindicate her worth as a beloved daughter of God. With her husband mute and perhaps even deaf (Luke 1:62), and with propriety and humility dictating that she bear her excitement with restraint, she would have been alone with her thoughts and communion with God all those months. By contrast, Zacharias, rendered speechless on account of disbelief, would have observed her self-control and trust in God throughout the months of her pregnancy. Surely, those months gave them both much to ponder concerning the miracle of God's grace to them in their twilight years.

That neither Elisabeth nor her husband made their news public underscores the fact that Mary in Nazareth would know nothing about Elisabeth's condition until the angel told her as a sign (Luke 1:36).

By the voice of two witnesses. Paralleling Gabriel's announcement to Mary of Elisabeth's pregnancy is the Spirit's revelation to Elisabeth of Mary's pregnancy. As soon as Mary "entered into the house of Zacharias, and [greeted] Elisabeth," the Holy Ghost bore witness to Elisabeth through her unborn son, John, that Mary would give birth to the Son of God (Luke 1:40–43). Realizing this truth, Elisabeth "spake out with a loud voice" (Luke 1:42), a stark contrast to the silent world in which she had been living for the past several months. Her spontaneous exultation reflects her awareness of the magnitude of this unparalleled truth.

Interestingly, Elisabeth blessed Mary not because of motherhood but because she "believed" (Luke 1:45). She first blessed Mary and only secondly blessed the sacred "fruit of [her] womb" (Luke 1:42). For Elisabeth, Mary had been chosen by God for a unique mission that would bless the whole world. Later Jesus used a similar description for the ideal disciple—one who hears the word of God, believes, and acts upon it (Luke 8:21).

As prophesied by Gabriel, John began his mission of preparing the way for the Savior even before he left his mother's womb. He leapt for joy at the sound of Mary's voice. He also echoed his mother's reverential response to the presence of Mary in his mission to "decrease" to allow Jesus to "increase" in the eyes and hearts of the people (John 3:30).

Like her son, Elisabeth is never portrayed as competitive. Although filled with wonder at her own long-awaited

Statues of Mary and Elisabeth at the Church of Visitation in Ein Kerem, Israel. "When Elisabeth heard the salutation of Mary, the babe leaped in her womb; and Elisabeth was filled with the Holy Ghost" (Luke 1:41).

miracle, when she learned of Mary's even greater miracle, she exclaimed, "Whence is this to me, that the mother of my Lord should come to me?" (Luke 1:43). Her words to Mary echo in her son's words about Jesus, "One mightier than I cometh, the latchet of whose shoes I am not worthy to unloose" (Luke 3:16). Of this exemplary relationship, biblical scholar Barbara Reid observed, "Mary and Elisabeth could easily be presented as rivals. Instead, they exemplify faith triumphing over personal ambition. They are mutually supportive and understanding, each accepting her own role in salvation history, and not threatened by that of the other. They serve as models of the power of cooperation over the destructiveness of competition."[12]

Mary and Elisabeth—two women—are the two requisite witnesses that reinforce the truth of God's grace in the life of each of them and in his plan for all of humankind. Additionally, Elisabeth's witness supports Mary's vow to submit to that plan.

Announcing Elisabeth's son. When "Elisabeth's full time came that she should be delivered, . . . her neighbours and her cousins heard how the Lord had [shown] great mercy upon her; and they rejoiced with her" (Luke 1:57–58). With the birth of her baby, Elisabeth's great news was finally made public, and relatives were invited to attend the ritual in which the child would be named and circumcised eight days after his birth. Elisabeth may have been the only woman present, as it was primarily men who attended and conducted the ritual. Envisioning her as the sole woman in a crowded room of men and lacking her husband's voice to represent her add poignancy to Elisabeth's final scene in scripture.

Without consulting the mother, a quorum of men assumed the child would be named "Zacharias, after the name of his father" (Luke 1:59). Elisabeth did not remain silent put protested, "Not so; but he shall be called John." The men were not deterred, reasoning that "none of thy kindred . . . is called by that name" and, turning away from the mother, attempted with hand signals to communicate with Zacharias instead (Luke 1:60–62).

In the cases of both John and Jesus, God had named the two miraculous sons and commanded angels to convey the message to Zacharias and Mary respectively. That Zacharias was still unable to speak complicated the communication of God's will when John was to be named. How Elisabeth learned the name for her son is not given. That the name was revealed to her from God is the easiest explanation, considering Elisabeth's faith and ability to recognize revelation. The alternative would be that Zacharias wrote a message to her to convey God's pronouncement, which would have necessitated that Elisabeth be literate, an unlikely condition.[13] Only after Zacharias confirmed in writing the words that Elisabeth spoke, "His name is John," was his tongue loosed. But it was his unexpected support of his wife's testimony that caused the men to marvel, even before Zacharias was again able to speak (Luke 1:63).

The meaning of her son's God-given name carries significance when considered through Elisabeth's perspective of the astonishing gift of motherhood after years of infertility. Reflecting her profound experience with the Divine, John's name in Hebrew is Yôḥānān (ḥnn), meaning "Yahweh [Jehovah] has given grace."[14] Eventually their neighbors, relatives, and all of the people throughout "the hill country of Judea" recognized the Lord's grace on Elisabeth and Zacharias as they marveled and mused about their miraculous son: "What manner of child shall this be!" (Luke 1:66).

Steady and prolonged faith. Elisabeth's faith in God was steadfast during circumstances that were humiliating and painful. Her patience and trust were in God's timetable, not her own. She accepted that God was mindful of her and through her could do great things. Her advanced age underscores the strength of her faith, even though she had not been granted her heart's desire for decades. Her assurance reflects a peaceful conviction of God's goodness, no matter what the future held. No wonder God chose Elisabeth to prepare, support, and bless young Mary for her own divine mission. Elisabeth exemplifies one who looks to God for a reason to hope even amid long years of uncertainty and disappointment.

Additionally, Elisabeth was a Spirit-filled woman who pronounced blessings and testified of truth. She blessed Mary, Mary's unborn Child, and Mary's belief, and assured Mary that God's word would be fulfilled. At the ceremony when her son was named and circumcised, she proclaimed truth to a crowd of neighbors, most of whom were men. In so doing, she was criticized. But in the end, her word was confirmed. She was a reliable witness both to Mary and to the general public. In fact, she has been called the first mortal in the Gospel narratives to proclaim a Christological confession, or truth about Christ (Luke 1:43).[15] Elisabeth shows us how God calls and enables women to stand as witnesses for him.

Like Elisabeth, many of us may discover that God's greatest blessings come near the end of a faithful life. In that moment, he also shows us that he was responding with love to our prayers all along. Through the Spirit, Elisabeth learned that Mary's unborn Son was not only *the* Lord but "my Lord" (Luke 1:43). Her example prompts each of us to profess the same truth even when the miracle is not yet evident.

POINTS TO PONDER

1. When have you been a reliable spiritual guide for younger women? Has there been an older woman who spiritually supported you sometime in your life?

2. In what ways are women uniquely capable of assisting each other?

3. Have you prayed for a righteous desire for many, many years only to have it granted when you least expected it? Did you respond with disbelief, like Zacharias, or with gratitude, like Elisabeth? How did the experience bolster your faith in God?

The Substance of Hope

BY ELSPETH YOUNG

ANNA
חנה

"Favor or Grace" (Greek form of the Hebrew Hannah)

The prophetess named Anna never heard Jesus preach and never witnessed any of his miracles; she saw him only once, and that was when he was a baby. Luke presents Anna as the female witness of the Christ child, in parallel with the male witness, Simeon, when Mary and Joseph visit the temple to offer sacrifice according to the law (Luke 2:22–38). Anna's loyalty to God, endurance, and patience amid prolonged tribulation exemplify characteristics for later believers who would hear and see Jesus during his ministry. In fact, at the end of his Gospel, Luke describes the believers mirroring Anna's faithful behavior: "continually in the temple, praising and blessing God" (Luke 24:53).

ANNA'S PLACE OF RESIDENCE

Women such as Anna were often in regular attendance at Herod's Temple in Jerusalem. They were welcome to join their families for festival pilgrimages, even though they were not required by law to do so. They were not obligated to do so but often chose to take sacrifices to the temple after a miscarriage or after their menses. The proper sacrifice in such a case was a dove, but because of the high price of doves due to high demand, the rabbis ruled that a woman could offer one dove to cover all her bodily emissions, including multiple miscarriages, since her last visit to the temple (*mKer* 1.7).

Jewish women such as Anna and Mary also participated in certain aspects of ritual performance connected to temple service.[1] They prayed at the temple, most of the time voluntarily, but at other times in accordance to special requirements of sacrifice, such as after childbirth. Women were allowed to take the Nazarite vow, in which they promised to devote themselves to God for a certain time. For example, one woman became a Nazarite in the hope that her son would safely return from war (*mNaz* 3.6). In the ceremony performed at the temple to end their Nazarite period, women brought their own sacrifices, had their hair cut (*mNaz* 4.4–5), and performed the act of waving the sacrifices themselves (*mQidd* 1.8). At least sometimes,

LUKE 2:36–38

HEROD'S TEMPLE IN JERUSALEM:
HOLY PROGRESSION AND INCREASED EXCLUSIVITY

The temple edifice was designed to communicate increased exclusivity and holiness the closer one came to the sanctuary. The outer court allowed Gentiles to enter the temple precincts but not beyond a low wall (called a *soreg*) that separated it from the Court of the Women. The low wall functioned as a division between the Court of the Gentiles and the inner areas of the temple, into which only Jews who were not ritually impure were permitted entry. Three divisions amplified this Israelite progression to holiness: the Court of the Women was first and was open to men and women, the second division was for Jewish men only, and the third for priests only. The last of these divisions itself contained three sections: the Place of Sacrifice, the Holy Place (the outer room), and the Holy of Holies (inner room), which measured thirty feet square, a perfect cube (*War* 5.5.4–5). The architecture of Herod's Temple

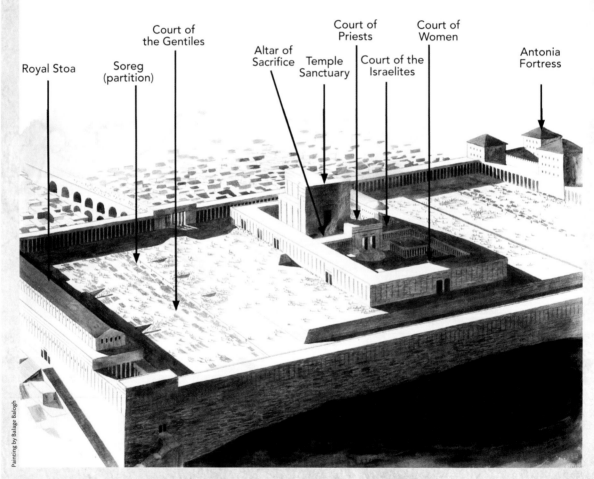

Herod's Temple, as seen from the east. The Court of the Women was likely where Mary encountered Anna and where the widow would have contributed her two coins to the temple treasury.

had a physical reminder of separation for women that no former Jewish temple had; the presence of that demarcation is considered by some to have been influenced by the Greco-Roman patriarchal cults.[2]

In describing the progression designated by the layout of the temple complex, Josephus underscored the perception that Jewish women were considered less pure than Jewish men: "All such as ever saw the construction of our temple, of what nature it was, know well enough how the purity of it was never to be profaned; for it had four [surrounding] courts, encompassed with cloisters round about, every one of which had by our law a peculiar degree of separation from the rest. Into the first court everybody was allowed to go, even foreigners; and none but women, during their [time of impurity], were prohibited to pass through it; all the Jews went into the second court, as well as their wives, when they were free from all uncleanness; into the third went the Jewish men when they were clean and purified; into the fourth went the priests, having on their sacerdotal garments; but for the most sacred place, none went in but the high priests, clothed in their peculiar garments" (*Apion* 2.102–105; *mKel* 1.6–9).

Although the elegantly crafted Court of the Women was typically as far as a Jewess could penetrate the temple precinct, women were not segregated from men in this court. It was a bustling area of activity for both men and women—where Nazarites completed the period of their vows, where lepers were pronounced clean, where blemished priests prepared the wood for the altar, and where men and women offered their monetary donations to the treasury (*mMid* 2.5–6). On Passover, priests sat in the Court of the Women after completing their work with the paschal sacrifice (*tPes* 4.12). Because the director of the weekly course of priests pronounced women clean after childbirth at the Nicanor Gate in the Court of the Women after their purification rituals were complete, most likely this was where Anna encountered Mary as she presented her offering forty days after she gave birth to Jesus (Luke 2:22–24).[3]

Photo by Kent P. Jackson

A warning against improper entrance to the inner courts of the temple was probably placed at the soreg. Two copies of the inscription have been found: the first, uncovered in 1871, is in the Istanbul Archaeology Museum; this one, discovered in 1935, is in the Israel Museum in Jerusalem. The inscription, translated from Greek, reads: "No outsider is to enter the protective enclosure around the temple; whoever does will have only himself to blame for the death that follows."[4]

women were allowed to participate in the actual ritual sacrifice of their animal offerings, not out of necessity but to "gratify the women" *(bHag* 16b). Finally, women also contributed their handiwork to the temple as a sacrificial offering, including curtains they wove for the inner temple *(mShek* 8.5).

ANNA'S APPEARANCE IN THE NEW TESTAMENT STORY

Descendant of Asher. Anna is introduced through her lineage. She was "the daughter of Phanuel, of the tribe of Aser [Asher]" (Luke 2:36). Despite nothing being known about Phanuel except his lineage, also given only here, Anna was acknowledged as a person in conjunction with a male progenitor, as was customary of the time. Anna's roots went back to Asher, the eighth son of Jacob and the second son of Leah's handmaid, Zilpah (Gen. 30:12–13). That an Asherite was living in Jerusalem at this time illustrates that the nation of the Jews was made up of representatives from potentially any of the twelve tribes, not only Judah, Levi, and Benjamin.[5] Sometime earlier, Anna's ancestors had moved from their tribal territory in northern Israel to Judea, where she lived in proximity to the temple in Jerusalem.

Anna's age. Anna is described as a widow "of a great age." Clues invite us to calculate her age more precisely, but we are still left with questions. The Greek text indicates that Anna was married for seven years and then widowed for eighty-four years (Luke 2:36–37). Assuming she was married by age 14, which was typical for Jewish girls, she would have been 105 years old when she encountered Mary, Joseph, and the baby Jesus at the temple. Such a probability is highly unlikely in any era. Perhaps the story was told to connect Anna to the apocryphal widow named Judith, who also achieved the age of 105 *(Jdt* 16.23), was always in the manner of fasting *(Jdt* 8.4, 6), awaited God's salvation *(Jdt* 8.17), and prayed at the temple *(Jdt* 9.1).

In addition to numerical symbolism inherent in Anna's age, J. K. Elliott applied historical and literary clues to argue that perceiving Anna as a woman who had lived more than a century has merit. She concluded, "Luke wants us to know that his female counterpart to Simeon in the temple was no ingénue but a centenarian of stature and experience who invited comparison with Judith, a character famed for her thanksgiving, and for her nationalistic fervour."[6] In other words, her age and her geographical roots may be more symbolic than actual elements of the story, included to establish Anna as a trustworthy witness.

Luke's message is that Anna waited and longed for the Messiah day and night with fasting and prayer (Luke 2:37). The implication is that she had sacrificed all (being displaced, widowed, and without other family), to emerge a new creature, different from her former self and wholly turned to God, in order to prepare for the Messiah. The widow Anna may have been overlooked and marginalized by others, but she was known and loved by God.

Prophetess. Anna is called a "prophetess" who was praying at the temple in Jerusalem, although her prophetic words or testimony are not recorded. The text summarizes her witness as speaking of the Lord out of gratitude "to all them that looked for redemption in Jerusalem" (Luke 2: 38). That she spoke truths concerning the Messiah through her prophetic gift necessitates her having been influenced by the Holy Ghost.

Anna resembles many strong Old Testament women who contributed their prophetic voices to bolster Israel's faith in Jehovah. She was like an earlier prophetess with the same name, Hannah, who was similarly found praying at the sanctuary and later professed great truths about the coming of Jehovah (1 Sam. 1–2).[7] Anna/Hannah is the feminine form of the name John, which means "grace; favor; or gift of God." Indeed, both prophetesses by that name acknowledged God's gifts to them and humankind through the birth of a son.

Early Christians were aware of the need for all believers to prophesy, or bear witness, of divine truth to spread the good news. For example, on the day of Pentecost after the Savior's Resurrection, the apostle Peter cited the Old Testament prophet Joel as teaching that men and women would prophesy in response to the Spirit being poured out upon them (Acts 2:18). In addition to Anna, named in the opening chapters of the New Testament, four daughters of Philip were known to prophesy of Christ after his Resurrection and could therefore also be called prophetesses (Acts 21:9). Knowing Anna was a prophetess makes her testimony both authoritative and trustworthy.

Anna's long life of waiting and preparing, fasting and praying for significant periods of time at the temple, was finally rewarded through a personal witness of the Christ child. She identified the baby but not because of something Mary, Joseph, Simeon, or anyone else said. She knew as a prophetess; she knew in the same way that Simeon knew—because the Holy Ghost was upon her (Luke 2:25).

Thereafter Anna "spake of him [the Christ] to all them that looked for redemption in Jerusalem" (Luke 2:38). In Greek, the verb describing Anna's act of speaking is in the imperfect tense, suggesting an ongoing activity.[8] We are not told how much longer Anna lived after she saw the baby Jesus, but the wording here implies that she continued to bear witness of Christ for the remainder of her days. Through the New Testament, Anna reminds readers today that only Jesus Christ will satisfy our longing for redemption. Although Luke recorded the response to witnesses spoken by the shepherds, Zacharias, Elisabeth, John the Baptist, and Jesus, he did not record public reactions to Anna's testimony. Nonetheless, that is no reason to conclude that her witness was not also accompanied by awe at the grace of God.

BETWEEN THE LINES

Luke presents Anna as a trustworthy witness not only because of her advanced age but because of a lifetime of unwavering faith and the commitment to share that faith with others. Other widows in Jerusalem are similarly portrayed in the New Testament as stalwart servants of God whose prayers were powerful and whose witnesses reflected their clear awareness of God's goodness. By extension, they served an important function in establishing the early Christian movement.

Importantly, such accounts of widows more often focus on their willing efforts to help others in a vulnerable condition rather than on their own destitution. The message is that all disciples, regardless of their challenging circumstances, will make their lives better and achieve a higher level of fulfillment than previously imagined by selflessly serving others.

POINTS TO PONDER

1. How does Anna exemplify both what Moroni wrote, "For ye receive no witness until after the trial of your faith" (Eth. 12:6) and what the early Christians were promised, "No chastening for the present seemeth to be joyous, but grievous: nevertheless afterward it yieldeth the peaceable fruit of righteousness to them that are exercised thereby" (Heb. 12:11)?

2. How do Anna and other widows in Jerusalem inspire you to recognize ways to serve even in your own "want"?

THE WIDOWS

The largest group of the poor and marginalized in Jewish society would have been the women, and the most marginalized group of women would have been the widows. Legally, widows had the same status as slaves and children in society. They were exposed to judgments and abuse that often left them in hopeless poverty, leading Jesus to censure Jewish scribes who "devour widows' houses" (Luke 20:47; Mark 12:40). The Hebrew word for widow, *almanah,* means "unable to speak" or "not spoken for."[1] The Greek word for widow, *chēra,* means "forsaken" or "left empty," an image that recalls Naomi. Both terms indicate the plight of women whose husbands die before them.

Widows often had no family ties in a society in which kinship gave one her identity. According to the rabbis, "A woman acquires her freedom [literally, "acquires herself"] in two ways . . . by a bill of divorce and by the death of her husband" (*mQidd* 1.1). That freedom came at a profound cost for both the divorcee and the widow because they suffered debilitating loss after their change of status (*bGitt 12b*). For this reason, rabbis viewed remarriage as the best solution for previously married women.

To be widowed and childless was a shameful circumstance. When the woman's husband died, his estate would have gone to their son. If the son died, the estate would then pass to the closest male relative.[2] Childless widows were left to fend for themselves. Advanced age was no excuse for women to ease up on the daily demands of domestic work. An elderly woman in poor health would likely continue to push herself to complete her requisite chores until she collapsed in exhaustion. Whether at her own home or that of a family member, poor widows were expected to work.

In addition to Anna the prophetess, the New Testament relates stories of other widows, such as the woman who sacrificed her last coins at the temple, the one who suffered as an invalid for eighteen years, and those supported by Tabitha, perhaps herself a widow.

The Windows of Heaven

BY AL R. YOUNG

THE WIDOW
WHO GAVE ALL

In parallel to Anna near the beginning of Luke's Gospel is, near the end, the story of another widow at the temple in Jerusalem. Like Anna, this widow gave "all the living that she had" to the temple (Luke 21:4), or as Mark reported it, she gave "of her want . . . even all her living [Greek, *bios,* 'life']" (Mark 12:44).[1] Her name is not given; instead she is known by her donation, "two mites," together worth a "farthing," or a quarter of a penny (Mark 12:42).

The widow, despite her want, gave generously at the temple that day. It was probably not the first time. Liberality had become second nature to her. Going to the temple with all that she had to offer suggests that God was the sole focus of her hope. Decades later, Paul wrote to Timothy about widows in the church who were "widows indeed, and desolate," meaning they were left all alone to survive. Paul indicated that such a woman either "trusteth in God, and continueth in supplications and prayers night and day," or "liveth in pleasure," or wantonly (1 Tim. 5:5–6). The widow who gave all at the temple was clearly of the first group.

The event occurred during Passover week when large numbers of Jews from all over the empire entered Jerusalem and made their offerings at the temple. Representatives from the upper 10 percent and the impoverished 90 percent mingled together at the holy site. The wealthy visitors' extravagant robes and ostentatious greetings would draw attention their way (Mark 12:38). The widow in her poverty and with her meager offering of two small coins must have presented a stunning contrast to the manifestation of opulence and affluence. Clothed in a widow's simple attire, she would have been easily overlooked, ignored, or forgotten. But not by Jesus.

According to Mark, Jesus called his disciples to hear the lesson to be learned. "This poor widow hath cast more in, than all they which have cast into the treasure: For all they did cast in of their abundance; but she of her want did cast in all that she had, even all her *bios*" (Mark

LUKE 21:1–4

MARK 12:41–44

141

Photos by Tanner M. Young

Above: The copper lepton, or mite, was the Judean coin of least worth at the time of Christ.
Two mites were the equivalent of a farthing (a fourth of a penny) in the King James Bible.

Right: The obverse and reverse of a first-century mite, similar to the coins the widow offered at the temple.

12:43–44). In truth, the wealthy gave of their overflowing abundance, which too often was obtained by ruthless methods. While the scribes "devour[ed] widows' houses, and for a pretense [made] long prayers," the impoverished and defenseless widow, with less than enough, gave all. It was extraordinary. Hers was a selfless, pure sacrifice; theirs was a self-serving display without even a hint of sacrifice. In this way, the widow is a type of Christ. He too was self-sacrificing when few noticed and fewer still tried to understand. In giving his life for all, Jesus exemplified his teaching that giving of oneself far outweighs gifts of money and often sincere giving involves suffering (Mark 8:34; 9:35; 10:42–45).

THE WOMAN HEALED IN THE SYNAGOGUE

*T*he Gospels relate many examples of men whom Jesus healed on the Sabbath day in the presence of disapproving Jewish leaders. Luke alone tells of him healing a woman on the Sabbath. For eighteen years she "was bowed together, and could in no wise lift up herself" (Luke 13:11). The woman is not called a widow specifically, but the description of her visible infirmity indicates she was likely alone and had to fend for herself. The absence of any complaint on her part and her desires to be grateful and to worship God set her apart from the ruler of the synagogue and other men who were witnesses of this miracle. Verses and chapters following her story indicate that Jesus was ministering across the Jordan River in Perea when he encountered the bent-over woman, suggesting she resided in that region.

Despite her pain and discomfort at being the object of scorn and mockery, the "woman which had a spirit of infirmity eighteen years, and was bowed together, and could in no wise lift up herself" went to worship God on his holy day. "And when Jesus saw her, he called her to him" (Luke 13:11–12). The woman did not approach Jesus, but he went to her when he saw her pitiful condition, saying, "Woman, thou art loosed from thine infirmity. And he laid his hands on her: and immediately she was made straight, and glorified God" (Luke 13:12–13).

The ruler of the synagogue was indignant at Jesus' response to the woman, accusing him of dishonoring the Sabbath by performing this work at that moment when there were six other days a week when he could have helped the woman. Jesus pointed out that the ruler of the synagogue would not hesitate to "loose" a farm animal if it were bound and unable to get to water on the Sabbath. He called him a "hypocrite" for judging that animals deserved freedom more than this invalid woman, a "daughter of Abraham" (Luke 13:14–16). In an additional motion to validate the woman's importance to God, Jesus identified the woman's infirmity as the doing of Satan, not a result of her gender or sins (Luke 13:16).

Immediately upon being able to finally stand up straight, the woman "glorified God" (Luke 13:13). Her

LUKE 13:10–16

Photo by Kent P. Jackson

Remains of a first-century synagogue in Gamla northeast of the Sea of Galilee. Jesus may have attended this synagogue during his Galilean ministry.

WOMEN IN THE SYNAGOGUES

The main purpose of a synagogue was to provide an appropriate place to assemble for Sabbath worship and for a public reading of the Torah. Women were neither required to attend the synagogue nor expected to respond to the public call to read the Law. Jewish law forbade women to take infants in arms outside the home on the Sabbath (*mShab* 18.12), which discouraged women from opportunities to hear the Law being read. Notwithstanding the reasons they might not attend, women were likely often in attendance and participating alongside the men in the synagogue. Multiple examples of evidence suggest that women were not segregated from men in first-century synagogue worship.[1] Clearly, the synagogue was not considered the same kind of sacred space as the temple, because not only were Jewish women welcomed but also God-fearers and Gentiles, who also were allowed to attend to hear the scriptures read and the teachings presented.

spontaneous expression of gratitude at being "loosed" rings with authenticity considering that she had learned to be content in whatsoever state she was in, as evidenced by her custom of worshipping the Lord at the synagogue.

The reference to the woman as "a daughter of Abraham" is significant. This is the only use of the phrase in the New Testament, but the indefinite article (*a*) used by Jesus suggests that other women could likewise share in the blessings of Abraham. Additionally, he considered the woman a daughter of the covenant before he healed her; being healed was not a condition of her being so called.

TABITHA AND THE WIDOWS IN JOPPA

תביתה   Δορκάς

"Gazelle" (Aramaic) or "Dorcas" (Greek)

*A*mong the stories that establish Peter as an authorized representative of Jesus Christ in the early years after the Resurrection are seven verses about a Jewish Christian woman named Tabitha, whom Peter raised from the dead. Tabitha was beloved in her town because of her compassionate service rendered to both women and men. She is the only woman in the New Testament described by the Greek word for "disciple." Her example and the miracle surrounding her restoration to life generated additional converts to Christianity in the early days of the church.

TABITHA'S PLACE OF RESIDENCE

Tabitha lived in the port city of Joppa, some thirty-four miles west of Jerusalem. This is the same port from which the Old Testament prophet Jonah departed in his attempt to escape a mission call from God. Joppa was home to other Christians in addition to Tabitha, giving evidence for the spread of Christianity to Jews outside Jerusalem and Galilee before Peter received the revelation to proselyte among Gentiles, too (Acts 10). Tabitha was known in the city for her good works, her kindnesses toward widows in Joppa contrasting sharply with what was occurring among Christians in Jerusalem, where widows from Greek backgrounds were ignored and neglected in favor of Jewish widows from Hebrew backgrounds (Acts 6:1).

TABITHA'S DAILY WORK

Luke introduces Tabitha by name, including the Greek form of her name (Dorcas), and by the fact that she was a "disciple" known for being "full of good works and almsdeeds" (Acts 9:36). Adopting names in different languages was a common practice of Jews who lived outside predominantly Jewish communities where the population included a significant number of Grecians.[1] It is also possible that Luke may have included the Greek version of Tabitha's name as a courtesy to his Greek-speaking audience.

ACTS 9:36–42

145

WORD STUDY: *DISCIPLE,*

mathētēs (masculine) or
mathētria (feminine)

Tabitha was known not by her illness but by her reputation for doing "good works and almsdeeds." The Greek term translated "almsdeeds" is elsewhere translated "acts of charity" or "acts of mercy," a term akin to the Hebrew ḥesed, which suggests loving kindness in a relationship of trust.[2] In other words, Tabitha shared similarities to Rahab and Ruth; they too were full of almsdeeds. As an example of Tabitha's acts of mercy, widows in Joppa showed Peter "coats and garments which Dorcas made, while she was with them" (Acts 9:39). Because Jesus and his apostles commanded disciples to do good for others as a sign of their love and gratitude to God (Matt. 25:35–36; Rom. 12:1; Gal. 6:10; Col. 3:17), Tabitha's selfless acts of kindness qualify her as a *mathētria.*

By labeling Tabitha a "disciple," Luke applies for the only time in the New Testament the Greek noun in the feminine form: *mathētria.* Furthermore, Tabitha's being called *a* female disciple (indefinite article) rather than *the* female disciple (definite article) further indicates that Christian women as well as men were known as disciples of Christ.

HISTORICAL CONTEXT

At the same time, Gentile Christian widows were being ignored and neglected in Jerusalem, Christian widows in Joppa exercised remarkable faith to secure a miracle for a woman who had devoted her life to helping them and others. The absence of contention in Joppa and the comparison between the cultures of the two cities opened the door for missionary work further than may at first be evident. Luke's placement of the story in his larger Gospel provides the clue, as it is tucked between the accounts of two monumental events in the history of the early Christian church—the astounding vision of Saul/Paul on the road to Damascus that prepared him to be the missionary to the Gentiles and Peter's vision directing him to take the gospel to Gentiles in addition to the Jews. Both the life and the story of Tabitha facilitated the spread of the gospel of Jesus Christ beyond the borders of the Jews.

After the initial explosive growth of Christianity in Jerusalem in the early days and years after the Resurrection of Christ, the gospel spread along the coast. Although the efforts and travels of other apostles are not known, Luke records that "Peter passed throughout all quarters" to visit and strengthen "the saints" where they lived (Acts 9:32). Jewish towns at the geographical edge of Israel experienced a growing number of Christian converts, and Peter visited the towns to minister among those new Christians. One such town was Lydda, where Peter healed a paralytic Christian man named Aeneas who had been bedridden for eight years (Acts 9:33–35). Word of the miracle further increased interest in Peter and the power of Jesus Christ.

News of Aeneas's miraculous healing spread to Joppa, ten miles northwest of Lydda, where Tabitha was also afflicted with illness—an illness that had taken her life just before Peter's visit to Joppa. Luke's focus on Peter's ministry to Tabitha fits his pattern of citing parallel stories of a man and a woman. In this case, Peter's miraculous act for the woman is more remarkable even than that performed for the man: Aeneas was raised from his sickbed, but Tabitha was raised from the dead.

TABITHA'S APPEARANCE IN THE NEW TESTAMENT STORY

The faith of Tabitha's friends. Luke implies that a lengthy illness had taken Tabitha's life: "it came to pass in those days, that she was sick, and died" (Acts 9:37). Her death must have very recently occurred because her body had not yet been buried, although it had been prepared for burial. Someone, most likely the widows who mourned her, "had washed" her body and "laid her in an upper chamber." Twice in the verses containing Tabitha's story the "upper chamber" is mentioned (Acts 9:37, 39). An upper room was the setting for sacred events at the conclusion of the Savior's mortal ministry (Luke 22:12–13; Acts 1:13) and also where authorized representatives of the Lord miraculously brought someone back to life (Acts 20:7–12; 2 Kgs. 4:10, 32–34).[3] By emphasizing this otherwise unnecessary detail, Luke acknowledges the sacred surroundings where another great miracle proclaiming the power of God was about to occur.

The fact that Tabitha was already dead did not preclude Tabitha's friends from seeking help from Peter. Certainly, these friends included "all the widows [who] stood by . . . weeping" and also male disciples (the Greek word has a masculine plural ending) who sent two men to Lydda to take Peter back to Joppa (Acts 9:38–39).[4] The implication is that men were also recipients of Tabitha's works of charity. Their message of urgency drew Peter to the upper chamber where Tabitha's body lay.

As if to substantiate their plea to Peter, the widows took him to the upper chamber "shewing the coats

Tabitha lived in the port city of Joppa, which was about thirty-four miles west of Jerusalem. Today the remains of ancient Joppa are surrounded by the modern city of Tel Aviv.

and garments" Tabitha had made, presumably for them (Acts 9:39). Because the Greek verb used here literally means "to show oneself," some have proposed that the widows showed themselves dressed in the clothing Tabitha had sewed for them.[5] More specifically, the verse describes both "coats," or outer garments such as a cloak or robe that sometimes had sleeves and reached to the feet, and "garments," or clothes worn next to the skin, such as a linen or wool sleeveless tunic or robe.[6] Men and women wore both the types of clothing that Tabitha sewed. Perhaps she included the widows in her sewing or weaving efforts or lodged them under her roof.[7] Their profound grief and Luke's labeling them as "widows," however, indicate that they were without family support and needed others to help them receive daily essentials.

The verse also clarifies that Tabitha did not donate clothing as alms because she had no need of it for herself. She wove the fabric and/or sewed the clothing herself. In other words, she gave of herself—her time and her gift with textiles—not merely the needed clothing. Furthermore, there is no evidence that she was wealthy, only that her good works included selfless acts of kindness toward those in need. Her faith and works in Christ naturally blended to create a genuine disciple.

Tabitha lives again. Luke does not indicate whether Peter knew Tabitha previously. The summons from the men, the emotional gratitude shown by the widows, and the display of Tabitha's gifts of clothing prompted Peter, moved by compassion, to turn to God for help. His divine petition, however, was not for the public. "Peter put them all forth," even those who loved and mourned Tabitha. Alone in the upper room, he knelt and prayed for a miracle (Acts 9:40). Then turning to face the body, in a command that sounds very close to the Savior's words to the daughter of Jairus as he brought her back to life: "Talitha cumi" (Mark 5:41, meaning "little girl, arise"). Peter spoke with authority, "Tabitha, cumi." The similarities—upper room, the command, the outcome—combine to reinforce the reality that the power emanating from Jesus continued to bless his disciples through his authorized servants.

Tabitha "opened her eyes: and when she saw Peter, she sat up. And he gave her his hand, and lifted her up" (Acts 9:40–41). Peter then "called the saints and widows," men and women of faith who believed that Peter could draw on the Savior's power to save, and "presented [Tabitha] alive" (Acts 9:41). As a model disciple himself, Peter depended on the power of God and then gave the glory to the Lord for the miraculous raising of Tabitha from the dead. The ripple effect of good that occurred because of this miracle went beyond Tabitha, the widows, and the Christians in Joppa. Others were touched by the event and were persuaded to believe on Jesus Christ (Acts 9:42).

Tabitha as a type of Christ. Tabitha's discipleship in providing clothing, or a *covering,* for others may be seen in symbolic terms. Daniel Belnap has proposed that as the Lord offered Adam and Eve clothing to cover their nakedness in the garden, the woman with the issue of blood was healed by touching the clothing of Jesus, and the resurrected Lord promised to "endue," or clothe, his disciples from on high, so Christ and his redeeming mission can be seen in terms of "investiture," a term that can mean mercifully covering or adorning another. In this way, because she selflessly clothed others with the work of her hands, the disciple Tabitha is a type of Christ.[8]

Christian examples of good works such as those performed by Tabitha, in areas populated by Gentiles and Jews alike, created a foundation of trust and compassion on which the missionaries could later build when Paul and others carried the message of Jesus to "the uttermost part of the earth" (Acts 1:8). Tabitha's story is indicative of innumerable believers, men and women, whose lives of discipleship carved a path through the Roman empire where the gospel would find root and flourish.

POINTS TO PONDER

1. Why do you think those who have the least of this world's resources and power are often the most generous?

2. How do these widows inspire you to enjoy life even when personal conditions are far from ideal?

3. What insights do these women provide into being a disciple of Christ?

And Martha Served

BY ELSPETH YOUNG

MARTHA AND MARY

מרתה

"*Lady* or *Mistress*" (Aramaic)

מרים

*Meaning uncertain,
from* Miriam *(Hebrew)*

*M*artha and Mary are mentioned in three different settings in the New Testament, one in Luke and two in John. These Gospel accounts of the sisters' interactions with the Savior teach lessons that address many of our own daily conflicts and frustrations. Because both women had fervent faith in Christ, their differing personalities and talents can be observed from other angles, rather than competitively or hierarchically in order to label one as better than the other. Additionally, consideration of the Savior's teachings before and after his visits with Martha and Mary create a larger context in which to identify gospel principles.

The story is meant not to describe ideal roles of female disciples but to teach all disciples how to respond to the word of God.[1] The lesson could have just as well been illustrated with examples of men, but Luke selected these women to illustrate the process involved in becoming true disciples.

MARTHA'S AND MARY'S PLACE OF RESIDENCE

Shortly after the Feast of Tabernacles had concluded, Jesus went to Martha's home in Bethany to teach his gospel. Bethany was a small village about two miles east of Jerusalem on the other side of the Mount of Olives. Luke's account shows an independent Jewish household, without evidence of parents, husbands, or children. The focus is clearly not on the two sisters but on what they show us about Jesus. Notwithstanding, the story invites us to better understand the lives of Jewish Christian women in Judea during the ministry of Jesus Christ.

MARTHA'S AND MARY'S DAILY WORK

Showing hospitality to guests. About the same time as he visited Martha's home, Jesus called and sent out seventy men with specific instructions for preaching the gospel, including depending on the hospitality of gracious people

LUKE 10:38–42
JOHN 11:1–6, 17–46
JOHN 12:1–12

Photo by Kent P. Jackson

The modern town of Bethany is in the same place as the New Testament village of Bethany, on the opposite side of the Mount of Olives from Jerusalem. A church and a mosque mark the Palestinian village today.

who would feed and shelter them as itinerant missionaries (Luke 10:1–24). Receiving the disciples by attending to their needs and listening to their message is equivalent to receiving and heeding the words as from Jesus himself (Luke 10:16; D&C 1:38). Jesus instructed the Seventy to gratefully accept what food and drink were set before them (Luke 10:7–8). When Jesus and some of his disciples visited Martha's house, she and her sister responded as gracious hosts, much like those the Seventy hoped to find on their missions.

Luke places a conversation between Jesus and a Jewish lawyer immediately before he introduces Martha and Mary (Luke 10:25–27). In response to a lawyer's questions, "What shall I do to inherit eternal life?" and "Who is my neighbor?" (Luke 10:25), the Savior invited the lawyer to show mercy to others, such as feeding, sheltering, and caring for anyone who stands in need, if he would be "his neighbor" (Luke 10:30–37). Professed belief alone is not enough. Martha's attempts in "much serving" indicate her acceptance and interpretation of this teaching (Luke 10:40).

Illustrating his teaching that he who is greatest ministers to others (Luke 22:26–27; Matt. 20:26–28), Jesus served others, including the wounded man on the road to Jericho and Martha and Mary. In return, Mary allowed him to serve her by receiving his gift, and Martha responded with her desire to serve him. Whereas the parable of the good Samaritan portrays a man serving, the story of Martha and Mary says that women too can exemplify true belief and discipleship through serving and learning. Giving service is part of being Christian for both men and women. True disciples of Christ produce works that center on their love for Christ and their willingness to learn and follow his gospel.

Martha may well have been of sufficient status to have a servant who would typically have prepared meals for guests, but Martha elected to do the service herself out of love for Jesus.[2] Perhaps after hearing Christ's parable of the good Samaritan, she chose to welcome the Savior into her home with a great display of hospitality. Her name literally means "mistress" or "lady." As the lady of the house, she appears to have taken that role seriously, but she soon discovered that her plan required more than she had the ability to produce.

Jewish funeral and burial practices. The work of Martha and Mary from time to time included burial preparations for a family member who had died (John 11:17–46). The Jews of that time did not practice embalming to postpone the body's decomposition. Most likely Martha and Mary would have anointed and wrapped the body in preparation for burial.[3] A tradition of care for the body was observed. Funeral associations, or *collegia,* were made up of women who were trained as professional mourners. Women taught this trade to their daughters, including wailing and loud expressions of grief which occurred in the days following the burial.

"After death the body was washed, its eyes were closed and its mouth and other orifices were bound shut. A mixture of spices was applied to the body, perhaps as a preservation or perhaps to ward off the smell of decomposition for those who visited the tomb later. It was then dressed in its own clothes or placed in a linen shroud. Next, a procession, including musicians, family, and (if the family could afford it) professional mourners followed the corpse to the tomb. It was customary for mourners to continue to visit the tomb for 30 days, to anoint the body again or to check to be sure the person had not been buried prematurely."[4]

The practice of washing and dressing the body signaled that the person was gone. Mourners, prayers in memory of the deceased, and burial concluded the ritual that marked the ending of the person's life. After at least a year had elapsed and the body had decomposed, the bones were placed in an ossuary, a small chest made of stone, leaving room in the tomb for subsequent burials. In another custom, the bones were placed in a receptacle carved into the burial chamber along with the bones of progenitors who had "gathered to their fathers," or "gathered to their people."[5]

HISTORICAL CONTEXT

Martha and Mary's encounter with Jesus appears to have transpired soon after the Feast of Tabernacles, approximately five to six months before the Savior's crucifixion. This annual feast was celebrated in Jerusalem, less than two miles away from where Martha and Mary resided. During the Feast of Tabernacles that preceded his visit to Martha's house, Jesus taught sermons that encouraged believers to show their faith by their actions. It is possible that the sisters heard those sermons.

At a time when many in Jerusalem expressed division and confusion over the Savior's identity, Jesus

She Is Come Aforehand

BY ELSPETH YOUNG

taught how they could know for themselves who he was: "If any man will do his will, he shall know of the doctrine, whether it be of God, or whether I speak of myself" (John 7:17). Putting faith into action by coming to him to drink of living water, following him through the darkness, and living what he teaches would eliminate any confusion about his identity. Because these were the most recent public teachings of Jesus and were given just a short distance from Bethany, these may have been the principles that shaped Martha and Mary's expectations when the Savior visited them soon afterwards.

MARTHA'S AND MARY'S APPEARANCES IN THE NEW TESTAMENT STORY

Setting 1: At Martha's house about six months before the crucifixion. Luke's inclusion of this story has been seen as either "the keystone of the changed status of women thanks to Jesus and his teachings"[6] or as reinforcing the submissive, silent role valued in Greco-Roman matrons.[7] The story does show, however, that Jewish women could be independent followers of Christ and fully accepted by him without male intermediaries or representatives, such as fathers, brothers, or husbands.[8]

The honor Martha and Mary showed Jesus indicates that this was not their first encounter with him. Scripture further implies that the women were already disciples: "And [Martha] had a sister called Mary, which *also sat at Jesus' feet,* and heard his word" (Luke 10:39; emphasis added). As an introduction to the sisters, this statement clarifies that both women had previously been taught by the Master.

The verse could also be translated, "And Martha had a sister Mary who also having sat at the feet of Jesus was listening to/used to listen to his word."[9] Because both sisters were introduced as disciples, Luke never intended a conclusion that Martha's service was unacceptable. Similarly, Jesus did not consider educating women as time wasted. He viewed women as intellectually and spiritually capable of studying and understanding God's word.

Martha was cumbered about much serving. The scriptures introduce the story with "Now it came to pass, *as they went,* that he entered into a certain village" (Luke 10:38; emphasis added), indicating that Jesus was likely in company with others when he was welcomed into Martha's home in Bethany. Perhaps overwhelmed and frustrated by the number of visitors, she became, as the scripture relates, "cumbered about with much serving" (Luke 10:40). The Greek word translated "cumbered" means being pulled in different directions, preoccupied, and distracted. Likely, she wanted to listen to the Lord, but her commitment to hospitable service took her away from him to focus on the task at hand. When Martha became cumbered about, her reaction introduced contention and threatened the goodwill of the Savior's visit.[10]

Although hospitable and responsible, Martha was also harried and impatient. She complained to Jesus, "Lord, dost thou not care that my sister hath left me to serve alone? bid her therefore that she help me" (Luke 10:40). Her protest implies her perception that she alone was ministering or serving, the Greek word here referring to her as doing work of a *diakonos*. She was blind to differing modes of service rendered by others at the time, including her sister, Mary, and the Savior himself.

No one but Martha appears to have been upset by the current arrangement. She alone detected a problem through her accusation, "Lord, dost thou not care that my sister hath left me to serve alone?" Her complaint was not only towards her sister; Martha was also accusing the Savior of not caring, of not acknowledging her hard work. Closer scrutiny of the verb tense suggests that Martha was noting a pattern in Mary's behavior, as if to say, "Mary has abandoned me in the midst of service before; this isn't the first time I've been left to serve alone."[11] In other words, in her accusation, Martha was also digging up Mary's past offenses. In his response, Jesus refused to rebuke Mary.

The Savior's caution to Martha. The Savior's reply to Martha reveals his perspective that she was a person worthy of direct conversation. With a voice of caution he acknowledged Martha's efforts to serve and her resultant frustration, "Martha, Martha, thou art careful and troubled about many things" (Luke 10:41). The Greek word translated "careful" means being worried, anxious, and full of cares. The Greek word translated "troubled" means bothered by surrounding circumstances or disturbed, as in a crowd of people. The Savior's words to Martha were meant not to devalue her contribution to the hospitable nature of his visit or to discourage her in her chosen way to show that hospitality but to acknowledge the right Mary had to show hospitality through listening and learning from him. His words to Martha underscore that Mary's actions are included in what is essential for all those who desire to follow him and be a *diakonos* independent of their chosen manner of service.

One thing is needful. The answer to Martha's conflict was recognizing that "one thing is needful" (Luke 10:42). The profound power of simplicity is implied. But "simple" means something different to each of us. In the case of Martha, scholars have long argued the meaning of the one needful thing. Some contend that Jesus is merely telling Martha to prepare one dish rather than a smorgasbord for her guests. Such a response, however, trivializes the story's intent and ignores the underlying problem. The standard of "needful" is found not in our output but in our motives. Embracing the "one needful thing" takes into account why we serve. In the grand scope of life, only one thing is needful. Regardless of the manner in which we serve, that which is essential is accepting and following Christ with all our heart and mind.

The rest of the Savior's response to Martha assigns goodness to Mary's efforts without saying anything about Martha's efforts. "But one thing is needful: and Mary hath chosen that good part, which shall not be taken away from her" (Luke 10:42). The King James Translation of the passage does not justify us in creating a dichotomy between the sisters' varying approaches to serving the Master. It does, however, caution Martha and the rest of us about the need to respect and honor those who manifest discipleship in ways different from ours.

Setting 2: In Bethany after the Feast of Dedication and before Passover. During the three months that led up to Passover (and to the Savior's crucifixion), Jesus traveled to Perea, east of the Jordan River, some twenty-five miles east of Jerusalem. As part of his ministry there, Jesus challenged his listeners to deeper discipleship, his teachings underscoring pure motives and commitment similar to what he taught Martha. The Savior was in Perea when Martha and Mary summoned him with news that their brother, Lazarus, was seriously ill. Jesus' response provides the second account of his interaction with the sisters. Timing would prove to be an essential part of this lesson. Jesus purposely delayed his return to arrive in Bethany four days after Lazarus had died.

The death of Lazarus. The fact that Martha and Mary had a brother is not disclosed in scripture until the account of events only weeks before the Savior's own death. Lazarus is first known by his relationship to his sisters (John 11:1–2). The siblings are also the first ones specifically named as "loved" by Jesus (John 11:5, 36). They were his friends. Furthermore, there is no trace of tension between sisters. They are portrayed as united in grief for their brother and faith in Christ.

The operative word in the miracle of Jesus raising Lazarus from the dead is *wait*. The scriptural narrative teaches that God's blessings occur according to his timetable, which is not always ours. Martha and Mary sent word to Jesus that his friend and their brother, Lazarus, was sick, but they were required to *wait* several days for a response. They had put all their trust and faith in Christ. As soon as their brother had fallen seriously ill, they sent for Jesus as their only hope to save their brother. They had perfect faith that if Jesus came, he would cure Lazarus. But Jesus delayed his coming—until after Lazarus died.

Jesus explained to his disciples that Lazarus's "sickness is not unto death, but for the glory of God" and "to the intent that [they] may believe" (John 11:4, 15). Then Jesus *waited* two more days in Perea before commencing his trek back to Judea. Learning that Lazarus had in reality died, these believers were required to *wait* to finally understand what Jesus meant as he orchestrated the moment for much more than merely allaying fears and preventing pain. Jesus purposefully delayed his arrival in Bethany to help his disciples understand the transcendent truth of power over death, made clearer precisely by the necessity to wait.

Martha's testimony. Reflective of the personalities exhibited during their first encounter, Martha hastened to meet Jesus the moment he came into sight. Mary sat still in the house. As soon as Martha met him, she said, "Lord, if thou hadst been here, my brother had not died" (John 11:21). When Mary first saw him, "she fell down at his feet, saying unto him, Lord, if thou hadst been here, my brother had not died" (John 11:32). The sisters' statements of confidence in the Savior's power were identical. Both were aware of the many miracles Jesus had performed in Jerusalem, but this miracle would be very different. By delaying his return, Jesus led Mary and Martha to the edge of their faith. That is the place where he can teach us most of all.

When Jesus met Martha on the outskirts of Bethany, he told her, "Thy brother shall rise again" (John 11:20–23). Martha's calm response to the Savior, after the unexplained requirement to wait, would surprise us if we had not noted her changed heart since the previous October. A more typical response for this setting would be disappointment, frustration, or even anger. More easily, we might expect Martha to echo her earlier complaint, "Lord, don't you care?" None of these complaints, however, colored Martha's reaction. She communicated neither bitterness nor accusations against Jesus. Because she had found the One who is "needful," her entire hope resided in him.

Martha had faith that even now God would give him power to do whatever he asked (John 11:21–22). In contrast to one of the Twelve who struggled to believe without first seeing (John 20:29), Martha believed even though she did not completely understand. Her response reflected her stretched faith: "I know that he shall rise again in the resurrection at the last day" (John 11:24). Jesus was going to expand her understanding of his power, however, to bring life in mortality as well as in the hereafter.

Jesus explained to Martha some of his greatest truths concerning the resurrection: "I am the resurrection, and the life: he that believeth in me, though he were dead, yet shall he live: And whosoever liveth and believeth in me shall never die." He then asked her, "Believest thou this?" (John 11:25–26).

With a voice full of faith, Martha answered, "Yea, Lord: I believe that thou art the Christ, the Son of God, which should come into the world" (John 11:27), or in other words, I *have come to believe* (present perfect tense) that thou art the Christ. In the Gospel of John, the Redeemer would not only raise everyone from the dead but would raise them either to "life" or to "damnation," depending on whether they did good or evil (John 5:28–29). Martha's testimony indicates that she knew that her brother would be resurrected to "life" because he was a follower of the Savior.[12]

Her statement of belief is the ideal example of faith and echoes that of the apostle Peter (Matt. 16:13–19). Elder Bruce R. McConkie observed, "Women as well as men have testimonies, receive revelation from the Spirit, and know of themselves of the Lord's divinity. Martha's testimony of Christ's divine Sonship is as plain, positive, and sure as was the same testimony borne by Peter."[13] Considering that this conversation between Jesus and Martha occurred before Jesus became the firstfruits of the resurrection underscores the profound nature of Martha's faith and testimony in Jesus as the Christ.

Deepening the sisters' testimonies. Mary wept as she fell at the feet of Jesus when she encountered him, and seeing her weep, Jesus wept also (John 11:32–35). Despite their great faith that Jesus could have saved their brother had he been there, with their pre-Resurrection limitations Martha and Mary did not yet understand the breadth of his powers. They could not yet imagine a happy outcome in mortality.

The family was surrounded by mourners and friends who did not distance themselves from Jesus when he joined them and took charge, even though they were not described as believers, as are Martha and Mary. Of note, although the sisters were true followers of Jesus, they were still fully integrated in their Jewish community. Their Jewish neighbors provided the traditional support expected at a time of family loss. However, when they uttered, "Could not this man, which opened the eyes of the blind, have caused that even this man should not have died?" (John 11:37). Jesus did not simply "groan;" he was angry. While the neighbors appeared grief-stricken and united at the time, he knew they would be among those who would urge their leaders to oppose him and Lazarus.[14]

Martha, Martha

BY ELSPETH YOUNG

This church in Bethany depicts images of Mary, Lazarus, and Martha above the entrance.

Jesus waited to go to Bethany until four days after Lazarus died. This delay did not merely dispel the Jewish myth that the spirit remained near the lifeless body for three days but, more importantly, gave his disciples something better to believe. In a few weeks' time, Christ's body would be the one lying in a tomb. The Savior engineered this circumstance with Lazarus to teach both male and female disciples that he had power to call his own body back to life. Lazarus was not resurrected on this occasion, but it was as close a circumstance as any to help the disciples appreciate the miracle of resurrection. After four days, in a hot climate the body would have begun to decompose and smell. The body's appearance would have also begun to change. Martha cried out, "By this time he stinketh," when Jesus ordered the stone cover removed from Lazarus's tomb (John 11:39). He then turned to Martha with a message just for her: "Said I not unto thee, that, if thou wouldest believe, thou shouldest see the glory of God?" (John 11:40).

After a prayer of thanks to his Father, Jesus gave the order, "Lazarus, come forth." And like a sheep who knows his shepherd, "he that was dead came forth, bound hand and foot with graveclothes: and his face was bound about with a napkin" (John 11:43–44). Lazarus walked out of the tomb—very much alive. The miracle of bringing Lazarus back to life after his body had begun to decompose was tangible proof of the Savior's promise: "He that believeth in me, though he were dead, yet shall he live" (John 11:25). The miracle gave reassurance to believers that death is not permanent because of the love of God.

By a requirement to wait upon the Lord, Martha and Mary were profoundly strengthened to surmount an even greater loss with the Savior's departure. They asked him for healing, and he gave something better—he brought restoration to a new and better life.

Mary as missionary. The miracle of raising Lazarus from the dead created an excitement and reverence for the Savior previously unknown. The miracle's publicity also triggered a serious plan to stop the Master from further notoriety. Chief priests and Pharisees gathered to scheme a way to kill Jesus but also "consulted that they might put Lazarus also to death; because that by reason of him many of the Jews went away, and believed on Jesus" (John 12:10–11). The assumption is, therefore, that Lazarus would be the chief missionary to spread the news that the Messiah is come: the Holy One of Israel is here with power in his wings. Interestingly, no mention is made in this connection of Lazarus as a missionary. But Mary is.

"Then many of the Jews which came to Mary, and had seen the things which Jesus did, believed on him" (John 11:45). Mary's ministerial message would not have focused on the doctrinal truths she learned at the Savior's feet. Her witness, borne of the Spirit, would echo what her inquirers saw and felt in the Master's presence. Her gift of listening and pondering enabled her to lead others to Christ and his saving power. Scriptural evidence of Mary's service to the Savior, however, does not end here. Learning at the feet of the Savior prepared Mary for another remarkable, even singular, opportunity to serve her Redeemer.[15]

During the weeks after Lazarus was raised from the dead, Jesus ministered in Ephraim, Samaria, Galilee, and Perea. But because of requirements of the law of Moses, he returned to Jerusalem in the spring for Passover. And the Jewish leaders knew he would. So did Martha, Mary, and Lazarus. The third and final scriptural account of the sisters' interaction with Christ took place six days before Passover, at the beginning of the greatest week in history—the week of his atoning sacrifice.

Setting 3: Simon's house in Bethany days before the crucifixion. Jesus was invited to Bethany to dine (John 12:1–9; Matt. 26:6–13; Mark 14:1–9). Martha was again serving, and Mary was again at Jesus' feet. Matthew and Mark record the event occurring in the home of "Simon the leper." He could have been the father of Martha, Mary, and Lazarus because, as his eldest daughter, Martha was acting as hostess. This home may have been the same residence that Luke earlier called "Martha's house." The law of Moses allotted inheritance to daughters only in the absence of brothers (Num. 27:8). In this case, we know that Martha and Mary had a brother, so the home would not be Martha's by inheritance from her father. Perhaps Martha was a widow and the house was her inheritance upon her husband's death. If that is true, Simon could have been Martha's husband who died of leprosy. Though the answers to these questions remain a mystery, we are given clues about Martha's and Mary's actions and attitudes during the evening.

Only a few months separated Christ's visits to Bethany in Luke 10 and John 12, but during the

Photo by Kent P. Jackson

Entrance to the traditional tomb of Lazarus in Bethany near the church

interim, Martha's attitude and motive in serving changed. Substantiation that she accepted Christ's counsel is evident when, during the later visit, Martha was still the one serving supper to Christ and his disciples, just as she had before, but this time she is hardly noticed.

The scriptural account reads, "Then Jesus six days before the Passover came to Bethany, where Lazarus was which had been dead, whom he raised from the dead. There they made him a supper; and Martha served: but Lazarus was one of them that sat at the table with him. Then took Mary a pound of ointment of spikenard . . . and anointed the feet of Jesus. . . . Then saith one of his disciples, Judas Iscariot, . . . Why was not this ointment sold . . . and given to the poor?" (John 12:1–5).

Women did not customarily eat with men when guests were present, nor did they even enter the room when men dined. But Mary seemed perfectly at ease as she entered the room when Jesus, Lazarus, and other disciples were dining—to anoint him. She knew that her attendance was not an intrusion into an all-male gathering. The men seem to have understood and accepted that same fact. Different from the earlier encounter recorded in Luke 10, at this supper the focus was on Christ and with Mary anointing his feet. In the periphery, we note the presence of Lazarus, recently raised from the dead, and also a disciple who was unhappy with Christ's attention to Mary's service. This time the disciple who complains is not Martha but Judas Iscariot.

Six days before Passover could have meant that this event occurred on Saturday evening, soon after the Sabbath ended. If that was the case, Martha could not have begun dinner preparations until after sunset, making dinner later than usual and potentially adding stress to preparing a meal for the large group of visitors. The fact that Martha is easy to miss in the scene is a great compliment to her changed heart and genuine delight in service.

While Martha quietly served the company their supper, doing what she loved to do, Mary was free to share her gift with the Savior. Somehow, somewhere, amid all the opportunities to learn at Jesus' feet, Mary had come to accept a truth that apparently no one else on record yet understood. When talk of the Master's death brought denial and defense from other disciples, Mary recognized that his departure was inevitable. Of Mary's early understanding, Elder Bruce R. McConkie taught, "Again Jesus announces that the Lord Jehovah shall die (Isaiah 53:9), and in doing so lets us know that Mary, at least, foreknew and realized what her beloved Lord would soon face."[16] Rather than fighting against that truth, Mary sought to sustain the Savior in his greatest mission, for completing the very purpose for which he came to earth.

Mary's preparatory anointing. Mary spent her resources to anoint Jesus with spikenard, "a fragrant oil derived from the root and spike (hair stem) of the nard plant which grows in the mountains of northern India."[17] The spikenard she selected cost 300 denarii (John 12:5; Mark 14:5, translated "pence" in the KJV). Assuming one denarius was payment for a day's labor (Matt. 20:2) and 200 denarii could provide a meal for five thousand men (Mark 6:37, 44), Mary's offering represented nearly a year's wages.[18]

According to Mark, Mary presented an alabaster "box," or a vial or cruse, of pure, undiluted spikenard to anoint his head in acknowledgment of his impending death and subsequent anointing with spices. Alabaster is a translucent stone that can be carved to create beautiful containers. While not uncommon in the ancient Near East, alabaster was nonetheless obtained only at considerable cost. Furthermore, she "brake the box" to access the fragrant oil, suggesting the vial had a narrow neck (Mark 14:3). Once opened, it could not be resealed. She would use all the precious oil to anoint the Lord.

In John's account, Mary "took" the perfume, suggesting that she had a larger supply from which she "took" some to anoint Jesus' feet.[19] She then dried his feet with her hair, which in effect allowed her head to be anointed by Jesus.[20] Raymond Brown posits that in antiquity one anointed the head of a live person and the feet of a corpse.[21] In other words, this was the anointing that one would typically receive at one's burial. Nicodemus and Joseph of Arimathea would perform a similar ritual immediately after Jesus' death (John 19:38–42).

Judas complained sanctimoniously about Mary's extravagance. It is ironic that he who would betray Jesus to the Jewish leaders in the next day or so for thirty pieces of silver, estimated at 100 denarii, complained at Mary's use of a precious perfume to reverence the Savior. "Mary thought [even this expensive ointment] not good enough to anele Christ's sacred feet," a nineteenth-century biblical scholar observed. "Judas thought a third part of it sufficient reward for selling His very Life."[22] Or, as another scholar wrote, Mary "gives up money for Jesus and enters the house to honor him (Mark 14:3–9), and Judas . . . gives up Jesus for money and leaves the house to betray him (Mark 14:10–11)."[23] Impervious to Judas's complaints, Jesus refused to rebuke Mary and instead defended her, received her act of discipleship, and extolled her actions as prophetic. "Let her alone: *for she hath preserved this ointment until now, that she might anoint me in token of my burial.* For the poor always ye have with you; but me ye have not always" (JST, John 12:7–8;

emphasis added). This passage, which includes insights from the Joseph Smith Translation, further underscores Mary's early understanding that Jesus must die because she had procured the spikenard in advance and saved it for that very purpose.

Mark and Matthew observe yet another manifestation of the Savior's respect for Mary's service. Speaking to those disciples in attendance, Jesus emphasized Mary's influence on future generations because of her openness to revelation *before* his death: "[Mary] hath done what she could: and this which she has done unto me, shall be had in remembrance in generations to come, wheresoever my gospel shall be preached; for verily she has come beforehand to anoint my body to the burying" (JST, Mark 14:8; Matt. 26:12–13). She also instinctively performed a service that the Twelve would need to be taught to do.

At the Last Supper, Jesus instructed the Twelve to do to others as Mary had done to him. While washing the apostles' feet, he explained, "For I have given you an example, that ye should do as I have done to you. Verily, verily, I say unto you, The servant is not greater than his lord: neither he that is sent greater than he that sent him" (John 13:15–16). By washing their feet, Jesus wanted his disciples to remember that they were not above the opportunity to serve, even in the most humbling tasks.

Some of the people present interpreted her actions as anointing him as the Messiah—as prophets, priests, and kings were anointed on their heads in connection with a call to serve (Ex. 28:41; 1 Sam. 10:1; Ps. 23:5). According to Jesus, her actions underscore her early understanding and support for the Savior's mission to die that all might live. Her choice of service to Jesus, reverently focusing on his feet, indicates that she knew he was to die and would live again. And just as the pleasant fragrance of the perfume filled the house, so the power of the gospel of Jesus Christ spread through the world to bring deeper understanding to those who loved and followed the Master.

BETWEEN THE LINES

Where were Martha and Mary when the Savior's body was buried? The women of Galilee never had the opportunity to anoint the Savior's body after his death. Surprisingly, that task, traditionally performed by women, was performed by two men: Joseph of Arimathea and Nicodemus were allowed to prepare and bury the body of Jesus (John 19:38–40). They would have been trusted by both Pilate and the Jewish leaders to be unbiased witnesses in this potentially volatile execution. By contrast, the leaders would not have wanted members of Lazarus's family to have a high-profile role considering the notice they received when the miracle of Jesus restoring Lazarus to life four days after he died became known.

Nicodemus "brought a mixture of myrrh and aloes, about an hundred pound weight" for anointing the body for burial (John 19:39). No mention is made of who furnished the myrrh and aloes, only that Nicodemus "brought" them. Mary "took" ointment from a greater supply to anoint Jesus' feet days before and was the custodian of the perfume that remained. Jesus either observed or instructed Mary's use of the remaining expensive ointment when he said, "Against the day of my burying hath she kept this" (John

12:7). Philip F. Esler and Ronald Piper have suggested that Mary may have given the spices to Nicodemus to anoint the Savior in her place because she was not allowed to participate.[24]

Various approaches to acceptable service. The short account of the Savior's visit to Martha's home and the responses of the two sisters reflect the Savior's acceptance of various modes of demonstrating discipleship as long as motives are pure. Like the innkeeper in the parable (Luke 10:34–35) and those who fed and sheltered the Seventy (Luke 10:5–9), Martha represents the hosts who supported itinerant missionaries without counting the cost. Mary represents such itinerant missionaries as the Seventy who were moved by the Spirit to go from place to place to preach the word while depending on the hospitality of hosts like Martha. Jesus' teachings in this story show his perspective that women were free to choose how to serve and how to show discipleship, just as men could choose.

Prototypes of the family of Christ. Collectively and individually, Jesus loved Martha, Mary, and Lazarus. This family is known not by who their ancestors were but solely through their association with Jesus, associations marked by friendship, family relationships, and love. The settings in which we encounter them resonate with family gatherings, dinners, tragedies, and ways in which family members look out for each other and serve in various ways. They were united by their love for Christ and for each other. As such they exemplify what discipleship with the Savior means.

The stories of Martha and Mary communicate that all women and men can be included in the Lord's family. Through these examples, Christ championed not a separate cause for women but the cause for all the honest in heart, all those who desire to follow him. The Lord's great contribution was not to glorify the specific greatness of womanhood but to rejoice with each willing heart and mind, regardless of gender or status. He did not ignore women or treat them as doormats, a common occurrence in every era. But neither did he put women on pedestals or call them *more* spiritual or *more* charitable or *more* helpful than men. He responded to his female disciples with the same love and care with which he responded to his apostles and other male disciples. In various settings, the Savior taught Peter, Martha, and us that he came to serve, not to be served (Mark 10:45; Matt. 20:28). The focus is rightfully on him.

POINTS TO PONDER

1. How does the slippery slope of being "cumbered about much serving" rob us of wisdom and transform order into contention?

2. How is Martha's discipleship valued by Jesus?

3. What do you see as the equivalent today of service rendered by Mary? by Martha?

The Miracle of Forgiveness
BY AL R. YOUNG

THE WOMAN TAKEN IN ADULTERY

*W*hen Jewish leaders brought to stand before Jesus a woman whom they had found in the very act of adultery, their plan was to test Jesus with the hope of framing a charge against him. That they used the woman merely as a prop by which to advance their scheme highlights the second-class status of women and, in particular, of women accused of breaking the law of Moses in their society. No one even spoke to the woman, let alone asked her for an explanation. In fact, she appears in the story as a silent, helpless victim of whatever ruling men chose to inflict on her. The story is told to showcase the wisdom and mercy of Jesus in contrast to the vindictive and hypocritical attitudes of the men who concocted the trap. Considered an example of the application of Christ's teachings for sinners generally, further analysis renders unforgettable the story of this unnamed woman and its message of hope for all.

THE WOMAN'S PLACE OF RESIDENCE

The woman taken in adultery most likely lived in Jerusalem, where Jewish customs and rabbinic rhetoric strongly communicated that women were profoundly second class. She would have daily encountered the religious elite as they publicly demonstrated how to eschew the filth and decadence of the world.

Surrounded by religious teachings and laws that cautioned men about women's inferiority, women in Jerusalem, more so than in the villages, would have often been reminded of such sayings as the following: "Better is the churlishness of a man than a courteous woman" (*Ben Sira* 42.14). "The shame of a woman [at not being married] is greater than the shame of a man" (*tKet* 12.3; 6.8). "Women are gluttonous," implying that men are not (*mToh* 7.9; *tToh* 8.16). Rabbis warned men, "He that talks much with womankind brings evil upon himself and neglects the study of the Law and at the last will inherit Gehenna/hell" (*mAboth* 1.5). Other Jewish sages taught, "Do not converse much with women, as this will ultimately lead

JOHN 8:2–11

167

you to unchastity" (*bNed* 20a) and "Of the woman came the beginning of sin, and through her we all die" (*Ben Sira* 25.24).

THE WOMAN'S DAILY WORK

The scriptures give nothing of her background except to label her an "adulteress," which implies she was married. Even if she was unhappy in her marriage, under Jewish law she could not initiate a divorce. Only a man could obtain a divorce. Her husband, on the other hand, could be rid of her with a simple writing.[1] Finding a wife guilty of adultery was legal grounds to rid oneself of her.

Whatever this woman's circumstances were before she was caught in adultery, her options afterwards would not be enviable. If her husband had not already discarded her, he certainly would after she was publicly exposed. To survive, she likely would have begun by begging, then stealing, and then, out of options, become a prostitute. As a divorcee, she would be at the mercy of a society that shunned her.

HISTORICAL CONTEXT

In the King James Version of the Bible, the story appears in John's Gospel during events occurring at the Feast of Tabernacles in October, approximately six months before Jesus was crucified (John 7:2). Chronologically, that would place this event shortly before the Savior's visit to Martha's house where he taught that only "one thing is needful" (Luke 10:38–42). In response to Jesus' teachings during the Feast of Tabernacles, the Jews in Jerusalem showed diverse responses, causing "divisions" among them (John 7:12–53). To his confused listeners, Jesus provided the means to know for certain that he was sent from God: "If any man will do his [God's] will, he shall know of the doctrine, whether it be of God, or whether I speak of myself" (John 7:17).

In addition to his teachings, Jesus' actions in his final months in mortality gave his audience clear evidence of his true identity; their choice was then to accept or reject him. Considering the story in this context is fruitful in that it offers another example of Christ's superior wisdom for those in Jerusalem who were confused about whether he was the One they sought.

As the incident opens, Jesus was seated at the temple "early in the morning," not long after sunrise, with a crowd of people around him eager to hear his words (John 8:2).

THE WOMAN'S APPEARANCE IN THE NEW TESTAMENT STORY

Given the reaction of Jewish leaders to his forthright teachings earlier in the week, it is not surprising that some of the scribes and Pharisees hatched a plan to "[tempt] him, that they might have [evidence] to accuse him" (John 8:6). They brought before him an unnamed woman "taken in adultery, in the very act" and, mockingly addressing him as "Master," or teacher, asked what should be done to her, considering that "Moses in the law commanded us, that such should be stoned" (John 8:3–5).

The Pharisees' trap. From the perspective of the Pharisees and the scribes, this trap ingeniously placed Jesus in an impossible position between honoring God's law to Moses, by which adultery was punishable by death, and the Roman law, which had recently taken away the right of the Jewish Sanhedrin to impose capital punishment (A.D. 30). As the Pharisees saw it, Jesus could either side with Jewish law and run afoul of the Romans or offend the Jews by honoring heathen law above God's law. Despite their perception that the Pharisees had set the perfect trap, it is hard to imagine the Romans making any response to the execution of an adulteress by the Jewish leadership; infidelity in a Jewish marriage would not have been viewed as a threat to Roman law or sovereignty.

That Jewish leaders concocted such a trap is further evidence of their recognition that Jesus was an observant Jew who respected and understood the law of Moses. He also interpreted it differently from the way the scribes and Pharisees interpreted it; Jesus embraced the principles upon which the law of carnal commandments was based, and he emphasized the importance of motive in one's obedience to God's law. Whereas scribes and Pharisees primarily viewed the law as means to identify sin and mete out the requisite justice, Jesus demonstrated that the God of the Jews also poured out profound mercy. From the beginning of his ministry, his teachings underscored the need to prepare the way of the Lord through repentance, the essential bridge that every sinner must cross to receive God's gift of forgiveness. Any interpretation of the story of the adulterous woman that omits the need for repentance misinterprets the fullness of Christ's teachings here and diminishes the cost of true discipleship with him.

The role of the unnamed woman in their devious trap was to stand as a silent, despised, and disposable prop to be used as a means to humiliate and trip Jesus from the place of high interest and respect he held among his followers. Once the instigators had obtained their objective, the woman could easily be discarded or even killed as a tool that was no longer needed. She was allowed no voice to protest, to explain, or to plead for mercy. All the while the men presented their case to Jesus, she was forced to stand by passively, with some of her clothes likely torn away (Ezek. 16:38–39). Humiliated by her sin being made public, she could do nothing but await her fate, which she undoubtedly expected would be death.

The scene also exposes the double standard that seems to have become so commonplace at the time that the accusers did not even appear to notice that the charge of adultery under the law of Moses equally condemns the man as well as the woman. Where was the guilty man who should have been standing right next to the woman in an equally humiliating stance? If she was condemned to death, he should die as well. That oversight provided Jesus a clue to unraveling what they thought was a fail-proof trap. The woman's accusers, the witnesses who had caught her in the "very act" of adultery, had already implicated themselves.

Jesus stooped down. Jesus' response to the woman's accusers was surely not what they expected. He "stooped down, and with his finger wrote on the ground, as though he heard them not" (John 8:6). His posture seemed to completely remove him from the debate. Some have suggested that he communicated his lack of interest or even boredom at the proceedings when he stooped down.[2] Others have seen in his visible rather than audible response evidence that he was distancing himself from the accusers, refusing to be contaminated by their ruse.[3] Most likely he was not writing legible words in the dirt, as tempting as it may be to imagine what they might have been. First, dirt does not make a reliably legible surface for communication; second, literacy was rarely expected; and third, his message was to be communicated to the guilty by the Spirit rather than through written words. By doodling in the dirt, Jesus directed the accusers to face each other and begin to acknowledge their own guilt in this case.

The first to cast a stone. Seemingly impervious to their queries, Jesus finally "lifted up himself, and said unto them, He that is without sin among you, let him first cast a stone at her" before again stooping down to resume his "writing" (John 8:7–8). It must be remembered that the Pharisees' trap centered on an understanding and acceptance of God's law to Moses. Jesus, therefore, applied the law to further awaken the accusers to a sense of their own guilt. In so doing, he also alerted them that he was fully aware that at least one of the accusers was also the adulterous man in this case.[4]

The law was precise in who could first cast a stone at those found guilty of adultery. "The hands of the [two or three] witnesses shall be first upon him to put him to death, and afterward the hands of all the people" (Deut. 17:6–7). A case of adultery required at least two witnesses to prosecute, and if the accused were charged, only the witnesses could commence the stoning. The law did not specify that witnesses be free from sin to bring an accusation of guilt for adultery, only that there be at least two witnesses.

So why did Jesus add, "He that is without sin among you . . ."? Knowing that the only ones he could be addressing were the men who had witnessed the woman "in the very act," the added condition of "without sin" in this case could also apply only to them. In other words, Jesus was revealing to them that obviously at least one of these two witnesses was also an adulterer and should be standing alongside the woman they had charged.

"And they which heard it, being convicted by their own conscience, went out one by one, beginning at the eldest, even unto the last" (John 8:9). Their ruse was exposed. Their immoral and hypocritical trap was thwarted. Because no one but the two witnesses could first cast a stone to punish the guilty, after the conscience-convicted "witnesses" slithered away, the others soon followed, with the elders being next in the order of succession in the stoning.[5] Their departure left Jesus alone with the silent and mortified woman. Without passing formal judgment on her, Jesus had cast suspicion on the motives and complicit involvement of the "witnesses" in this immoral trap.[6] He succeeded in silencing his distracters, demonstrating that his "wisdom is greater than the cunning of the devil" (D&C 10:43). As was often the case, his response to naysayers also afforded opportunities to teach weightier matters. The most valuable lesson was reserved for the unnamed woman and for all of us who have likewise sorrowed because of our sins.

BETWEEN THE LINES

Standing up again after the crowd had dispersed, Jesus addressed the woman for the first time: "Woman, where are those thine accusers? hath no man condemned thee?" (John 8:10). Her answer included addressing him by the respectful title *kyrie* (otherwise translated "sir"), "No man, Lord." There is no evidence to suggest that she had ever met Jesus or heard his teachings.

The Savior's next statement to the woman requires exploration. He told her, "Neither do I condemn thee: go, and sin no more" (John 8:11). It is too easy to understand his words to mean, "I forgive you; in my eyes, you have no sin. Just don't sin again." It is equally shortsighted to explain the story as evidence that because Jesus does not judge, neither should we.

When Jesus was earlier in Jerusalem, he proclaimed that he indeed does judge; in fact, he taught, "the Father . . . hath committed all judgment unto the Son" (John 5:22). The Savior's higher law therefore cautions against judging the faults and weaknesses of others (Matt. 7:1–2); that is his role. Adultery is a sin in the eyes of God and offensive to the Spirit. In fact, any and all sin offends the Lord (D&C 1:31). Without repentance, this woman would remain in her sin even at the Final Judgment. But under the law of Moses, Jesus could not condemn her because he was not a witness.

Under the law of Christ, we, like this woman, are condemned without formal witnesses. The witness of the Spirit will testify against us and invite us to turn our hearts and wills to Christ and to desire to repent. It might also be noted that under the law of Christ, adultery is not a capital crime. Through Christ, God judges us all, "but his judgment is salvation, not condemnation."[7] Jesus' objective in the case of the humbled adulteress was to lead her to desire to repent and subsequently sin no more. Similar in his purpose for healing physical illnesses, Jesus used this circumstance to lead the woman to become a new creature with a new life.

The Joseph Smith Translation adds an insightful ending to verse 11: "And the woman glorified God from that hour, and believed on his name" (JST, John 8:11). From this note of epilogue, the woman accepted Jesus' invitation to repent and became a new creature in Christ. In reality, the woman's accusers were offered the same gift of mercy, to repent and sin no more, but only the woman appears to have accepted it.[8] If we are wise, her story can motivate us to do likewise.

POINTS TO PONDER

1. In your opinion, what purpose did Jesus' choice to stoop down serve in the exchange with the Pharisees and scribes? What may be a parallel posture today and when might taking such a stance prove wise?

2. How does the woman in this story inspire you to similar faith to repent, regardless of your specific sins?

A Damsel Came to Hearken

BY ASHTON YOUNG

RHODA

Ῥόδη

"Rose" (Greek)

A young slave named Rhoda was part of a Christian household in Jerusalem where an assembly of believers regularly congregated. Although without status in the greater society, Rhoda held status as a disciple of Christ. She recognized and spoke truth, even though her testimony was challenged by fellow Christians. The strength and preservation of her voice in scripture underscores the growing freedoms for marginalized women among the Jews in the wake of the Savior's teachings and ministry.

RHODA'S PLACE OF RESIDENCE

Rhoda was a young slave who worked as a domestic servant to her owner, Mary, mother of John Mark, who lived in Jerusalem (Acts 12:12–13). Other early Christian women, such as Chloe and Lydia, headed households that most likely included slaves. But Chloe and Lydia were Greco-Roman women. Most Jewish families could not afford to own slaves. Rhoda's position in Mary's household implies that Mary was probably more well-to-do than other Jewish Christians at the time. This observation is substantiated by Luke's description of her home as the meeting place for Jewish Christians in the years following the Resurrection of Christ: "The house of Mary the mother of John, whose surname was Mark; where many were gathered together praying" suggests that Mary was a patroness of sorts for the early Jewish Christian congregation in Jerusalem (Acts 12:12).

RHODA'S DAILY WORK

If the master or mistress of a household converted to Christianity, so did the slaves within that household. Because Rhoda's mistress, Mary, was a converted Christian, most likely Rhoda was also a Christian and participated in prayer meetings like the one occurring when Peter was miraculously released from prison.

Domestic maidservants like Rhoda performed a variety of household tasks in addition to caring for children in the home. We are not told how Rhoda came into

ACTS 12:12–16

servitude. She may have been born to an enslaved mother, sold into slavery to pay a debt, or elected to become a slave as a means of security or even social status.

When Peter knocked on the door of the gate of Mary's home, Rhoda was expected to answer the summons (Acts 12:13). The hour was late, probably well into the night, considering that the angel came to Peter in prison after he was asleep and Peter was giving direction to the Christians in Mary's house before day broke (Acts 12:6, 18). Rhoda's service in the home was expected at any time of day or night.

HISTORICAL CONTEXT

Mary and her fellow Christians congregated specifically to pray for Peter, who was imprisoned by "Herod the king" (Acts 12:1). The Herodian client-king over the land of Israel at this time was Herod Agrippa I, brother of Herodias (Mark 6:17–28) and grandson of Herod the Great (Matt. 2:16). His death in A.D. 44 is reported at the end of Acts 12, which supplies a time marker for the rest of the events in the chapter, including the story of Rhoda. In order to gain favor with the Jews, Herod Agrippa I had "killed James the brother of John with the sword" (Acts 12:2). Because his heinous act achieved the desired outcome among the Jews, he next imprisoned Peter, intending to execute him in the same way (Acts 12:3–4).

While the Christians prayed "without ceasing" for Peter, an angel freed him from his chains and led him outside the prison and back into the city (Acts 12:5–10). As soon as he realized what had happened, Peter went directly to the home of Mary, mother of John Mark, where he must have known he would find safety and shelter. There the group of Saints was joined in prayer for him (Acts 12:11–12). Rhoda was one of them.

RHODA'S APPEARANCE IN THE NEW TESTAMENT STORY

Rhoda could not see who knocked, but she recognized Peter's voice. She had obviously heard his voice enough in the past to allow her to instantly identify him, even though she could not have expected him. Luke reports, "And when she knew Peter's voice, she opened not the gate for gladness, but ran in, and told how Peter stood before the gate" (Acts 12:14). Not only did she know Peter by his voice but her joy at knowing he was safe and no longer imprisoned was so overwhelming that in her exuberance she forgot to open the gate to let him in. Leaving Peter outside in the street, she ran to announce the good news to the "many" who were assembled inside. Because the Greek word for "many" in verse 12 is masculine, the assembly of Christians in Mary's home was made up of both men and women.[1]

Rhoda could easily be seen as scatterbrained, flighty, and immature from her initial reaction in leaving Peter outside the gate. Seen another way, however, she was so sure Peter was there that she could announce it as an accomplished fact, even without opening the door to verify her conclusion. She did not need proof; rather, she needed to spread the gladness of the message that distracted her from opening the gate for him. Her first desire was to share the good news with the others who were praying for this very miracle.

"Thou art mad," Mary and the others told her (Acts 12:15). Considering that Rhoda's testimony was truthful and offered with sincere motives to a believing audience, such a response is unexpected but perhaps not surprising. Although we pray for miracles, we may miss seeing them even when they are on our front doorstep. Like Zacharias who prayed for a child and then could not believe it when an angel announced Elisabeth would bear a son, this congregation of Christian men and women hesitated to believe that God would answer their prayers in such a miraculous way.

When Rhoda "constantly affirmed" that she knew what she testified was true, the group of faithful Saints told her, "It is his angel" (Acts 12:15), or spirit. Their dismissive attitude communicated their feeling that this young slave girl must be delirious or naïve. Although she was welcomed as a Christian sister, she was still a slave and a girl, which apparently made her witness questionable. But Rhoda would not be dissuaded. She knew what she heard was truth. As a Christian, she was also learning to believe that her testimony of truth was not one whit behind that of her social superiors.[2] Having "put on Christ," she demonstrated a changing society in which she believed "there is neither bond nor free, there is neither male nor female: for ye are all one in Christ Jesus" (Gal. 3:27–28). The assembly might not accept her statement, but she was free to give it. Her actions also follow the pattern of a converted disciple: she first heard, then acted, and then testified.

Throughout the exchanges between Rhoda and the assembly inside the house, Peter continued knocking outside the gate, his presence potentially a confirming witness of Rhoda's testimony. "But Peter continued knocking: and when they had opened the door, and saw him, they were astonished" (Acts 12:16). They believed only when the gate was opened and they heard Peter's voice offer explanation.[3] This situation is similar to that in which the male disciples accused women from Galilee of an "idle tale" when they reported the tomb of Jesus was empty. Only after Peter and John investigated by going to the tomb and seeing for themselves was the women's testimony believed. Ironically, while Peter stood outside the gate waiting for entrance, he again experienced consequences of a woman's testimony of truth being discounted.

BETWEEN THE LINES

Rhoda's story shows that even though the gathered Christians did not believe her at first, the testimony of a slave girl was considered important enough to preserve in scripture. Furthermore, the slave girl is shown speaking to her social superiors. Even when those superiors called her "mad," she continued to reaffirm the truth she had learned. Rhoda's response shows remarkable courage and reflects her faith in truth that is not seen. Rhoda knew that Peter actually could be outside the gate of Mary's house rather than in prison. She had no difficulty believing that their collective prayers were answered and that Peter really was outside waiting to enter.

Rhoda is also presented in Acts 12 as a contrast to Herod Agrippa I. She was exuberant in her faith, young, and without any social status in contrast to Herod's royal power, elite status, and armies at his command. By the end of the chapter, Herod is dead (Acts 12:19–23) and Rhoda and the Christians are empowered through God's mercy and strength to take the gospel of Jesus Christ far beyond Jerusalem's borders (Acts 12:24). Rhoda demonstrates that God often chooses the weak and foolish to confound the "wise" and "mighty" so that "no flesh should glory in his presence" (1 Cor. 1:27–29).

POINTS TO PONDER

1. How does Rhoda's example embolden you to express faith?

2. After considering the response of the Christian assembly in Mary's house to Rhoda's testimony, how can you increase your ability to see God's miracles for which you have prayed?

3. Considering that James was killed in prison while Peter was miraculously set free, what might you conclude about the prayers of the faithful on behalf of someone in need? What does this story illustrate about the wisdom and purposes of God in contrast to our finite perspectives? How may it inform your prayers?

WOMEN OF GALILEE

The women of Galilee are identified in the New Testament as a group of faithful followers of Christ. Some of their individual stories are told but without their names. Where we do know their names, we are not given any specific story to appreciate their path to discipleship of Jesus. Nonetheless, their presence in Jerusalem during the Savior's suffering on the cross and at the empty tomb cannot be ignored. In what must have been deliberate, the Savior chose these women to be the first witnesses of his Resurrection. His words and actions repeatedly reinforced the truth that women are not second class but worthy of the same blessings from God that men can receive.

Female disciples of Jesus who lived in Galilee are mentioned in two instances in the New Testament: first, women whose lives were transformed by Jesus and who subsequently ministered to him in his travels; and second, women who attended the Savior at his crucifixion, burial, and the empty tomb. With only a few named in both instances, it is impossible to determine how many of those in the first group were also included in the second group of Galilean women. Furthermore, no two of the four Gospels provide in the Passion narratives the same list of names of women who attended the Savior. Considering that some may have been part of both groups, however, adds dimension and clarity to the ministering women of Galilee.

MINISTERED TO JESUS OF THEIR SUBSTANCE

Luke reports that Mary Magdalene, Joanna the wife of Chuza, Susanna, and "many others" in Galilee received the Savior's healing from "evil spirits and infirmities" and in turn ministered to him (Luke 8:2–3). The Greek term translated "many others" is feminine, thereby communicating that there were many Galilean women in addition to the three named.[1] With their lives transformed, these women formed an important core of the Savior's unofficial entourage as he and the Twelve traveled "throughout every city and village" (Luke 8:1). They were not, however, merely tagging along. This group of Galilean women travelled openly with Jesus and his itinerant company as they freely moved from village to village. Regardless of the women's situation at home, their choice to be away from home and family for days at a

From the northwest borders of the Sea of Galilee, looking toward the village of Magdala.

time would have been viewed as inappropriate even by rural Jewish standards. Notwithstanding cultural perceptions, Jesus accepted the presence and support of these women.

In their reverence and gratitude to the Master, these good women "ministered unto him of their substance" (Luke 8:3), meaning they gave to him from their own resources. In the second century, Tertullian described these generous Galilean women as "certain rich women" in a tribute to their discipleship and indication of their economic status (*Marc* 19.1). The Greek verb translated "ministered" is *diakoneo,* which is derived from the noun *diakonos* and is variously translated "deacon," "minister," and "helper." An added dimension of the term is apparent when one considers that the same Greek verb is used to describe what angels did for Jesus after he was tempted of Satan: "the angels *diakoneo* unto him" (Mark 1:13; Matt. 4:11).[2]

The scriptural implication is that these Galilean women had access to ample resources and the freedom to dispense them as they chose. They also appear to have had the support and blessing of family members to be relieved of traditional domestic duties in order to serve the Savior in this way. We are not told the marital status of Mary Magdalene and Susanna, but Joanna was either married or had been married. Did these women attend the entourage during the day and return to their own homes at night? Were any of them related to one of the male disciples? Did their children ever accompany them, or had they already

WORD STUDY: *DIAKONOS*

The same Greek verb used to describe the action of the women who ministered to Jesus in Luke 8:2–3 is used to describe actions both by Peter's mother-in-law and by Martha, who was "cumbered about much serving" (Luke 10:40). The verb is also used to describe servants of the Lord who are found "watching" for him to return (Luke 12:37) and who wait to serve him in the parable recorded in Luke 17. It describes giving assistance, such as table service or ministering to another's needs, including delivering messages.[3] In the noun form, *diakonos*, the term eventually was used to identify a priesthood office, "deacon," or specific ecclesiastical service, but originally the word meant "servant" or "helper."

From a Greek's perspective, being a *diakonos* was not a virtue; ruling always trumped serving. Jesus transformed the meaning of the term for his followers when he taught that the person who is servant is greater than the one being served (Matt. 20:26–28; Mark 10:43–45; Luke 22:25–27). As the perfect example, Jesus came to serve, not to be waited upon. Through his teachings and example, Jesus made the term an essential qualifier for all who would be his disciples. He assigned attributes that were totally new in comparison to the Greek understanding. "It is clear that Jesus is not merely bringing about a radical change in the academic estimation of human existence and action [with his enhanced meaning of the term]; He is instituting in fact a new pattern of human relationships."[4]

For Christ, when we serve our neighbor, we are serving him and his Father (Matt. 25:40). Being a *diakonos*, as Jesus used the term, means being selfless and devoid of pride in one's offering. It is waiting upon or ministering to another out of genuine love. The Savior magnified the nobility of service, including table service, when he washed the feet of his apostles and told them to do likewise (John 13:12–16). Ultimately, the full measure of what it means to be a *diakonos* in the teachings of Jesus involves suffering and self-sacrifice, he being the supreme example when he gave his life out of love for us.

reared their children? Whatever the circumstances, their commitment to the Savior was not episodic; these women followed him in Jerusalem—to his crucifixion, his burial, and his Resurrection.

THEY STOOD BY JESUS IN HIS SUFFERINGS

Although the women of Galilee are not mentioned between the description of their miracles of healing and the Passion narratives, their support and love for Jesus was ongoing. Jesus was sentenced to die by crucifixion, a most shameful punishment in the eyes of Jews and Romans, which would have kept those concerned with their reputations away from the scene. Yet here was a significant group of women who appeared uninterested in what anyone else thought of them or of any danger to which such devotion might expose them. It was the women who remained near him and with him through his death and burial who give an extraordinary show of genuine love and support. Luke initially identifies them as "the women that followed him from Galilee" (Luke 23:49) but later specifies some of them as "Mary Magdalene, and

Joanna, and Mary the mother of James, and other women that were with them" (Luke 24:10). By contrast, in their confusion and fear, the male disciples "forsook him, and fled" (Matt. 26:56; Mark 14:50).

Two men are later identified in their lament and support for Jesus, namely Nicodemus and Joseph of Arimathaea. They had the political clout to secure the body of Jesus and ensure his body a proper burial. But it was this undefined company of women who were always in the wings, looking for a way to help, seeking for solace in their profound grief and love for the crucified One. Because the burial ceremony could not occur until after the Sabbath, the women watched "how his body was laid" and prepared spices and oil for anointing the body for a more fitting burial later (Luke 23:55–56). The last thing Jesus is recorded as saying before his Passion, "Watch" (Mark 13:37), which was exactly what the women did. They were accustomed to care for Jesus in life and were not going to abandon him in death.

THEY WERE THE FIRST WITNESSES OF THE RESURRECTION

"In the end of the sabbath, as it began to dawn toward the first day of the week," Matthew recounts, "Mary Magdalene and the other Mary" went to the tomb where the body of Jesus had been laid (Matt. 28:1). Two angels of the Lord with "their countenance . . . like lightning, and their raiment white as snow" rolled away the stone that sealed the entrance to the tomb and addressed the women while the guards trembled with fear (JST, Matt. 28:2–4). "Fear not ye; for we know that ye seek Jesus, which was crucified. He is not here: for he is risen, as he said. . . . And go quickly, and tell his disciples that he is risen from the dead" (JST, Matt. 28:5–7).

That Jesus appeared first to women after his Resurrection is not likely to have been invented because it would have been very unusual for women to be chosen as the first witnesses rather than men. Celsus, a second-century polemicist against Christianity, reduced the Christian faith to the imaginations of "a half-frantic woman" (*Cels* 59–60).[5] His description carries with it evidence of dismissive attitudes men harbored for women's testimonies at the time. The apostle Paul later testified that multiple men saw the resurrected Christ (1 Cor. 15:4–8) but made no mention of women who were also witnesses, let alone that they were the first witnesses. This silence suggests that even believers recognized that citing the testimonies of women would not be convincing for their cause.

DIFFERING ACCOUNTS

Because many interpretations exist of what happened the morning of the Resurrection and who first witnessed the empty tomb, scholars continue to explore and discuss it. Unfortunately, the authors of the four Gospels report conflicting narratives of that Sunday morning. The confusion may have been created by the lack of credence given to women's testimonies. Because witnesses of the divinity of Jesus were considered important and trustworthy for future leaders of Christianity, variations among the accounts may

WOMEN PRESENT IN THE PASSION NARRATIVES

Matthew	Mark	Luke	John
27:56; 28:1	15:40–41; 16:1, 9	23:49, 55–56; 24:10	19:25; 20:1, 11–18v
Mary Magdalene	Mary Magdalene	Mary Magdalene	Mary Magdalene
Mary the mother of James and Joses	Mary the mother of James and Joses	Mary the mother of James	Mary the mother of Jesus
Mother of Zebedee's children	Salome		Sister of mother of Jesus (and/or) Mary wife of Cleophas
		Joanna wife of Chuza	
Many other women	Women from Galilee		

The parallel accounts may also suggest that the mother of Zebedee's children may be named Salome because the two descriptions appear in otherwise identical lists in Matthew and Mark. Or was she "the other Mary" (Matt. 27:61), who may also be Mary the wife of Cleophas (John 19:25)? Salome may also be the sister of Mary the mother of Jesus, if the sister of the mother of Jesus is not Mary the wife of Cleophas.

These last suggestions are made more confusing by the fact that John's portrayal of the women at the crucifixion does not make it clear whether three women or four were there (John 19:25). Is Mary the wife of Cleophas the same person as the sister of the mother of Jesus (suggesting that the mother of Jesus and her sister were both called Mary, a not uncommon practice in the Roman empire), or are Mary and the wife of Cleophas two different women? A third-century Gnostic text asserts that three women always walked with the Lord and that all three were named Mary—his mother, his mother's sister, and Mary Magdalene "his companion" (GPhil 59.6–9).[7]

Joanna the wife of Chuza does not appear to have a parallel listing. Susanna is the one Galilean woman named among those who previously ministered to Jesus but is not identified in the Passion scenes, unless her name was transcribed as Salome. Nothing more is known of either this Salome or Susanna.

also reflect a "rivalry for authority" among early Christians.[6] Although the specific reason for the diverse accounts in the Gospels is unknown, the scriptures are clear that the first witnesses were women.

When aligning the four accounts side by side, several observations as well as questions become apparent. First, the prominent witness of Mary Magdalene is unquestionable in all but the Gospel of Luke, which records that the resurrected Christ appeared to Peter whereas the women merely reported the empty tomb (Luke 24:10, 33–34). Second, parallel listings may identify the same women, even though they may be described differently. For example, Mary the mother of James and Joses could be the same woman as Mary the mother of Jesus, who was previously reported to have had additional sons, namely "James, and Joses, and Simon, and Judas" (Matt. 13:55; Mark 6:3). This difference in identification could explain the apparent absence of Jesus' mother in the synoptic Gospels when she is so prominent in John's account of the crucifixion (John 19:25).

During the weeks following the Savior's Resurrection, "the women, and Mary the mother of Jesus" were numbered among the one hundred and twenty faithful disciples of Christ (Acts 1:14). When these disciples bore witness "with other tongues" (Acts 2:4) of the "wonderful works of God" (Acts 2:11) on the day of Pentecost, the apostle Peter explained the phenomenon by citing an ancient prophecy: "And it shall come to pass in the last days, saith God, I will pour out of my Spirit upon all flesh: and your sons and your daughters shall prophecy. . . . And on my servants and on my handmaidens I will pour out in those days of my Spirit; and they shall prophesy" (Acts 2:16–18; Joel 2:28–29). The New Testament bears witness that early female disciples verified the truth of Joel's prophecy.

In verses surrounding his brief comment that Mary Magdalene, Joanna, and Susanna were healed or changed by Jesus, Luke recounts the stories of other women in Galilee whose lives were forever changed through encounters with the Savior. Notably, we read of the widow of Nain (Luke 7:11–15), the woman who loved the Savior so much that she washed his feet with her tears (Luke 7:36–50), the daughter of Jairus (Luke 8:41–42, 49–56), and the woman who was healed of a serious illness by touching the hem of the Savior's clothing (Luke 8:43–48). Were these women among the Galilean women who shared their resources along with Mary Magdalene, Joanna, and Susanna? Was one of them the mother of James and John, Zebedee's children?

Although no conclusive answer to those questions is possible, we can at least think of these women as representative of the faithful Galilean women who later attended the Savior. By exploring the stories of those individuals healed in Galilee, we can better appreciate the women who stood by Jesus through his suffering on the cross and at his tomb. More importantly, they can teach us about coming to Christ and laying hold on his Atonement.

THE WIDOW OF NAIN

*I*n a spontaneous act of compassion, Jesus recognized the profound despair of an unnamed widow in an otherwise undistinguished village and returned her only son to life. Although scripture does not record any of her words, the widow of Nain can represent any of us in seemingly hopeless circumstances when we do not have words or even the presence of mind to pray for help. The story also highlights a special sensitivity the Savior has for mothers, which may also carry implications for his love for his own mother.

The village of Nain was one of many small communities in Galilee. Jesus would have probably been to Nain in his childhood and young adulthood because it is only seven miles southeast of his hometown of Nazareth. In fact, he may have been previously acquainted with the widow and her son, considering that upon first seeing the funeral procession, he knew that the woman was a widow and that the dead man was her only son.

Without her son, this widow in Nain had no means of support and would be left a vulnerable target for exploitation. She would no longer have anyone to care for her, no home to shelter her, and only insurmountable troubles to threaten her for the remainder of her mortal life. In this helpless state, she is portrayed in the story as voiceless and powerless, walking alongside the body being carried to its burial. Although surrounded by mourners, she might as well have been alone.

The impoverished widow appeared incapable of even articulating a plea for help. With her only hope forever gone, she seemed drenched in despair and misery. The Savior's compassion for her is palpable. Within a year or two, it will be his mother whose heart will break when his body is laid in a tomb.

Jewish burials typically occurred the day the person died, adding drama to the scene as the shock of loss would still be fresh. Professional mourners and musicians, usually women, accompanied funeral processions. The company would attract instant attention with loud wailing and banging (Matt. 9:23). Those seeking ritual purity would avoid potential contact with a corpse, but Jesus seemed drawn to the funeral scene.

LUKE 7:11–18

Jesus approached the mourning mother and uttered a seemingly impossible command, "Weep not" (Luke 7:13). As the only One with power to give hope and joy in the face of loss, the Savior brings life even when we have not asked. With a touch of his hand and the power of his word, the young man suddenly sat up and spoke. Although we are not told what he said, his act of speaking is evidence that he was no longer dead.

With awe, the onlookers acknowledged that "a great prophet is risen up among us" (Luke 7:16). The result of the miracle was that "this rumour of him," or in Greek, the *logos,* or "word," spread from the village throughout the land (Luke 7:17). Similarly, the good news of Christ, who is the Word, will eventually spread to every nation, tongue, and people.

The story of the widow of Nain illustrates the compassion of Jesus; he was influenced neither by others' pleas nor by another's intercession. Even when Jesus "delivered [the revived son] to his mother" (Luke 7:14–15), the widow's voice is not heard in scripture. Paul taught that because of the grace of Christ, "the Spirit . . . maketh intercession for us with groanings which cannot be uttered" when "we know not what we should pray for as we ought" (Rom. 8:26). No doubt the widowed mother knew no words to convey her depth of awe and gratitude.

The miracle occurred because the Lord desired to mend a mother's despair. Through his atoning sacrifice, broken hearts are healed, families are restored, and life is forever better. Through his example, we learn what it means to be a Christian. James, the brother of Jesus, learned that lesson and subsequently taught that "pure religion" involves visiting "the fatherless and the widows" (James 1:27).

PETER'S MOTHER-IN-LAW

*A*lthough the totality of what we know of Peter's mother-in-law comes in two or three verses in each of the synoptic Gospels, each account offers a slightly different emphasis and insight into one event when the Savior healed an unnamed woman of an unidentified illness. His miracle on her behalf is noted not only by the woman's restoration to health but by her desire and ability to minister to others immediately afterwards. The story further illustrates the breadth of power Jesus possessed to heal any person of any ailment, thereby rendering those healed better than ever before.

Peter's mother-in-law was a simple, ordinary woman who became ill in a small fishing village called Capernaum on the Sea of Galilee. The house where she lay sick was Peter's, not hers. We are not told whether his mother-in-law had her own home or whether she was simply visiting or residing in Peter's home. If she was residing and not merely visiting there, she was almost assuredly a widow. That she was with her daughter and son-in-law rather than a son may also indicate she had no living sons.

The setting for the healing of Peter's mother-in-law recalls Jesus at the nearby synagogue in Capernaum where he healed a man who was possessed of "an unclean devil." Apparently people in Galilee knew that they could find Jesus in such holy places as the local synagogue. Upon hearing from his disciples about the sick woman, Jesus left immediately and entered the home where she lay (Luke 4:33–38).

The home was the site of the miracle for Peter's mother-in-law, however, not the synagogue. By going to her rather than requiring her to come to him at the synagogue to perform the miraculous healing, he revealed his respect for the home, a location watched over by women. To him, the home can be sacred space, an appropriate location for demonstrating his power. His actions in that home underscore that the place where women were most often found could also become a holy sanctuary or a place of worship.

MATTHEW 8:14–15
MARK 1:29–31
LUKE 4:38–39

♥

Fishing near Capernaum at the time of Christ.

Luke the physician stressed the seriousness of the woman's illness by calling it "a great fever"; Mark and Matthew give no qualifiers. Furthermore, in Luke's account, Jesus did not touch the woman when he healed her but "stood over her, and rebuked the fever; and it left her" (Luke 4:38), a detail that communicates awe from the perspective of a physician. In Mark and Matthew, however, Jesus touched the woman in restoring her health. In the book of Matthew, "he touched her hand, and the fever left her" (Matt. 8:15). In Mark's Gospel the healing is even more personal and tender: "And he came and took her by the hand, and lifted her up; and immediately the fever left her" (Mark 1:31).[1]

All three accounts witness that, after her miraculous return to health, she arose and served or ministered to those in the house. Luke reports that she did this "immediately" (Luke 4:39). Her ability to stand up and do something may be noted simply as proof that she was indeed completely and immediately healed and able to resume her customary duties in hospitality to guests. However, something more may be implied here.

The dramatic healing of his mother-in-law may have served as a critical step toward Simon Peter's commitment to follow Jesus. According to Luke, Simon Peter accepted the Savior's call to full-time discipleship shortly after he saw his mother-in-law minister to them and his fishing nets filled to overflowing with fish through the power of Jesus. After witnessing discipleship in his mother-in-law, he left catching fish behind, "forsook all," and began to "catch men" to follow Christ (Luke 5:1–11).

The doctrine of restoration promises not simply a return to the way we were before our weakness but, because of the Savior's gift, a restoration to a better condition than we have ever experienced. In the case of Peter's mother-in-law, the woman's restoration to health returned to her a more liberating condition in addition to eliminating the disease. She had the ability to resume life but with new life in her. Her ministering was thereafter infused with greater purpose and power. In a way related to the parable of the woman who hides leavening in three measures of flour, Jesus spotlighted a woman's menial work, usually invisible to the world, to teach that what he touches becomes greater and better (Matt. 13:33).

Furthermore, the Greek verb translated "ministered" in all three instances is *diakonei,* the same verb used to describe what women in Galilee did for Jesus during his travels (Luke 8:2–3) and how the angels served him (Mark 1:13). Because of the healing she received through Jesus, this woman was enabled to serve like the angels and become more like the Savior. When such service is rendered by a woman, it should not then be looked down upon as subservience.

Artist's rendering of Peter's home in Capernaum on the north shore of the Sea of Galilee.

Artwork by Balage Balogh

THE MOTHER OF JAMES AND JOHN

The mother of Zebedee's children, James and John, is perhaps the woman most difficult to accurately track in the New Testament. Her name may have been Salome, if Matthew and Mark were describing the same list of women in their Passion narratives (Matt. 27:56; Mark 15:40). Just as plausible, she could have been named Mary, described as "the mother of James" (Luke 24:10) or "the other Mary" (Matt. 27:61), who may also be Mary the wife of Cleophas (John 19:25). In addition to being one of the Galilean women who stayed near the Savior during his suffering on the cross and his burial, the mother of James and John is portrayed earlier in the Gospels. The teaching she received from Jesus earlier in his ministry informed her faithfulness to him at his death.

Her two sons, James and John, were chosen by Jesus to be members of his first Quorum of Twelve Apostles, and they were also two of the three apostles selected to witness events on the Mount of Transfiguration and in the Garden of Gethsemane. Her husband was presumably Zebedee, the father of James and John, but he never appears in scripture. She is never called the wife of Zebedee but always the mother of James and John. In the absence of more specific information, this attribution indicates that she was a widow.

In Matthew's account, the mother of James and John approached Jesus to worship him and to request that her sons be given a place of prominence in his kingdom (Matt. 20:20). Matthew records that she herself said, "Grant that these my two sons may sit, the one on thy right hand, and the other on the left, in thy kingdom" (Matt. 20:21). In Mark's Gospel, James and John ask Jesus for this privilege directly, without their mother's intervention (Mark 10:35–37). In both accounts, the other ten apostles were offended by the petition (Matt. 20:24; Mark 10:41).

Jesus responded that this good mother did not know what she asked and inquired whether her sons were capable of accepting his "cup" of suffering. James and John answered, "We are able" (Matt. 20:22; Mark 10:39). The

MATTHEW 20:20–28

MATTHEW 27:55–56

❦

Savior then instructed all his apostles that true greatness is measured by one's willingness to serve others rather than by exercising authority over others as the world defines it. Through a lifetime of ministering to others, followed by giving "his life [as] a ransom for many," Jesus demonstrated what it means to be "chief among [them]" (Matt. 20:25–28).

By willingly standing by the suffering Savior at the foot of the cross, attending his burial, and watching over the empty tomb, the mother of James and John appears to have understood and accepted Christ's lesson about suffering and service (Matt. 27:55–56). Her actions witness a woman who had lost herself in the service of her Lord even when tragedy and confusion surrounded her.

She was completely consumed by her love for Jesus to the extent that she no longer cared about what others thought of her or her sons or whether they had achieved greater status. She cared only that their beloved Teacher was not left to suffer alone. It has even been argued that she made a complete commitment to sacrifice and service before her sons did, given that they fled while she remained anchored at the scene of shame under the cross.[1] The record concludes with her example as a nameless servant of the Lord who embraced his teachings and example when answers were unseen.

THE WOMAN WHO LOVED MUCH

A Galilean woman whose name is unknown found Jesus dining with a Pharisee and could not hold back her profound expressions of gratitude and love for the Lord. The uninspired Pharisee judged the woman to be a sinner and Jesus to be a charlatan from his observations at dinner. The communication between the woman and the Savior, however, reveals that Jesus forgives the repentant individual who establishes a new course of life.

THE WOMAN'S PLACE OF RESIDENCE

Luke tells of a Pharisee named Simon who resided in Nain, where he must have had several opportunities to encounter Jesus of nearby Nazareth. This "woman in the city," probably a resident, spotted Jesus as she walked by, and she entered Simon's home. Most of the Jewish villages at the time had only a couple hundred residents, which made it easy for them to know too much about each other and also for them to quickly recognize newcomers.

The scriptures introduce her simply as "a woman in the city, which was a sinner" (Luke 7:37). Apparently, the woman was well known from the town and, from the fact that the Greek verb here is in the imperfect tense, we understand that the woman *used to be* a sinner but was a sinner no longer.[1] She was also a woman of some means, as evidenced by the fact that she carried with her on that occasion an alabaster vial filled with expensive ointment.

We do not know her specific sins, only that they were "many" (Luke 7:47). The most common assumption is that she was a prostitute because her sins were publicly known, she greeted him with kisses, she caressed his feet, and she was a woman of means.[2] One opinion even portrays her as a publican who had earlier received baptism from John along with other repentant tax collectors.[3] She could have been guilty of any number of actions that offended God and constituted reason for Jesus to acknowledge her sins as "many."

LUKE 7:36–50

190

It is not important to know the woman's past sins, only that she had changed and become a new creature in Christ. In fact, one lesson from the story is that one cannot deduce another's sinful life by observing outward appearance. Simon the Pharisee knew of her sins because he belonged to the town but expected Jesus to know of them by inspiration if he really were a prophet.[4] Simon knew of her sins but not that she had changed.

HISTORICAL CONTEXT

Hospitality in Jewish culture expected hosts to greet their guests with kisses and often to offer fragrant ointment to dispel unpleasant odors. The fact that Jesus was reclining at dinner suggests that Simon had adopted the Greco-Roman custom of dining—legs extended behind and feet exposed while reclining at a three-sided table, called a *triclinium,* which rested on or near the floor. He would have left his sandals at the door. The imagery of a woman stepping into this scene provides a poignant portrayal of contrasts. Simon was respectable, titled, named, inhospitable, and a Pharisee—a separatist from the unclean and impure. She was a former sinner, without name or title, genuinely hospitable, and *inseparable* from Christ, that is, she was complete only by being with him. If Jesus faced away from the entrance, the woman could have fallen at Jesus' feet without his knowing that she was there—until she began weeping and anointing his feet with her tears and the ointment.

Although restrictive rules about women being seen in public would likely have been relaxed in Galilee in comparison with Jerusalem, Simon's reaction to the woman's entrance implies that he expected Jesus to observe the laws of piety and separation with exactness. For the pious, table fellowship was reserved for those who strictly observed dietary and purity regulations. The custom made a clear separation between God and those of the fallen world.[5] By contrast, sharing a meal for Jesus was not an occasion to publicly express one's religious purity but a chance to extend his grace to the outcast and marginalized. He therefore ate with the "publicans and sinners," reaching out to offer them acceptance, repentance, and complete forgiveness despite the fact that Pharisees and scribes found the practice repugnant (Luke 7:34; 15:2).

Soon after entering Simon's house, the woman uncovered her hair, loosed it, and then wiped her tears from Jesus' feet with it. For a woman to appear in public without a head covering and her hair unbound could send a variety of messages to an observer, depending on the circumstance. New Testament scholar Charles H. Cosgrove surveyed accounts from the ancient Mediterranean world that indicated that a woman's unbound hair could signal sexual promiscuity, evidence of grief or mourning, or an expression of religious devotion, and if she was a girl, that she was unmarried.[6] Cosgrove highlights an account of a Greek woman who entered the shrine of Aphrodite to express profound gratitude for the blessing of being reunited with her husband. She "places her hands and face on the goddess's feet, lets down her hair, and kisses the feet of the goddess. In this setting, the loving attention to the feet and the letting down of the hair are clearly acts of thankful veneration."[7]

THE WOMAN'S APPEARANCE IN THE NEW TESTAMENT STORY

Because the woman in Luke 7 (according to Luke's retelling of the story) approached Jesus, fell at his feet, unloosed her hair, and began weeping, her actions communicated to her first-century audience deep grief, such as for her sins, or a manifestation of grateful devotion. By teasing out the scriptural text, we can conclude that the woman must have already repented of her sins before that evening, likely after a previous encounter with the Savior's message of salvation. Again, she had been a sinner but was one no longer. Evidence of such is her sincere expression of gratitude toward Jesus. When she knew that Jesus was at Simon's house, she made preparations to demonstrate her gratitude to him by anointing his feet with the ointment.

Actually being in the presence of Jesus after her repentance may have been even more emotional for the woman than she anticipated. She "stood at his feet behind him weeping" when she found him "and began to wash his feet with tears, and did wipe them with the hairs of her head, and kissed his feet," and her tears flowed with the ointment (Luke 7:38). Repentant and profoundly humble, she fell at her Savior's feet and kissed them with overwhelming reverence. Because she wiped his feet with her hair rather than a cloth may suggest that her tears were spontaneous and she had not prepared another means to wipe them.[8] Her loosened hair could also reflect a broken heart and indicate that she had forgotten about herself in her overwhelming focus on her Redeemer. Clearly, her appearance was not a cry for attention, which could be turned against her. She appeared so immersed in her quest that she was completely unaware of Simon's judgment of her as impertinent and inappropriate.

By contrast, Simon's self-righteousness bore unspoken witness that he felt no need for the Redeemer. His assumption that Jesus did not know the woman or her reputation as a sinner was incorrect. Simon's conclusion from those assumptions, that Jesus could not be a prophet, was therefore also incorrect.[9] Speaking to himself, Simon mused, "This man, if he were a prophet, would have known who and what manner of woman this is that toucheth him: for she is a sinner" (Luke 7:39). Simon took offense when Jesus showed respect and appreciation for this woman. She felt amazingly free to show her gratitude for Jesus in such an unconventional way, recognizing that he understood her and unashamedly accepted her expressions of love even while Simon callously spoke of her with disdain.

While the woman wept in humble adoration, Simon silently rebuffed Jesus for allowing a sinner to touch him thus, concluding this was sufficient evidence that Jesus was no prophet. Knowing Simon's thoughts, Jesus told him the parable of two debtors, both of whom were subsequently forgiven by their creditor: "There was a certain creditor which had two debtors: the one owed five hundred pence, and the other fifty. And when they had nothing to pay, he frankly forgave them both. Tell me therefore, which of them will love him most?" (Luke 7:41–42). In a question pointed to Simon but also meant to be heard by the woman, Jesus asked, "Tell me therefore, which of them will love [the creditor] most?" Scholars have argued that the word "love" used here means "thank" or "be grateful."[10] Simon logically and accurately answered, "I suppose that he, to whom he forgave most," concluding that depth of gratitude follows forgiveness (Luke 7:42–43).

Just as Simon had neglected to show Jesus proper hospitality when he entered Simon's home, neither did Simon and other Pharisees accept baptism when it was offered—unlike the publicans, who did accept (Luke 7:29–30). Christ acknowledged the woman's soul-felt repentance by telling Simon, "Her sins, which are many, are forgiven; for she loved much: but to whom little is forgiven, the same loveth little" (Luke 7:47). If Simon were truly listening, he would have known that Jesus felt little if any love from him, which in turn blocked Simon's ability to receive the Lord's blessings. Because he refused the Savior's proffered gift of repentance and baptism, Simon missed out on the blessing of forgiveness and knowing gratitude.

At this point, the story suddenly shifts focus. For the first time in the dialogue, Jesus addressed his words directly to the adoring woman. His message was meant specifically for her when he proclaimed, "Thy sins are forgiven. . . . Thy faith hath saved thee; go in peace" (Luke 7:48–50). By speaking directly to the woman, Jesus challenged Simon the Pharisee to really look at her and see her penitent heart. His chastisement was for Simon and not for the woman. Visibly, she had become a new creature in Christ. Her outward response to her new world was clearly now immersed in selfless love and profound appreciation.[11]

The Savior's forgiveness of the woman was not a consequence of her love for him at that moment or for her tears and expensive ointment. He frankly forgave her because she had sincerely repented. Her love for him grew out of his cleansing gift that allowed and enabled her to repent. The apostle John taught, "We love him, because he first loved us" (1 John 4:19).

Who among us loves the Savior most? In reality, those who recognize they have sinned, fallen short, and are forever lost without the atoning blood of Jesus Christ feel the exquisite love of the Redeemer most profoundly. Bankrupt in spirit and burdened by sin, we come to Christ as unprofitable servants. In such a helpless plight, none of us would claim that our sin is a mere fifty-pence problem. Our debt is greater than we can ever repay, time immemorial.

This woman personifies the authentic disciple of Christ. Through her sincere acceptance of the Lord's Atonement, the Galilean woman who loved much teaches us to reverence our Redeemer because of his dual gifts of repentance and forgiveness. No sinner is so low as to be outside the power of the Atonement. The natural response for us will then be much as it was for this loving woman—to fall at his feet and, out of profound love and gratitude, wash them with our tears.

I Shall Be Whole

BY AL R. YOUNG

THE WOMAN WHO TOUCHED THE HEM OF HIS GARMENT

*A*Galilean woman who is known in scripture for her disease rather than by her name or subsequent life figures in one of the most memorable stories of the Savior's healing power and compassion. She, who wanted no one to see her, attracted the complete attention of Jesus, which in turn drew the villagers to see at her in a way they never had before. With the woman's simple touch of faith, the Savior brought her back into society and into his family as his "daughter."

THE WOMAN'S PLACE OF RESIDENCE

The woman's dramatic healing occurred in one of the many villages surrounding the Sea of Galilee, probably Capernaum, where there was a synagogue and a Jewish population that daily tried to live the complex and sometimes contradictory tenets of the law of Moses. Because the woman suffered from a blood disorder, her neighbors would have shunned her because she was ritually unclean. According to the law of Moses, a blood disease rendered the sufferer ritually unclean, and anything or anyone she touched was consequently unclean (Lev. 15:25–31). Her bed, eating utensils, and the food she prepared were tainted.

After battling the disease for a dozen years, she may have been left to live alone where no one else could mistakenly touch something she had touched and be in turn reduced to an unclean state. If she had once had a husband and children, they are not mentioned in the story. Most likely, her family members no longer touched her, and her friends had abandoned her long before.

The woman was plagued by "an issue of blood" for twelve long years (Mark 5:25; Luke 8:43), as long as Jairus's daughter had lived. She was not dead, like Jairus's daughter, but in consequence of the hopeless circumstance that isolated her from society, she might as well have been. Menstruation symbolized death in large part because a lack of menstruation signified conception and life. Luke reports that the woman had "spent all her

Matthew 9:18–26
Mark 5:21–43
Luke 8:40–56

195

living upon physicians" without a positive resolution (Luke 8:43). This description implies that she had been a wealthy woman at one time—but no more. This woman represents depletion in nearly every way—physically, socially, financially, and emotionally—but not spiritually.[1] In the midst of all her distress, buried in the impossibility of her circumstance, she had one shining hope to return to normal life.

THE WOMAN'S APPEARANCE IN THE NEW TESTAMENT STORY

In an undisclosed previous circumstance, the woman had heard enough about Jesus to more than hope; she knew he could heal her. Her fear was in her ability to get close enough to touch him and to do so without drawing any attention to herself. She had no one to intercede on her behalf as Jairus did for his daughter. With a boldness and determination that must have stretched her weakened body to its limits, the woman devised a means to access her Savior without anyone's notice. Having no one to talk to, she talked to herself, allowing the reader to know her thoughts: "If I may touch but his clothes, I shall be whole" (Mark 5:28). She may have connected the fringe on the border of his garment with priesthood power.[2]

Accustomed to being invisible to society, the woman tried to get close enough to Jesus while a large crowd of people accompanied him and Jairus down the narrow, winding, village street. Approaching Jesus from behind reflects her marginalized place in society and presents a striking contrast to Jairus's face-to-face encounter with the Healer. Her hesitancy and her desire to touch him anonymously may be attributed in part to expectations for modest women to be circumspect in public and not touch a man or ask him to help her. As she reached out, somehow she succeeded in touching the border, or hem, of the Savior's robe as he passed by (Luke 8:44).

"And straightway the fountain of her blood was dried up; and she felt in her body that she was healed of that plague" (Mark 5:29; Luke 8:44). She knew her greatest prayer was suddenly and finally answered. She would be relieved if then she could simply fade away from the crowd without anyone knowing she had been there. One senses how horrified she would be if the public's attention were turned on her, shunned as she had been for so long.

Yet Jesus did not stop at healing her when only she and he recognized the miracle. He purposely turned a street full of neighbors, who were trained to shun and isolate the unclean, to look at her and watch him touch her and praise her for her remarkable faith. At the very moment she knew her body was healed, Jesus turned to ask, "Who touched me?" (Luke 8:45). The surrounding crowd was oblivious to the miracle that was unfolding. The full import of what was happening was between the woman and the Lord alone. Jesus was not afraid of touching those he blessed; touch was often part of his healing. Neither was he upset at being touched by a woman, even one who was diseased. He had a further gift to offer to this woman—but it would require even greater faith on her part.

The scriptures hint of the drama that must have accompanied that moment. "And when the woman saw that she was not hid, she came trembling, and falling down before him, she declared unto him before all the people for what cause she had touched him" (Luke 8:47). Her trembling is palpable as she awaited the sentence Jesus would pronounce. He began by addressing her as "Daughter" (Luke 8:48). Her faith in him qualified her for admission into his family. By publicly calling her "Daughter," he also showed his profound sensitivity to her emotional state, considering the intimate nature of her problem.[3]

Finally, Jesus told the woman, "Be of good comfort: thy faith hath made thee whole; go in peace" (Luke 8:48). In this additional display of compassion, Jesus announced in the presence of her neighbors that this woman's healing came as a result of her remarkable faith rather than pointing to his own essential power in the miracle. In doing so, he declared her honorable and erased any temptation to shame her in the future. Because of her exceeding faith in him, Jesus openly numbered her among his family and pronounced her whole. She was healed both inwardly and outwardly.

By touching merely the hem of his garment, the woman may have believed that she could be healed without rendering the Savior unclean and without calling down further denunciation and disgust from her neighbors. The Savior appreciated her courage and initiative but knew she was capable of more. He challenged her to stretch her faith and publicly acknowledge what she had done without knowing how he would respond.

The incident also teaches us about the Savior. He was "astonishingly free from the need for public honors, and also from the need to dominate women."[4] He declared that the woman's manifestation of faith saved her. Faith in Christ is the basis for salvation. Her witness was not honored by Jewish courts of law or believed by men generally, but it was accepted and confirmed by Christ. In one dramatic moment, he reinforced the divine truth surrounding the dignity of all God's children, including this seriously marginalized woman. Her subsequent life promised to be dramatically different after her encounter with Jesus that day.

This story also shows something of Jesus' sensitivity to women's fears and challenges. Suffering alone as she did for so many years and known only by a disease that men could easily ignore, the woman discovered that Jesus was more than a divine Healer. The Savior understands and is not ashamed of intimate health issues unique to women.

The Savior's Atonement extends beyond mending physical pain. He heals broken hearts and sick souls. He makes us whole, spirit and body. When we wholeheartedly come to Christ in our distress, knowing that he is our only hope, he renews, enlarges, and enhances the quality of our lives through his atoning blood.

I Say unto Thee, Arise

BY AL R. YOUNG

THE DAUGHTER
OF JAIRUS

On the brink of adulthood and the blessings of marriage and family, a twelve-year-old girl died before her father and Jesus could arrive to help her. A child, she is known not by her name but by her relationship to her father, Jairus, who spoke and acted on her behalf. The girl's story underscores that God is fully capable of addressing the needs of each of his children at any given time and responds at the moment and in the manner that is most efficacious for each one.

Luke describes the girl as Jairus's "only daughter" (Luke 8:42). The context also indicates that she is his only descendant.[1] She could be considered Luke's parallel example to the only son of the widow of Nain to show God's concern for his daughters as well as his sons. The girl was dying at the age of twelve, just as she was nearing the time of marriage and potential childbearing. As the daughter of a prestigious village leader, she would likely have been quite sheltered and gently nurtured, being taught to run a house and care for a family by her mother in the privacy of their home.

Although we know Jairus was distraught over the possibility of losing his beloved daughter, the girl's death at such a critical age could also signal loss of his own life's value. Without posterity, a man's life was quickly forgotten. Furthermore, her death could create financial distress if she were espoused and the groom's family had already paid their obligation for the bride-price. Jairus would be expected to refund it all.

With all that could have been at stake for Jairus, it is not surprising that he boldly approached Jesus to petition his help. His posture, however, reflected intense vulnerability. He knelt at Jesus' feet as he pleaded, "My little daughter lieth at the point of death: I pray thee, come and lay thy hands on her, that she may be healed; and she shall live" (Mark 5:23).

At his word, Jesus could have blessed the young girl and returned her to full health and her parents to complete relief. He healed others from afar, without a need

MATTHEW 9:18–26

MARK 5:21–43

LUKE 8:40–56

to touch or even see the sick person. This circumstance was different, however. News of the girl's death arrived before Jesus had reached her bedside (Mark 5:35). Jairus may also have needed healing, which warranted the prolonged heartache. Perhaps his faith in Jesus Christ needed to be stretched and deepened. Jesus calmly counseled the distraught father, "Be not afraid, only believe" (Mark 5:36). His instructions make one thing certain: the Lord had more to teach Jairus before answering his specific petition.

Along the way to the ruler's home, as Jairus tried to rush the Savior through the crowded, narrow streets of the village and "people thronged" Jesus, his agenda was interrupted (Luke 8:42). Jesus suddenly stopped to ask who among the crowd had "touched" him (Luke 8:45). A female figure other than Jairus's daughter commanded the Lord's attention in that moment. While his daughter lay dying at home, Jairus stood helpless as Jesus took precious time to minister to a trembling woman who was probably sitting or lying on the ground with the crowd of people looking down at her. Jairus heard the woman's amazing acknowledgment that she was the one who had "touched him" and the Savior's response to her, "Daughter, be of good comfort: thy faith hath made thee whole; go in peace" (Luke 8:47–48).

In the same instant, the power of the moment was broken when "there cometh one from the ruler of the synagogue's house, saying to [Jairus], Thy daughter is dead; trouble not the Master" (Luke 8:49). Jesus heard the same report and, without evidence of frustration or impatience, told Jairus not to fear but "believe only" and his daughter would be made "whole" (Luke 8:50). One senses the collision of emotions that were simultaneously thrust upon Jairus and his struggle to know how to respond.

Another chaotic scene met them as they approached Jairus's home. According to Mark's account, professional mourners, probably women (Jer. 9:16–17; Ezek. 32:16), had already surrounded the house and "wept and wailed greatly" to announce the death of the girl (Mark 5:38). The mourners mocked Jesus when he told them the girl was not dead but merely sleeping, so he sent them out, permitting only the parents and his close disciples to be with him and the dead girl (Mark 5:39–40). To the public, he understated the crisis by saying that the girl was merely sleeping. But privately, in the home of Jairus, Jesus told the girl to "arise," not simply to awaken.

With the crowd of mourners shut out, Jesus took the girl "by the hand" and commanded her, "Talitha cumi," meaning, "Damsel, I say unto thee, arise" (Mark 5:41). The scriptures report that the girl arose immediately and even walked, to the astonishment of those present (Mark 5:42). Jesus asked that the girl be given something to eat, which suggests that food would assist her return to health but also to supply additional evidence that she indeed lived again (Mark 5:43).

As one of the awestruck bystanders who witnessed the unbounded faith of the unclean woman in proclaiming her presence to Jesus, Jairus was given a firsthand example of what it means to "fear not" and "believe only." How different would Jesus' words sound—that his daughter, though dead, would be made whole—after witnessing active belief and fearlessness in this outcast woman? Was anything too hard for the Lord?

In the Lord's masterful choreography of simultaneous needs and requests for help, he orchestrated answers that blessed each party in the most poignantly personal and beneficial ways. By first witnessing the faith of the woman who touched the hem of Jesus' robe, Jairus stretched the limits of his belief to see a more spectacular miracle than that of his daughter restored to health. Jesus made the girl whole after she had died and in so doing infused her father with deeper understanding and commitment.

Whether the two women ever met each other, the stories of the daughter of Jairus and the woman with the issue of blood will always be intertwined because of the way that all three New Testament accounts present them. Both woman and girl were previously outside society—unclean—but with the touch of the Master, each was subsequently restored to communal life. The number "twelve" figures in both. Both are called "daughter," the girl was so referenced by her father and the woman was similarly endeared by Jesus. Jesus insisted that the woman's healing be public, whereas he required privacy when he restored the girl to life. At the same time, each was healed outwardly and publicly, but both were inwardly or privately healed, too, to a level of wholeness that the world cannot see. The woman touched Jesus to be healed; Jesus touched the girl to heal her. Together these two events reinforce one important doctrinal truth: faith in Jesus Christ saves. And although it is not stated, we sense that Jesus would know and respect the names of this young girl and this woman. They were not forgotten to him.

The worth of one young girl to the Savior, regardless of whether she married, independent of the number of children she bore, is illustrated in this story. In requesting that the parents not share the details of the miracle, Jesus showed that he genuinely cared about this child, with no wish to enhance his own reputation or to bring shame on those who had ridiculed him. Outside, the world mocks; inside, one sees clearly. In addition to the stories of Jesus' raising the son of the widow in Nain and Lazarus the brother of Mary and Martha, this story of the raising the daughter of Jairus anticipates the Resurrection of Jesus. He has the power over death. He is indeed the light and the life of the world.

JOANNA

יוֹחָנָה

"God Has Been Gracious"
(a feminine version of the masculine Hebrew name John)

The Galilean Joanna was a married woman who followed Jesus and supported him in his travels. She was one of the women who stood in the shadows as the Savior suffered on the cross, watched where his body was laid in a sepulcher, and reported to the men that the tomb was empty on the third day. She is named only in Luke's account among two lists of Galilean women, but in both instances, she is named second to Mary Magdalene. Although it is impossible to conclude anything about Joanna beyond these scant facts, they do allow a few suppositions.

Luke identifies Joanna's husband as "Chuza Herod's steward" (Luke 8:3). This Herod was Herod Antipas, tetrarch of Galilee during the Savior's ministry. His official residence in Galilee was likely in the provincial capital, Tiberias, on the western side of the Sea of Galilee. Because the tetrarch's servants and assistants, along with their families, generally lived in the palace or nearby and traveled with the client-king when he traveled, Joanna most likely lived in or close to Tiberias, which is only a short distance from Magdala, where Mary Magdalene lived. The two women are named together in the Gospel of Luke and were likely close acquaintances in their devotion to Christ.

The root of Joanna's name is Hebrew, as is her husband's, suggesting they were both of Jewish descent ensconced in a Hellenistic society. As steward for the tetrarch, Chuza may have been a slave, a freedman, or a free man; his employment alone would not have made him wealthy. On the other hand, the client-king's steward may have been a nobleman; the context does not provide enough information for us to be certain. There is no indication that Chuza was a disciple of Jesus or that he traveled with his wife, but his responsibilities as a servant in Herod's court would likely have made travel with Jesus very difficult, if not altogether impossible.

That Joanna had means to support Jesus from her reserves suggests that she was freeborn.[1] It may also suggest that Chuza married above him in status, a common practice of freedmen. Joanna appears to have been free to

LUKE 8:2–3; 24:10

202

travel and dispense of her resources at will, without the need for Chuza's permission. Or Chuza might have been grateful to Jesus for healing his wife, if indeed such a healing had happened, and therefore supported Joanna's desire to assist the miracle worker.

If Joanna were of a higher social status, then she had an increased opportunity for a better education, including language skills in Aramaic, Greek, and maybe even Latin. Her connection to Herod's court through her husband's position would have been instrumental in helping her and the other Galilean women learn the whereabouts of Jesus during his trials and crucifixion in Jerusalem so they could attend him. She also may have been Luke's source of information about Herod's sole encounter with Jesus (Luke 23:6–12). The scriptural accounts bear witness that she attended the Savior at his death and was among the first to see him after he rose again.

In large measure, Joanna and the women of Galilee remain anonymous, putting the focus and importance where they should be—on Jesus Christ. In a personal and almost palpable way, Joanna was a recipient and an eyewitness of the Savior's sacrifice not only at the end but during his mortal ministry. The Atonement was efficacious in her daily life in Galilee. Her enduring discipleship bears witness to the retroactive and infinite power of the Atonement.

Joanna also reminds us that men and women hold equal value in the eyes of God and that lack of a title or position of authority does not exclude someone from having a remarkable spiritual witness. She prods us to use our agency wisely to come to him, no matter how hopeful or hopeless our circumstance or how little or greatly marginalized we may feel in society. Without fanfare or many words, Joanna and the other Galilean women reinforce the poignant principle that it is by hearing the Lord's teachings and doing them that we join his family.

POINTS TO PONDER

1. From your experiences, what strengths come from being a *diakonos* as the Savior used the term?

2. What risks did Joanna and the other women take by openly following and standing by Jesus in his ministry and death? How does your discipleship with the Savior ease fears about what others may think of you?

3. What humble and repentant followers of Christ could you miss by judging righteousness solely by outward appearances?

4. How has your gratitude increased after knowing you have repented of your sins and been forgiven by God?

5. Have you ever noticed divine healing after witnessing another person's miraculous recovery? How would you describe the Lord's healing choreography in your experience?

As It Began to Dawn

BY ELSPETH YOUNG

MARY OF MAGDALA

Μαρία

Meaning uncertain (Greek form of the Hebrew *Miriam*)

*M*ary Magdalene is one of the best-known characters in the New Testament, yet we know surprisingly little about her. In all but one of the twelve times that she is mentioned in the four Gospels, she is either named alone or first in a list of women. The sole exception is in John's account of the women who stood by the cross in which the mother of Jesus is listed first (John 19:25). Nevertheless, in the Gospel of John, Mary Magdalene is the premier witness of the Resurrection and the only one commissioned to tell others the stunning truth. The primacy of her name in these accounts, the frequency of her mention, and her role on the morning of the Resurrection suggest that she was a prominent and respected disciple in the first century. From the earliest interpretations of her, however, she has been assigned polar opposite roles: at one extreme, a repentant sinner who quietly served; at the other, the apostle to the apostles.

MARY'S PLACE OF RESIDENCE

Mary was designated by her connection to her hometown rather than by her relationship to a parent or husband. She was Mary from Magdala, an identifier that suggests that she traveled and was therefore known in other geographical areas. Magdala is the Aramaic name for an impressive first-century city of some 1,000 to 1,500 inhabitants situated about four miles north of Tiberias on the western shore of the Sea of Galilee.[1] Its Greek name, Taricheae, means "salted fish," indicating the area's fame for a salted-fish export industry located there.[2]

MARY'S DAILY WORK

Because it was not unusual for lower-class women to acquire any one of a number of trades, Mary Magdalene may have been a fisherwoman and involved in the local trade, which could have given her access to the means to minister to Jesus in his travels.[3] The Babylonian Talmud

MATTHEW 27:55–61; 28:1–10
MARK 15:40–47; 16:1–10
LUKE 8:1–3; 23:49, 55; 24:9–11
JOHN 19:25; 20:1–18

From atop Mount Arbel, looking down at Magdala, where Mary Magdalene lived.

introduces another possibility for her trade. The name Magdalene could be interpreted to signify she was a hairdresser (*bHag* 4b).

Nothing in scripture reveals anything about Mary Magdalene's family. She could have been married and perhaps involved in the family fishing business with her husband. Just as possible is that she was a widow or unmarried with skills to support herself. The details of her personal relationships were obviously not germane to the authors' purpose. There is no evidence, however, that she was related to the family of Jesus or those of any of his apostles. Likewise, nowhere in scripture is she called a sinner.

HISTORICAL CONTEXT

In two of the Gospels, Mary Magdalene is reported to have been possessed by demons and healed by Jesus (Luke 8:2; Mark 16:9). Unbelievers may have embellished her previous condition to discredit her witness or her example, much as they did to Jesus when they accused him of being possessed by Beelzebub, the prince of demons (Mark 3:22).[4]

Only Luke and Mark mention that she had been possessed by "seven devils" (Luke 8:2; Mark 16:9), a detail that Luke, a physician, would have noticed. Jews generally did not understand what caused diseases and often considered serious illnesses as originating from the devil.[5] Early Christian commentators linked

From the Sea of Galilee, looking toward Magdala and Mount Arbel on the left.

Mary and the seven devils with the seven deadly sins,[6] although nowhere else in the New Testament when Jesus healed someone possessed, such as the man with a legion of evil spirits (Luke 8:26–39), the two possessed of devils (Matt. 8:28–34), and the daughter of the Syrophoenician (Matt. 15:21–28), did he consider the possession a result of sin. Others have suggested that her strong spiritual sensitivities may have become unbalanced in the face of life's challenges, leading her to be "dispossessed of herself."[7]

The number seven in scripture often connotes wholeness, a complete period of time, or totality. Mary's ailment involving seven devils may say more about the magnitude of Christ's power to heal than her previous spiritual, emotional, or moral health. In announcing Mary's cure, Luke may be confirming that through the power of Christ, Mary was completely healed, she was made whole, or she was completely liberated from her illness.[8] In this sense, she is a prototype of all of us: enslaved by the pull of a fallen world, only Christ can free us.

After her healing, Mary Magdalene remained faithful to Jesus and free from the malady that previously plagued her. Her role in the Passion scenes underscores her subsequent faith, service, and leadership rather than any concerns in her former life.

MARY'S APPEARANCE IN THE NEW TESTAMENT STORY

Witness of the crucifixion. The Gospels unanimously attest that Mary Magdalene was among the Galilean women who followed Jesus to Jerusalem and became active witnesses of his crucifixion.[9] The male disciples scattered; the women of Galilee stood as sentinels and witnesses. The synoptic Gospels depict Mary as standing far enough away from the cross as if to communicate her censure of what was happening yet close enough to show her support for Jesus (Matt. 27:55–56; Mark 15:40; Luke 23:49). In John, Mary Magdalene stood with Mary, the Savior's mother, close by the cross (John 19:25). Her stance in that

The Church of Saint Mary Magdalene was built in Jerusalem in 1888 by Russian czar Alexander III to commemorate Mary Magdalene's discipleship during the ministry of Jesus. It is a prominent landmark on the Mount of Olives, where it faces the Kidron Valley and walls of the Old City.

Gospel reflects her commitment in the face of the shame associated with death on a cross.

Because time did not allow for the customary sprinkling of spices and perfumed ointment on the strips of cloth used to wrap around the body before burial, the official burial ceremony could not occur until after the Sabbath.[10] Mary and other women watched where the body was laid and returned home to rest for the Sabbath.

First to the empty tomb. The synoptic Gospels as well as traditions that predate their writing agree that Mary Magdalene and at least one other woman from Galilee were the first to discover the empty tomb early on that first Easter morning.[11] Even though John identifies only Mary Magdalene at the scene (John 20:1), in her report to the apostles, she states, "We know not where" he is (John 20:2), implying that at least one other person accompanied her in making the initial discovery, as Matthew, Mark, and Luke report. Some New Testament scholars propose that John 20:2–10 was not part of the original text but was added later to conform more closely to the other accounts.[12] By reading verse 11 after verse 1, John's testimony suggests that the resurrected Christ appeared to Mary when she first discovered the empty tomb rather than upon her return after Peter and the other disciple verified that the tomb was empty.

Prepared to anoint the dead body of Jesus for whom she still mourned, Mary and perhaps other Galilean women were confused when they looked into the empty tomb. The pre-Resurrection world could explain the absence of the body only by a theory involving tomb robbing. When the two angels at the tomb told them that Jesus was not there but had risen and that they must tell the apostles what they had learned, Mary was eager to obey.

Matthew's account is unique in its report of the resurrected Christ appearing to Mary Magdalene and the other Mary along the way as they returned to tell the male disciples their news. The two women fell at his feet, and he gave them the commission to tell the other disciples to meet him in Galilee (Matt. 28:9–10).

The male disciples did not believe her. Mary may have been confused but she was not in doubt, even after the male disciples refused to believe her witness (Luke 24:10–11; John 20:3–8). According to John, Peter and another disciple ran to the tomb, witnessing that the burial clothes were folded, with those that covered the head separate from the burial strips that had clothed the rest of his body. The scene bespeaks a calm and orderly departure rather than a robbery. If indeed the resurrected Lord was the one who folded them, the neatly wrapped clothing suggests a solemn and reverent reflection, even awe, at what had just occurred. After the two apostles saw for themselves that Mary's report was true, they "believed," or were convinced, of Mary's witness and quickly departed again, not yet understanding that "he must rise again from the dead" (John 20:4–10).

With Mary Magdalene alone at the tomb, John directs the reader to follow her quest and subsequent revelation. Undoubtedly other disciples could have testified of their own parallel experience of seeing the resurrected Christ, but it is Mary's personal encounter with the resurrected Christ that is preserved. According to John, after everyone else had run away, Mary remained at the empty tomb, seemingly determined not to depart until she learned what had happened to the body of Jesus. She continued vigilant, ever loyal.

First to witness the resurrected Christ. Mary Magdalene did not recognize the Savior when he first appeared and spoke to her, calling her by the nonspecific term "Woman" (John 20:13). The generic term may invite each of us, whether man or woman, to put ourselves in her place to become a potential witness of truth. She did not at first recognize Jesus and assumed that he was the gardener. Perhaps her eyesight was blurred by tears, or perhaps Jesus' physical appearance had been purposely changed to forestall recognition. The risen Lord may have wanted her to first know him through her spiritual eyes and ears rather than through her physical ones. In a similar way, disciples on the road to Emmaus could not recognize the resurrected Christ because "their eyes were holden" (Luke 24:16). Importantly, Mary neither comprehended the Savior's Resurrection when she discovered the empty tomb nor when she actually saw him with her natural eyes.

When the Lord then said her name, "Mary,"

First-century tomb, viewed from the inside, in Midras, Israel.

Photo by Kent P. Jackson

her spiritual eyes were opened (John 20:16). Suddenly her encounter with the resurrected Lord had become very personal. In an example of what Jesus taught by way of metaphor in John 10, Mary heard the voice of the Good Shepherd when "he calleth his own sheep by name, and leadeth them out" (John 10:3).

"Touch me not." Immediately upon her recognition of him, Mary Magdalene fell at his feet and addressed him as Rabboni (John 20:16). Although the term is properly translated "teacher" or "master," it was often reserved for deity and therefore more honorific than "rabbi."[13] Her use of the term implies that she could see that Jesus had somehow changed.

Coinciding with her recognition was what appears to have been an instinctive attempt to touch him. The Lord's response, "Touch me not," is in the present imperative (John 20:17), which suggests a continuous action more precisely rendered, "Don't keep touching me."[14] The term has been variously interpreted to mean "Stop holding me;"[15] "Do not hold on to me;"[16] "Don't cling to me;"[17] "Hold me not" (JST, John 20:17), or to discontinue whatever it was she was doing.[18] Taken together, these several explanations combine to suggest that the Savior was asking Mary not to hold him back from what he still needed to do. Mary may have anticipated that Jesus had returned to remain with his followers forever and resume their association. In her anxious desire not to lose him again, she therefore wanted to cling to him to keep him there.

The Savior could not stay because he had not yet ascended to his Father. One final event in his great victory—returning to the presence of his Father—remained to be accomplished. Later that day, however, he would specifically invite others to touch him: "Handle me, and see; for a spirit hath not flesh and bones, as ye see me have" (Luke 24:39).

BETWEEN THE LINES

Many have asked why Mary Magdalene received this remarkable experience. We could just as easily ask, Why not? We do not need a unique calling, title, or relationship with the Savior different from that of any other disciple to receive a spiritual witness. We need a broken heart, faith in him, and an opportunity for him to teach us. If for no other reason, she may have received this blessing simply because she lingered in a quiet spot rather than running off to talk with others. Church leaders have observed that we would have more spiritual experiences if we did not talk so much about them.[19] Mary Magdalene teaches us to be still and *learn* that he is God (see Ps. 46:10; D&C 101:16).

The Savior's singling out of women to be his witnesses cannot be anything but deliberate. His words and actions repeatedly reinforced his truth that women were not second class but worthy of the same blessings from God as men could receive. According to all four of the Gospel writers, the women were proven credible. Considering that the Gospels were written in the decades after the Resurrection of Jesus, it is arguable that Mary Magdalene became a prominent and respected member of the Christian community, although she is not mentioned in Luke's Acts of the Apostles or in any of the apostles' epistles.

POST–NEW TESTAMENT PERSPECTIVES OF MARY MAGDALENE

The dearth of further details about Mary from the Gospels only stirred imaginations of later Christians to elaborate on history and morph her into whatever image fit their purposes. Portrayed in one of two extremes, she was seen as either a penitent prostitute or the wife of Jesus, neither of which has scriptural or historical foundation. On the other hand, both history and scripture agree that she was a faithful disciple, teacher, and leader among the early Christians.[20]

The earliest Christian fathers did not mention her much, but what does remain of their writings puts her in a favorable light and portrays her as a real person. For example, Tertullian explained that Mary wanted to touch the resurrected Savior out of love and not out of curiosity or disbelief, which Thomas later manifested. The Lord refused Mary her desire not because it was inappropriate but because the time was not right: he had not yet ascended to his Father (*Prax* 25).

Other early Christian writers described Mary Magdalene as the chief apostle. Drawing on the Greek word *apostolos,* which means "one who is sent forth," they noted the Magdalene's assignment from the resurrected Lord, to go to his brethren and give her witness that he had indeed risen from the dead (John 20:17). As a result of this description, Christians of the Middle Ages assigned her the title of apostle of the apostles.[21]

A number of Gnostic Christian texts, discovered in 1945 in Nag Hammadi, Egypt, depict Mary Magdalene as one of the main speakers and in a prominent position among the disciples. Gnosticism stressed that only through secret knowledge (*gnosis*) was one granted salvation rather than through the Atonement of Jesus Christ. Its emphases on the spiritual over the physical disparaged mortality and the creation of a physical world and perceived physical bodies as prisons for spirits.

In apocryphal *Sophia of Jesus Christ,* probably written in the second century, the resurrected Christ met "his twelve disciples and seven women" in Galilee to teach them and give them authority to preach his gospel (*SophJesChr* 119. 4–15).[22] Of those seven women, Mary is the only woman named, and the only woman whose questions are included. In *The Dialogue of the Savior,* she is one of three disciples in conversation with the Lord, the other two being Judas and Matthew. In that text, after one of Mary's comments, the narrator observes that she "uttered this as a woman who had understood completely" (*DSav* 139.11–13).[23] In the same text, the Savior assigns a favorable attribute to Mary by telling her, "You make clear the abundance of the revealer" (*DSav* 140.17–19).[24] The superior value of knowledge over service is highlighted.

Some Gnostic Christian literature describes Simon Peter in a negative light and in competition with Mary Magdalene for supremacy among the disciples. One of these is the apochryphal *Gospel of Thomas,* in which Mary Magdalene and Salome along with three male disciples ask Jesus questions and are in turn taught by him. It ends with Simon Peter saying, "Let Mary leave us, for women are not worthy of life" to which Jesus responded, "I shall lead her in order to make her male," maleness (according to the text) being a requirement for obtaining the kingdom of heaven (*GThom* 51.18–26).[25] The text invites distrust of traditional Christian authority, using Mary as a symbolic alternative all the while considering "maleness" as a nonphysical attribute that is desirable to all who "know."

In the apocryphal *Gospel of Mary,* named for Mary Magdalene, she comforted the male disciples after the risen Lord departed, telling them, "'Do not weep and do not grieve or be irresolute, for his grace will be entirely with you and will protect you. But rather let us praise his greatness, for he has prepared us and made us into men.' When Mary said this, she turned their hearts to the Good, and they began to discuss the words of the [Savior]" (*GMary* 9.12–24).[26] She then shared special revelation that she alone received from Christ, teachings that reflect typical Gnostic searches for the soul's progress through ethereal realms. Peter challenged her because he did not think the Savior would tell such truths to a woman rather than to his male disciples. Levi, one of the men present, responded to Peter, "If the Savior made her worthy, who are you indeed to reject her? Surely the Lord knows her very well. That is why he loved her more than us" (*GMary* 18.11–15).[27] Again, the unknown author of this text uses Mary Magdalene to denigrate Peter's authority as the one to whom Jesus gave the keys, adding fuel to schisms that were increasingly dividing Christians in the second century.

By the fourth century, the tone shifted among early church fathers.[28] Rather than seeing the Magdalene as more knowledgeable than male disciples and more trusted by the Lord, they focused on the Lord's command that she not touch him and the fact that she had once been possessed by seven evil spirits. They explained Jesus' command to mean that she was not worthy to touch the risen Lord because she lacked faith and understanding. She was sent to the male apostles not to proclaim the Resurrection, as the scriptural text explains, but to receive strengthening in her weakness from the men.[29]

Also beginning in the fourth century, church fathers countered interpretations of Mary as the apostle to the apostles being spread through the *Gospel of Mary* and other texts by conflating her with known sinners to create a new persona. By the end of the sixth century, in one sermon Pope Gregory the Great combined all three women into one, officially marking Mary Magdalene as a repentant sinner for more than a dozen centuries. He identified the seven devils that once possessed Mary as seven sexually promiscuous vices.[30] Suddenly three individual disciples became one promiscuous and licentious woman while three women of faith, courage, generosity, and intellect were blurred and forgotten in the retelling.[31]

Furthermore, after Mary was transmogrified into a sinful woman, it was easy to identify her with any other female sinner in the New Testament, including the adulteress in John 8 and the Samaritan woman in John 4. It is noteworthy that whereas the Christian fathers of the Latin Church undermined the prominence of Mary Magdalene as a teacher, witness, and leader by conflating the multiple women named Mary in the New Testament, none of the Eastern churches confused any of the Marys with prostitutes and adulteresses.[32]

Although multiple known and unknown authors have taken creative license to mold Mary Magdalene into any number of images for their own purposes, the New Testament Gospels contain the only truths about her that we know for certain. The focus of these Gospels, individually and collectively, is to bear witness of Jesus Christ as the Son of God and Savior of the world. They did not aspire to detail the lives of those who followed him. The testimony of Jesus' mortal ministry, however, could not be told without including Mary Magdalene. As an early disciple and generous *diakonos,* she became a trustworthy witness that he was indeed the Redeemer of the world. As one who ministered her substance to Jesus as he traveled, stood near him as he suffered and died on the cross, and brought spices to anoint his body in the tomb, she remains an example of the power of bearing testimony of the Savior by our actions.

POINTS TO PONDER

1. What significance do you see in Luke's mention that Mary Magdalene was healed from seven evil spirits?

2. How does the story of Mary of Magdala strengthen you when your testimony is not believed?

3. What are the implications of conflating four individual women into one?

WOMEN OF SAMARIA

$\mathcal{T}$he territory called Samaria, sandwiched between Jewish Galilee and Judea, and the people who lived there had been disenfranchised by the Jews for centuries, even though they shared the same political and religious history. In turn, the Samaritans had grown to distrust and often repel Jews who ventured through their land. Mount Gerizim was the center of Samaritan worship, which included the anticipation of a mortal messianic figure who would destroy those who alienated the Samaritans. In stark contrast to this prolonged contention between Jew and Samaritan, Jesus welcomed opportunities to speak positively about Samaritans and gave the command to take the gospel to them in the days immediately after his Resurrection.

THE LAND OF SAMARIA

The territory called Samaria in the first century A.D. was the region just north of Judea and south of Galilee. Initially, this territory was the land inheritance given to the two tribes of Joseph (Ephraim and Manasseh) when the children of Israel first conquered the land. Soon after their arrival, Moses' successor, Joshua, established the region as the first religious center for the Israelite nation. Mount Ebal to the north and Mount Gerizim to the south border the site of ancient Shechem. Shortly after the death of King Solomon in the tenth century B.C., in protest against high taxes, the northern ten of the twelve tribes of Israel created a separate kingdom (1 Kgs. 11:26–12:26). In about 880 B.C., King Omri of the northern kingdom established a new capital city called Samaria (1 Kgs. 16:16–24). The Old Testament capital city of Samaria was known as Sebaste in New Testament times.

THE PEOPLE OF SAMARIA

The northern kingdom of Israel came to an end in 722 B.C., when the Assyrians invaded and conquered it, scattering most of the Israelite inhabitants to diverse parts of the Assyrian empire, where they quickly lost their identity as children of Israel (1 Kgs. 11:13–17; 2 Kgs.17:5–8; 18:9–11).

In the centuries between the Assyrian conquest and the Savior's ministry, the Samaritans became an ethnically and religiously diverse people, made up of a mixture of Israelites who were not scattered by the Assyrians and various other peoples transported to the region by the Assyrians (2 Kgs. 17:24). The desired effect was to "undermine the cohesion and culture" of the Israelites, which was far more effective when Israelites were taken away from their homeland than when they were allowed to remain.[1]

During the sixth century B.C., the Babylonians conquered the Assyrian empire and also the kingdom of Judah, including Jerusalem with its temple. The Babylonians deported the Judahites to Babylon, where they remained in exile until 538 B.C., when Cyrus the Persian king allowed them to return to their homeland. Evidence of the Judahite disdain for the Samaritans was apparent when they offered to assist in reconstructing the temple of Israel in Jerusalem. Their offer rebuffed and themselves accused of threatening the purity of Israel's race and religion, the Samaritans created obstacles that temporarily halted the Israelite reconstruction. The books of Ezra and Nehemiah reflect the growing tension between the groups and teachings intended to officially separate the ethnically mixed Samaritans from those of pure Israelite lineage with their orthodox practice of Judaism.

By New Testament times, the contention and distrust between the two peoples had continued over seven hundred years. Jewish rabbis warned their people against Samaritans with such claims as "he that eats the bread of the Samaritans is like to one that eats the flesh of swine" (*mSheb* 8:10). The enduring animosity between the Jews and the Samaritans encouraged most Jews to avoid Samaria by traveling between Galilee and Jerusalem by way of the Jordan River Valley. In skirting Samaria, Jews could avoid contact with the Samaritan people.

SOCIAL HIERARCHY IN SAMARIA

Although one of the several wives of Herod the Great was a Samaritan woman named Malthace (*Ant* 17.1.3; *War* 1.28.4), in general Samaritan women were considered by the Jews to be the lowest of the low. Collectively, Samaritan women and men were the *am ha'eretz,* the people of the land, the nobodies. Because it was assumed that only the poorest farmers were those who had been allowed by the Assyrian invaders to remain on the land, first-century Jews enforced legal, social, and religious practices to perpetually disenfranchise and alienate Samaritans as unquestionably "other." Seen from that perspective, Herod's marriage to a Samaritan was an attempt to garner support by forging connections with all factions who inhabited the land he was commissioned to rule.

In ways that would have sounded shocking to most Jews, Jesus referred to Samaritans in honorable terms. For example, of the ten lepers he healed, Jesus clarified that the only one to return to offer thanks was a Samaritan (Luke 17:15–16). In the parable, a Samaritan, rather than a Jewish priest or Levite, exemplified true compassion for one in need (Luke 10:33–35). And a Samaritan woman was the first person to whom Jesus openly identified himself as the Messiah (John 4:25–26). When Samaritans refused to provide hospitality to Jesus and his traveling party and James and John desired to call down fire from heaven to destroy the village, Jesus rebuked his followers and took a different road back to Jerusalem (Luke 9:51–56). At the conclusion of his forty-day ministry, the resurrected Christ commissioned his disciples to take the gospel not only to the people of Judea but also to the people of Samaria (Acts 1:8).

SAMARITAN RELIGIOUS BELIEFS AND INFLUENCE

Notwithstanding their mutual animosity with the Jews, many Samaritans maintained religious connections to the Torah, the God of Moses, and their relationship to Father Abraham. The story of Simon Magus in Samaria indicates that religious interpretations and practices claiming God's power through sorcery were also influential in the area at the time (Acts 8:9–17). Nonetheless, an early Christian disciple named Philip found success in preaching the gospel of Jesus Christ among the Samaritans (Acts 8:5–8, 14–17). For first-generation Jewish Christians, perhaps in response to the Savior's inclusive teachings and instructions about Samaritans, being willing to accept Samaritans as fellow believers did not pose as great a challenge as embracing believing Gentiles later proved.

Although they shared the same religious foundation with the Jews and likewise believed in only one true God, Samaritan beliefs were distinct from Jewish beliefs in notable ways. Samaritans believed that God created humankind in the image of angels. They accepted the Torah (Genesis through Deuteronomy) as God's word but not the later books in the Hebrew Bible (Joshua through Malachi) or rabbinic teachings such as those later recorded in the Mishnah. In the beliefs of Samaritans, Moses was the last true prophet. He received God's law, the Torah, not on Mount Sinai but on Mount Gerizim. Not surprisingly, then, Mount Gerizim was the most sacred spot on earth and the true house of God. Samaritans also anticipated the coming of a messianic figure, called the *Taheb* (meaning "restorer"), suggesting one who would restore true worship of God and the Samaritans to their rightful place in the house of Israel. According to their beliefs, the *Taheb* would come as a mortal man and live 110 years, finally destroying all those who believed the instructions of Ezra and rejected the Samaritans.[2]

Notably, in Deuteronomy, which was acceptable to the Samaritans because it was in the Torah, is the prophecy that the messianic figure to come would be a prophet like unto Moses (Deut. 18:15, 18). The Samaritans believed the anticipated *Taheb* would restore the gift of prophecy not held since Moses. The Book of Mormon clarifies that this prophet like unto Moses is indeed Jesus Christ (1 Ne. 22:20–21; 3 Ne. 20:23).

As a people, the Samaritans also believed in the importance of temple worship and ritual in their collective religious expression. In about 430 B.C., after a century of being denied access to the temple in Jerusalem, Samaritans created a temple worship site on Mount Gerizim (*Ant* 11.8.2, 7). The Samaritan

Photo by Kent P. Jackson

A Samaritan temple stood atop Mount Gerizim until it was destroyed by the Jewish Maccabean rulers in 128 B.C.

temple functioned for more than two hundred years, until the Jewish Maccabean rulers destroyed it in 128 B.C. After the loss of their own temple and still being forbidden to visit the temple in Jerusalem, the Samaritans resorted to Mount Gerizim as their holy space for sacrifice and other rituals. That was the situation when Jesus ministered among the people of Samaria.

Living Water

by Elspeth Young

THE WOMAN AT THE WELL

$\mathcal{T}$he Savior met a Samaritan woman doing her daily task of drawing water at a well. He helped her to see her weaknesses and created an environment in which she could learn his identity through the witness of the Holy Ghost. When filled with this knowledge, she abandoned her sins and became the catalyst that brought an entire Samaritan village to Christ. The Samaritan woman's story is found in only one of the Gospels, but it is one of the best-known narratives in scripture. Her story contains profound doctrinal teachings and hopeful implications for all who desire to follow Jesus Christ.

THE WOMAN'S PLACE OF RESIDENCE

The Samaritan woman was drawing water from Jacob's Well, near the foot of Mount Gerizim. In New Testament times, the village where she resided was called Sychar; it was known in the Old Testament as Shechem and is near the Palestinian city of Nablus today. Here Jacob purchased land shortly after his favorable reunion with Esau (Gen. 33:18–20), thereby giving the well its name. Strong Jewish, Christian, Muslim, and Samaritan traditions confirm this location as the site of Jacob's Well, which is reportedly more than one hundred feet deep and seven feet wide.

HER DAILY WORK

Every day, preferably in the cool of the morning or the evening, women went to the well to fetch water for their homes and families. The daily ritual required women to be physically strong and agile. Each woman walked to the well carrying a lengthy rope, a leather or animal-skin vessel for collecting the water, and a clay pot to transport the water back to her home. These items were too valuable to be left by the well for public use. After manually drawing water from the well, the woman would carry her now heavy water pot back to her home, only to repeat the chore the next day.

Jesus was resting at Jacob's Well "about the sixth hour," or six hours past sunrise, which would be around

JOHN 4:3–42

219

Photo by Kent P. Jackson

View from Mount Gerizim toward Mount Ebal. The New Testament village of Sychar was located near the modern city of Nablus between the two mountains.

noon (John 4:6). It was an unusual time for a woman to go to the well because of the heat of the day and because the need for water was greater at the beginning of the day. An unnamed Samaritan woman, however, had approached the well to draw water at midday when Jesus spoke to her. One senses that no one else was around. Perhaps that is what the woman preferred—to perform her daily chore without encountering others. The fact that she had been married to five different men and was currently living with a man who was not her husband (John 4:17–18) would mean that her own people, as well as the Jews, would have ostracized her. Jesus lived in a culture that discouraged public communication of men with women, yet we find him at the well, deep in theological discussion with a woman and a clearly imperfect one at that.

HISTORICAL CONTEXT

According to the Gospel of John, Jesus was returning to Galilee after spending Passover in Jerusalem (John 2:13), where a Pharisee and Jewish ruler named Nicodemus had sought out Jesus in the middle of the night to learn more of his teachings (John 3:1–21). After leaving Jerusalem to return to Galilee, the disciples who traveled with Jesus went into Sychar to buy something to eat, leaving him alone at the well (John 4:6, 8).

When the disciples returned to rejoin Jesus, they "marveled that he talked with the woman"—a Samaritan woman—but did not dare ask him why (John 4:27). Cultural perceptions that denigrated women, especially Samaritan women, were socially ingrained, even in the Savior's disciples. A mid-first-century Jewish regulation warned that Samaritan women were ritually impure because they were "menstruants from their cradle."[1] The disciples' reaction to Jesus speaking to a woman, and a Samaritan woman at that, indicates how unexpected and unusual his behavior was in their culture.

THE WOMAN'S APPEARANCE IN THE NEW TESTAMENT STORY

Jesus seemed to orchestrate his timing and route to encounter the woman, traveling right through the middle of Samaria, rather than taking the alternate route through the Jordan Valley. He also met her before she had heard of him, whether through his teachings or his miracles. He made no requirement that she be living in a particular way before he could speak with her. Through both his words and his actions, Jesus convincingly taught, "I am not come to call the righteous, but sinners to repentance" (Matt 9:13). But the woman of Samaria knew none of that. She saw only a thirsty man sitting at the well. He had no rope or leather pouch with which to draw water to quench his thirst, so he asked her for a drink (John 4:7). Perhaps from his speech or his clothing, the woman recognized that the man was not a Samaritan but a Jew.

When she addressed him, her greeting was not only without any evidence of respect but filled with awareness of the animosity that separated her people from his. "How is it that thou, being a Jew, askest drink of me, which am a woman of Samaria? For the Jews have no dealings with the Samaritans" (John 4:9). Clearly the woman was on her home turf. The Jewish stranger was the one out of place. Initially, they did not communicate on the same level. Yet the Savior showed that he can speak in whatever language we understand.

Jesus offered her the gift of living water. She had gone to the well seeking life-sustaining water. He offered her something better. He offered living water, which sustains life eternally. Jesus said to her: "If thou knewest the gift of God, and who it is that saith to thee, Give me to drink; thou wouldest have asked of him, and he would have given thee living water" (John 4:10). As yet, the woman had no idea that she was conversing with the One who would selflessly suffer to make that miraculous living water obtainable. She did not yet realize the One she was speaking with had the power to give her eternal life. Her response shows, however, that she was gaining respect for the man and had an interest in his proffered gift. For the first time she addressed him as *kyrie* (translated from the Greek as "sir" or "lord"), adding, "Thou hast nothing to draw with, and the well is deep; from whence then hast thou that living water? Art thou greater than our father Jacob, which gave us the well . . . ?" (John 4:11–12).

In his answer, Jesus emphasized that the water he offered was not like the water in that well. No rope or leathern bucket was necessary for his promised water. In reference to the water in Jacob's Well, Jesus said, "Whosoever drinketh of this water shall thirst again: But whosoever drinketh of the water that I shall give him shall never thirst; but the water that I shall give him shall be in him a well of water springing up into everlasting life" (John 4:13–14). Wells and springs can symbolize the abundant life that Christ alone gives. To Joseph Smith, the Lord revealed, "Unto him that keepeth my commandments I will give the mysteries of my kingdom, and the same shall be in him a well of living water, springing up unto everlasting life" (D&C 63:23).

The Samaritan woman was quick to respond to his explanation. Her interest in the gift was deepening, and the awe she had for this man was increasing. "Sir," she petitioned, "give me this water, that I thirst not, neither come hither to draw" (John 4:15). She may have hoped to escape the physical labor and social rejection associated with daily trips to the well, or perhaps she had a feeling that there was a better life where thirst is eternally quenched.

Jesus removed her objections and feelings of unworthiness. Jesus did not commence the conversation by pointing out what the woman needed to change in order to recognize and follow him. Rather, he began by opening her eyes to possibilities that exceeded anything she could have imagined. When her problematic lifestyle was finally verbalized, instead of being offended, she reverenced the stranger even more. "Go, call thy husband," Jesus invited, "and come hither" (John 4:16). She answered, "I have no husband." In his response, Jesus complimented her for telling the truth before he spelled out the full story: "Thou hast well said, I have no husband: For thou hast had five husbands; and he whom thou now hast is not thy husband" (John 4:17–18). "Sir," she immediately replied, "I perceive that thou art a prophet" (John 4:19).

By following the Savior's line of thought, we discover that he not only met her where she was physically but also spiritually. He knew that she was looking for a messiah who was a prophet like unto Moses (Deut. 18:15, 18). As a result of this interchange, she began to consider a greater identity for this man: he might be a prophet.

Her misconceptions, however, first needed to be removed. Remembering that he was a Jew and she a Samaritan, she protested, "Our fathers worshipped in this mountain [meaning Mt. Gerizim]; and ye say, that in Jerusalem is the place where men ought to worship" (John 4:20). Jesus indicated that the temple in Jerusalem would be destroyed just as the Samaritan temple on Mount Gerizim had been (John 4:21). Finding truth and proper worship does not depend on a specific location. To the correct aspects of Samaritan messianic expectation, Jesus therefore added detail concerning their anticipated prophet's mortal origins: "Ye worship ye know not what; we know what we worship: for salvation is of the Jews" (John 4:22). Jesus was a Jew, born into the tribe of Judah. As much as the Samaritan woman may not have wanted to acknowledge it, salvation for her and all humankind comes only through Jesus Christ, who was born a Jew.

Jesus led her to learn truth through the Spirit. In leading their discussion, Jesus created an environment that enabled the woman to learn his identity. He responded with "the hour cometh, and now is" (John 4:23) to suggest both a future and present application; there is only one true way to recognize the Christ, and it is the same in every era. The apostle Paul identified that true way when he taught that no man can know that Jesus is the Lord except by the Holy Ghost (1 Cor. 12:3).[2] To the woman, the Savior said, "True worshippers shall worship the Father in spirit and in truth: for the Father seeketh such to worship him. For unto such hath God promised his Spirit. And they who worship him, must worship in spirit and in truth" (JST, John 4:23–24).

Learning in spirit and in truth necessitates the tutelage of the Holy Ghost. His mission is not to speak of himself but to bear witness of Christ and guide us to truth (John 16:13). That is precisely what the Holy Ghost did for the woman at the well. She carefully listened to Jesus, but it was the Holy Ghost who revealed the messianic thread throughout his teachings. Once taught by the Spirit, she began to put it all together and professed, "I know that Messias cometh, which is called Christ: when he is come, he will tell us all things" (John 4:25).

Then, and only then, did Jesus unequivocally declare himself the Messiah. The King James Version records the Savior's response as "I that speak unto thee am *he,*" with the "he" in italics (John 4:26). Italics are used in that translation to indicate words that were added by translators when they deemed them necessary for a translated passage to fit English grammar or syntax. Reading the passage without the italicized *he,* however, illuminates a deeper truth in what Jesus said. One of the Lord's titles is "Jehovah," which may be translated "I Am," as in The Always Existing One. In his Gospel, John records several statements in which Jesus bore witness of himself as the great "I Am."[3] In the passage in John 4:26, then, we see that Jesus was confirming his identity to the woman by saying, "I Am speaketh unto thee."

Bringing others to know Christ. As soon as the woman received the confirming witness, she "left her waterpot, and went her way into the city, and saith to the men, Come, see a man, which told me all things that ever I did: is not this the Christ?" (John 4:28–29). Perhaps the water pot signifies the woman's former life, including her dependency on a sinful world in order to survive. One drinks living water; one does not carry it. A water pot is therefore not necessary.

Different from divine commands that silenced unclean spirits or the soothsayer slave girl in Acts 16 whose statements of the divinity of Christ were true, although not borne of the Holy Spirit, Jesus did not prevent the woman from sharing her new discovery. Her desire was to bear witness from a pure and meek heart. Much as she left her water pot behind to bear witness of divine truths to her neighbors, so she turned away from her former life and turned steadfastly to the Savior.

Nourishing the seed of conversion, the Samaritan woman found that her greatest desire was to share the good news with everyone in her village. No doubt some of those who believed her message were individuals who previously had mistreated her. With a "testimony of Jesus" (Rev. 19:10), she was filled with the gift of prophecy, and through her, others came to know the true worship of God. Initially, they believed in

Jesus because of "the saying of the woman." But after hosting him as a guest in their village for two days, they believed because of the witness of the Spirit. The new Samaritan converts then proclaimed to the woman, "Now we believe, not because of thy saying: for we have heard him ourselves, and know that this is indeed the Christ" (John 4:42). At a time when few Jews knew the true identity of Jesus, a little village in Samaria, inspired by an ostracized woman of ill repute, proclaimed the truth of truths, the declaration of declarations: "This is indeed the Christ, the Saviour of the world" (John 4:42).

BETWEEN THE LINES

Much can be learned from the fact that Jesus selected a marginalized Samaritan woman to learn truth from the Spirit and proclaim that truth to others by the same Spirit. In nearly every way she is an anomaly among the recipients of revelation. Quite a different conclusion would be achieved had the recipient been a man of the respected class. The exchange between Nicodemus and Jesus in John 3 provides a near perfect contrast in parallel circumstances. In addition to their opposite positions in society, Nicodemus and the Samaritan woman manifested different attitudes about others' opinions toward them and experienced very different outcomes after their personal encounter with Jesus.

Nicodemus and the woman at the well were at opposite ends of the social hierarchy. As a man and a Pharisee, Nicodemus would have commanded respect in society. He wielded power, was well respected, among the best educated, and considered by many to be a master teacher. The woman at the well was a *woman* and a Samaritan, a double reason to be labeled unclean by the Jews. With her unsavory past, she would have received no respect in any community. He would have been recognized as a religious individual. She would be identified with the gravest of sinners.

Their reasons for conversing with Jesus were just as diverse. Nicodemus elected to converse with the Lord at night. No one would be able to see a prestigious rabbi being taught by a craftsman from Galilee. Her exchange with Jesus was at midday in the midst of her daily chores. Nicodemus sought to learn from the Savior after noting the many miracles Jesus had performed in Jerusalem. He visited Jesus on his own terms, not the Lord's. On the other hand, Jesus met the woman where she was, without any show of miracles or previous introduction.

Finally, they experienced opposite results from their individual discussions with Jesus. Nicodemus returned to his daily routine, presumably keeping his conversation with Jesus a secret. She left her water pot behind and spread the good news to all those who would hear her. With all his power, position, and opportunity for learning, Nicodemus would not admit the identity of the man with whom he spoke. But the woman at the well acknowledged what she saw. Is not that the miracle? This woman who does not even have a name in our scriptures opened her mind and heart to be spiritually taught. She who had neither title, nor position, nor formal education, nor a stainless past could see the thirsty stranger as he truly was: the Savior and Redeemer of the world.

Life-changing revelation came to her, revelation as profound as we find in scripture. But her conversion was not in the dramatic fashion of Alma the Younger or Saul on the road to Damascus. In a quiet and contemplative way, the Samaritan woman received a clear witness while in the midst of doing ordinary household chores. In her humble way, she therefore encourages any who feel disenfranchised to trust in the Lord's invitation to drink from his living water and experience his love and power to save them.

POINTS TO PONDER

1. What characteristics did the Samaritan woman possess that encouraged her to trust in the Jewish stranger whereas Nicodemus did not?

2. How is each one of us in a sense marginalized and alien in this fallen world? How does the story of the Samaritan woman at the well strengthen our faith to follow God's plan for us?

3. Artwork depicting the woman at the well is frequently found in Latter-day Saint temples and meetinghouses. What in her story inspires others who worship the Lord?

WOMEN AMONG THE ARISTOCRACY

mong the diverse women throughout the Roman empire in the first century were a very few who belonged to the upper class. At least five elite women are depicted by New Testament authors. These women gained their elite status through the men in their families, who enjoyed prestigious positions in the Roman government or military, which in turn conferred distinction, citizenship, power, and even at times titles upon the women. During the first century, elite women enjoyed greater freedom than other women to participate in public religious expression and civic duties. The lifestyle and privileges enjoyed by these women placed them in a world completely unlike that of women of lower social classes.

SOCIAL HIERARCHY AMONG THE ARISTOCRACY

Exclusive categories of the rich and powerful defined the upper classes in the Roman empire. The emperor was the wealthiest and most powerful of all Romans, and he could raise in status men he favored and relegate to invisibility those of whom he disapproved.[1] Since the establishment of an imperial monarchy in Rome, greater productivity in numerous areas of the empire improved economic conditions generally, and qualified men from outside of Italy were given membership among the elite.

Within the upper class were three clearly defined orders: senators, equestrians, and decurions. Male Roman citizens always bore three names, the most important name being that of the clan (*gens*) or extended family. Roman women, on the other hand, officially had only one name, the feminine form of her father's clan name. Hence the daughter of Claudius would be Claudia and of Julius would be Julia. In families with more than one daughter, the girls would be distinguished simply by calling them "older" or "younger" (*major* and *minor*), if there were two; if there were more, the feminine forms of the Latin words for "first" (*prima*), "second" (*secunda*), "third" (*tertia*), and so on would be used. Beginning with the wife of Caesar Augustus, however, women of the elite were given an additional name to reflect their connection with important men in their lives. Thus Augustus's wife, Livia Drusilla, was later known as Julia Augusta.

The senatorial order. The most prestigious and exclusive order was made up of six hundred senators. These men controlled military, legal, and religious affairs. They came from prestigious families of tremendous wealth and pedigree. Wealth, along with family connections and political offices, were the key characteristics of senators.[2] At least two senators are named in the New Testament: Sergius Paulus, the senatorial governor of Cyrus (Acts 13:7); and Gallio, senatorial governor of Achaia (Acts 18:12). No names of women of the senatorial order are included in scripture.

The equestrian order. The second highest order among the elite was the equestrian order, members of whom often became governors of smaller provinces because they had money and could maintain peace within their jurisdiction. The emperor chose men to represent him in these assignments who had characteristics similar to those he possessed. Their individual merits and accomplishments, often in an impressive military career, rather than family connections, qualified them for distinction.[3]

In the New Testament, three equestrians are named: Pontius Pilate,[4] Marcus Antonius Felix,[5] and Porcius Festus.[6] The wives of two of these three governors have roles in the early years of Christianity. Pilate's wife briefly appears in scripture in connection with the trials, or hearings, immediately before the crucifixion of Jesus, and Felix's wife, Drusilla (one of the Herodian women), heard the apostle Paul's testimony firsthand.

The decurion order. Rome was not concerned with the way individual cities and regions were governed as long as the requisite taxes were collected and the people remained loyal to the empire. Direct leadership of the various areas was therefore assigned to local aristocrats who had already proven their allegiance to Rome. These men made up the largest and least prestigious group in the elites—the decurions. Each city in the empire organized its own order modeled after Rome and selected rich men to serve as city magistrates.[7] Wealth, reputation, family lineage, and military service were considerations for inclusion in the order. Often a governmental position was handed down within prominent families. Two men in the New Testament were probably decurions and also Christians: Dionysius, a member of the Areopagus, a council of governing elders in Athens (Acts 17:34), and Erastus, the city treasurer of Corinth (Rom. 16:23). Even though this group was only a very small proportion of the entire population, many of the Christians named by Paul and Luke in their New Testament writings were likely local aristocrats and may have been considered part of the decurion class. For example, Luke briefly mentions "devout," "honorable," or "chief" women among those who became Christians in Antioch, Berea, and Thessalonica (Acts 13:50; 17:4, 12).

The Jewish aristocracy. In addition to owning land, the Jewish elite were bankers and merchants in such commodities as wood, oil, grain, and wine.[8] Because of their unique religious dynamic, however, leading Judeans were rarely accepted into the ruling classes of the Roman state as were their wealthy counterparts everywhere else in the empire. Yet four generations of the family of Herod stand out as Jewish aristocrats being granted Roman citizenship, official Roman names, and the honorary title of *ornamenta praetor* within the most prominent orders.[9] From the perspective of most Jews, however, Herod the Great, an Idumean (descendant of Esau), did not possess the requisite ancestry to rule them. Until the reign of Herod's grandson, Herod Agrippa I, Judeans struggled to abandon the view that Idumeans were outsiders and should not be trusted. Agrippa I finally gained favor with many Jews by persecuting Christians in Judea (Acts 12:1–3).

RELIGIOUS INFLUENCE AMONG ARISTOCRATIC WOMEN

Religious rites in the home and for family were long considered the domain of women. Roman women assumed responsibility for prayer to heal family members and to ensure their own fertility and safe pregnancy. They also participated in religious rites associated with the birth of their children and at funerals, but responsibilities for involvement at civic religious rituals and feasts belonged to men.

Women's involvement in religion significantly increased during the New Testament era. Elite Roman women participated more in public religious life after witnessing imperial women, such as Livia, wife of Caesar Augustus, head the cult that deified the emperor. Even earlier, in the era of the Roman republic, Roman matrons held such important positions as Vestal Virgins in native cults and for such newly imported deities as *Magna Mater,* or "the Great Mother," as the Greek and Anatolian goddess Cybele was known. In the imperial period, they imported additional religions, such as the cult of the Egyptian goddess Isis to whom they prayed, "Thou . . . didst make the power of women equal to the power of men."[10] Involvement in these female cults and mystery religions gave women status which they could not obtain in other public venues.[11] Few of the rites are known today because of the secrecy attached to them. What is known is that many first-century Greco-Roman women were attracted to them and actively participated in the rituals. With notable examples of imperial women leading religious worship, increased female participation and leadership in religion generally likely encouraged similar curiosity and eventual membership in the Christian movement as well.

Although their commitment to Judaism was often only cursory, to avoid outright revolt among the people the Herodian elite respected the holy days and observed the outward signs of compliance with the law of Moses. When they were in Caesarea, Rome, or Antioch the same aristocrats would have been difficult, if not impossible, to distinguish from their Gentile associates. Other Jewish elites, including many of the Sadducees, showed intense devotion to purity rules and other religious observances as evidenced in the archaeological remains of ritual baths in their homes in Jerusalem.

ARISTOCRATIC WOMEN AT HOME

In Roman culture and among provincial elites eager to imitate Roman customs, people did not sit at tables to dine but ate while reclining on couches around a *triclinium,* or U-shaped table.[12] While resting on one elbow, diners ate with the opposite hand and communicated to the one next to them by leaning "on [his]

"CHIEF WOMEN NOT A FEW"

The following three prominent women are given only a mention in the New Testament but are illustrative of those who were drawn to the message of Jesus Christ.

Chloe *(Greek, "verdant, blooming")*
1 Corinthians 1:11

Chloe's voice or "those of her household" are heard through Paul's lengthy epistle outlining the consequences of divisive practices. "For it hath been declared unto me of you, my brethren, by them which are of the house of Chloe, that there are contentions among you" (1 Cor. 1:11). Paul obviously trusted the report, because he wrote one of his longest and most detailed letters to rectify the problems. Chloe appears to have been wealthy enough to support a household, presumably made up family members, slaves, or freedmen and freedwomen who worked for her. She probably had a business that required her or her employees to travel and thus could deliver the letter

The ancient Agora ("gathering place") and Stoa (covered promenade) where the Areopagus met in Athens. Although Paul achieved little success when he taught scholars and philosophers about the "Unknown God," a woman named Damaris became a believer and follower after hearing him teach (Acts 17:19–34).

outlining their concerns to Paul. The Corinthian Saints may have been more closely acquainted with Chloe because she was a known and respected Christian rather than through her business ventures.

Damaris (*Greek, "heifer"*)
Acts 17:34

Showing that the gospel of Jesus Christ blesses men and women equally, Luke named a man and a woman as the fruit of Paul's preaching in Athens during his second mission. Damaris is the female convert named there: "Howbeit certain men clave unto [Paul], and believed: among the which was Dionysius the Areopagite, and a woman named Damaris" (Acts 17:34). The fact that Luke knew her name suggests that she became or remained a strong witness for Christ and contributed to the Christian community. In the scriptural context, Damaris was in the company of the intellectual and cultural elite of the city when Paul preached. One early manuscript of Acts adds the description "of honorable station" to Damaris's name, suggesting that she was respectable in her own right and not merely by association.[13]

Apphia (*Greek, meaning uncertain; a term of endearment*)
Philemon 1:1–2

Paul addressed a letter to "Philemon our dearly beloved, and fellowlaborer, and to our beloved Apphia, and Archippus our fellowsoldier, and to the church in thy house" (Philem. 1:1–2). The letter reveals that Philemon was a slave owner who was patron of the church in Colossae. A woman named Apphia is noted with him along with a man named Archippus who apparently worked with Paul to spread the gospel of Jesus Christ as a "fellowsoldier." The most logical assumption is that Apphia is Philemon's wife and Archippus was their son. If this was a family unit, Apphia lived in relative wealth with servants and accommodations to host church meetings in her home. Unfortunately, no other information clarifies Apphia's identity or contribution.

bosom" (John 13:23, 25). This reclining position also explains how someone could wash a diner's feet without disrupting the meal (John 12:3; Luke 7:36–38).

Nicer Jewish homes often featured rooms that opened to a courtyard with an outer wall and gate that separated the courtyard from the street (Acts 12:13). These mansions had at least three floors: the upper floor for family residence, the ground floor for reception and guest rooms, and the floor below ground for servants. The largest homes covered areas of some 6,300 square feet. Most homes of the Jewish elite were built in the upper city of Jerusalem overlooking the Temple Mount from the west in what is today called the Jewish Quarter.

ARISTOCRATIC WOMEN IN PUBLIC LIFE

Under Augustan legislation at the end of the first century B.C., elite women who had given birth to three children could be legally exempted from male guardianship. Livia, wife of Augustus, became the model

Photos by Kent P. Jackson

Terraced houses in Ephesus. These elegant homes, dating from the Roman era, belonged to elite families in Ephesus. Exquisite mosaic floors and painted walls hint at the luxury the residents enjoyed.

Roman matron and traditional mother, the *materfamilias,* in addition to her public persona as benefactress and representative of the gods. Although rarely given direct governing power, elite women were often awarded state titles to symbolize civic virtues that the emperor applauded.

Wealthy Roman, Greek, and Jewish women often had a voice and power in the public sphere. Among the urban elite in Asia Minor, men ruled at the highest levels of government, but a few wealthy women in Greco-Roman societies are known to have held such municipal offices as magistrate, a member of the magisterial board, or a member of the finance committee.[14] Notwithstanding the evidence that women of the elite were becoming increasingly influential in society, men still dominated political and economic policy.

Romans distinguished themselves by rank through their clothing. By their dress, jewelry, hairstyles, and public display of wealth, elite women attempted to maintain their reputation as respectable matrons while hoping to catch one of their equals in a lapse. Roman women never wore a toga, the official attire of elite Roman men, but they wore a tunic that reached to the ankles and was covered by a gown, called a *stola,* that was belted at the waist. They wore jewelry such as rings, bracelets, and earrings for pierced ears.

Beginning with Livia (wife of Caesar Augustus) and Octavia (daughter of the emperor Claudius and wife of the emperor Nero), imperial women set the fashion for hairstyles for women of all classes to imitate, as funerary monuments demonstrate. Greco-Roman artifacts of the day suggest that women kept their hair long and wrapped it in various styles rather than letting it fall freely around their shoulders. During the first century, wealthy Roman women began wearing elaborate hairstyles with more complex and higher curls around the face, indicating the need for something akin to a curling iron.[15] For the elites, a woman was not considered "well dressed" unless "she has embellished her hair" (*Met* 2.9).

Images of women on Roman coins and in marble sculptures may depict popular hair styles.[16] An elite woman had scores of slaves at her bidding, including personal maids to care for her appearance. Women visited the baths in the mornings; men typically preferred the afternoons. Slaves applied fragrant oils during a massage and after a bath. These oils were also sprinkled on clothes so the fragrance would cover unwanted odors.[17] A comb with extra fine teeth could remove lice, which were a frequent problem. Oil was used to treat women's hair, and beeswax kept in place braids, curls, and other intricate hair arrangements.[18] Archaeological remains indicate that women used white or red face powder and black or brown paint for brows and lashes. A blue mixture for eyelids was believed to have medicinal properties. The fingernails and toenails of wealthy women were usually painted white. Both Paul and Peter expressed concern over sophisticated and complex hairstyles adorned with gold and pearls (1 Tim. 2:9–10; 1 Pet. 3:3).

Sketches by Elspeth Young

Images of women on Roman coins and in marble sculptures may depict popular hair styles, many of which would likely have required the time and remarkable skills of a slave to create. Covering one's hair with a veil or other headdress continued to be socially acceptable.

ARISTOCRATIC WOMEN IN THE NEW TESTAMENT STORY

The sole Roman aristocratic woman featured in the New Testament was the wife of Pontius Pilate. Four women of the Herodian family also appear in the New Testament record, namely Herod's granddaughter Herodias and three of his great-granddaughters: Salome (daughter of Herodias) and Drusilla and Bernice (nieces of Herodias). Because they were members of the elite, we find additional details about them in Roman and Jewish histories.

Upon Awakening

BY ELSPETH YOUNG

PROCLA, WIFE OF PONTIUS PILATE

Procla

"Renowned" (Latin)

*A*lthough her appearance in the New Testament is brief (only thirty-eight words) and she is unnamed there, Pontius Pilate's wife is known for her attempt to prevent her husband's involvement in the death of Jesus of Nazareth. As a Roman, she lived in Caesarea but seems to have accompanied her husband to Jerusalem and may have become acquainted there with aspects of Jewish culture. Later histories record her name as Procla, or perhaps Claudia Procla, and suggest she was a God-fearer or perhaps even a proselyte to Judaism. Subsequent Christian myths magnify and embellish her support for Christians. The scriptural text, however, highlights her sensitivity to spiritual promptings through dreams and her courage to speak out against unjust punishment.

PROCLA'S PLACE OF RESIDENCE

When in Jerusalem, the governor Pilate and Procla likely resided in the palace that Herod the Great built on the west side of the city, near the present-day Jaffa Gate. Their permanent residence would have been in Caesarea at Herod's exquisite palace on the manmade promontory that jutted into the Mediterranean Sea. The scriptures do not mention them in connection with Caesarea, however, but only their being in Jerusalem during Passover.

The New Testament provides no explanation for Procla's cognizance of Jesus to lead to her having a dream about him. As a Roman, Procla would likely have been unfamiliar with Jewish customs before her husband received his assignment to govern Judea. Although her dream may have been an inspired, one-time occurrence, it may also indicate an existing familiarity with Jewish issues or an awareness of Jesus before his trial. Even though both Greek and Roman traditions expected women to be modest and heed their husbands' commands, influential and strong women often privately counseled their husbands to behave in a more moral fashion. Pilate's wife is a New Testament example of this type of influence when she advised him against involvement in the vendetta against Jesus.

MATTHEW 27:19

This engraved stone memorial refers to Pilate as "Prefect of Judea" in conjunction with the dedication of a building he sponsored in Caesarea. Translated, the inscription reads: "To the honorable gods (this) Tiberieum Pontius Pilate, Prefect of Judea, had dedicated . . ."

Photo by Kent P. Jackson

HISTORICAL CONTEXT

According to the Byzantine historian John Malalas (*Chron* 10.14.1) and the apocryphal work *Paradosis Pilati,* the name of Pilate's wife was Procla.[1] She is only mentioned in relation to her husband, Pontius Pilate, so background from her husband's life and policies in the Jewish territories provides some context for her surroundings. Pontius Pilate was appointed governor of Judea (A.D. 26–36) under Tiberius Caesar. According to Josephus, Pilate was especially insensitive and oppressive toward the Jews, seeking to abolish their peculiar laws and offending them by displaying in Jerusalem imperial banners bearing the image of Caesar (*Ant* 18.3.1; *War* 2.9.2). The powerful treasurer of the Jewish temple apparently agreed to some of the Roman governor's projects because Pilate used temple funds to build an aqueduct to Jerusalem.

Josephus notes that Pilate killed the Jews who protested his building decisions (*Ant* 18.3.2; *War* 2.9.4) and mistook as a threat to the peace a number of Samaritans who were seeking for vessels around Mount Gerizim that they believed had been buried by Moses. He sent troops in to break up the crowds, killing many in the melee. Later protests resulted in Pilate's dismissal from office in A.D. 36 (*Ant* 18.4.1). The Jewish client-king who was appointed a few years later to oversee Jerusalem, Herod Agrippa I, described Pilate to his friend the emperor Caligula as "naturally inflexible, a blend of self-will and relentlessness" (*Embassy* 301).

PROCLA'S APPEARANCE IN THE NEW TESTAMENT STORY

Procla's dream and concern for Jesus. In the final scenes leading up to the crucifixion of Christ, only Matthew recounts Procla's involvement. On the morning of the crucifixion, Jewish "chief priests and elders" took Jesus, charged with treason against Rome, to stand before Pilate, the governor of Judea. Pilate could not find cause for executing Jesus. He knew the Jewish leaders were accusing Jesus out of "envy," so he sought to defuse the contention by offering to release a prisoner, whether Jesus or Barabbas, as a Passover gift to the people, as was his custom. While Pilate sat in the "judgment seat," Procla sent word to him: "Have thou nothing to do with that just man: for I have suffered many things this day in a dream because of him" (Matt. 27:19). Having been warned in a dream of Jesus' innocence, she warned her husband to show mercy to the accused.

The impressions she received through her dream were motivating enough to cause her to intervene at a most public and formal moment in

A bronze coin issued by Pontius Pilate features a libation ladle with Tiberius's inscription on the obverse and the laurel wreath, a symbol of power, on the reverse.

the proceedings—when Pilate was seated in the chair of judgment. She was willing to ignite her husband's fiery temper by causing him to be interrupted to advise him against his decision. In the apocryphal *Acts of Pilate,* after receiving Procla's warning but before he told the Jewish delegation of it, Pilate explained, "You know that my wife is pious and prefers to practice Judaism with you" to which the Jews answered, "Yes, we know it" and then told them about Procla's dream (2.1). When nothing he said or did changed their minds, Pilate "washed his hands before the multitude" and, describing Jesus as Procla had done, said, "I am innocent of the blood of this just person," thereby consenting to their request (Matt. 27:20–24). Whether Procla was indeed inclined toward Judaism or later to Christianity is not verifiable from other sources.

Revelation through dreams. Matthew's Gospel opens with stories that show how God's revelations through dreams are trustworthy. The magi were warned not to return to Herod, Joseph was instructed to take Mary and Jesus to Egypt, and he was told when it was safe to return to Judea from Egypt—all three revelations communicated to these men in the form of dreams (Matt. 2:12–13, 19–20). Toward the end of his Gospel, Matthew again demonstrates the communication of God through a dream, but this time a woman was the recipient of the revelation. Whether all she learned about Jesus came solely from that dream or whether she had previous information to indicate that he was "just" or righteous is not clear from the passage. What is clear is that she took a stand to communicate the dream's message.

The scriptures also cite her words sent to Pilate, not a paraphrase. The dream and its poignant message caused her "[to suffer] many things this day" because of what she had learned through the revelation (Matt. 27:19). One of the costs of true discipleship with the Savior involves suffering, drinking from the same "cup" of affliction that he drank (Rom. 8:17–18; Matt. 20:22), because "without sufferings [we] cannot be made perfect" (JST, Heb. 11:40). The dream produced such discomfort as to propel Procla to act, even to plead for Jesus, whereas the Jewish leaders pleaded for Barabbas. How her suffering informed her thoughts and actions after the death and Resurrection of Jesus remains unknown.

THE HERODIAN WOMEN

$\mathcal{W}$ealthy women of the aristocracy in Jewish society could influence local policy only by working through the powerful men in their family.[1] Because they were excluded from most official positions of power, elite Jewish women exercised influence from behind the scenes, prodding their husbands or other men to represent their particular perspectives. Women of the family of Herod are the most notable examples of women who exercised powerful influence on governmental actions.

RELIGIOUS INFLUENCE AMONG THE HERODIANS

During the reign of the Hasmonean dynasty (142–63 B.C.), just before the Roman era, leadership over the Jewish territories was directly linked to religious functions. Those sentiments did not change when the Romans took control. Although the temple and high priestly families were still considered to be the center of government by the Jewish people, Herod was ethnically an Edomite, with a lineage that went back to Esau, son of Rebekah and Isaac (descendants of Esau were called Idumeans in New Testament times). Josephus considered him to be a "half Jew" (*Ant* 14.15.2). His ancestors were forcibly converted to Judaism during the Hasmonean rule. The Romans considered Herodians loyal to Caesar and also Jewish, even though they were not blood Israel. Additionally, the family could claim patronage of Israel or Rome, depending on which was most advantageous at the time. Nearly always, Rome trumped.

HERODIAN WOMEN IN PUBLIC LIFE

The family of Herod. Jewish society permitted men to be married to more than one woman at the same time, although monogamy was preferred and was far more common. The principal issue was financial: only the wealthy could afford multiple wives. The short list of polygamists included Herod, who had ten wives (*Ant* 17.1.3). When one considers the women of Herod's own generation and those who were born later, the number is significant. The complexity of the large family tree is increased by the number of marriages that many of the Herodian women contracted and the frequency with which they married male relatives.

238

The women of the house of Herod in Jewish histories have been described as "a flock of screaming, bright-plumaged birds."[2] Not unlike other provincial courts in the Roman empire at the time that were ruled by Hellenistic monarchs, Herod's name was Greek, as were the names of nearly all of his female descendants. Many of the names were replicated generation after generation. Herod's influential sister Salome, his wives, his daughters, his sons' wives, the wives of his brothers and their sons, his granddaughters, and his grandsons' wives present vibrant images in history of intrigue, power, and bold feminine involvement.

The intrigue, distrust, and executions within Herod's court are often attributed to Herod's ambitious and ruthless sister, Salome. Jealousy and competition defined her relationship with Herod's second wife,

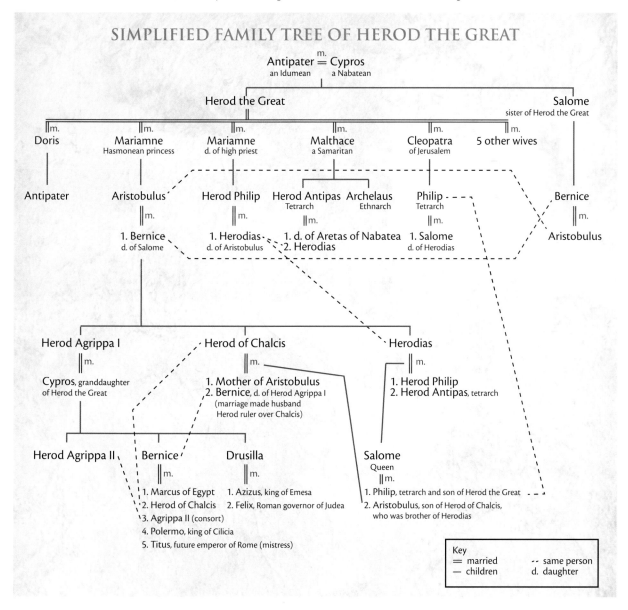

SIMPLIFIED FAMILY TREE OF HEROD THE GREAT

Mariamne, whose royal Hasmonean family prestige could trump her own. Mariamne's family agreed to the marriage with the anticipation that Herod would bestow the position of high priest on Mariamne's brother. But then, fearing such a move would add greater prestige to his wife's family, Herod assigned the priesthood position to an obscure Jew from Babylon (*Ant* 15.2.4). To sever her own restrictive marriage with her uncle at a time when Jewish women could not initiate a divorce and to destroy her sister-in-law Mariamne at the same time, Salome accused her husband of adultery with Mariamne, an accusation that resulted in his immediate death and eventually Mariamne's death, too, in response to Herod's vengeful jealousy and paranoia (*Ant* 15.5.9; 15.7.3). In recounting the malicious saga, Josephus maintained Mariamne's innocence while assigning blame for this plot to Salome, who is portrayed as having been successful in her determination that none of Mariamne's children would survive to inherit power (*Ant* 16.1.2).

None of these dramatic and calculating Herodian women appear in the New Testament, but the detritus that their decisions and influence left behind shaped the players who remained. At his death, Herod the Great divided his wealth and power among his remaining sons, leaving none of them as wealthy and powerful as he had been. While Herod was a client-king, three of his sons held the title of either ethnarch or tetrarch to rule a fraction of the area he had governed. Herod's sons never attained the level of social and political clout with the Romans that Herod achieved.

In the third and fourth generations after Herod the Great, the Jewish political elite turned to his descendants through his second wife, Mariamne, and their son Aristobulus. Herod the Great's daughter and granddaughters, who could claim a distinguished heritage from both the great Herodian and the Hasmonean dynasties, would again splash color, revenge, and infidelity upon the pages of history. This time, however, they and some of their deeds are also chronicled within the pages of scripture. The New Testament reports that they also heard the teachings of Jesus Christ from believers. But they, like the rest of the Herodian clan, responded like "a reed shaken with the wind," bending to the intoxicating breezes of power, ambition, and luxury rather than taking a stand for truth.[3]

HERODIAS

Ἡρῳδιάς

"Heroic"

As her name indicates, Herodias inherited a politically strong family lineage. Not only was she the granddaughter of Herod the Great through her father Aristobulus but she was also the granddaughter of Herod's sister, Salome, through her mother, Bernice. In addition to this double dose of Herodian blood, Herodias was a granddaughter of the Hasmonean princess Mariamne, who bequeathed to her descendants a Jewish priestly lineage that Herod and his sister, Salome, could not claim. Herodias also had two full brothers: Herod Agrippa I and Herod. Herodias and Herod Agrippa I make striking appearances in the New Testament, though not as followers of Christ or believers in him.

HERODIAS'S MARRIAGES

In an attempt to compensate for killing Mariamne and their son Aristobulus, Herod the Great arranged marriages for the children of Aristobulus. For Herodias, he chose an uncle, Herod Philip, who was the son of Herod the Great with another woman named Mariamne, this one the daughter of Simon the high priest (*Ant* 17.1.2). To this husband, Herodias bore a daughter named Salome (*Ant* 18.5.4).

During a visit to Rome with her brother, Herod Agrippa I, Herodias met Herod Antipas, her husband's half-brother, who was the son of Herod the Great and his wife Malthace the Samaritan. Antipas was tetrarch in Galilee and Perea and was married to the daughter of the Nabataean king Aretas (Luke 3:1; *Ant* 18.5.1). Antipas fell in love with Herodias and determined to divorce or desert his wife. Herodias likewise fell in love with Antipas. The two married immediately, leaving their spouses without warning. Divorces such as these were legal and acceptable for Roman nobility, but they were offensive to the Jews, as Josephus wrote: "Herodias took upon her to confound the laws of our country, and divorce herself from her husband, while he was alive, and

MATTHEW 14:3–11

MARK 6:17–28

LUKE 3:19–20

241

was married to Herod [Antipas]" (*Ant* 18.5.4). Likewise, their blatant disregard for marriage bonds conflicted with the teachings of John the Baptist (Mark 6:17–18).[1]

The so-called marriage between Herodias and Antipas provoked political ramifications. When the wife of Antipas heard the news of her husband's desertion, she traveled to her father's kingdom in Petra to inform him of her husband's actions. King Aretas attacked and destroyed Antipas's army in retaliation (*Ant* 18.5.1–2).

HERODIAS'S APPEARANCE IN THE NEW TESTAMENT STORY

Herodias never encountered Jesus and may never have met John the Baptist, but she knew what they taught. Both secular history and scripture portray Herod Antipas as less competitive than other rulers and appreciative of the teachings of John the Baptist. Herodias, however, wanted vengeance against John for condemning her marriage to Antipas. Mark wrote in his Gospel: "Herodias had a quarrel against [John] and would have killed him; but she could not: for Herod feared John, knowing he was a just man . . . and when he heard him, he did many things, and heard him gladly" (Mark 6:19–20).

When Salome, Herodias's daughter by her first husband, danced for Herod Antipas and in return was promised anything she desired "unto the half of [his] kingdom," Herodias directed her to request the head of John on a charger. She had finally found a way to be rid of him (Mark 6:22–24). To explain John's martyrdom, Matthew focuses more on Herod Antipas's lack of backbone than on Herodias's conniving (Matt. 14:3–11). Luke considers Herod Antipas's guilt about marrying Herodias and John's bold condemnation of his moral turpitude to explain John's imprisonment (Luke 3:19–20). Herod Antipas tried to silence his conscience by killing John the Baptist but was haunted by far more guilt after John was dead (Luke 9:7–9; Matt. 14:1–2).

Josephus claims that Herod Antipas put John the Baptist to death for political reasons. Antipas envied John's popularity and feared that the Jews would hear John's rebuke against him and rebel. If he could not control the Jewish people, the Romans would replace him, as they had his brother Archelaus, and put a Roman governor in his place. So Antipas imprisoned John and then executed him. Whatever the true impetus, Herodias abused her influence to orchestrate the evil deed, and Antipas abused his power when he ordered that John be killed.

HISTORICAL POSTSCRIPT

Not content with Antipas's title of tetrarch of the Jewish territories Galilee and Perea and jealous that her brother Herod Agrippa I had been granted the title of king by the Romans, Herodias urged Antipas to petition the new emperor, Caligula, for the same honor that had been given Agrippa. She longed for the title of queen. According to Josephus, Herodias was miserable with jealousy and pleaded with Antipas, "Let us go to Rome, and let us spare no pains nor expenses, either of silver or gold, since they cannot be kept for any better use than for the obtaining of a kingdom" (*Ant* 18.7.1). Antipas was reluctant, satisfied with his current station and fearful that the request would not end well for him, but he eventually succumbed to her endless entreaties. The year was A.D. 39.

Agrippa I learned of his sister's plan and warned Caligula of Antipas's shortcomings before the couple arrived in Rome. Herodias must have known that Caligula was a close friend to her brother, but she did not expect the emperor's cutting reaction. Caligula flatly refused

The fortress-palace of Machaerus was built on the eastern shore of the Dead Sea in modern-day Jordan. According to Josephus, it was the site where Herod Antipas put John the Baptist to death (Ant 18.5.2).

their request and denounced Antipas, removing him as tetrarch. To heap even greater shame on the greedy couple, he gave to Herodias's brother Agrippa the gold and silver they had offered Caligula to sweeten their request. Moreover, the emperor added Antipas's territories of Galilee and Perea to Agrippa's kingdom, making him ruler over all the Jewish territories his grandfather Herod the Great had ruled. Finally, Caligula banished Antipas to Lyon in faraway Gaul, in what is now modern-day France (*Ant* 18.7.2).

Knowing that Herodias was the sister of Agrippa I, Caligula offered her freedom from exile and the restoration of her fortune. Much to his surprise, Herodias refused, saying, "Thou, indeed, O emperor! actest after a magnificent manner . . . in what thou offerest me; but the kindness I have for my husband, hinders me from partaking of the favor of thy gift; for it is not just that I, who have been made a partner in his prosperity, should mistake him in his misfortunes" (*Ant* 18.7.2). Preferring banishment in obscurity to separation from Antipas, this woman who had squandered so much opportunity leaves the stage of history.

SALOME, DAUGHTER OF HERODIAS

Σαλώμη

Greek form of the Hebrew Shlomzion, "peace of Zion"

Although not named in scripture, the daughter of Herodias is named Salome in Josephus's history and is known by that name today. She was the daughter of Herodias (a granddaughter of Herod the Great and his wife Mariamne the Hasmonean princess) and Herod Philip (a son of Herod the Great and another Mariamne, the daughter of Simon the Jewish high priest) (*Ant* 17.1.2; 18.5.4). At the bidding of her mother, Salome obtained favor from Herod Antipas, yet another son of Herod the Great, and requested the head of John the Baptist on a platter. Outside the New Testament story, Salome is better known as the queen of Chalcis (in modern-day Lebanon).

SALOME'S MARRIAGES

Salome was married first to her great-uncle Philip, son of Herod the Great and Cleopatra of Jerusalem (*Ant* 17.1.3). Philip was the tetrarch in Caesarea Philippi and the northeastern area of the Holy Land (Luke 3:1). In A.D. 34, after Philip died childless, Salome was married to her cousin Aristobulus, a son of her mother's brother Herod (*Ant* 18.5.4); both were thus great-grandchildren of Herod the Great. Salome was granted the title of queen when Aristobulus became king of Chalcis, a distinction inherited from his father, who had become king of Chalcis after his marriage to Bernice, daughter of his brother Herod Agrippa I,

SALOME'S APPEARANCE IN THE NEW TESTAMENT STORY

Salome's age when her mother left her father and began living with Herod Antipas is not known; however, because she had not yet been married, she was likely still a child. Furthermore, daughters of Jewish members of even the nominally elite were sheltered to some degree from worldliness to ensure their purity when they were married.

In what Mark describes as a lavish birthday party for Herod Antipas, to which the elite landowners, military commanders, and other prominent members of the elite

MATTHEW 14:3–11

MARK 6:17–28

LUKE 3:19–20

244

Photo by Kent P. Jackson

An image of Salome, daughter of Herodias, is on the capital of this column of the Church of Agia Sophia in Monemvasia, Greece. The church commemorates the ministry of John the Baptist.

Artwork by Ashton Young

According to a custom established by Hellenistic rulers, Salome's image was represented on coins issued in Judea. Here she wears a crown in the form of a hat, and her hair hangs loosely below it.

residing in Galilee and Perea were invited, a celebratory supper was served (Mark 6:21). Into the room came Salome, possibly a bright-eyed and playful child. She "danced, and pleased Herod and them that sat with him," prompting the delighted tetrarch to offer her whatever she wanted, even "unto the half of my kingdom" (Mark 6:23). Embellishments of the biblical story usually portray Salome in a salacious dance to appeal to Herod Antipas's sensual side, but the scriptures give no indication that such was the case.

It is more plausible, considering Salome's likely tender age, that her dance was the dance of an innocent child, endearing her to the guests. If such a description is accurate, the response that Antipas gave, "Ask of me whatsoever thou wilt, and I will give it thee" (Mark 6:22) is still completely appropriate. Salome's not knowing how to answer and instead running to her mother, inquiring, "What shall I ask?" (Mark 6:24), further argues for her being an innocent child. Matthew explains that Salome was "instructed of her mother" to request John's life (Matt. 14:8). Speaking as her mother had told her to do, Salome may not even have comprehended what she requested: "in a charger the head of John the Baptist" (Mark 6:25). In recounting that Herod Antipas indeed kept his promise to give her whatever she asked and suffered from nightmares afterwards, the scriptures do not chronicle the influence, if any, John's death had on Salome.

HISTORICAL POSTSCRIPT

Salome, the daughter of Herodias, is known in history for more than her dance before Herod Antipas. Although her mother failed to achieve the title of queen, Salome attained it. She was the first and probably the only client-queen in Judea to have her likeness and title engraved on a coin. Salome, daughter of Herodias, died sometime between A.D. 54 and 61.[1]

DRUSILLA

Δρούσιλλα

Feminine form of Drusus, of the Livius clan

Drusilla was born in A.D. 38 and given the same name as that of the Roman emperor Caligula's sister who died the same year. Drusilla's father, Herod Agrippa I, and Caligula were close friends, having grown up together in Rome. Like her older siblings, Drusilla was given the opportunity to hear Paul bear witness of Jesus Christ but indicated no willingness to change the course or purpose of her life.

DRUSILLA'S MARRIAGES

As he did for his other children, Agrippa II and Bernice, Herod Agrippa I arranged a marriage for Drusilla, who was still a young child. He chose for her the son of a wealthy king in the east, near the Euphrates River. After Agrippa I died in A.D. 44, however, the man backed out of the agreement, choosing not to convert to Judaism as marriage into a Jewish family required. So, through her brother's arrangement, Drusilla married Azizus, king of Emesa in Syria, who converted to Judaism in order to marry her (*Ant* 19.9.1; 20.7.1).

Drusilla's being a married woman, however, did not deter Antonius Felix, the Roman governor of Judea (A.D. 52 to about 59), from pursuing her. Felix had for many years been a slave of Antonia, mother of the emperor Claudius in Rome. Later in his life he was freed by her, granted the high social rank of equestrian, and appointed governor of Judea by Claudius (*Ant* 20.8.9; *War* 2.12.8). Felix was attracted to Drusilla by her great beauty but had no intention of converting to Judaism and being circumcised in order to marry her. Instead, he persuaded her to abandon her husband and her Jewish faith, escape Bernice's jealous maltreatment, and marry him (*Ant* 20.7.2).

Drusilla was his third wife, but all three of his wives were of royal birth, an indication that a freedman could achieve significant power and status in the empire. Even though his assignment as Roman governor was to keep order among the Jews, Felix more often sided with the Hellenists than the Jews (*War* 2.13.7). There is no evidence that Drusilla tempered such biases against her people.

ACTS 24:22–27

DRUSILLA'S APPEARANCE IN THE NEW TESTAMENT STORY

The New Testament describes Drusilla and her husband, Felix, as listening to Paul's teachings when he was imprisoned. She heard Paul's testimony before her sister, Bernice, did. Luke calls Drusilla a "Jewess," suggesting that she could have explained to her husband about Jewish beliefs and why the prisoner's witness would upset many Jews (Acts 24:22–24). Felix "trembled" in reaction to Paul's teachings of "righteousness, temperance, and judgment to come" but found no crime in his behavior or beliefs to justify his being held in custody. Drusilla said nothing to defend Paul or the truths he spoke.

Luke reports that Felix "sent for [Paul] the oftener, and communed with him," including being willing to free him if Paul paid him a bribe, but Luke does not mention Drusilla again (Acts 24:24–26). Paul refused the bait while continuing to fearlessly preach against their blatant disregard for the laws of God. "Willing to show the Jews a pleasure," Felix kept Paul imprisoned for two years, until Felix was replaced in office by Porcius Festus (Acts 24:26–27), who was soon afterwards visited by Agrippa II and Bernice.

HISTORICAL POSTSCRIPT

The New Testament does not explain why the Romans replaced Felix as ruler of the area, but Jewish and Roman historians do. Both Josephus and Tacitus wrote that Felix was forced out of office because he failed to quell riots that erupted between the Jews and the Syrian Gentiles in Caesarea (*Ant* 20.8.7; *War* 2.13.7; *Ann* 12.54). Drusilla was denounced along with her husband.

Felix and Drusilla had one son together, whom they named Agrippa. Josephus reports that their son and perhaps also Drusilla died in the A.D. 79 eruption of Mount Vesuvius (*Ant* 20.7.2).

What Is Truth?

BY AL R. YOUNG

BERNICE

Βερνίκη

"Victorious" (Greek)

*F*ourth-generation Herodian nobility, Bernice and her siblings, Herod Agrippa II and Drusilla, inherited Herodian blood from both their father, Herod Agrippa I, and their mother, Cypros. Far more is known about Bernice from extrabiblical sources than from the New Testament, where she appears silently supporting her brother as they listen to Paul's defense of his faith after his arrest. Although the Romans did not give Bernice an official title, she enjoyed political influence and power through her brother, who was known as "king Agrippa" in the New Testament (Acts 25:13).

BERNICE'S MARRIAGES

In A.D. 44 Bernice's father, Herod Agrippa I, ordered the execution of James, one of the original twelve apostles of Jesus, and died shortly thereafter (Acts 12:1–2, 21–23). Having been born in A.D. 28, Bernice was sixteen years old when her father died. Her brother, Agrippa II, was seventeen, and their younger sister, Drusilla, was six (*Ant* 19.9.1).

Bernice had already been married twice by the time her father died; Agrippa I had selected both husbands for her. Her first marriage was to Marcus, son of Alexander the Egyptian, a magistrate and a younger brother to Philo. Marcus died soon after the marriage, and Agrippa I gave Bernice, his eldest daughter, to his brother Herod to be his wife. Through this marriage arrangement, Agrippa secured the kingdom of Chalcis for his brother to rule, thereby augmenting the region that Rome entrusted to the Herodians (*Ant* 19.5.1). After Bernice bore him two sons, Berenicianus and Hyrcanus, her second husband died in A.D. 48 (*Ant* 20.5.2).

Bernice was then just twenty years old and twice widowed. Her father had by that time been dead four years, which removed pressure on her to marry again quickly. The emperor of Rome at the time, Claudius, looked to the only living son of his friend Agrippa I to succeed his father. Claudius, however, thought Agrippa

ACTS 25:13–26:32

II too young at age seventeen to immediately assume his father's position as client-king in the Jewish territories, but the emperor awarded him power incrementally. When Bernice's second husband died, Claudius
assigned the region of Chalcis to Agrippa II to rule (*War* 2.11.6). Later Agrippa II was assigned responsibility for the temple in Jerusalem, including the right to appoint the high priest of the Jews and the power to
call the Sanhedrin into session. Shortly afterwards, he received the right to rule Galilee and Perea as well
(*Ant* 20.8.4).

Bernice moved in with her brother, who never married, and assumed the role of his consort. Josephus
and others imply that their incestuous relationship caused a scandal even among their licentious peers (*Ant*
20.7.3; *Sat* 6). To squelch the rumors, Bernice persuaded Polemo, king of Cilicia, to be circumcised and
marry her. He agreed because of her riches, but the marriage did not last long. With her decision to leave
her husband, she also abandoned Judaism (*Ant* 20.7.3) and returned to live with her brother.

BERNICE'S APPEARANCE IN THE NEW TESTAMENT STORY

As consort and queen to her brother Agrippa II, Bernice makes her appearance in the New Testament.
During a visit to the Roman governor Festus in Caesarea on the Mediterranean coast, the royal couple
heard of a Christian Roman citizen imprisoned there. The apostle Paul had been arrested in Jerusalem
and taken to Caesarea, where Roman governors had detained him to avoid angering the Jewish Sanhedrin
(Acts 25:13–21).

Luke describes the scene when Agrippa and Bernice entered the court "with great pomp" along "with
the chief captains, and principal men of the city" (Acts 25:23). Festus ordered that Paul, imprisoned for his
testimony of Jesus Christ, be brought in to plead his case before these two Hellenized Jewish dignitaries.
Although arrogant and noncommittal, Bernice and Agrippa were nonetheless taken aback by Paul's delivery of his message, and they concluded that he was innocent of the charges made against him.

When Festus accused Paul of being "mad" for believing that Jesus Christ was resurrected and was a
light to both Jew and Gentile, the prisoner defended the truth. Paul then turned to Agrippa, saying, "For
the king knoweth of these things, before whom also I speak freely: for I am persuaded that none of these
things are hidden from him; for this thing was not done in a corner" (Acts 26:22–26). Paul's words imply
that Agrippa was already aware of Jewish witnesses of the resurrected Jesus, Jewish prophecies, and Jewish
laws pertaining to morality and justice. He may have been reminding Agrippa and Bernice of their responsibility to follow the customs they pretended to respect (Acts 26:2–3).

Agrippa's response in the King James Version, "Almost thou persuadest me to be a Christian," represents a missed opportunity to embrace truth that could have anchored the shifting morals of the
Herodians.[1] Of Agrippa's reaction, Elder Neal A. Maxwell observed: "Golden moments happen in many
ways and in many situations. They are caused and furthered under the direction of the Spirit. Such moments are usually framed in 'a tiny moment' of time but involve all eternity!"[2] Rather than face the protests

of angry Jews and upset the Roman status quo, like a reed shaken in the winds, Agrippa shifted responsibility to a higher court by returning to Paul's appeal to Caesar. Agrippa equivocated that had Paul not made the appeal, he would have set him free. Although Bernice's reaction is not recorded, she presumably agreed with her brother.

HISTORICAL POSTSCRIPT

In the days leading up to the First Jewish Revolt in A.D. 66, Bernice returned to Jerusalem to make a vow, similar to the Nazarite vow, according to which she would shave the hair of her head, abstain from wine, and offer sacrifice. The vow also necessitated that she remain in Jerusalem for thirty days. Upon her arrival, Bernice witnessed the widespread Roman barbarity incited by Florus, the new Roman governor over Judea, against Jewish revolutionaries who attempted to free Israel from Roman occupation (*War* 2.14.6–9).

According to Josephus, Bernice stood barefoot before Florus's tribunal and pleaded for mercy for the Jews. She begged him to stop the massacre and destruction, but he rebuffed her. Fearing that her own life was at risk, Bernice sought refuge in the Hasmonean palace in Jerusalem where she was protected by guards until her brother returned to the city (*War* 2.15.1–2).

With Bernice looking on from a palace window in the upper city of Jerusalem, Agrippa II made a lengthy speech to the Jews in an attempt to calm their desire for revenge against the Romans. He warned them that the outcome would be irreversible for Jews everywhere but especially in Jerusalem. He further told them that God condemned the immoral behavior of the Jewish rebels and would no longer fight with them, concluding, "Have pity, therefore, if not on your children and wives, yet upon this your metropolis, and its sacred walls; spare the Temple, and preserve the holy house, with its holy furniture, for yourselves; for if the Romans get you under their power, they will no longer abstain from them, when their former abstinences shall have been so ungratefully requited" (*War* 2.16.4). As Bernice and Agrippa wept, the revolutionaries temporarily ceased their rampage. Soon, however, the mob resumed their attacks and burned down the palaces of Bernice and Agrippa (*War* 2.16.5; 2.17.6).

Seeing that nothing would stop the uprising, Agrippa and Bernice withdrew and stood beside Vespasian, the Roman general, in the attacks in Galilee (*War* 3.9.8; 4.1.3). In Vespasian's bid for supreme power over the empire in A.D. 68, Bernice contributed financial support and gained his admiration. She also

Titus destroyed Jerusalem during the Jewish revolt of A.D. 70. The Herodian princess Bernice was his mistress until he became emperor of Rome in A.D. 79.

Photo by Kent P. Jackson

attracted the romantic attention of Vespasian's son Titus (*Hist* 2.2, 81). Although he was ten years younger than she, the relationship lasted for years (*Tit* 7).

Bernice, daughter of Herod Agrippa I and great-granddaughter of Herod the Great, might have become empress of Rome as the wife of Titus but for her Jewish nationality and the anti-Jewish sentiment in Rome at the time. Bernice did not join Titus in Rome until A.D. 75. It was generally assumed that Titus would soon marry her (*Tit* 7), and Bernice tried to hasten the event. When she publicly presented herself as his wife, however, Titus ended their relationship because of Roman dislike of the Jews (*Hist Rom* 66.15).

After news came of the death of Vespasian in A.D. 79 and Titus emerged as the new emperor, Bernice returned to Rome in the hope of sharing the imperial throne with him. Said to be more wise in his judgment after coming to the throne than he ever was before, Titus sent Bernice away, albeit reluctantly (*Hist Rom* 66.18). Titus died after two years as emperor and was remembered for ruling in "mildness"; he "died at the height of his glory" (*Hist Rom* 66.18).

An inscription in Athens bears the name "Bernice" and calls her "queen," indicating that she was recognized as a Jewish client-queen beside her brother, Agrippa II. She likely forged connections with the city of Athens in her frequent travels between the Jewish territories and Rome. Nothing more is known of Bernice after her hopes of marriage to Titus failed.

POINTS TO PONDER

1. How may these Herodian women inspire us to positively influence public discourse and decisions?

2. Drusilla reacted to Bernice's cruelty toward her out of jealousy for her beauty. Are relationships in your life being harmed by allowing jealousy to color your perceptions and reactions?

3. Although Bernice failed to embrace the testimony of Paul, she manifested genuine concern for the Jewish people and risked her life in an effort to save them. How does that action inspire you to find hidden qualities of goodness in those who initially appear to have none?

4. How are the examples of the Herodian women meaningful in illustrating the potential dangers inherent in attaining public prominence?

5. What value do you find in the inclusion of Herodian women in the New Testament account? Collectively and individually, what do these women teach us?

WOMEN IN GRECO-ROMAN SOCIETY

$\mathcal{A}$fter Peter received the revelation to regard people of all nations as acceptable to God (Acts 10), the Greco-Roman world beyond the Jewish synagogues was opened for missionary labors. The Romans welcomed the complex variety of cultures, languages, and beliefs that accompanied a diverse population and exhibited a remarkable tolerance toward the Jews wherever they lived. The special privileges afforded Jews translated into freedoms for early Christians in their initial efforts to take the gospel to the "uttermost part of the earth" (Acts 1:8).

Greco-Roman society featured a strict social hierarchy, including formal patron-client relationships, expectations for women to become wives and mothers, and expanding freedoms for women in public life, particularly in comparison to the Holy Land. Those opportunities extended to women receiving some education when their occupation or station warranted it. The diversity of cultural backgrounds and perceptions of women's roles in society and in the church created unprecedented challenges as well as greater stability and power to cement the foundation of Christianity.

THE LAND OF THE ROMAN EMPIRE

By the early first century, the Roman empire covered some 2.2 million square miles over a swath of the world from Spain to Israel, a breadth of geography comparable to the lower forty-eight states in the United States that covers some 3 million square miles. An extensive and well-built road system and reliable maritime transportation made all points of the empire accessible and affordable for even the lower classes. Establishing the *Pax Romana* ("Roman peace"), Augustus Caesar (27 B.C.–A.D. 14) enacted laws to ensure peaceful coexistence among the diverse peoples within the empire.

Although most of our knowledge of the Greco-Roman world of the first century A.D. comes from accounts of city life, no more than 7 percent of the total population lived in cities.[1] Rome was the largest city in the empire with a population of over 1 million, followed by Alexandria in Egypt, whose population neared 600,000; Carthage in northern Africa and Antioch in Syria each had a population of around 500,000; and Ephesus, on the western coast of Asia Minor, had some 400,000 residents.

A maze of narrow, winding streets was commonplace in such older cities as Jerusalem and Damascus, but newer cities were laid out with a grid of much wider streets crossing at right angles. Nearly a quarter of the land incorporated into a newer Greco-Roman city was reserved for public space. A main street called the *cardo,* often with colonnades and awnings for shade over the various shops that lined the street, and a central marketplace called the *agora* were standard features of these cities. Also important to the cities were temples, shrines, monuments to important statesmen or heroes, theaters, gymnasiums, and civic centers.

Aqueducts delivered fresh spring water to public fountains, baths, and homes of the wealthy. The city of Rome in the first century boasted more than two hundred public baths, accessible to all classes. Public baths were a popular place for socializing and conducting business among Greco-Romans but would have been offensive to observant Jews.

Photo by Kent P. Jackson

The Upper Cardo in Jerusalem. The Romans rebuilt parts of Jerusalem after the A.D. 70 destruction, including a cardo, whose remains are still visible at the southern end of the city.

The Roman agora in Athens was built east of the ancient agora and included a large concert hall (odeion) and a temple to Ares. It became the new place for assemblies in the city.

THE PEOPLE OF THE ROMAN EMPIRE

By New Testament times, the Roman empire had become a confluence of multiple races, cultures, and belief systems among some fifty to sixty million people. Despite the variations in language and customs from region to region in the empire, some common cultural patterns were evident throughout.

A common language was a unifying factor within the empire. With the spread of Hellenism under Alexander the Great (332 B.C.), Greek had become the *lingua franca* in the East. Despite the widespread use of Greek, the New Testament suggests that local languages did not disappear from among the Jews living throughout the empire. On the day of Pentecost shortly after the Resurrection of Jesus Christ, Luke refers to the multiplicity of languages spoken among the Jews (Acts 2:5–11). Over five hundred inscriptions from early Jewish catacombs in Rome indicate that most Roman Jews spoke Greek, with a smaller proportion using Latin. The inscriptions also reveal all levels of literacy skills among Roman Jews, of whom a significant number had little or no education.[2]

Proper names of Jews in ancient Rome indicate that they assimilated with their pagan neighbors more than one might have imagined. Although Semitic names were not uncommon, the catacombs disclose that Jewish girls were often given Latin names that were current among the Romans. Semitic names were adapted or translated into Latin or Greek, such as Annia (from Hannah) or Aster (from Esther), or some Jewish girls received names derived from those of such pagan goddesses as Aphrodisia or Isidora.[3]

Referred to as the Jewish diaspora, populations of Jews began spreading beyond their native land in the centuries before Jesus was born. After the Assyrian invasion in 722 B.C. and the Babylonian captivity in 586 B.C., many Jews relocated to Alexandria for economic reasons. In 63 B.C., the Roman general Pompey sent many Jews to Rome as slaves. By the time of Christ, more Jews lived outside their homeland than in it; about 50,000 Jews lived in the city of Rome itself.[4] Most of the dispersed Jews lived in Greek-speaking cities, with 200,000 in Alexandria constituting the largest population of Jews in one city. Presumably, Joseph and Mary would have found refuge in such a Jewish community when they fled to Egypt with the baby Jesus to escape Herod's edict (Matt. 2:13–15).

Life expectancy increased in the Roman empire due to prolonged times of peace, even though a relatively high infant and child mortality and serious diseases kept death a constant reality for even the wealthiest Romans. Approximately a third of children died before they reached ten years of age, in contrast to other preindustrial societies in which nearly half the children died before age five.[5] A sharp increase in mortality for women between ages fifteen and twenty-nine indicates the high death rate associated with childbirth.[6] If a woman survived until menopause, she was almost certainly a widow and would have given birth to about six live children in order to leave behind two surviving descendants.[7] Overall, the average lifespan is estimated to have been under thirty years for both men and women.

RELIGIOUS TOLERANCE FOR JEWS

Romans, like the Greeks and Persians before them, were remarkably tolerant of other religions, unless they feared that a particular religion threatened their native culture and the empire's peace. Furthermore, individual cultural or racial groups freely adopted customs from other groups in the empire. For example, according to Josephus such Jewish customs as fasting, Sabbath observance, and abstinence from certain foods were adopted by many non-Jews (*Apion* 2.40).[8]

Jews in particular received special privileges in the late Roman republic by decree from Julius Caesar. A brief history of how such preferential treatment was won is important background for understanding the New Testament. By the middle of the first century B.C., a Jewish community in Rome was already politically influential when Julius Caesar contested with Pompey for supreme power over the empire. Roman Jews were "wholeheartedly on Caesar's side," mainly because Pompey was the general who attacked Jerusalem in 63 B.C. and desecrated the temple by entering the Holy of Holies.[9] In return for their support in his victory, Caesar conspicuously awarded special rights and liberties to Jews throughout the empire.

Privileges for the Jews throughout the empire included full freedom of worship, including assembly for religious purposes, Sabbath day observance, rights to raise money for maintenance of Jerusalem and the temple, exemption from compulsory military service, and permission to use Jewish courts of law as a legal substitute for Roman courts (*Ant* 10.14.1–26). Subsequently, large numbers of Jews relocated to Rome to enjoy the protection the government afforded while at the same time retaining their religious distinction. Caesar's successors largely continued these policies favorable to Jews (*Embassy* 157–59).

Because of their special status, Jewish congregations were found throughout the empire and were free to aggressively seek converts to their unique beliefs and practices. A number of prominent Romans and "high-born ladies" became proselytes of Judaism and opened the door for Christianity (Horace, *Sat* 1.4.140–43; Origen, *Cels* 3.9).[10] Even in Ephesus, where the Greek fertility goddess Artemis, or Diana, as she was called by the Romans, was the patron deity, Christian missionaries such as Prisca preached the gospel and established a vibrant branch of the church. Thessalonica, the trade center of Macedonia with a population of 200,000, retained a strong Greek culture, a cult of the god Dionysus, a cult of the Egyptian deities Isis and Serapis, and a significant Jewish synagogue in the city. Yet Christians found success in missionary efforts there, including "chief women not a few" among their converts (Acts 17:4).

Initially, Romans viewed Christians as part of Judaism and afforded them the same tolerance they gave to the Jews. By the reigns of Domitian (A.D. 81–96) and Trajan (A.D. 98–117), however, Christianity had become viewed as a threat to peace in the empire, and tolerance for Christians was replaced with a test of loyalty. Residents were required to worship the emperor, a requirement that would ferret out clandestine Christians, who would refuse to comply.[11]

SOCIAL HIERARCHY

Social order and class were well defined throughout the Roman empire. Status took into consideration wealth, education, citizenship, patron or client class, free or slave, male or female, married or unmarried, and whether a person voluntarily aligned himself to Rome or was conquered.[12] A middle class was practically nonexistent, except for a very few of the lesser elites, who were referred to as the "respectable

Travel was relatively accessible and affordable for anyone living within the Roman empire during the first century A.D. due to the sophisticated network of fifty thousand miles of roads that connected the various regions, and boats of all types sailed to the various ports around the Mediterranean. Travel within the empire was also comparatively safe because the *Pax Romana* had reduced piracy on the seas, robbery on the roads, and military threats at the borders. Many segments of these ancient roads survive today, a testament to superior Roman engineering and construction.

populace." Wealth, family connections, and community figured far more prominently in determining social status than gender.

The patron-client system. The elite in society retained their exclusive status in part by a two-party system that assigned either a patron or a client role in every relationship. The patron wielded more power and status than his or her clients and provided them legal protection and even financial support at times. In return, the client was expected to show gratitude and honor to the patron by supporting any political action the patron embraced. Not surprisingly, because the elite controlled most of the resources and power, they were always the patron in a relationship with anyone in a lower class.

Patrons received tangible benefits for assisting clients, including the confidence that their clients would support them in elections for public office or erect monuments to honor them. Similarly, one could not secure a loan, Roman citizenship, property, or receive support to pursue the arts or a public office without the backing of a patron. Clients rendered free services to their patrons, publicly attested to their patron's wealth and power, and never sued their patrons. Women could serve as patrons as readily as could men as will be shown from New Testament examples. Acting as patroness allowed women wider involvement in most social levels of society and opportunities for contributions in economic, cultural, religious, and political arenas. Although important to solidifying class divisions, "the institution of patronage was in many respects gender-blind."[13]

Patricians. Most Roman aristocrats, called patricians, owed their wealth to land ownership. The top 1 percent of society was made up of the senator, equestrian, and decurion classes. Evidence suggests that Phebe and Prisca belonged among the upper classes, probably in the decurion order or among the rich *liberti,* or "rich freedmen."

Rich freedmen. Former slaves who had been granted Roman citizenship and succeeded in accumulating a measure of wealth were considered more respectable than the lower classes. The taint of their slave origins, however, kept them from the decurion class.[14] The upper classes looked down on this group because, in comparison to the upper 1 percent, craftsmen and craftswomen performed work that could and often was done by slaves.[15]

Plebeians (plebs). The lower class made up the remaining 99 percent of society and bore the burden of producing the necessities for their own survival and paying the heavy taxes that enabled the minority elite to enjoy a life of luxury and ease. Plebs often found it necessary to form *collegia,* or collective associations, to participate in the societal network and develop leverage and collective bargaining power in society. These organizations, usually numbering between forty and three hundred members, were formed by individuals with similar interests or trades. The *collegia* functioned much like trade guilds, or unions, which looked after the needs of their members in exchange for regular dues.[16]

Because of the overwhelming number of plebs, they were subdivided within their class. On the higher end were peasant farmers, artisans, or traders in small ventures in the villages. Artists, scientists, and

ROMAN CITIZENSHIP

Only about five million of the more than fifty million inhabitants of the empire in the first century were "free and full Roman citizens."[17] Apart from cities in Italy, no city in the empire, including Roman colonies, had a majority of the population that were Roman citizens. In principle, a knowledge of Latin was a requirement for citizenship.[18]

A person could become a citizen in a variety of ways. Being born to a citizen father was the most prestigious way to receive citizenship, but some citizens were awarded citizenship following an impressive display of loyalty to Rome, after discharge from the military, and in conjunction with manumission from slavery if the candidate was in service to one of the upper class with citizenship. Purchasing citizenship also occurred, but it was the least meritorious way to receive it, especially when it was granted by an unscrupulous governor who personally profited from the exchange.

Roman citizenship offered significant benefits, chief among them exemption from paying property tax and the tribute tax to Rome. They also had full legal protection, including immunity from being beaten without a trial and torture as a form of punishment, the right to appeal to a higher court, and safety measures when making legal contracts. As an example of a citizen's privileges, the murder of a citizen would be investigated by the authorities but not the murder of a noncitizen.[19]

Beginning in A.D. 4, the Roman state established a system to register citizens at birth in an official log. When soldiers were granted citizenship, they were given a certificate much like an identity card today. Others with citizen status may have received a letter, signed by the emperor, which recognized the bearer as a citizen.[20]

HOMES OF THE POOR

First-century houses were built of adobe and covered with plaster, typically with a single story that opened onto a courtyard. Wealthier Greeks had homes with more than one story, walls decorated with paintings or mosaics depicting pastoral and mythological scenes, and floors covered with mosaic tiles. Apparently, a few early Christians had homes large enough to accommodate meetings of "the whole church" of Christians in their area (see Rom. 16:23; Philem. 1:22).

By the first century, most people in large cities lived in crowded, poorly ventilated, multistoried apartment buildings, called *insulae*, which were built around a common courtyard. Individual domiciles within the *insulae* consisted of one or two rooms. Because stairs were the only way to access higher floors, the first floor was the most expensive and desirable in the building. Apartments generally did not have kitchens, so residents cooked on a brazier near an outside opening or purchased food from city vendors. Toilet facilities in the *insulae* were chamber pots located in small spaces under the building's stairs or public latrines in the city. Those living in apartments on the upper floors often threw waste out their window to the street below, adding to the odors and detritus that permeated the big cities.[21] Plebeians washed in public baths or went without bathing. Most city-dwelling Christians of the first century probably lived in one of these small apartments, in the home of their master or former master, or in a room behind their place of business.

The poor spent nearly all their waking hours outside their homes and in the streets. Privacy was a luxury, and disease was unavoidable. Pleasant aromas, such as those from bread baking, would be overwhelmed by the stench of wet garbage, animal and human waste, rotting fish and meat, and sweat from masses of people living in close proximity. Juvenal commented that sleep was impossible in such neighborhoods (*Sat* 3.232–38). Merchants kept their businesses opened until sundown and tried to be home by dark for safety. Soldiers who patrolled the streets were primarily concerned for the safety of the wealthy residents and their property, and the poor were often left to fend for themselves when the criminal element emerged at night.

doctors were not highly regarded by the elite because their work focused on the private realm rather than public policy. Artists in particular had lower status because Greek slaves produced most of the works of art in the first century A.D.

The lowest of the plebeians included such entertainers as gladiators, athletes, and actors, all of whom were barred from holding public office and had few legal protections. Although women athletes were honored in the Greek territories, as is evidenced in an inscription from A.D. 45 that lauds victorious women in foot races and maybe even chariot racing at the Greek games,[22] they were nonetheless considered plebs, in sharp contrast to the high value society places on professional athletes and actors today.

GRECO-ROMAN WOMEN AT HOME

After Augustus's domestic policies were enacted in 18 B.C., marriage officially began when the wife commenced living in her husband's home rather than with a formal marriage ceremony. According to this legislation, for a Roman marriage to be considered legal, both parties had to be citizens, have free status, be of legal age, and have familial consent. For the Romans, marrying for love or physical attraction was irresponsible.[23] Men are described in early Roman literature as more likely loving women who were not their wives.[24]

Roman law and behavior codes were addressed to adult men, as heads of their households. Women and children were referred to in third person. The wife's performance of her extensive duties was subject to the husband's approval, as Arius Didymus observed in a letter to Caesar Augustus: a "man by nature has rule over [his household]. For the deliberative element [or faculty] is worse in a woman, is not yet in children, and is not at all in slaves"(*Ethics* 149.5). An outgrowth of this perspective allowed a man to prosecute his unfaithful fiancée or wife, while not being required to remain faithful to her.

Children. The birth of a boy was celebrated on the eighth day after his birth and of a girl on the ninth day by officially naming them and welcoming them into the family.[25] Pagan writers were condescending toward Jews because, unlike the Romans, Jews tended to have larger families and reared all their children.[26] Wealthy Romans may have preferred fewer children in order to keep an estate intact for the next generation, and fewer children among poor Romans resulted from concerns over feeding a large family and adequately equipping children to succeed in adulthood.[27]

Age at marriage. Women in Roman society could marry as young as twelve years old, which was legally determined to be the age of puberty, even though not all young brides were yet sufficiently physically mature for marriage. The larger issue was therefore not the girl's physical readiness but that Roman men desired brides who were "pure and undefiled in body and mind when their husbands took them."[28] Not all Roman girls married young, however. Some waited until their late teens or even early twenties to marry, especially in the larger cities. Most important in arranging a marriage was consideration of financial and political gain to ensure an estate for one's posterity. Consequently, husbands were usually in the early stages of their careers and typically older than their wives, usually between two and thirteen years older, with about a quarter of young brides marrying men twenty or thirty years older than themselves—the same generation as their fathers.[29]

Wedding customs. Weddings in the first century A.D. usually included a banquet after the wedding party accompanied the bride and groom from the bride's family home to the groom's house. One account describes the bridal party when they arrive at the new home: the bride anointed the door posts with fragrant oils and the groom lifted the bride over the threshold. Then he ceremonially offered his wife fire and water as symbols of her authority over the domestic realm.[30]

Valued characteristics in a wife. For many aristocratic men, the ideal woman's most noble characteristics revolved around being demure, quiet, and efficient. Some men considered women their equals only if women submitted to them (Martial, *Epig* 8.12). Pliny the Younger applauded the emperor Trajan for his wife's visible virtues of modesty and obedience, giving credit to the husband "who has fashioned and formed her habits" (*Pan* 83.5–8). One of the early Christian fathers, Tertullian, assumed in his day that "a female would rather see than be seen" (*Virg* 17). Juvenal described the ideal Roman wife as one who did not cheat on her husband but tolerated his extramarital affairs, who did not reject his friends, who did not abandon his gods for foreign religions, who did not make a public spectacle of herself, and who managed his household well (*Sat* 6). In view of such expectations, a wife who became a Christian would create serious family conflicts.

GRECO-ROMAN WOMEN IN PUBLIC LIFE

By New Testament times, the classical Greek custom that valued the seclusion of women in the home was beginning to change.[31] Typically, however, the farther east one traveled from Rome, the less freedom women were allowed. For example, under the reign of Claudius (A.D. 41–54), laws were amended to allow citizen women to freely administer their own property after the death of their fathers. By comparison, women in Greece continued to be subject to male guardianship of their inheritance.[32] Jews living amid Greco-Romans likely assimilated into the more liberal culture than did those living in the Jewish territories, where a number of Jewish groups resisted encroaching Hellenistic mores. The threat of losing their unique identity as God's chosen people made many Jewish religious leaders suspicious of outside influences.

Notwithstanding the greater freedoms afforded women in Roman-influenced cities, some literary and philosophical leaders sought to return women to traditional roles identified with home and family and away from public discourse and the public eye.

EDUCATION FOR WOMEN

Formal education and expectations for literacy were not considered essential for most women and men in the empire. Except for Greek, Latin, and to a lesser extent Hebrew, none of the dozen or so languages spoken within the empire were used in written form. Even though most Greek or Hellenistic cities supported at least one school, schools were small and rarely employed more than a few teachers at once.[33] Teachers were often freedmen or slaves and not highly regarded among the elite (Suetonius, *Gram* 17; Pliny, *Ep* 3.3.3). School supplies were also expensive, especially paper. Wooden tablets covered with a layer of wax were preferred for school exercises, business documents, and letters because they could be reused. Given that there was no incentive for laborers to obtain an education, literacy remained low among the general populace and was slow to spread even among the elites.

The spoken word retained tremendous value for the educated, and oratory was more respected than writing. Similarly, learning to speak Greek or Latin was important to those who desired greater social or political prestige, were involved in commerce, or hoped to gain a better position as a slave.[34] Furthermore, engaging in written communication did not require literary skills. An author could assign a slave to do the actual writing by dictating the message. Similarly, one did not have to be literate to engage in legal agreements as there were those trained and hired to assist. Evidence of written communications by women in Rome, Egypt, and elsewhere in the empire prove that women were among the literate, but such a skill was rare. More than social rank or wealth, one's occupation determined literacy.

Considering that girls married young, even those who did attend school or were tutored at home were frequently educated at only a rudimentary level. Until they turned fourteen, boys and girls from wealthy families were educated together. Afterwards, boys began specializing in skills for a public career, such as public speaking, and girls usually returned home to prepare for marriage.

Some educated men stressed the importance of educating women and argued for elevating women to equal social status with men.[35] For example, the philosopher Seneca believed that women have the "same inner force, and the same capacity for nobleness as men."[36] The physician Soranus recommended that midwives be literate so as to study others' theories and experiences and thereby add to their own expertise (*Gyn* 1.3). Medical knowledge in antiquity was more likely to be transmitted through written works rather than by oral teaching.[37]

Not all men were as generous in their attitudes towards educated women, however.[38] Pliny the Younger reflects his conformity to the patriarchal ideal in restricting women's education when he stated his pride for his wife who remained silent and hidden while she watched his public display of intellect: "If I am giving a reading she sits behind a curtain nearby and drinks in every word of appreciation" (*Ep* 4.19). Juvenal opposed educating women because of his perception that education had an erosive power on marriages. In a long poem highlighting female faults, he denigrated Roman women who knew Greek and debated with men about social and political issues. He was disgusted by women whose education was superior to that of their husbands, especially female grammarians: "I hate the woman who . . . observes all the rules and laws of language, who like an antiquary quotes verses that I never heard of, and corrects

Replica of a wax tablet like those used by schoolchildren to practice their writing. The impression of a seal is also shown.

her unlettered female friends for slips of speech that no man need trouble about: let husbands at least be permitted to make slips in grammar!" (*Sat* 6.434–456).

Among educated women of the time were writers, poets, and historians.[39] Women of high status could be heads of households, painters, philosophers, and lawyers. A first-century Jewish woman named Mary was reputed to be one of the most accomplished scientists of the ancient world. Her skills and some of her experiments as an alchemist were preserved in a third-century encyclopedia of scientific knowledge, including many procedures that were advanced for that time. The French word for the double boiler, *bain-marie,* uses her name in a modern reminder of this woman's scientific contributions.[40]

CHRISTIAN WOMEN

Evidence of success in attracting women from diverse social backgrounds in Greco-Roman society to belief in Christ is abundantly apparent in the New Testament. Their diversity in cultural and religious background reflected the melting pot of typical Greco-Roman cities. By contrast to the strict societal hierarchy in Greco-Roman culture, Christian communities described in the New Testament did not follow class divisions. Some Christians, for example, were slaves or former slaves, and few had much status in their cities, let alone citizenship.

The apostle Paul saw the strength of the church not in divisions or hierarchies but in sharing God-given gifts with others. God gave women a variety of gifts as he did men, and the congregation was stronger and more whole when they each contributed (1 Cor. 12:12–13). Women were allowed to pray and prophesy in Christian worship meetings (1 Cor. 11:5), study the scriptures daily (Acts 17:11–12), be baptized without their husbands' approval (1 Cor. 7:13), and serve as traveling missionaries, teachers, and co-workers with Paul. Because Christian women were educated in the scriptures and served in visible leadership roles, other women would have been attracted to the faith, regardless of their religious or social backgrounds.

In contrast to the Roman model of the family in which the husband retains the authority and deciding power in the family, Christian teachings included mutual affection, cooperation, and responsibility between the husband and the wife. Paul placed limitations on the husband's authority over his wife when he wrote to men, "Love your wives, even as Christ also loved the church, and gave himself for it . . . so ought men to love their wives as their own bodies" (Eph. 5:25, 28; 1 Cor. 7:1–5).

In concert with the teachings of Christ, a Christian bishop in Alexandria named Clement wrote: "As far as respects human nature, the woman does not possess one nature, and the man exhibit another, but the same; so also with virtue. If . . . self-restraint and righteousness, and whatever qualities are regarded as following them, is the virtue of the male, it belongs to the male alone to be virtuous, and to the woman to be licentious and unjust. But it is offensive even to say this. Accordingly woman is to practice self-restraint and righteousness, and every other virtue, as well as man, both bond and free; since it is a fit consequence that the same nature possesses one and the same virtue" (*Misc* 4.8.58–60).[41]

With the successful spread of Christianity in such areas as Ephesus, Corinth, and Philippi, church leaders encountered different challenges among their female converts, depending on the women's religious background. Apparently, some Gentile Christian women overstepped the bounds of their newly acquired roles. A few appeared immodest in their hairstyles, and others spoke out in tongues without translation, perhaps attempting to "rule" or take over during church services, thereby causing conflict and contention in the meeting (JST, 1 Cor. 14:34; 1 Cor. 11:5). Considering that some among them were repentant prostitutes (1 Cor. 6:9–20) whereas others were respectable and wealthy patronesses (Acts 13:50; 17:12; Rom.

16:1–2), one may imagine the growing pains experienced as a novice congregation practiced conducting worship services by the Spirit so that "all things be done decently and in order" (1 Cor. 14:40).

Add to the mix Christian women with pagan backgrounds and Jewish Christian men who had been called as leaders but who may have found equality with women still somewhat uncomfortable, considering the prevalent rabbinic views of women with which they had grown up. Although the specifics surrounding Paul's concerns about women are unknown, one senses a clash of cultures and religious backgrounds as Christian converts tried to carve out a new collective identity.

Useful lessons are evident from the accounts of specific women of the New Testament who accepted the gospel of Jesus Christ in a more liberal Hellenistic environment than when the early Christian church remained within the shadow of Judaism. We begin with the Syrophoenician woman and her daughter who encountered Jesus in their Gentile community and then turn, in roughly chronological order, to those to whom Paul introduces us: Eunice and Lois, Lydia, the unnamed Philippian soothsayer, Phebe, Prisca (or Priscilla) and her husband, Aquila, and Christian women in Rome.

Blessed Are the Meek

by Elspeth Young

THE SYROPHOENICIAN WOMAN

The first recorded instance of Jesus taking his gospel to anyone other than the children of Israel is his healing of a Gentile girl at the request of her mother. The mother, not known by her name or the name of a husband or son, is described by where she resided, which indicates her ethnicity, culture, and religion. According to Mark, she was "a Greek, a Syrophenician by nation," which means she was a Gentile, an outsider from the Jews (Mark 7:26). Focused on his Jewish audience, Matthew used an Old Testament label for the woman: he called her "a woman of Canaan" (Matt. 15:22), probably because Phoenicians were descendants of the Old Testament Canaanites. Thus, the Syrophoenician was a triple outsider—a woman, of an outside race, and from an outside religious tradition.[1] Compounding these marks of undesirability, her daughter was possessed by an unclean spirit, increasing her impurity in the eyes of Jews.

THE SYROPHOENICIAN WOMAN'S PLACE OF RESIDENCE

In a rare departure from the Jewish territories, Jesus took his apostles to Gentile territory along the Phoenician coast of Syria, in what is today called Lebanon. Matthew and Mark both relate that he found a place to stay in the area around Tyre and Sidon but do not specify the village (Matt. 15:21; Mark 7:24). In the first century, Tyre and Sidon were prosperous port cities. Tyre had become a Roman colony, and Sidon, some twenty miles up the coast, was under Rome's direct rule. Neither of these areas had large populations, and both were flanked by numerous smaller villages. It is likely the Syrophoenician woman lived in one of the numerous Syrian villages closer to Tyre that was ignored by the Romans and their military.

Because of the military importance of the region, by A.D. 23 Rome had stationed four legions of soldiers in Syria to defend against invasion from the Parthians east of the Euphrates River.[2] Rome's military presence in Syria guarded against revolts in any of the independent kingdoms in the region, including Emesa, north of Damascus; Palmyra, east of Damascus; and the

MATTHEW 15:21–28
MARK 7:24–30

267

Syrophoenician landscape. More people lived in one of the numerous small villages in the Syrophoenician countryside than in large cities, such as Antioch or Tyre.

Jewish territories, south of Damascus. The principal city of Syria was Antioch, the third largest city in the empire (behind Rome and Alexandria) with approximately 500,000 inhabitants.

THE SYROPHOENICIAN WOMAN'S DAILY WORK

The scriptures do not record anything about the Syrophoenician's livelihood, but it is known that Syria produced leather, wine, and linen. Purple dye and cloth were known to have been made in Tyre.[3] The coastal area had always been prime real estate for trade by land and by sea. The Syrophoenician woman could have been involved in any of these industries, but her primary concern was her daughter. Caring for the needs of the afflicted girl may have taken most of her time and effort. When she left her daughter and went to find Jesus and plead for help, the woman may have experienced added stress if the girl had to be left alone.

HISTORICAL CONTEXT

The Savior's encounter with the Syrophoenician woman probably occurred at the beginning of the third and final year of his ministry. Upon leaving the coastal area, he passed through other Gentile villages in the area of Decapolis (Mark 7:31) before performing the miraculous feeding of the four thousand (Matt. 15:32–38; Mark 8:1–9). In contrast to the feeding of the five thousand, which occurred in the Jewish territory of Galilee, the feeding of the four thousand can be understood to have included Gentiles. Although the time to take the gospel directly to the Gentiles had not yet come, Jesus taught his disciples that peoples "of every kind" would be gathered into the gospel net (Matt. 13:47).

Why Jesus traveled to the Phoenician coast is not explained, but the implication is that he did not go to teach the Gentiles his gospel. He may have left the Jewish territories for a respite and to teach the Twelve without interruption by the Jewish multitudes. Upon his arrival at the Gentile coast, underscoring his desire to be secluded, he "entered into an house, and would that no man should come unto him" (JST, Mark 7:24).

Into this private world of the Son of God burst the Syrophoenician woman. Her bold interruption was fueled not by idle curiosity or her own needs but by a desperate desire to save her daughter.

THE SYROPHOENICIAN WOMAN'S APPEARANCE IN THE NEW TESTAMENT STORY

Both Matthew and Mark record the woman's side of her discussion with Jesus, a perspective often omitted in scriptural stories of women: "For a certain woman, whose young daughter had an unclean spirit, heard of him, and came and fell at his feet" (Mark 7:25) and "cried unto him . . . O Lord, thou Son of David; my daughter is grievously vexed with a devil" (Matt. 15:22). Although the woman was probably more often at home caring for her daughter than out in public, she had somehow "heard of him" and learned about his power to heal. Matthew indicates that the woman even shouted or "cried" out after him to draw the Savior's attention, which prompted his disciples to urge him to send her away (Matt. 15:22–23). This woman, however, would neither turn away nor be silent. Her request for help, "O Lord, thou Son of David," was in the form of a prayer. Like desperate mothers in any era, her concern was for her afflicted daughter, and she was willing to do whatever she could to secure her only hope of saving her daughter.

The Savior first ignored her, then told her that his mission was to Israel only, and finally said that she was not fit for the feast prepared for the lost sheep of Israel (Matt. 15:23–26). It appeared that he meant to deny the woman's request, although she had approached him with greater respect and faith than did most of the Jews. His disciples reproached her, trying to protect their Master from her persistent pleas. In a stunning show of fortitude and faith, she refused to accept his rejection and instead "worshipped him," trusting in the knowledge she had gained of him before she ever met him (Matt. 15:25).

Three times Jesus declined her request on behalf of her daughter. His third objection was a proverb: "Let the children of the kingdom first be filled; for it is not meet to take the children's bread, and to cast it unto the dogs" (JST, Mark 7:27). Jews were prone to label non-Jews as Greeks, pagans, sinners, and even dogs because they were seen as "not yet matured, prepared, and worthy to receive" God's word.[4] In what is easily recognized as

Roman ruins in Tyre.

Tyre in the first century A.D. was a prosperous port city and a Roman colony.

an ethnic insult, no doubt often heard along the areas bordering the Jewish territories, it is shocking and disconcerting to consider the Savior saying that his gospel was not yet available to this pleading woman, a "dog." Jehovah had promised Old Testament prophets that his gospel would go first to the children of Abraham and only afterwards to the Gentiles (Abr. 2:8–11). Rather than hearing the gospel directly from the Lord, Gentiles would hear it though the preaching of the disciples of Christ and through the witness of the Holy Ghost (3 Ne. 15:21–23).

Despite the pain and humiliation this exchange must have created in the woman, she did not slacken her efforts. In a manner that was at once humble and assertive, both witty and profoundly serious, she claimed only the crumbs: "Truth, Lord: yet the dogs eat of the crumbs which fall from their masters' table" (Matt. 15:27). Her words call to mind the remnants that were carefully gathered after the Savior miraculously fed the multitudes (John 6:12–13; Matt. 14:20; Mark 8:19–20) and the morsels we share during the sacrament of the Lord's Supper as a reminder of the covenant we make when we become spiritually begotten as sons and daughters of Christ (Mosiah 5:7–8).[5]

Jesus' reaction indicates that he was not offended by her refusal to back down and go away. He did not scold her for being disrespectful and presumptuous. Instead, he blessed her for having unwavering faith—but only after that faith had been sufficiently tried. Nonetheless, the woman's unshakeable hope seems to have amazed even the Savior. "O woman," he responded, "great is thy faith: be it unto thee even as thou wilt" (Matt. 15:28). This woman's exemplary belief and commitment caused the Savior to make an exception to his promise to Father Abraham. His response also underscores his boundless love for all God's children. Even when he sought privacy in a nation of idol worshippers, "he could not deny [those who petitioned him]; for he had compassion upon all men" (JST, Mark 7:24).

BETWEEN THE LINES

The Syrophoenician has been likened to Rahab because she "takes the initiative and asks boldly for the kindness she so desperately needs . . . , receives the mercy for which she had asked . . . , and . . . like Rahab, because of her faith she is a first exception to the rule about Canaanites" being invited into the covenant of God.[6] Just as other Gentiles joined Israel as Rahab did, so would innumerable Gentiles become stalwart Christian disciples after the example of the Syrophoenician.

At another time in his ministry, Jesus taught a crowd of Jews in Galilee that it would be more tolerable for people in Tyre and Sidon at the Day of Judgment than for them because Syrophoenicians were more likely to repent after seeing so many miracles (Matt. 1:21–22; Luke 10:13–14). Certainly, this woman bears out that teaching. Her faith transcended the ethnic and religious differences that defined her and her Healer. With an eye of faith, she saw beyond current conditions and refused to be offended by what clearly appeared to be discriminatory practices to claim inclusion within the family of Christ.

The description of the woman's expanding faith and her exchange with Jesus is the focus of the scriptural account rather than the actual healing of the daughter. The scriptures simply report that upon hearing the Savior's exclamation about her faith, the Syrophoenician knew that her prayer for her daughter was answered. "And her daughter was made whole from that very hour" (Matt. 15:28). Before returning home to see the physical evidence that her daughter was restored to health, she knew the girl "was made whole," another testament of faith in that which is true but is not seen.

The Syrophoenician's daughter was not the only one healed in this story. By being completely selfless and entirely open to her need for the Redeemer, the mother was also blessed and healed, even before she knew that she too needed the Physician. By having her faith in Christ so tried and recognizing that her love for the Savior surpassed any other consideration, she was strengthened spiritually and emotionally to withstand subsequent challenges as a lone disciple of Jesus Christ in her community. It would be a decade or more before missionaries took the gospel to other Gentiles in her area. But the brief encounter between Jesus and this Gentile woman gives us a glimpse of miraculous consequences that would result from the Lord's revelation to Peter to expand the gospel's reach to all kindreds, tongues, and peoples (Acts 10). By being stripped of pride and void of offense, the Syrophoenician woman provides a powerful example of unquenchable faith and hope.

POINTS TO PONDER

1. Why do individuals who were outside the household of faith often become some of the greatest exemplars of Christian living? Why would Jesus note that it would be more tolerable for Gentiles in Tyre and Sidon at the Day of Judgment than for the "children of the kingdom" who had long been surrounded by God's truth?

2. How does the Syrophoenician woman strengthen your resolve to refuse to take offense from what others say about you?

Established in the Faith

BY ELSPETH YOUNG

EUNICE AND LOIS

Εὐνίκη

"Good or happy victory"
(Greek)

Λωΐς

"More pleasant or
more desirable" (Greek)

The scriptures name Eunice and her mother, Lois, in the last letter that Paul wrote before his death (2 Tim. 1:5). In giving encouragement and instruction to a young, inexperienced Christian leader named Timothy, Paul applauded Timothy's mother and grandmother, Eunice and Lois, respectively. The apostle attributed his protégé's strong faith to the example and influence of two Christian pioneers. Like the mothers of the stripling warriors in the Book of Mormon, these two matriarchs infused a son with early and unwavering faith in the Lord, faith that would sustain him through life's challenges (Alma 56:47–48). Most of what is known of these two women is on account of Timothy's stalwart leadership and commitment to Christ rather than through a specific story about them.

EUNICE'S AND LOIS'S PLACE OF RESIDENCE

Their Greek names and the location where Timothy and his mother lived when they met Paul and were baptized indicate that Eunice resided in a village called Lystra in the province of Galatia. Although Luke does not call her by name, Eunice is introduced in scripture at the beginning of Paul's second mission (Acts 16:1). No clues are given concerning Lois's conversion and baptism, but she was probably living with her daughter in Lystra. Her conversion to Christianity would have constituted yet another chapter in the success story of Paul's first mission to Galatia. Lois's name, like that of her daughter's, is Greek, suggesting that both were born and reared in a Hellenistic community outside the land of Israel.

Because it was in a valley some distance from the main trade route through the area, Lystra was not a well-known or much-frequented town. Many inhabitants followed Greek religion and culture, as was evidenced by the villagers who mistook Paul and Barnabas for the Greek gods Zeus and Hermes after the missionaries healed a man who had been crippled since birth (Acts 14:8–13).

ACTS 16:1–3
2 TIMOTHY 1:5; 3:14–15

273

HISTORICAL CONTEXT

Paul invited Eunice's son, Timothy, to accompany him on his second mission. In that context, the reader learns of Timothy's parentage: he was "the son of a certain woman, which was a Jewess, and believed; but his father was a Greek" (Acts 16:1). Eunice was a Jew with a Greek name who "believed," meaning she had already converted to Christianity when Paul returned to Galatia, whereas his Greek father was neither a Christian nor a God-fearer. *Timotheus,* a Greek name, reflects his father's influence; the meaning of that name, "honored of God," suggests his mother's heritage. A Jewish scholar argued that Timothy would have been considered Greek rather than Jewish because "when the Israelite woman moved abroad to join her gentile husband, her children were considered Gentile."[1]

Eunice's Gentile husband must have been present in the home when their son was young because Timothy was not circumcised as an infant, a procedure on which Eunice would have insisted had she not been under the influence of an unbelieving husband. After Eunice and Timothy were converted to Christianity, because the Jews "knew that [Timothy's] father was a Greek," Paul asked Timothy to undergo circumcision (Acts 16:3) so that he would be more acceptable to Jews when he preached the gospel of Christ. The passage implies that were it not for the requirements of the Jews, Paul would have preferred for Timothy to have remained uncircumcised.[2]

Paul may have had Eunice and her husband in mind when he counseled Corinthian Saints who were married to unbelievers, "If the unbelieving [spouse] depart, let him depart" (1 Cor. 7:15). Through revelation, Joseph Smith learned that during the New Testament era, unbelieving husbands would teach their children to give "heed to the traditions of their fathers and [believe] not the gospel of Christ" (D&C 74:4).

In an epistle to Timothy, Paul mentioned that Timothy had been taught the "holy scriptures" as a child (2 Tim. 3:15). Since his father was a Greek and presumably unacquainted with the scripture to which Paul referred, Eunice and maybe even Lois were probably his scriptural tutors. That this mother and daughter were united in their

Photo by Kent P. Jackson

The view from atop the buried remains of Lystra in Galatia.

And He Shall Direct Thy Paths

BY ELSPETH YOUNG

faith and care for young Timothy is underscored in Paul's observation of their joint example in Timothy's solid foundational beliefs.

EUNICE'S AND LOIS'S APPEARANCE IN THE NEW TESTAMENT STORY

In his final epistle, Paul wrote to Timothy to strengthen him to carry on in faith after he was gone. Among Timothy's sustaining blessings was a supportive and believing family. From a Roman prison Paul wrote him, "When I call to remembrance the unfeigned faith that is in thee, which dwelt first in thy grandmother Lois, and thy mother Eunice; and I am persuaded that [is] in thee also" (2 Tim. 1:5). Paul's observations imply that Lois was a long-time believer who taught her daughter to have "unfeigned faith," and she in turn taught her son.

Through the challenges and uncertainties that must have surrounded them while they lived among those who followed different beliefs, Paul's counsel appears to echo the example of Timothy's mother and grandmother: "For God hath not given us the spirit of fear; but of power, and of love, and of a sound mind. Be not therefore ashamed of the testimony of our Lord" (2 Tim. 1:7–8).

The site of the ancient Galatian city of Lystra (modern Turkey), where Paul met Eunice and her son, Timothy.

Another verse of scripture in the same epistle hints that Eunice and Lois were somewhat literate, too. Continuing in the spirit of encouragement, Paul wrote to Timothy, "But continue thou in the things which thou hast learned and hast been assured of, knowing of whom thou hast learned them; and that from a child thou hast known the holy scriptures, which are able to make thee wise unto salvation through faith which is in Christ Jesus" (2 Tim. 3:14–15).

Although Paul became a father figure to Timothy (1 Tim. 1:2, 18; 2 Tim. 1:2; Phil. 2:19–20), his mother's influence would have shaped him as a child. Women in both the Jewish and the Greco-Roman cultures were responsible for the early education of their children. By acknowledging that Timothy had learned the scriptures in his childhood, Paul provides another indicator of the early spiritual influence of Eunice and Lois. To teach truths from scripture, they must have been somewhat educated. Furthermore, Eunice and Lois had learned sufficient to recognize that the gospel Paul taught was consistent with the scriptures they had received from Judaism and that it built upon them.

BETWEEN THE LINES

In 18 B.C., Augustus Caesar established laws to increase excellence and good character in Roman society. In addition to making divorce a criminal offense, his agenda encouraged mothers to accept the primary responsibility of transmitting morals and virtue to their children. The mother was also expected to train her daughters in domestic arts in preparation for their own marriage.[3]

In the case of Timothy, the evidence suggests that Eunice and Lois shared child-rearing responsibilities as mother and grandmother (2 Tim. 1:5).[4] In the early second century A.D., an exchange of letters between a Greco-Egyptian mother and grandmother indicates a similar commitment to child care across generational boundaries.[5]

We see the fruits of Eunice's and Lois's teachings and faith in the stalwart discipleship and leadership of their son and grandson. Timothy's religious understanding was grounded in scripture and faith, most likely taught in his home, which prepared him to become a fervent witness that indeed salvation comes only through Jesus Christ.

POINTS TO PONDER

1. What additional lessons would have been available to Timothy and fellow Christians in the community of Lystra because of the partnership between Eunice and her mother?

2. Paul described Timothy's faith as "unfeigned." What does this communicate about those who taught him how to develop authentic faith?

She Worketh Willingly with Her Hands

BY ELSPETH YOUNG

LYDIA

Λυδία

Meaning uncertain; perhaps "She who comes from Lydia" (Greek)

ydia holds the distinction of being the first known Christian convert in what is today called Europe. As a resident of a Roman colony and a believer in the God of the Jews, she and other women held prayer meetings despite the lack of a synagogue. Lydia ran a textile business in purple cloth or dye and was responsible for those of her own household. When the Christian missionaries came to her city, Lydia took the lead in embracing the truths they shared. Because of her faith and generosity, she was instrumental in establishing Philippi as a center of Christianity and a safe haven for the apostle Paul.

LYDIA'S PLACE OF RESIDENCE

Founded in 360 B.C., Philippi was named for Philip II, the Greek king of Macedonia who was the father of Alexander the Great. The Romans conquered the city in 168 B.C., and Mark Antony made it a Roman colony in 42 B.C. after defeating the assassins of Julius Caesar there. As a colony, Philippi was home to Roman military veterans and their families, who were sent from Italy to establish a firm Roman presence in the area, although local aristocrats who obtained Roman citizenship would also have lived there. Eventually the city became one of the largest and most prestigious Roman cities in the East.

The layout of Philippi, its official religion, the dress styles of its inhabitants, and its currency echoed those of Rome. Like other Roman colonies, Philippi had a central forum with a temple to Jupiter, a basilica for settling law cases and business deals, monuments to the emperor and other distinguished citizens, a theater, an amphitheater, and public baths. Such pagan cults as one to the goddess Diana/Artemis and another to Isis depended upon priestesses and priests, respectively, to lead the organizations.[1]

Unlike cities in the empire that were not colonies, Roman colonies such as Philippi used watchmen to curtail crime and mete out punishment. The magistrate in Philippi empowered two guards, called *lictors,* to carry bundles of rods for use in administering punishment as well as to signify their authority. Additionally,

ACTS 16:12–15, 40

279

Photo by Kent P. Jackson

Like other Roman colonies, Philippi had a central forum, or agora, with a temple to Jupiter, a basilica for settling legal cases and finalizing business deals, monuments to the emperor and other distinguished citizens, a theater, an amphitheater, and public baths.

the magistrate was to ensure that no Roman citizen was bound or beaten without provocation. That is exactly what happened to Paul and Silas during their first visit to Philippi. They did not divulge their citizenship until after they had spent the night in the stocks, having been beaten without a trial (Acts 16:37).

Notwithstanding an overwhelming Roman presence, a significant local population remained in the area of Philippi, including those who provided services and luxuries to the Roman expatriates. Lydia's name, occupation, and place of origin all indicate that she was one of the Greek merchants who established a business in the city, where she lived among Roman citizens and colonists. Philippi was known for its trade guilds, such as fabric workers, dyers, tanners, and leatherworkers. Along any given commercial street could be found several establishments of the trade for which the street was named. Such an arrangement facilitated cooperation for equipment and raw materials and established a community of common interests. Businesses located closest to the city center were those most valued and respected by the Romans and those that did not produce noxious odors or filth.

A stream that runs near the edge of where the city of Philippi thrived in Lydia's day is called Lydia's River today. It may well have been the location of the women's Sabbath prayer meeting (Acts 16:13).

LYDIA'S DAILY WORK

Manufacturing related to making clothing was perhaps "the most important industry in the ancient world."[2] Men and women, free and slave, worked in the cloth trade in New Testament times. Jobs were available to women as spinners, weavers, fullers, dyers, and seamstresses (Cyprian, *Dig* 7.8.12.61). Studies of clothing manufacture in Pompeii suggest that men performed most of the weaving and women were more often the seamstresses and menders.[3] Lydia was a "seller of purple," meaning she was a dealer in purple cloth in Philippi (Acts 16:14).

Producing and preparing cloth suitable for making clothing was a complex process that required multiple skills and many workers. After weavers produced cloth from natural fibers, fullers cleaned it with natural oils or gums in preparation for its being dyed. The cloth was steeped in a cleansing solution, then stamped, felted, bleached with sulfur fumes, and finally ironed flat with a fuller's press.[4] The process produced foul odors that necessitated fullers situating their businesses outside the cities. If Lydia's business was selling purple cloth rather than dying it, her shop would likely have been a city-center business.

Purple dye was arguably the most exotic and expensive of all the dyes and therefore contributed substantially to the clothing trade. The most likely source of the purple dye was the glands of Mediterranean mollusks, or small shellfish, a secret discovered and guarded for centuries by the Phoenicians. Producing the dye was a messy and foul-smelling business that combined the mollusk glands with urine.[5] To produce even one gram of purple dye required the glands of some eight thousand mollusks, thereby explaining the high cost of purple cloth. Dyed purple cloth ranged from light lavender to deep violet. According to ancient inscriptions, the city of Thyatira, Lydia's hometown in Asia Minor, had a flourishing dyers guild and was especially famous for its manufacturing of the expensive and luxurious purple dye.

Because Lydia was head of her own household and had a home sufficiently large to host and lodge missionaries indefinitely (Acts

A stream runs near the edge of where the city of Philippi thrived in Lydia's day. A modern town nearby is called Lidia.

Mollusk shell. The most likely source of purple dye was glands of Mediterranean mollusks, or small shellfish. Thousands of mollusks were needed to produce even small amounts of purple dye, thereby explaining the high cost of purple cloth.

16:15, 40), she was likely wealthy. She probably ran a business selling the finished purple cloth rather than a shop that created the dye. Nonetheless, even though purple cloth was viewed as a luxury in her day, as a tradeswoman dependent on her business to sustain her livelihood, Lydia would have been seen as lower in status. Furthermore, even among the Greeks, it was unusual for a woman to run her own business unless she inherited it from her father or a deceased husband. The scriptures, however, do not convey anything about Lydia's family except that she went to Philippi from Thyatira in Asia Minor. She may have imported purple-dyed cloth or the actual dye from Asia Minor and sold it to the wealthy residents of Philippi for a profit. Perhaps she was a widow whose father or late husband ran the family business in Thyatira and she began a branch of the business in Philippi.

Because of the tight-knit community that surrounded merchants such as Lydia, her moral character would have been known. A reputation for honesty and quality workmanship was essential for anyone to succeed in business. In view of the fact that she ran a household, Lydia's business must have been quite successful and her reputation in the city favorable.

LYDIA'S APPEARANCE IN THE NEW TESTAMENT STORY

Lydia went to Philippi from Thyatira, a city in western Asia Minor (Acts 16:14). At the time, Thyatira was home to a strong Jewish presence, which provides a possible explanation for Lydia's introduction to Jewish beliefs and practices and her learning to worship God on the Sabbath day (Acts 16:13–14).

Many would-be converts to Judaism considered some requirements of the Mosaic law too great a sacrifice, especially circumcision for men. Not surprisingly, more women became full converts to Judaism than men. Likewise, throughout the empire, more women than men showed interest in foreign religious practices.[6] Those who did not fully convert but who adopted the Jewish belief in one God, observed dietary laws and the Sabbath, appreciated the moral teachings in Judaism, and "feared God" were called God-fearers. In his travels, Paul encountered many women who were God-fearers and often found them to be prominent women of the community who regularly attended the local synagogue (Acts 14:1; 17:4, 12; 18:4).

When the Christian missionaries met Lydia, she was a God-fearer in a city where few Jews lived, a circumstance not surprising for a Roman colony (Acts 16:14). A *minyan,* or quorum, of at least ten adult male

Jews was required for a synagogue. In the absence of a synagogue and its ready-made audience to which they could introduce their witness of Jesus Christ, Paul, Silas, Luke, and other missionaries searched for an alternative venue. They found a group of women praying together near the city's river on the Sabbath day, and as Luke reported the scene, "we sat down, and spake unto the women which resorted thither" (Acts 16:13).

An obvious deterrent for Lydia fully converting to Judaism was the Jewish requirement to avoid Gentiles, an impossibility in her profession in a Roman colony. Nothing in Judaism, however, prevented a group of women from meeting on the Sabbath to worship Jehovah.[7] Lydia's active religious leadership role in Philippi in the absence of a quorum of men indicates that women were likely more often active participants in Judaism, especially in Greco-Roman cities, than previously supposed. As the missionaries spoke to the women, Lydia was one "whose heart the Lord opened, that she attended to the things which were spoken of

Public domain

Woman selling produce. Several inscriptions and reliefs found in Ostia, the harbor of Rome, depict marketplace scenes with which Lydia would have been familiar. Although this one dates to the second or third century, it resembles first-century representations found at Pompeii.

Paul" (Acts 16:14). She would have heard in Judaism truths she loved in addition to testimonies of Christ's sacrifice and the teachings that men and women, Jew and Gentile, free and slave, were "all one in Christ Jesus" (Gal. 3:28). Upon hearing the good news of Jesus Christ, Lydia accepted the witness and "was baptized" and so was "her household," who were probably relatives, children, and slaves (Acts 16:15).

BETWEEN THE LINES

Surprisingly, Paul does not mention Lydia in his letter to the Philippians, although her influence in the Church, both spiritually and financially, is sensed throughout the epistle. Paul wrote more openly to the Philippians than to any other Christian congregation, freely divulging his personal journey to conversion (Phil. 3:5–8). He clearly trusted the members there would not use his words against him. Furthermore, the Philippian branch of the church was the only one from which Paul had received gifts, likely in part from Lydia's financial resources (Phil. 4:15–18; see also 2 Cor. 11:9).

The absence of Lydia's name in the epistle, however, has prompted several explanations that would include her, albeit indirectly. Paul's letter to the Philippians does name two women, Euodias and Syntyche, who "laboured with me in the gospel" (Philip. 4:2–3). He implores them to "be of the same mind in the

Lord," or to cease contention, which wording does not indicate whether the disagreement was between the two women or with Paul.[8] Perhaps Euodias and Syntyche had a quarrel that was damaging good feelings within the branch. Some have suggested that the name Lydia could have been a nickname for one who came from Lydia in Asia Minor and the true name of the seller of purple was either Euodias or Syntyche, given their mention in Paul's letter.[9]

The other suggestion for Lydia's inclusion in the letter is more controversial: What if Lydia is the "true yokefellow" Paul addresses in verse 3?[10] The Greek term translated "yokefellow" variously means marriage, couple, companion, and spouse. Clement of Alexandria (A.D. 150–215) interpreted Philippians 4:3 to indicate that Paul was married: "Even Paul did not hesitate in one letter to address his consort. The only reason why he did not take her about with him was that it would have been an inconvenience for his ministry." Clement noted that other apostles did take their wives "that they may be their fellow-ministers in dealing with housewives. It was through them [the wives] that the Lord's teaching penetrated also the women's quarters without any scandal being aroused" (*Misc* 3.6.53). Many scholars believe, however, that Paul could not have been married, and therefore they consider his yokefellow to have been a male missionary companion. Others remain open to the possibility that Paul addressed his wife who resided in Philippi and have gone so far as to identify that wife as Lydia. Without additional information, however, we cannot know for certain.[11]

That which may or may not be lacking in the epistle to the Philippians, however, cannot diminish Lydia's example and contribution reported by Luke. A woman who was a patroness and God-fearer orchestrated an environment conducive for the worship of Jehovah in the absence of a synagogue. Before meeting the Christian missionaries, Lydia reflected the blended influences of Hellenism and Judaism in her social independence and religious commitment. Her conversion to Jesus Christ and subsequent financial support to the church were invaluable to the growth and stability of the Philippian branch. Through her contact with influential and powerful clientele, Lydia

Photo by Kent P. Jackson

Remains of a gate or other entrance to ancient Thyatira in Lydia (modern Turkey), where Lydia's family originated.

would have been a welcome source for contacts for the missionaries to teach. Surrounded by reminders of luxury and working with clients who possessed endless wealth, Lydia discerned the greater value of the gospel of Christ over worldly riches.

Lydia and her household formed the foundation of believers that would attract and stabilize future converts, including the men who would share leadership duties for the fledgling branch (JST, 1 Cor. 14:34). Lydia's achievements also show that women did not have to be from the upper class to contribute to the broader society. She was from the working class, albeit the high end of it. Her resources, then, would not be limitless. Notwithstanding, her actions after her baptism indicate a leader with a generous heart.

Lydia shines in scripture as a golden convert. She understood the gospel. She listened. She led all of her household into baptism after her. She shared her resources with the missionaries. In contrast to the jailor in Philippi who first tried to silence Paul and was interested in the gospel only after the jail was destroyed, Lydia was eager to learn as soon as she met the missionaries. She had nothing to gain professionally through her conversion to Christianity and plenty to lose. She willingly offered her home for church needs, making it the most logical place to establish the first Christian congregation in the city. In this way, Lydia can be seen as a benefactor, or patron, of the Philippian branch.

Paul's first mission to Philippi closes with the missionaries leaving prison and entering Lydia's home (Acts 16:40). As the home of Mary, the mother of John Mark, was the sanctuary for those praying for the imprisoned Peter and where Peter went after his miraculous release from prison (Acts 12), so was Lydia's home the place to which Paul and the other missionaries went directly after their miraculous release from prison to find an emerging community of Christian Saints praying for their safety. The missionaries "comforted them, and departed," leaving Lydia and her fellow converts to build up the church in Philippi.

POINTS TO PONDER

1. Why is Lydia's example as a faithful Christian woman without known family connections relevant today?

2. How did the Roman environment in Philippi color the religious climate either in favor of or against the spread of Christianity?

3. What challenges and opportunities in the church would Lydia have faced with her business background?

4. How does what we know of Lydia inspire greater commitment as a member missionary?

THE SLAVE-GIRL SOOTHSAYER

The Christian missionaries' initial efforts to preach the gospel in Philippi included the story of another woman besides Lydia. The girl was a fortune-teller of sorts whose declarations of the unknown created a lucrative business for the men who owned her. This slave girl, whose name is never given, was interested in the Christian missionaries and their message. Her approach and response to them, however, differed significantly from Lydia's reaction.

The slave girl's story elucidates a different public role that women in Greco-Roman cities had to influence the economic and religious tone around them. It also provides a glimpse into the world of Greco-Roman slavery, particularly when a young woman was owned by men. Although what happened to the girl after this story is not given, her reaction to the missionaries became a catalyst for spreading the gospel of Jesus Christ in Macedonia.

THE SLAVE-GIRL SOOTHSAYER'S DAILY WORK

The girl is known in scripture not by her name but by her work. She was a slave whose owners presented her as a soothsayer, a source for oracles and for divining unseen truths. Possessed by an unclean spirit, the girl uttered messages that may have come from voices in her head, which her owners translated into "facts" that the public would be willing to pay to hear.

Trust in magical incantations, potions, and sorcery was commonplace in the Greek world. Greeks believed that the prophetesses of Delphi were able to predict the future through inspiration from the god Apollo, who assumed the form of a python snake.[1] Because of similar claims, the soothsayer girl in Philippi is therefore sometimes called the pythoness or snake girl. She made money in public for her owners and in the process heard the message of salvation preached by Paul and the other missionaries. Even though what she proclaimed publicly about the missionaries and their message was true—they represented the Most High God and taught the only way to be saved—her performance "grieved" or annoyed Paul (Acts 16:18).

ACTS 16:16–18

HISTORICAL CONTEXT

Slavery was an accepted part of the social fabric of the Roman empire. No one questioned its moral implications. Any free person in the empire could own a slave. Slaves were bought and sold, hired out and given away as gifts, misused and abused, promoted and trained for greater service, set free, and even given citizenship. Some slaves were held in high esteem by their masters, trusted and loved as a member of the family. By New Testament times in Rome, at least 40 percent of the total population was enslaved.[2] Outside Italy, slaves made up only 10 percent of the population.[3]

A person became a slave if captured in war, abandoned as an infant, born to slaves, or indebted beyond the ability to pay. Some people even chose to be slaves to secure more stability and increase their social status. If a slave had a gracious master, life could be more predictable and less demanding than life as a poor free person. With rare exception, slaves could count on three meals a day, lodging, clothing, and health care. Those who served members of the upper class were often given a superb education or at least trained in special skills that would increase their options after they were freed. You could not distinguish slaves from masters by sight since they were ethnically the same and because some slaves lived a higher-class life than the free poor.

In Greco-Roman thought, slaves were not inferior by nature; it was their status as slaves that made them inferior. While working for their masters, slaves could earn and save money to eventually buy their freedom or be granted freedom as a reward for excellent, extended service. In short, slavery did not have to be a permanent position; it was more often a process or temporary condition to endure while carving out a better standard of living. Because of the security associated with employment for a compassionate master, unskilled women in particular often continued working for their former owners after gaining freedom.

Female slaves often worked as domestic servants in wealthy households as spinners, seamstresses, kitchen help, wet nurses, and nannies. They were trained to be ladies' maids, hairdressers, or midwives, or educated to read for their mistresses. Child slaves working as entertainers provided an income for their owners or travelling companies, as did the soothsayer in Philippi (Acts 16:16–19).

Slaves' clothing was dictated by the work they performed rather than their owner's generosity.[4] In one case, slaves working in a mill wore only threadbare rags akin to a loin cloth (Apuleius, *Met* 9.12). The same source also described slaves clothed in richly extravagant uniforms, including an abundance of jewelry, and "curly-haired boys in beautiful clothes" to advertise the wealth and refined taste of their owners (*Met* 2.19). Generally, female domestic slaves wore a simple linen tunic that fell below the knee with "a dainty, bright red band tied up under her breasts" (*Met* 2.7). Many slaves worked barefoot.[5]

Christ introduced dramatic changes to the way slaves should be viewed. His gospel considered every man, woman, and child as the offspring of God, with complete access to all that salvation promises. In Christian thought, no one was denied spiritual fulfillment because "there is neither Jew nor Greek, there is neither slave nor free, there is neither male nor female; for you are all one in Christ Jesus" (Gal. 3:28). Through his gospel, Jesus Christ gave every individual a reason to hope.

Christian leaders neither promoted resistance to slavery nor enjoined masters to treat their slaves as equals; Christian leaders functioned within the prevailing laws and customs. For example, Paul invited Philemon to receive Onesimus, his runaway slave, home again as a brother, but it was up to Philemon the Christian master to choose whether he would adhere to Roman privilege or Christian conscience (Philem. 1:10–19). The apostles spoke directly to Christian masters, as one would expect, but also directly to Christian slaves, and encouraged them to show integrity in their servitude. Paul counseled, "Servants, be obedient to them that are your masters according to the flesh, with fear and trembling, in singleness of your heart, as unto Christ" (Eph. 6:5; Col. 3:22). Similarly, Peter instructed, "Servants, be subject to your masters with all fear, not only to the good and gentle, but also to the froward" (1 Pet. 2:18).

Paul used the imagery of slavery to describe his complete submission to Christ. He considered slavery to sin the only shameful form of servitude. His writings acknowledge that mortal life is replete with injustices and inequalities, and only faith in Christ offers the comfort and perspective to trust in the eternity created by a loving Savior.

THE SLAVE-GIRL SOOTHSAYER'S APPEARANCE IN THE NEW TESTAMENT STORY

After the baptism of Lydia and her household, the missionaries encountered "a certain damsel possessed with a spirit of divination" who apparently worked for a group of Romans in Philippi's marketplace and "brought her masters much gain by soothsaying" (Acts 16:16). The fact that she had more than one owner suggests that the girl's divination skills were lucrative enough to support the business ventures of at least two individuals. For "many days" the girl followed after the missionaries and cried out, "These men are the servants of the most high God, which shew unto us the way of salvation" (Acts 16:17–18). The New Revised Standard Version translates the girl's exclamation as, "These men are slaves of the Most High God, who proclaim to you a way of salvation," which suggests that she was more resistant to the Christian message than is indicated by the translation in the King James Version.

Perhaps the girl's behavior irritated the missionaries because she saw them as her competitors with similar abilities to "tap into the spirit world."[6] Paul's reaction to her, however, indicates that the girl's "witness" was far more serious than mere competition for attention. After several days of her performance, Paul "turned and said to the spirit [that possessed the girl], I command thee in the name of Jesus Christ to come out of her. And he came out the same hour" (Acts 16:18). The Christian missionaries were teaching about the only trustworthy way to receive inspiration, and the truth was being echoed and even mocked by a counterfeit means. Paul was annoyed with the spirit that tormented the girl, not with the girl herself.

The situation is akin to those when Jesus encountered individuals possessed by unclean spirits who testified that he was the Son of God (Mark 1:23–25; 3:11–12). Like the Savior, Paul also silenced the young soothsayer because her witness sprang from the same evil source as that of the unclean spirits. Turning to false spirits to learn truth is dangerous and eventually damning. So, in the name of Jesus Christ, Paul exorcised the spirit that possessed her.

The girl's owners, incensed by their loss of revenue, dragged the missionaries to the city magistrates and accused them of disturbing the peace and teaching customs that were contrary to Roman law (Acts 16:19–21). Furthermore, their accusers considered the missionaries Jews (Acts 16:20). In public perception and in laws enacted in Rome under Claudius, Christians and Jews were lumped together and considered troublemakers who could therefore legally be expelled from the city. What is not stated but is strongly implied by the reaction of the soothsayer's owners is that by exorcising the evil spirit from the girl, Paul showed his audience that his God is more powerful than the serpent or the Apollo cult it represented. This truth would have produced sufficient public consternation to justify the magistrate's imprisoning the missionaries.

The slave girl's encounter with the Christian missionaries opened unexpected doors of opportunity for spreading the gospel, however. Paul and Silas spent a most uncomfortable night in jail after being stripped, beaten, and held in the stocks, but they responded with songs of praise and were miraculously freed from their bonds. By morning, the jailor and all his household were converted to Jesus Christ, and they were baptized (Acts 16:22–34).

When the city magistrates learned that they had punished and imprisoned Roman citizens without a trial, they "feared" (Acts 16:34–38), which is an understatement. The ramifications for mistreating a Roman citizen without due process were serious: the magistrates faced punishment far worse than that which the missionaries had suffered during the night. With profuse apologies, the magistrates tried to make amends for their misconduct to save their own positions (Acts 16:39).

By not divulging their citizen status when they were arrested, the missionaries had in effect purchased the city by their sufferings for future missionary labors. A remarkable branch of the church emerged in the city, as evidenced in Paul's later epistle to the Saints there. The story of the slave girl set events in motion to expand and protect a strong Christian presence in the Roman colony of Philippi.

POINTS TO PONDER

1. What choice would the slave girl have had after she was freed from the unknown spirit and rejected by her owners? What do you think became of her?

2. How is the source we seek for learning truth critical to what we learn? How does the story of the slave-girl soothsayer alert us to dangers associated with relying on questionable sources in seeking truth?

Here Bring Your Wounded Hearts

BY ELSPETH YOUNG

PHEBE

Φοίβη

"Bright, radiant" (Greek)

*O*nly two verses in scripture refer to a Greco-Roman woman named Phebe. Such a brief and seemingly insignificant reference has often caused her to be overlooked as a valuable participant in the first-century Christian church. Nevertheless, a careful analysis of the two verses reveals three titles by which Paul described her. Those titles give insights into the character of Phebe herself as well as the roles filled by women in the early church.

In closing his letter to the Romans, Paul introduced Phebe to the Saints with these words: "I commend unto you Phebe our sister, which is a servant of the church which is at Cenchrea: That ye receive her in the Lord, as becometh saints, and that ye assist her in whatsoever business she hath need of you: for she hath been a succourer of many, and of myself also" (Rom. 16:1–2). Paul called her "our sister [*adelphē*]," "a servant [*diakonos*] of the church," and "a succourer [*prostatis*] of many," including himself. The meaning and function of each title hints that Phebe's role in helping spread Christianity was significant.

PHEBE'S PLACE OF RESIDENCE

Phebe was "our sister [*adelphē*]" in the church in Cenchrea. Cenchrea was one of two harbors that served Corinth, the capital city of Achaia, a region of Greece on the Peloponnese peninsula. Cenchrea was on the Aegean Sea to the east of Corinth, and Lechaeum was to the west on the Adriatic Sea. Only four miles separated the two ports, which caused many owners of smaller sea vessels to have their boats and contents hauled across the narrow isthmus to avoid sailing around the Peloponnese. Not until the early twentieth century, however, was a canal successfully created to allow boats to sail from port to port.

From Phebe's title of *adelphē,* we may observe that she was an active member of the Christian community in Cenchrea. She would have assumed responsibility to assist in practical, spiritual, and financial ways where there was need. Considering that her name is Greek and the third title indicates that she held prominent status, Phebe was likely a Gentile convert to Christianity.[1]

ROMANS 16:1–2

291

Photo by Kent P. Jackson

The harbor city of Cenchrea provided important access to Corinth from the east. Phebe was an active member of the Christian community in Cenchrea.

PHEBE'S DAILY WORK

Phebe was described by Paul as "a servant [*diakonos*] of the church at Cenchrea."[2] Romans and Greeks regarded a *diakonos* as someone who held a subservient and pedestrian position. Jesus redefined the term to be a crowning virtue. He made being a *diakonos* a foundational characteristic for any who would desire discipleship with him. For Christians, the term connotes a position of trust, such as a selfless servant, teacher, or missionary. In the early second century, Pliny gave evidence of two slave women who were *diakonais* and were tortured for being Christians (*Ep* 10.96). Not only was Phebe a valued teacher or missionary in the church but the context of Paul's commendation suggests that she was the *diakonos* who traveled from Cenchrea to deliver his letter to Rome.

Like the members of the house of Stephanas who devoted themselves "to the ministry [*diakonia*] of the saints" (1 Cor. 16:15), Timothy, whom Paul called "our brother, and minister [*diakonos*] of God"

(1 Thess. 3:2), and Tychikos, who delivered Paul's letter to the Colossians and the Ephesians and whom Paul recommends as "our beloved brother" and "faithful minister [*diakonos*] in the Lord" (Eph 6:21), Phebe was introduced by Paul as "our sister" and "*diakonos*." Similarly, Paul identified himself as a *diakonos* who preached the gospel in various locations (1 Cor. 3:5; 2 Cor. 3:6; 6:4; 11:23; Col. 1:23). Although the King James Version describes Phebe as a "servant" and a male servant of Christ as a "minister," the Greek word is the same. In other words, as a *diakonos,* Phebe performed similar missionary duties at home and away as did faithful male disciples of Christ. As a *diakonos,* she may also have served as Paul's intermediary or representative in delivering his words in a letter and "in whatsoever business she hath need of you" (Rom. 16:2).

PHEBE'S APPEARANCE IN THE NEW TESTAMENT STORY

Paul mentioned Phebe to the Romans as the bearer of his letter and introduced her plans for other work among them when she arrived. In his third description of her, Paul said that Phebe was a *prostatis* to him and many others. The term is the same one used in Paul's letters to describe male Christian leaders (1 Thess. 5:12; 1 Tim. 3:4; 5:17). The word connotes a benefactor, protector, or patron in the Roman patron-client sense as well as a leader of a group or club.[3] In the masculine form, it is often translated as "leader, president, superintendent, or patron."[4] In referring to Phebe as a *prostatis,* Paul viewed her as both prosperous and of high social standing.[5] But she was more than this. In some undisclosed way, she was of significant benefit to Paul specifically and to the church generally. Paul's terminology implies that Phebe was a patron to him personally.

It has been estimated that as many as 10 percent of patrons and donors in the Roman period were women.[6] Evidence that Christian women were afforded meaningful assignments explains in part why "chief women not a few" were among the early converts (Acts 17:4, 12). Capable and resourceful women would resonate with movements that needed and used their talents. In return, women of status, such as Phebe, could assist in obtaining recognition for the church from local government leaders through their connections and public influence. As an additional hint that Phebe was a patron, Paul as client provided the expected reciprocity important to the relationship by recommending her as his patron to the Romans.

Considering that Paul's examples of church leaders were men, Phebe did not supervise the branch of the church in Cenchrea or Paul's missionary efforts. More likely, she was a patron to Paul and other Christians by supplying needed financial, spiritual, and temporal support. Phebe's role in Cenchrea may have also extended to hosting the church there in her home. She did, however, have additional business in Rome, presumably church business, for which Paul requested the Saints there to support her (Rom. 16:2). Thus, Phebe's ecclesiastical commission reached beyond her hometown.

BETWEEN THE LINES

Paul wrote to the Romans at the end of his third missionary journey, in about A.D. 58, and spoke of his plans to take the gospel to Spain (Rom. 15:24–28). From hints throughout the letter, Paul appears to have been laying the groundwork for a different approach to missionary work than he had used previously. He had typically set up residence in a city as a craftsman tent maker without announcing beforehand his missionary intent or requesting support. He would then begin preaching in the local synagogue, where he could make crucial contacts, such as patrons who would support his future efforts in the area. He had the language skills to address both Greco-Roman and Jewish groups in all of his former missionary locations.

If indeed there was not yet a significant Jewish population in Spain, Paul might have been searching for another way to begin a mission there. Language could have been a barrier in Spain where Iberian, Punic, and local dialects were more prevalent than Latin or Greek.[7] Because he could not expect to find synagogues there, as was his custom, he would also need advice to find suitable resources and contacts in Spain, including lodging, travel, and translators.

Paul therefore revealed his travel plans, writing to the Roman Christians that "whensoever I take my journey into Spain, I will come to you: for I trust to see you in my journey, and to be brought on my way thitherward by you, if first I be somewhat filled with your company" (Rom. 15:24). After stopping in Jerusalem to deliver contributions from the Christians in Achaia and Macedonia, he would "come by you [in Rome] into Spain" (Rom. 15:25–28). These passages imply that he intended to stay in Rome only long enough to gather support for his proposed mission to Spain. By referencing the charitable Gentile Christians in Greece, he was planting seeds of generosity in the hearts of the Roman Christians and predisposing them to assist him in planning and financing a new and unique mission field.[8]

Furthermore, it is likely Paul had not yet been to Rome when he wrote this letter. Considering that most Saints in Rome would have known him only from hearsay and that some Jewish Christians continued to criticize his approach to teaching Gentiles, Paul probably faced a significant challenge in convincing the members there to trust him as a trustworthy and stalwart disciple of Christ. He needed a respectable patron to go before him and convince the Roman Saints to help him. Enter Phebe.

Considering the three descriptive titles Paul gave her, Phebe possessed the credentials to garner support for her recommendation of Paul and reassurance of his trustworthiness. Paul may have been inviting fellow Christians in Rome to offer Phebe their hospitality, knowing that she had been the financial enabler of much good in the area around Cenchrea and had the potential to facilitate the future mission to Spain. He therefore asked them to "assist her in whatsoever business she hath need of you" (Rom. 16:2). In Paul's mind, the Roman Saints would be honored to associate with one of Phebe's rank and could trust in her mission to raise funds for spreading the gospel. Robert Jewett suggests that Phebe's assignment, as a Christian patron, "was to create the logistical base for the Spanish mission."[9] She would have delivered the letter to the authorities of the respective Christian house churches in Rome and shared details for making

Paul's mission to Spain a success. If Jewett's theory is correct, Phebe would have needed skills in diplomacy as she interacted with the diverse leaders of the various branches and a quick intellect to correctly interpret the complex teachings and reasoning Paul uses in the epistle. Armed with such skills, she could convince them of Paul's integrity, orthodoxy, and loyalty to Christ and his work.

Although Paul's planned stop in Rome and mission to Spain were interrupted by his arrest in Jerusalem, Phebe's efforts in Rome may have paid off in an unanticipated way. As a prisoner, Paul appealed to Caesar and was taken to Rome as a prisoner. Unexpectedly, during the final week of a dangerous and difficult transport to Rome, Paul encountered Christians, "brethren," in Puteoli who offered to host him along the way (Acts 28:13–14). Next, other Christians came to meet him from Appii Forum and Three Taverns, areas some fifty miles distant from Rome. These encounters caused Paul to thank God and take courage (Acts 28:15). Finally, upon arriving in Rome, Paul was allowed to serve his sentence under house arrest, in far more favorable conditions than prison (Acts 28:16, 30-31). House arrest, however, required the prisoner to pay rent for his lodging and wages for the guards, which Paul obviously did not have. At least one patron would have been needed to orchestrate the plan, finance the logistics, and gain access to the officials whose command provided Paul such favorable circumstances during his imprisonment in Rome. Phebe easily fits the description and was likely the patroness who secured house-arrest lodgings for Paul where he could continue to preach the gospel and strengthen the Saints.[10] Her influence and testimony are heard through her actions rather than through any recorded words.

Paul's letter to the Roman Saints commending Phebe to them would have facilitated the work of the church among Christians whom neither Paul nor Phebe had ever met. Because of Paul's recommendation and her status as Christian benefactor and teacher, Phebe was empowered to receive needed hospitality and access to leaders in Rome. Her example in the New Testament gives evidence that not only did men serve as official representatives to various Christian branches but also women traveled to represent the church and facilitate communication between the various communities. Phebe also demonstrates how the missionary work was spread by traveling missionaries who encouraged unity, love, and understanding of members in diverse places.

POINTS TO PONDER

1. Do you see any significance in the fact that Phebe is described with such important terms and without any connection to a husband or male relative?

2. How does Phebe's example expand your perception of women's roles in the early Christian church?

3. What skills do you have that might not be considered traditional for your gender but could enhance your work within your own congregation?

Forsaking All

BY ELSPETH YOUNG

PRISCA

Πρίσκα

"Venerable" (Latin)

Prisca and her husband, Aquila, were Jewish Christians from Rome. Their prominence in missionary efforts and leadership in the various branches of the church where they resided is noted by Luke in Acts and in the frequent greetings Paul wrote in his epistles, including his final epistle. By this inclusion of their names in the narrative and letters, we are able to trace at least some of their missionary travels and subsequent influence.

In all, Prisca is named six times in the New Testament: three times by Luke, who refers to her as Priscilla, the informal, diminutive form of her name (Acts 18:2, 18, 24), and three times by Paul, who in his epistles uses her formal name Prisca once (2 Tim. 4:19) and Priscilla twice (Rom. 16:3; 1 Cor. 16:19). In all six of these references, she is named alongside Aquila. In four of the six occurrences, however, she is named before her husband: twice by Luke and twice by Paul.

Prisca and Aquila offered their home as a meeting place for Christians in more than one area and provided Paul with lodging and a livelihood as a tent maker to support himself during his missionary travels. They were independent craftsmen with resources to travel and host church functions in their home. Their scriptural identification as wife and husband reflects the emphasis that Caesar Augustus's reforms placed on restoring virtue to his empire by increasing the social prestige of marriage and family,[1] reinforces the Savior's respect for the institution of marriage, and illustrates the effectiveness of a married couple working as a missionary team to spread the gospel of Jesus Christ.

PRISCA'S PLACES OF RESIDENCE

Prisca's name and hints about her in the text indicate that she was freeborn and wealthy. Her name is Latin and is found in more than two hundred inscriptions of first-century Rome, only a small number of which indicate women named Prisca who had slave origins.[2]

ACTS 18:2–3, 18–19, 24–28

ROMANS 16:3–4

1 CORINTHIANS 16:19

2 TIMOTHY 4:19

Further evidence from ancient Rome connects this name not only with local aristocracy but also with Christianity.[3] One such tie is the Catacomb of Priscilla in Rome, which was originally a burial ground located on the country estate of the prestigious Acilian family. Descendants of the family included a consul under the emperor Trajan who was executed in the mid-90s for being a Christian (Dio Cassus, *Hist Rom* 67.14). Another tie to the name, wealth, and Christianity is the anciently named Santa Prisca church, located in the Aventine district, which was built on the probable site of Prisca and Aquila's home and house church in Rome. The fact that the church was named after the woman implies that the property was listed in her name. In other words, it is likely that Prisca rather than Aquila owned property in Rome.[4]

By contrast, Aquila's family origins were Jewish, from Pontus near the Black Sea in Asia Minor. His name, however, is Latin. He could have relocated to Rome for a number of reasons, including settling there as a freeborn tradesman seeking better opportunities for work. Just as plausible is the suggestion that he was taken to Rome as a slave and thereafter freed and given a Roman name.[5] It is estimated that about one in three residents in Rome at the time was a slave, increasing the probability that at least some of the Jewish population, including those who converted to Christianity, were slaves or freed men and women.[6] Often freed men and women were those who had risen above other slaves due to their intellect and skills. Aquila's tent-making skills and residence in Rome, together with his Latin name, fit such a description. Robert Jewett even suggests that Aquila might have been a slave of the Acilian family where he met Prisca and later was granted freedman status.[7] Whether he was freeborn or a freed slave, however, Aquila's trade as a tent maker alone would likely place him in the massive plebeian class of laborers without much hope of upward mobility.[8] Hope for improved circumstances would increase considerably, however, if he married a woman of wealth and prestige.

Some have argued that Prisca's name was, unusually, placed before her husband's because she was converted to Christianity before her husband or played a more prominent role in the Christian community than he did.[9] Others reject this idea because no distinctions between active and less active involvement in church membership were recognized in the early Christian church.[10] Those who argue for a humble Jewish background for Prisca on a par with Aquila's social status explain the connection between the Acilian family, Christianity, and the Catacomb of Priscilla to the Christian conversion of the prestigious family having been influenced by stories of Prisca's example and faith years after she lived rather than that she was an ancestor of the clan.[11] However, more of the unusual circumstances inferred about Prisca and her prominence in scripture can be explained by her having come from a prestigious and wealthy family in Rome. Considering the culture and mores of the time, her name was given first because she was of a higher social status than her husband and was recognized as the greater patron among their clients.[12] As a daughter of a wealthy family, she would have received an excellent education equal to that afforded sons of prominent Romans. She would have studied Roman and Greek literature, rhetoric, oratory, and philosophy. Roman women from the upper classes had much more choice about what life they would lead.

If that conclusion is accurate, it would explain how Prisca could excel in expounding the gospel to the erudite Apollos (Acts 18:24–26). It also explains the high degree of mobility Prisca and Aquila demonstrated in relocating from Rome to Corinth, then to Ephesus, and finally back to Rome. In each of these places, they also had means to own or rent domiciles large enough to accommodate as many as thirty people for worship services. History shows that women of rank and property were often attracted to the gospel of Jesus Christ. Many gave their wealth to the church and became missionaries, visiting families and individuals inferior to their previous associates (Marcarius Magnes, *Apoc* 3.5.5).

Considering other scriptural hints, Prisca must have become a Jewish proselyte before her conversion to Christianity. Implicated in Jewish unrest in Rome, Aquila and Prisca were driven from the city in accordance with Claudius's edict (Acts 18:2). Later, Prisca attended a synagogue in Ephesus, further indicating a connection with Judaism (Acts 18:26).

Under Roman law, freedmen were allowed to marry freeborn citizens.[13] Furthermore, mixed marriages between a Jew and a freeborn Roman citizen or between a Jew and a Gentile were not unusual. For example, Felix was a Roman freedman who married Drusilla, the daughter of King Herod, and was awarded the governorship of Judea. Josephus was a Jewish slave who received his Latin name when he was freed, and he married a Roman noblewoman. Timothy's mother, Eunice, was a Jewess who converted to Christianity and his father was a Greek (Acts 16:1). After scrutinizing the scriptural text about Prisca and Aquila in light of Roman culture, Jewett concluded, "A mixed marriage between a Roman noblewoman and a Jewish Christian freedman is the only circumstance that explains all the evidence about this couple."[14]

PRISCA AND AQUILA'S DAILY WORK

Husbands and wives were legally permitted to form business partnerships under Roman law, even if the woman's contribution to the partnership was money only.[15] Prisca and Aquila formed a business partnership as "tent makers," or more literally, "leather workers."[16]

Because the Greek word translated "tent maker" (*skēnopoios*) is obscure, scholars have proposed various interpretations for the occupation of Aquila and Prisca. The dominant view for years was that they were leatherworkers who purchased leather from tanners or traders and prepared it to be made into tents for military or personal use and other leather goods.[17] Tent makers also used wool or hair of animals indigenous to the area in which they worked. For example, camel or goat hair was common for tent making in the Holy Land, and because goats were widespread in Cilicia, Paul of Tarsus may have learned to make tents from their hair. Several long, narrow strips of woven animal hair were sewn together to form the tents. Cords connected the cloth to stakes secured in the ground to pitch each tent.

More recently, scholars have proposed that Paul's and Aquila's trade involved sewing linen awnings to protect street businesses and porticos from the sun.[18] Imperial craftsmen made awnings for such large venues as competitive games, city streets, and community plazas. In Corinth, tent makers would have found an additional market in making sails for boats. "Handkerchiefs or aprons" (Acts 19:12) may have been linen or leather fragments from Paul's tent-making business that were also often used as ties around individuals' robes or as headbands.[19]

Leatherworking involved two essential skills: cutting (requiring round-edged and straight-edged knives) and sewing various stitches (requiring awls of various sizes) to make the product both sturdy and waterproof. A stool and a workbench would have been all that was needed for a tent maker to perform his or her work. The requisite tools were portable, making it easy for Prisca and Aquila to move their trade from place to place as their missionary labors dictated.

In addition to tools, which they would have carried with them from the time they completed their apprenticeship, tent makers needed a sharpening stone, a stool and worktable, oil and blackening for treating leather, and storage space for their prepared goods to set up shop. Paul wrote of working "night and day" as a tent maker (1 Thess. 2:9), probably meaning that he began work before sunrise and continued most of the day until after sunset, with a break of a few hours at midday for a meal and nap, as was the custom among artisans in the ancient Mediterranean world.

Streets in ancient cities were lined with shops where merchants sold their wares. Several shops of a

The forum in Corinth with awnings over shops similar to what Prisca and Aquila might have manufactured. They also might have had a shop in a forum similar to this wherever they lived.

Artwork by Balage Balogh

certain trade tended to be located in the same general area with their workshops located close by, often attached to their residence. Tanners usually established their businesses near water because tanning leather required working with dead animals and the use of tannic acid, which produced noxious odors, and chemicals were easiest to discard by dumping them into a river or the sea.

Female merchant in butcher shop in Ostia, Italy. A clay relief portrays a woman selling poultry, which hangs from the roof of the market. Rabbits and chickens are stored in crates, the top of which she uses for her counter and for displaying baskets of other foodstuffs. Three male customers stand nearby, one of whom is buying a piece of fruit. The woman is dressed in simple attire with her hair drawn back in a simple bun, which distinguishes her from elite women.

In comparison to the shops of tanners, a tent maker's workshop would have been quieter and cleaner. It might be located in a room within the artisan's home, a ground-floor room in an apartment building, or a separate building altogether. Prisca and Aquila's shop was large enough to absorb at least one additional worker when Paul joined them. The setting would have been relatively quiet and devoid of offensive odors, so it could have been located within the city and near the businesses of other leather makers. A shoemaker wrote of listening to someone read out loud while he busied himself with his stitching.[20] Quieter shops were also known to have an opened door for those who simply wanted to come in and chat.[21]

Prisca and Aquila's workshop would have provided an ideal site to teach of Jesus Christ and his gospel. The location would have been perfect for informal and spontaneous discussions in which honest seekers of truth could find answers to their questions.

HISTORICAL CONTEXT

According to Josephus, Jews lived in Rome in large numbers from at least the time of Augustus (31 B.C.–A.D. 14) (*Ant* 17.11.1; *War* 2.6.1). The oldest and largest Jewish community in the city, across the Tiber River from the city center, dates back to the second century B.C. (Philo, *Embassy* 155). Because Christianity spread along the routes the Jews followed in their travels, it is not surprising to find early Christians among these Roman Jews and God-fearers. The conversion process likely began with visits from Christians to Rome and by Roman Jews visiting Jerusalem and other centers of early Christianity. Eusebius notes that Peter preached the gospel in Rome during the reign of Claudius (A.D. 41–54), some of the same years that Prisca and Aquila resided there (*Eccl Hist* 2.14). On the Day of Pentecost, only weeks after the Savior's crucifixion and Resurrection, Jews from all over the empire, including Rome, were taught and baptized by Peter and the other disciples. These new converts returned to their various homes and likely shared the good news with their Jewish neighbors (Acts 2). We are not told where Prisca and Aquila first encountered the gospel of Christ, but they were already Christians when they lived in Rome and before they moved to Corinth about A.D. 49.

While Claudius ruled the Roman empire, missionary efforts among the early Christians expanded and grew dramatically. Claudius, who commenced his rule in A.D. 41, affirmed the special privileges afforded Jews by his predecessors (Josephus, *Ant* 19.5.2–3; 19.6.3). Because Romans made no distinction between Jews and Christians until A.D. 64 when Nero singled out the Christians and not the Jews to be persecuted as scapegoats for the fire that destroyed much of Rome, these protective rights also extended to Christians. An incident sometime during Claudius's reign, however, compelled him to publicly reprimand this protected group, including banishing at least some from the city. The New Testament records that Aquila and Priscilla were "lately come from Italy . . . because that Claudius had commanded all Jews to depart from Rome" (Acts 18:2).

Unrest may have occurred when Jewish Christians proclaimed their testimonies of Jesus Christ in the synagogues. Suetonius, a second-century imperial biographer, wrote that Claudius expelled Jews from Rome due to prolonged uprisings or riots that were instigated among the Jews by "Chrestus" (*Claud* 25.4). That report agrees with Luke's account in Acts 18:2. Although Suetonius gave no chronological marker for the riots, in the fifth century, Orosius dated this exile of the Jews from Rome to the ninth year of Claudius's reign, or A.D. 49 (*Pag* 7.6). That year coincides with Luke's account, which places Prisca and Aquila in Corinth at the same time that Gallio was the Roman proconsul there, sometime around A.D. 50–52 (Acts 18:12–17).[22]

Photo by Kent P. Jackson

Claudius, emperor of Rome A.D. 41–54, banished Jews, including Prisca and Aquila, from Rome during his reign.

Questions also continue about the identity of "Chrestus," whom Suetonius names as the instigator of the riots among the Jews. The most plausible explanation links "Chrestus" with a title for Jesus. Much evidence suggests that outsiders to Christianity were prone to mispronounce or misspell the Greek forms for Christ and Christians by replacing the *i* with an *e,* thereby referring to the leader of the movement as "Chrestus" rather than "Christus" and his followers as "Chrestians."[23] Even as late as the third century, Tertullian complained that many mispronounced the name of the founder of Christianity and insisted that he was a "Christian," not a "Chrestian" (*Nat* 1.3.8–9). Suetonius likely confused Jesus Christ himself preaching in Rome with Jewish converts to the gospel of Christ preaching in his name, which fueled the conflict.

Classics scholar Harry J. Leon suggested a scenario that appears to satisfy the relevant facts. In that scenario, riots in Rome erupted between a few outspoken and influential Jews and Christians, leading Claudius to drastic action to protect the peace and safety of the city while honoring the Roman laws protecting the Jews and recognizing the majority who were not involved in the fray. Therefore, Claudius "expelled only those who had a prominent part in the disturbances and banned the rest from holding assemblies, for fear that new trouble would start. Among those expelled was Aquila, who was a leader of the faction that had accepted Jesus as Christ."[24] In other words, for the sake of peace amid competing factions, the emperor expelled those he considered troublemakers among Jews and Christians alike, making no distinction between them.

Similar unrest between Jews and Christians occurred in Jerusalem (Acts 6:9–15), Antioch of Pisidia (Acts 13:45, 50), Iconia (Acts 14:2, 5), and Lystra (Acts 14:19), as well as Corinth at the time Prisca and Aquila resided there (Acts 18:12–17). Echoes of rioting between Roman Jews and Christians that compelled Claudius to take such drastic action likely reverberated through many other synagogues in the empire. Unquestionably, the earliest conflicts with Christians involved the Jews, not the Romans.

PRISCA AND AQUILA'S APPEARANCE IN THE NEW TESTAMENT STORY

As Christian missionaries in Corinth. Corinth was a Roman colony and the capital of the Roman province of Achaia (today's Greece). It was the largest city in the area with a population of about 100,000 inhabitants, including a large proportion of freedmen. Flanked by its twin ports, Cenchrea and Lecheum, Corinth was the most important commercial and administrative center in all of Greece, attracting businesses, merchants, and travelers in large numbers. Artisans exported their wares from the city to destinations throughout the empire.

Corinth was also the center for the worship of the goddess Aphrodite, whose temple was located on the Acrocorinth, a hill fifteen hundred feet above the city. Strabo, a first-century geographer, estimated that the temple employed "more than a thousand temple slaves, courtesans, whom both men and women had dedicated to the goddess" (*Geogr* 8.6.20). The city had high regard for the temple prostitutes, who had their own seats at the city's theater.

The New Testament indicates that when Paul first came to Corinth as a Christian missionary, about A.D. 50, Prisca and Aquila had "lately come from Italy," but long enough before to have established a tent-making business there and presumably ties with the community (Acts 18:2). In his later letter to the Corinthian Saints, Paul identified Gaius, Crispus, and the household of Stephanos as the only ones he baptized in Corinth (1 Cor. 1:14–16). He made no mention of baptizing Prisca and Aquila. Additionally, when Paul first arrived in Corinth, he worked not with those he baptized but with Prisca and Aquila. In other words, Paul did not teach and baptize them; they were already converted Christians before they arrived in Corinth. Paul went to Corinth seeking them (presumably their reputation as stalwart Christians had spread), and when he "found" them (Acts 18:2), he commenced working with them, both as tent makers and fellow Christians.[25]

During the eighteen months Paul resided in Corinth at the home of Prisca and Aquila, Paul taught the gospel in the nearby synagogue, but nothing is said of his teaching in their home (Acts 18:8–10). If their home in Corinth was not used as a meeting place for Christians, it was the only city in which they resided that their home was not used as a house church. These months of association with Paul would have afforded Prisca and Aquila valuable lessons in discipleship as they witnessed his commitment to faith in Christ whether in times of success or of rejection and persecution. The same may be suggested for potential strength through example and word that Paul received in working alongside Prisca and Aquila.

As Christian missionaries in Ephesus. When Paul left Corinth for Syria at the end of his second mission, Prisca and Aquila accompanied him as far as Ephesus (the western coast of modern-day Turkey). Paul stopped there briefly, but Prisca and Aquila remained in the city for at least three years as patrons of a house church (Acts 18:19–21; 19:10). Paul spent most of his third mission in Ephesus, when he again associated with the missionary couple. He mentioned them both when he wrote from Ephesus to the Corinthian Saints in about A.D. 55.

View from Curetes Street in Ephesus. An east-west thoroughfare lined with shops, baths, and religious shrines and provided with a public latrine, Curetes Street ended at the Library of Celsus, the two-story façade of which stands today but was built after the New Testament era.

Photo by Kent P. Jackson

Josephus called Ephesus "the metropolis of Asia" (*Ant* 14.10.11). The city was the provincial capital and one of three hubs for communication from Rome to the East, the others being Antioch in Syria and Alexandria in Egypt. The city boasted a busy harbor that facilitated shipping and transportation on water or on land with major roads connecting cities to the East.

Ephesus, like most Greco-Roman cities, had a diverse and cosmopolitan population of various races, ethnicities, and religions. The city was home to some 250,000 people when Prisca and Aquila lived there but would double in size by the end of the first century. Approximately a quarter of the city of Ephesus had been allotted to a large Jewish colony.[26] Worship of the goddess Artemis/Diana proved to be lucrative and prestigious for the city. Built centuries earlier, the temple of Artemis was considered one of the seven wonders of the world. In addition to the cult activities there, the temple served as a bank with foreign rulers depositing significant sums of money there for safekeeping, giving temple officials plenty of funds to lend to others in exchange for considerable interest.

Roman aqueducts provided the city with running water to numerous public fountains, baths, and latrines; all were popular locations for socializing. A 25,000-seat theater with remarkable acoustics provided a view of the impressive colonnaded street that led to the harbor. That same street, half a mile long and thirty-five feet wide, was lined with a variety of shops. The city attracted practitioners of hedonism, licentiousness, sorcery, demonism, and magic on one hand and exemplary followers of Christ on the other. Like other prominent cities in the empire, Ephesus exuded tolerance for new ideas and welcomed opportunities to change, making such cities a fertile environment for introducing and spreading the gospel of Jesus Christ.

During their time in Ephesus, Prisca and Aquila heard Apollos, a Jew from Alexandria, "speak boldly in the synagogue" (Acts 18:26). Luke described Apollos as "an eloquent man, and mighty in the scriptures . . . [He] was instructed in the way of the Lord; and being fervent in the spirit, he spake and taught knowing only the baptism of John" (Acts

The Ephesian goddess Artemis is mistakenly called Diana, the name of a Roman goddess, in the King James Version of the Bible. Ephesus became a center for the worship of Artemis and attracted silversmiths, who sold replicas of her image in the city (Acts 19:24–41). Artemis personified wild nature.

Photo by Kent P. Jackson

18:24–25). Interestingly, early translations of the New Testament used by churches descended from Western Christianity, including the King James Version, list Aquila before Priscilla in recounting the story of their teaching Apollos, even though Prisca is named first in the earliest Greek manuscripts of Acts and retained in Eastern Orthodox traditions (Acts 18:26).[27] Prisca's name being listed first is particularly important when we note that in this passage, the missionary couple taught and converted this learned man to Jesus Christ. Naming Priscilla first underscores the probability that she was the leading gospel teacher for Apollos. It reflects her ability to teach, her grasp of scriptures and prophetic teachings from the Old Testament, and the convincing power of her witness.[28]

Apparently, all that Apollos knew and believed about "the Lord" was accurate, but his understanding was incomplete, likely not including knowledge of the gift of the Holy Ghost and the mission of Jesus Christ. His teachers would need to be capable of adding to his already informed understanding of God's will. In the Revised Standard Version of the Bible, the text reads, "Priscilla and Aquila . . . took him in hand and expounded the way to him in greater detail [more completely]" (Acts 18:26). Luke uses the same Greek word translated here as "expounded" to describe Paul's manner of teaching scripture (Acts 28:23). Together, Prisca and her husband effectively taught and converted to Jesus Christ the brilliantly impressive Apollos.

Thereafter, when Apollos felt inclined to go to Achaia to share these truths, Luke reports that the church in Ephesus wrote a letter of introduction to the members there to welcome him. Prisca not only knew the church members in Achaia, because of the months she had lived in Corinth, but probably also knew how to write a letter of recommendation. Although not specified in scripture, Prisca was likely at the center of composing the letter mentioned in verse 27. The results of her teaching and faith are also evident from Apollos's missionary success in Corinth and its environs: "For he mightily convinced the Jews, and that publicly, showing by the scriptures that Jesus was the Christ" (Acts 18:28). John Chrysostom (A.D. 337–407), who often wrote disparagingly of women, acknowledged Priscilla as Apollos's principal teacher: "She taught him the way of God and made him a perfect teacher" (*HomAct* 60).[29]

When Paul returned to Ephesus after Prisca and Aquila had been living there for a year, he found a thriving branch of believers, including Apollos, whom he considered a "brother" and friend (1 Cor. 16:12). In an epistle to the Corinthian Saints, probably written from Ephesus at this time, Paul sent greetings from "the churches of Asia." More specifically, he wrote of those in Ephesus who were well known by the Saints in Corinth: "Aquila and Prisca salute you much in the Lord, with the church that is in their house" (1 Cor. 16:19).[30]

Paul left Ephesus after being expelled from the theater filled with Artemis/Diana worshippers who threatened to riot against him and the Christian cause (Acts 19:24–31; 20:1). Prisca and Aquila may have departed from Ephesus at the same time. The next time we find them in scripture, they had returned to Rome (Rom. 16:3–5).

HOUSE CHURCHES

Private residences were frequently a gathering place for early Christians and a preferred location for teaching. That Christians met undisturbed for so long was likely due to their continued association with Judaism in the eyes of the Romans and the right afforded Jews to assemble for religious purposes. No buildings were constructed for the express purpose of Christian worship in the first century. Paul indicated that Christians in the various branches of the church met to worship in a member's "house."

Small, first-century apartments called *insulae* consisted of one or two rooms in a multistory building. When Christians met together in an *insula*, everyone else in the building would have heard what was being taught and discussed; nothing in such domiciles could be kept secret. Sometimes outsiders apparently wandered into such meetings (1 Cor. 14:23). In another example, Paul taught a group of Christians in a third-story apartment or home in Troas, on the coast north of Ephesus. The gathering extended late into the night, with at least one participant finding a place to sit on the window sill, perhaps an indication of the crowded conditions within or the need for air (Acts 20:7–12).

Only wealthy Christians would have had a house large enough to host the local Christian congregation. Their gatherings were not just once a week but as often as daily for a community prayer. Probably no more than fifty people could assemble in even such larger residences, but a couple of dozen worshippers would be a more likely number.[31] Possibly, a group of Christians in the area met at a home large enough to accommodate them and when the group became too large, a second branch of Christians was established in another home. Meetings to accommodate the "whole church" probably required renting a hall or the patronage of someone with a large home (Acts 15:22; Rom. 16:23).

Not only were women among those who embraced and spread the gospel of Jesus Christ but they often offered their homes as meeting places for Christians in their areas. Mary the mother of John Mark (Acts 12:12), Lydia in Philippi (Acts 16:1–15, 40), Phebe in Cenchrea (Rom. 16:1–2), and Nympha in Laodicea (Col. 4:15) likely hosted church meetings in their homes. Prisca and Aquila opened their house for

Artwork by Balage Balogh

Christians met in the home of one of their members, perhaps in the upper story above the family's workshop, as portrayed here. Prisca and many other women are known in the New Testament to have made their homes available for church assemblies.

church gatherings in Ephesus and Rome and possibly in other cities where they lived, although that is not specified in the scriptures (1 Cor. 16:19; Rom. 16:3, 5).

In some cases, the host of a house church was its financial patron or patroness. This patronage, however, did not mean authoritative leadership for a house church. Female patronage and male priesthood authority could have been the basis for at least some of the conflict involving women attempting to rule the Corinthian branch (1 Cor. 14:31–35). Women may have given financial support and patronage for the house church, but men were given the authority to direct the affairs of the local Christian community.

Paul often referred to Christians as being from "the household of God," perhaps as a reminder that local household affiliations were types of the one true Patron. Jesus Christ is "the head" and "corner stone" of the household of God (Eph. 1:22; 2:19–20; Col. 1:18).

Return to Rome. Prisca and Aquila went back to Rome, probably shortly after the death of Claudius in A.D. 54, when the edict against the Jews lapsed. In Paul's epistle to the Romans, written during his third mission and probably sent shortly after the couple returned, Prisca and Aquila were the first he greeted in a list of some twenty-eight people he names (Rom. 16). Paul called Prisca and her husband *synergous* ("co-workers" with him) in Christ Jesus in establishing Christian communities and teaching the gospel of Christ (Rom. 16:3).

Without giving details, Paul informed the Roman Saints that Prisca and Aquila "have for my life laid down their own necks" (Rom. 16:4). The circumstance is not preserved in scripture, but Paul may be referring to the disturbance in Ephesus after the Christian missionaries' success there threatened sales of silver images of the goddess Artemis/Diana and the craftsmen's livelihood. The city went into an "uproar," and Paul's safety was threatened (Acts 19:23–41; perhaps also 1 Cor. 15:32). Considering that setting, Prisca and Aquila may have used their political or social clout as patrons to set Paul free at the risk of their own lives. Had they simply been ordinary craftsmen recently moved from Corinth, they likely could not have accomplished such a feat.[32]

Paul's words of praise for Prisca and Aquila suggest that many Christians were aware of their courageous deed. He wrote, "Unto whom not only I give thanks, but also all the churches of the Gentiles" (Rom. 16:4). In so doing, the apostle acknowledged the couple's influence for good throughout the mission to the Gentiles. Paul's reference to all converted Christians from non-Jewish backgrounds feeling gratitude for this couple exemplifies the love, unity, and praise that Christians were to express and show to each other.

Again in Ephesus. When Paul wrote his last extant epistle, he again remembered Prisca and Aquila as faithful co-workers in the faith (2 Tim. 4:19). At the time of his writing, he was imprisoned in Rome, knowing that he would soon be executed for his faith in Christ (2 Tim. 4:6–8). The letter is dated at about A.D. 65, during Nero's persecution of Christians in the city. Paul addressed this epistle to Timothy, a church leader who had been in Ephesus (1 Tim. 1:2; 2 Tim. 1:1–5). No details are given to explain why or for what length of time Prisca and Aquila were in Ephesus and no longer in Rome, but Paul continued to view them as important ambassadors for the cause of Christ. His instructions to Timothy are simply, "Salute Prisca and Aquila" (2 Tim. 4:19).

Both of Paul's letters to Timothy reveal his concerns over the Saints in Ephesus and their susceptibility to apostasy in this later time, including issues involving women: their dress and demeanor in church services (1 Tim. 2:9–12), being "idle" and "busybodies, speaking things which they ought not" (1 Tim. 5:13), vulnerability to false teachings so as easily to be led away from the truth (2 Tim. 3:6). Imagining Prisca in such a congregation underscores why Paul often turned to her for help. As a knowledgeable, converted, and articulate teacher and disciple, Prisca and her example would provide a strong role model for women in the church.

BETWEEN THE LINES

Only six brief New Testament passages speak of Prisca, but they combine to paint a consistent image of an inspiring believer of Jesus Christ. She left a life of luxury and a position of status in Roman society to preach the gospel and fellowship the Saints. She selflessly utilized the privileges and resources she received, likely as a result of being part of a prominent family, to be a patron to the church in Jewish and Gentile communities in the Greco-Roman world. Her support and encouragement to Paul and countless other Christians were significant. Her legacy of service and unwearied devotion to the work of the Lord can be just as inspiring in today's world.

POINTS TO PONDER

1. How does Prisca expand and inspire your understanding of ways that women can contribute to the work of the Lord today?

2. What functions did Prisca and Aquila perform as leaders in the early church?

3. How do knowing that Prisca was married, a devoted missionary companion with her husband, and often a leader in their church work inform your perceptions of her and the institution of marriage?

CHRISTIAN WOMEN IN ROME

*I*n the final chapter of his letter to the Romans, Paul sent many more greetings than in any other of his extant letters (Rom. 16:3–15). Included in the greetings are twenty-eight individuals, more than one-third of whom are women. Two men (Narcissus and Aristobulus) are not directly greeted, probably because they were not believers; however, Paul did greet their households, which unquestionably would have included women. The Christian community in Rome was a unique setting for him, at least in part because he had not yet labored as a missionary there. Notwithstanding, Paul had previously worked in areas east of Italy with most of these Roman Christians whom he greeted, including many of the women. At the conclusion of his lengthy treatise to the Roman Saints, Paul's salutations to these individuals could help him build trust among the larger community of Saints in an area in which he was largely unknown.

HISTORICAL CONTEXT

The stories of how these residents of Rome encountered the gospel of Jesus Christ appear nowhere in scripture. Apparently, some were converted even before Paul was. If they were previously devout Jews, they could have been taught the gospel in Jerusalem when they traveled there for one of the Jewish holy days, as on the Day of Pentecost (Acts 2–3). Just as likely, Christian missionaries may have traveled to Rome to establish the church there and introduced some of them to Jesus Christ. The recipients of Paul's greetings in Rome included close friends and fellow laborers with Paul in Asia Minor or Greece and who later returned to Rome after the edict of Claudius ended. Prisca and Aquila fit this description, and many of the other women and men named in the letter may also.

Others were individuals whom Paul knew only by reputation, perhaps as leaders or patrons of Roman house churches. He included them in his greetings, possibly to show respect for their honorific positions in the community and the church. Due to the growing numbers of Christians in the city and the variety of the

ROMANS 16:3–15

310

The Imperial Forum in Rome. When first-century Christians lived in Rome, they would have known the rectangular plaza that formed the center of the city. The Forum, surrounded by important public buildings, was the place where commercial, cultic, and business activities occurred.

members' cultural and religious roots, house churches may have been created around different ethnic identities. For example, the church in Prisca and Aquila's home would have attracted Jewish Christians (Rom. 16:3–5); another congregation could have been made up of Hellenistic Christians (Rom. 16:14); and a third group could have been made up of those from other cultural backgrounds, including those whose names indicate slave origins (Rom. 16:15).[1] An estimated 40 percent of Italy's population were slaves, especially those with Greek names, suggesting that a good number of Roman Christians had slave origins.[2]

In addition to Prisca and her husband, Aquila, many others are greeted in pairs. The Greek conjunction *kai,* used in each case and translated "and," suggests that the pair was related through marriage or family. The scriptural context opens the probability that the pairs had served as missionary companions. Those who are named without any such familial connection may not have had Christian relatives, or Paul may not have known their family situation or a companion with whom he or she had labored.

THE APPEARANCE OF CHRISTIAN ROMAN WOMEN IN THE NEW TESTAMENT STORY

In addition to Prisca, Paul saluted eight other women in Rome. Exploring the verses of scripture in which they are named provides a glimpse of the various types of women who were stalwart Christians in the Greco-Roman world.

Mary (Latin, "a woman of the Marius clan"). "Greet Mary, who bestowed much labor on us" (Rom. 16:6). That Mary had labored "much" suggests that she had been active in the Christian faith for a significant length of time. Paul's brief description also indicates that he was acquainted with her because she had "bestowed much labor" on him and others, possibly after she was exiled from Rome during Claudius's edict.[3] Considering the preponderance of other women of the time bearing the same name, hers was either a Jewish name (the same name as that of the mother of Jesus) or the feminine form of the Latin name Marius. Romans almost always gave their daughters the feminine form of the father's name, even if there was more than one daughter in the family.[4] *Mary* has been found 108 times as a contemporary Latin name, which strongly suggests that the Mary to whom Paul sent greetings was a Gentile Christian from the Marius family in Rome.[5] On the other hand, the name has also been found eight times in the first-century Jewish catacombs of Rome.[6] If she was from a Jewish background and converted to Christianity,

Artwork by Balage Balogh

An artist's rendering of the Roman Forum in the mid first century A.D.

her residence in Rome implies a greater probability that her ancestors went from the Holy Land to Rome as slaves.

Junia (Latin, "a woman of the Junius clan"). "Salute Andronicus and Junia, my kinsmen, and my fellowprisoners, who are of note among the apostles, who also were in Christ before me" (Rom. 16:7). Paul's linking Andronicus and Junia with "apostles" has caused considerable debate from at least the sixteenth century over whether a woman could hold the title of "apostle"; whether the name Junia could be a diminutive form of a man's name, which removes claims of legitimate female apostles; or whether the couple was merely recognized and appreciated by the apostles rather than being apostles themselves.[7] Because no evidence of a masculine name related to Junia, such as Junias, is documented in ancient Rome and because Junia was a common Roman name for women, especially for slaves and freedwomen of the Junia family (some 250 times), the support for a female Junia in Paul's greeting is "overwhelming."[8]

The most logical explanation for Junia's role in the early Christian church is that she and Andronicus were a married couple who were "sent forth" to preach the gospel, the underlying meaning of the Greek word translated into English as "apostle." The terminology for Christian missionaries and other functionaries, such as "apostles," was still very fluid in those early years. As an unofficial term meaning anyone who was "sent forth," an *apostle* could be any male or female representative, leader, or called servant of the Christian faith.[9] Because Paul is frequently referred to as an apostle in the New Testament without clarifying whether he was one of the Twelve Apostles or one of many who were "sent forth," the term is likely a designation that could apply to all Christians who specifically worked and traveled as missionaries or who were witnesses of the Resurrection of Christ. That the names Andronicus and Junia were linked with the Greek conjunction that signifies they were related further supports the probability that they were a married couple.

Prisca and Aquila were hardly the only married couple who were missionaries of the time. Paul defended the practice of an "apostle" taking along his wife or sister to carry out missionary labors (1 Cor. 9:1–5). It is dangerous, though, to conclude that a woman was among the Twelve in the early Church from this reference alone, because the term *apostle* was obviously used in a much broader sense in the first century than in later eras. The New International Version translates the phrase as "They are outstanding among the apostles." Nonetheless, it appears that of all those called to represent and bear witness of Christ, Junia and her husband were among the greatest.

Paul called Junia and Andronicus his "kinsmen," or relatives, suggesting that they were from Jewish families. Like Prisca and Aquila, they could generate trust for Paul among the Jewish Christians in Rome. Paul also notes that they had been imprisoned with him. Considering the conflict that often erupted when missionaries opened new areas for preaching and the number of times Paul had been imprisoned, the description of being "fellowprisoners" was probably literal. Roman prisons held arrested persons in crowded, filthy, and dangerous conditions until they could be tried or punished (Acts 16:19–24).[10] Had Junia and her husband been imprisoned with Paul under such conditions, a strong bond of trust would naturally have formed.

Finally, Paul explains that Andronicus and Junia "were in Christ before me," which indicates that they were converted to Christianity before he was and underscores their long-time commitment to the work. Consequently, they could have been among the earliest Christians in Jerusalem. One scholar has even suggested that Junia could have been the same woman as Joanna the wife of Herod's steward (Luke 8:3), *Joanna* being the Hebrew form of the Latin name.[11] It seems more likely, however, that Andronicus and Junia could have been converted to Christianity on the Day of Pentecost (Acts 2:1) or been numbered among the "Grecians" in Jerusalem in the early days of the church (Acts 6:1).

Tryphena and Tryphosa (Greek, "delicate or dainty" and "luscious, or living luxuriously"). "Salute Tryphena and Tryphosa, who labor in the Lord" (Romans 16:12). No other information is given about these women beyond their involvement in missionary efforts, being workers "in the Lord." Because of the similarity of their names and Paul's report of their working together, many scholars assume they were sisters who were missionaries or held important roles in the local church.[12] They could just as likely have been unrelated missionary companions who traveled and lived together. The norm for early Christian missionaries seems to have been preaching and traveling in pairs.[13] Having a traveling companion would have been particularly beneficial for female missionaries, considering the uncertainties and dangers of public travel at the time. The wording suggests that Paul was personally acquainted with the women, possibly by having labored with them during his missionary efforts in the East. As leading Christians in Rome, they may have been exiled during the "Jewish" unrest. Contemporary listings of their names in Rome indicate that the two women were probably descended from slaves.[14]

Persis (Greek, "Persian woman"). "Salute the beloved Persis, which labored much in the Lord" (Rom. 16:12). Paul's reference to Persis as "beloved" indicates he was well acquainted with her. She may have been one of the exiles from Rome whom Paul met in Asia Minor or Greece. At some time in the past, he witnessed that she "labored much in the Lord" or made significant contributions to the spread of the gospel of Jesus Christ. Although her name could indicate slave origins from Persia, it has been found only three times in first-century Rome and as either a bondwoman or a free woman.[15]

Mother of Rufus. "Salute Rufus chosen in the Lord, and his mother and mine" (Rom. 16:13). Although we are not told the name of Rufus's mother, the short greeting indicates that she and her son were believers and well acquainted with Paul. Robert Jewett argues for considering this Rufus as the same man so named in Mark 15:21. In other words, Rufus may be the son of Simon of Cyrene, who carried Jesus' cross, which would mean his mother was the wife of Simon of Cyrene.[16] Paul's only added information about the mother of Rufus is that he acknowledged her as a mother figure to him as well, "his mother and mine." It is likely that this good woman had the disposition and economic ability to render appreciated hospitality to the missionaries.

Julia and Nereus's Sister (Latin, "a woman of the Julius clan"). "Salute Philologus, and Julia, Nereus, and his sister, and Olympas,[17] and all the saints which are with them" (Rom. 16:15). With no other description but their inclusion with the "saints," the frequent use of the Greek conjunction translated "and" suggests that at least some of these individuals were related to each other or were members of the same house church. It does not appear that Paul had met or worked with them. Julia and Philologos were probably husband and wife.[18] Nereus and his sister may have been biological siblings and also children of Julia and Philologus or children of another married couple who was not known to Paul.[19] Paul did not know the name of Nereus's sister, which suggests he knew the individuals in this group by reputation but not personally. The female Roman name Julia appears 1,400 times in Roman documents, indicating a descendant from a patrician family, a noble lady from the house of Julian. It is also possible that she was a freedwoman or the descendant of a freed slave associated with the prestigious Julian family.[20] Nereus's Greek name indicates that he was likely from a background of slavery, and therefore his sister would likely have also been a slave or a freedwoman.[21]

BETWEEN THE LINES

Early Christians gave more of themselves and their resources to help the poor and needy than the followers of other religions gave to their temples.[22] No cost was too great as they worked to spread the teachings and truths of Jesus Christ, motivated by their love and indebtedness to their Redeemer. These Christian pioneers "put heart and soul into all their acts of love. The freedom of self-determination in their labors gave an entirely voluntary character to all social work done by the early Christians."[23] They entered the gospel net as new creatures, receiving the Holy Spirit by baptism and the laying on of hands, and became confident and free. One early Christian leader, Cyprian (ca. 200–258), explained the change this way: "Doubtful things at once began to assure themselves to me, hidden things to be revealed, dark things to be enlightened, what before had seemed difficult began to suggest a means of accomplishment" (*Don* 4). The Christian women and men that Paul greeted at the conclusion of his epistle to the Romans are indicative of this newfound confidence in God and selfless acts of service.

In a broader sense, beyond what is understood by looking at these Christians individually, Paul's greetings to the Roman Saints served to establish a level of trust with a Christian community in which he was largely unknown. Those who had been co-workers with him would be able to recommend him and his teachings to the rest of the branch. Those he greeted were trusted members of the church in Rome and likely individuals of consequence. The details that Paul includes about many of these men and women appear to be more for the reader's benefit than for those he specifically greeted. In other words, the implication is that Paul felt a need to introduce these Roman Saints as trustworthy Christians to a congregation that does not know them or him very well.[24]

His repeated use of the second-person plural imperative, "Greet" or "Salute," communicated to a community of Saints collectively to welcome one another with a warm embrace, whether the other was male or female. Kissing or embracing a guest communicated that the newcomer was an acknowledged member of the extended family.[25] The pattern reflected in Paul's instructions to the Roman Christians illustrates what must have been appropriate Christian protocol in the early church as a way to communicate honor and sincere hospitality regardless of the recipient's ecclesiastical or social status. Early converts to Christianity would likely have found such a departure from traditional class systems revolutionary when they joined a community that emphasized divine worth over worldly status. Women were an integral part of this inclusive hospitality, leading, expanding, and strengthening the congregations of Christians in Rome.

POINTS TO PONDER

1. How might we improve our fellowshipping practices within our wards by applying the attitudes toward visitors and newcomers that Paul encouraged?

2. How may our current use of the title *Elder* give insight into the first-century use of the term *apostle*?

3. How might the use of married couples, siblings, and two female companions as effective missionaries in New Testament times redirect our understanding of what an effective missionary force looks like? How have recent changes in Church missionary policy redefined the demographics of our current missionary force?

CONCLUSION

The dramatic power of the brief Bible narrative is one of their most wonderful characteristics. By a few incidents, a word here and there, they create a vivid image of a personality that afterwards never dies from our memory. The women of Shakespeare have been set upon the stage with all the accessories of dress, scenery, and the interpreting power of fine acting, and yet the vividness of their personality has not been equal to that of the women of the Bible.[1]

—Harriet Beecher Stowe

More than twenty years ago, I encountered *Women in Sacred History,* by Harriet Beecher Stowe, one of the earliest works on women in the Bible. Surrounded by a father and brothers who were Protestant ministers, she grew up with a reverence for scriptural teachings. In her own reading of the Bible, however, she also discovered the roles women played throughout the biblical story, roles which the men in her family did not see. As a result of her serious inquiries, she found the power of story to be as compelling as the inspiring teachings. Her perspective of seeing these women as real people who could become our heroines invited me to look at scripture through their eyes. Stowe recognized the need to see these women in their cultural context and was not afraid to see them as flawed as we all are. With few other resources than the Bible, she wrote a stunning tribute to women in all their various roles.

In a complementary way, *Women of the New Testament* and its companion volume, *Women of the Old Testament,* provide a valuable avenue to insight by shining the spotlight on the remarkable lives of early Christian women. They exemplify the power of the gospel when it is "written . . . with the Spirit of the living God; not in tables of stone, but in the fleshy tables of the heart" (2 Cor. 3:3). Their enduring stories witness that believing women were valiant missionaries for Christ in word and deed. They remind us today that God works through his daughters *and* his sons to accomplish his great work for all of humankind. By studying the first-century Christian women, we better appreciate the meaning of discipleship and the strength created through community efforts where everyone's contribution is valued. Finally, these women's lives turn our hearts to Jesus Christ, the focus of all scripture.

This deeper study of the power of Jesus Christ as experienced among women in his day offers us something more than an increased reverence for Christ's power. If God sees the poor widow bent over for eighteen years and the group of women praying together by the river near Philippi, he can see each of us. And because he sees each of his children, he also knows the precise time to send one to minister, to bless, and to cheer. Elder Neal A. Maxwell of the Quorum of the Twelve Apostles realized the power of such a discovery. He testified, "The same God that placed the star in a precise orbit millennia before it appeared over Bethlehem in celebration of the birth of the Babe has given at least equal attention to the placement of each of us in precise human orbits so that we may, if we will, illuminate the landscape of our individual lives, so that our light may not only lead others but warm them as well."[2] Awareness of these women's stories is a reminder that God sees each of us, whether anyone else does or not. And, as he did for so many of the women of the New Testament, he has prepared missions whereby each of us, no matter how lowly our station, can assist him in his work.

On Resurrection morning, the two angels told the women to remember what Jesus taught them concerning his gospel and how he would be crucified and rise again. "And they remembered his words . . . and told all these things unto the eleven, and to all the rest" (Luke 24:4–9). As true disciples who hear the word of God to remember it and do it, these women inspire us to do the same today. Of equal importance, many of the women of the New Testament illustrate the true sense of community.[3] The ideal Christian community is created when engaged women and men work together in the spread of the faith and in their joined efforts to include all members in an active, authentically lived religion. With the blessing of Christ's Atonement and renewed commitment to keep our covenants with him, we cannot fail in that quest.

The stories of the women of the New Testament create lasting, fascinating images in our minds. Perhaps because they were not presented as being without flaws, they are endeared to us. They give us hope that the Atonement of Jesus Christ is every bit as much for us, too. That, however, was likely not the reason women were included in scripture. The purpose that propelled authors to write the testimonies and epistles included in our New Testament was to bear witness of Jesus Christ, not to showcase the disciples of Jesus, especially not to highlight his female disciples. Nonetheless, making our own personal journey to Christ is informed and enlightened by the examples of these women of the first century.

In the meridian of time, the Christian church commenced after multitudes heard both men and women bear witness of their Redeemer. Our recognition of the breadth of the Savior's power will likewise increase when we hear and appreciate the testimonies of all those who know the Lord—even those whose perspective may be different from our own. When both women and men fervently testify of the stunning reality of the Atonement in their lives, we are all blessed.

Appendix A

NEW TESTAMENT CHRONOLOGIES

The story of the New Testament fits within a single century. Contemporary secular histories allow us to create a general outline of events chronicled in the life of Jesus Christ and the opening era of the Christian church. Our calculations of approximate years must remain somewhat fluid, however, considering the absence of a standard calendar used by all historians during the Roman era.

DATING THE BIRTH OF JESUS

Time markers from various primary sources indicate that Mary probably gave birth to the Son of God before 2 B.C.[1] Although at first it might seem obvious that Jesus was born in the "year of the Lord," or *anno domini* (A.D. 1), our present calendar is inaccurate. The seeming contradiction of dating Jesus' birth to years B.C. ("before Christ") is explained by mistakes made in developing a dating system centuries after the Savior's mortal life. Specifically, at the behest of Christians in the sixth century, a Scythian monk named Dionysius Exiguus invented a calendar that reckoned time from the year that Jesus was born rather than from the era of the Roman emperor Diocletian (A.D. 284–305). Unfortunately, Dionysius made some miscalculations.

To compound the confusion surrounding the precise date of Jesus' birth, there is an apparent lack of consensus in reputable primary sources for events mentioned in the New Testament as coinciding with his mortal life. Specifically, the birth occurred near the end of Herod's reign (Matt. 2:1; Luke 1:5) and around the time of Augustus Caesar's "taxation" in the area when Cyrenius was governor of Syria (Luke 2:1–2). Additionally, during "the fifteenth year of the reign of Tiberius Caesar," Jesus "began to be about thirty years of age" (Luke 3:1, 23). In each of these cases, the accepted year of the political event would suggest errors in Matthew's and Luke's assigned dating for the year Mary gave birth to Jesus. These observations reveal further problems with pinpointing the exact year.

Political events as markers of time. A variety of suggestions have been made to reconcile apparent contradictions, some of which are briefly described here. The point remains, however, that chronicling the birth of Christ in the context of world history requires us to speak in terms of B.C. instead of "in the year of the Lord."

The death of Herod. Many scholars conclude that Herod the Great died no later than the spring of 4 B.C.[2] A principal support for this observation is Josephus, who claimed that Herod died just before Passover some thirty-seven years after he was named "king" of the Jews by the Romans (40 B.C.) and thirty-four years after he ordered the death of Antigonus (37 B.C.) (*Ant* 17.8.1; 17.9.3). Because Josephus counted parts of years as full years in his calculations, it would be more accurate to say that Herod died in the year *before* 3 B.C.[3] Furthermore, shortly before Herod's death, an eclipse of the moon occurred (*Ant* 17.6.4), which corresponds to a lunar eclipse in the land of Israel on the night of March 12–13 in 4 B.C.[4]

On the other hand, along with other problems with the 4 B.C. date for Herod's death, Jack Finegan contends that the twenty-nine days that separated the 4 B.C. eclipse and Passover that year were not sufficient to accommodate the numerous events in Herod's life that Josephus describes as transpiring during that time. He lists several reasons for concluding that a 1 B.C. date for Herod's death would be more appropriate.[5]

According to both Matthew and Luke, Jesus was born while Herod still lived, although not long before his death (Matt. 2:15, 19; Luke 1:5). That Mary and Joseph lived in a "house" and Jesus was identified as a *paidion* (Greek, "child") rather than *brephos* (Greek, "infant" or "newborn") when the wise men visited them, suggests that Jesus was born perhaps a year or two before Herod's death. This conclusion is supported by the use of the word *pais* for the "children" who were "two years old and under" to be killed by Herod's command (Matt. 2:16).

The taxation by Augustus. No known empire-wide census was conducted under Caesar Augustus, but a provincial census that included Judea was ordered during his reign. A political leader often conducted a census as a condition for calculating new taxes. Publius Sulpicius Quirinius, or Cyrenius, as he is known in the Gospel of Luke, acted as governor of Syria two different times under the direction of Augustus in Rome. His first term is dated at 3–2 B.C.; the second term began in A.D. 6 at the same time that Archelaus, son and successor of Herod, was deposed as ruler of Judea.[6] Immediately following Archelaus's departure, Augustus sent Cyrenius to "Judea, which was now added to the province of Syria, to take an account of their substance, and to dispose of Archelaus's money" (Josephus, *Ant* 17.13.5; 18.1.1). The problem in our search for the year Jesus was born is that this taxation and census by Cyrenius occurred during his second term as governor in A.D. 6 and therefore no longer during the reign of Herod the Great. Many scholars feel it is impossible to reconcile Luke's timing of the wondrous birth with Cyrenius's census and taxation of Judea with the currently available data (Luke 2:1–2).

In an attempt to harmonize the biblical and the historical accounts, some researchers have turned to Tertullian, who cited an otherwise unknown source naming Sentius Saturninius as the governor of Syria who initiated a census just before he left office (*Marc* 4.19). Considering that the process of census taking and taxation would require more than a year to finish, Saturninius's successor would likely have overseen its conclusion, allowing for a census during the possible time frame of Jesus' birth (6–2 B.C.). Unfortunately for our purposes, the next Syrian governor's name was Quintilius Varus rather than Quirinius/Cyrenius, and Quirinius/Cyrenius did not govern until 3–2 B.C., too late to be involved with Saturninius's census (Josephus, *Ant* 17.5.2).[7] To reconcile this challenge, some scholars have argued that Luke or a later copyist confused the name Quintilius with that of Quirinius.[8]

Finegan revised the assumed list of Syrian governors and contends that Cyrenius/Quirinius was not one of them but was instead Caesar's "first procurator in Judea" and associated with Saturninus, the Syrian governor at the time of the birth of Jesus. He further argues that rather than a census for taxation, Luke's wording could be understood as a registration for purposes other than taxation, such as the registering of all people within the empire, which indeed did occur in conjunction with Augustus Caesar's thirteenth consulship in the year 2 B.C.[9]

SELECTED GOVERNORS OF SYRIA UNDER CAESAR AUGUSTUS[10]

9–6 B.C.	Sentius Saturninus
6–4 B.C.	Quintilius Varus
3–2 B.C.	Sulpicius Quirinius/Cyrenius
1 B.C.–A.D. 4	Gaius Julius Caesar, adopted son of Augustus
A.D. 4–5	Volusius Saturninus
A.D. 6-?	Sulpicius Quirinius/Cyrenius
A.D. 11–17	Caecilius Creticus Silanus

FINEGAN'S REVISED LIST OF GOVERNORS OF SYRIA[11]

7 or 6–4 B.C.	Quintilius Varus
4–2 B.C.	Sentius Saturninus
2 B.C.–A.D. 1	Quintilius Varus (a second time)
A.D.1–4	Gaius Julius Caesar, adopted son of Augustus

The reign of Tiberius Caesar. Luke reports that Jesus was baptized and commenced his ministry in "the fifteenth year of the reign of Tiberius Caesar" when he "began to be about thirty years of age" (Luke 3:1, 23). Tiberius became the sole emperor of the Roman empire shortly after the death of Augustus Caesar in A.D. 14. In anticipation of the transition of power that came with the knowledge that Augustus's death was imminent, Tiberius received unlimited power in A.D. 13.[12] Accepting the possibility that either A.D. 13 or 14 was his first year's rule, "the fifteenth year" of Tiberius's reign would be about A.D. 27–29. Calculating the Savior's birth nearly thirty years before these dates and accounting for the absence of a year "0" in the Roman system places his birth year around 3–1 B.C.

Although far more extensive explorations of the problem surrounding attempts to date precisely the year of the Savior's birth have been conducted, this review underscores challenges to establishing an accepted date for when Mary gave birth to Jesus. For our purposes here, we consider that Jesus was born sometime between 6 B.C. to 2 B.C.

POSSIBLE TIME LINE FOR THE NEW TESTAMENT GOSPELS

40 B.C.	Before the Roman senate, Octavian declares Herod "king of Judea"
37 B.C.	Herod conquers the Hasmonean kingdom to officially begin his rule from Jerusalem
31 B.C.	Octavian becomes absolute sovereign of the Roman empire, assuming the name Augustus Caesar
29 B.C.	Herod executes his favorite wife, Mariamne, the daughter of Hasmonean royalty
20 B.C.	Herod begins building the temple in Jerusalem
21–15 B.C.	Mary is born
7–3 B.C.	Herod executes his sons by Mariamne the Hasmonean: Alexander and Aristobulus
6–2 B.C.	Mary gives birth to Jesus, the Son of God
4–1 B.C.	Herod dies five days after ordering the death of his eldest son, Antipater; his will named his son Archelaus as ethnarch over Judea; his son Herod Antipas as tetrarch over Galilee and Perea; and his son Philip as tetrarch over Gaulonitis, Trachonitis, Batanea, and Panias
A.D. 6	Archelaus is banished; Roman prefects begin rule in Jerusalem; Cyrenius took a census and taxed the inhabitants of Judea
A.D. 13	Tiberius is granted power equal to that of Emperor Augustus
A.D. 14	Death of Augustus Caesar; Tiberius becomes sole emperor of the Roman empire
A.D. 24–29	Jesus is baptized and begins his ministry[13]
A.D. 28–33	Jesus is crucified and is resurrected three days later

CHRONOLOGY WITHIN THE SAVIOR'S THREE-YEAR MINISTRY

The Gospel of John provides the best indicators of the four Passover celebrations that marked the Savior's mortal ministry. The order of events listed below within each year generally follows Luke's arrangement of them because he is the one author to state that he presented the testimony of Jesus Christ "in order" (Luke 1:1–4). Nevertheless, the order here is arguably not precise, because Luke does not mention events and women chronicled in others of the Gospels.

Mary, the mother of Jesus, requests his assistance at the marriage in Cana (John 2)

First Passover (John 2:13, 23)
The woman of Samaria at the well (John 4)
John the Baptist is imprisoned (Luke 3:19–20)
Peter's mother-in-law (Luke 4:38–39)

The widow of Nain (Luke 7:11–15)

The woman who loved much (Luke 7:36–50)

The Galilean women who minister to Jesus (Luke 8:1–3)

Mary, Jesus' mother, and his brothers hear him teach (Luke 8:19–21)

The woman who touches the hem of his garment (Luke 8:43–48)

The daughter of Jairus (Luke 8:49–56)

Second Passover (John 5:1)

Herodias schemes against John the Baptist (Mark 6:17–28)

Salome dances for Herod's birthday (Mark 6:22–23)

Herod Antipas orders the death of John the Baptist (Luke 9:9)

Third Passover (John 6:1–4)

The Syrophoenician woman and her daughter (Mark 7:25–30)

Peter is given the keys of the priesthood on the Mount of Transfiguration (Luke 9:28–36)

Jesus teaches Martha and Mary in Bethany (Luke 10:38–42)

The woman taken in adultery (John 8:1–11)

Woman bent over is healed on the Sabbath day (Luke 13:11–13)

Martha and Mary's brother Lazarus is raised from the dead (John 11)

Mother of James and John asks a favor for her sons (Matt. 20:20–26)

Fourth Passover (John 11:55; 12:1; 13:1)

Mary anoints Jesus in preparation for his death (John 12:3–8)

The widow who gave all (Luke 21:1–4)

Pilate's wife (Matt. 27:19)

Jesus' mother and other women of Galilee at the crucifixion (Luke 23:27–31; John 19:25–27)

Mary Magdalene and other Galilean women witness the empty tomb and the resurrected Christ
   (Luke 24:1–10; John 20:1–2)

CHRONOLOGY FOR THE FIRST-CENTURY CHURCH UNDER THE APOSTLES

Commencing with the forty-day ministry of the resurrected Christ, the chronology of the apostolic era of the New Testament relies on Roman and Jewish historical records that date the rule of political leaders mentioned in the scriptures in conjunction with events recounted in the early Christian church.[14] Stories of New Testament women are listed in the approximate time frame in which their appearance is chronicled in scripture. As in assigning dates in antiquity to either B.C. or A.D., we must allow some latitude since historians assigned dates according to national or political events, such as the year of an emperor's reign.

A.D. 28–33	Disciples of Christ, both men and women, teach the gospel in the areas around Jerusalem and bring thousands into the gospel net (Acts 1–8)
A.D. 33–36	Paul is converted (Acts 9)
	Peter raises Tabitha from the dead in Joppa (Acts 9:36–43)
A.D. 41–44	Death of James brother of John; Peter is imprisoned (Acts 12)
	Rhoda and Mary mother of Mark greet Peter when he is freed (Acts 12:12–13)
A.D. 47–48	Paul's first missionary journey (Acts 13–14)
	Eunice, Timothy, and perhaps Lois are converted in Lystra (Acts 16:1)
A.D. 49	The Jerusalem Conference (Acts 15)
	Claudius's edict banishes "Jews" from Rome
A.D. 49–51	Paul's second missionary journey (Acts 16–18)
	Lydia is converted in Philippi (Acts 16:14–15)
	Slave-girl soothsayer (Acts 16:16–18)
	Chief women are converted in Thessalonica and Athens (Acts 17:1–4)
A.D. 50–52	Gallio is Roman deputy in Corinth (Acts 18:12–17)
	Prisca and Aquila anchor the church in Corinth (Acts 18)
A.D. 52–55	Paul's third missionary journey (Acts 18–21)
	Prisca and Aquila in Ephesus and Rome (Acts 18; Rom. 16:3–4)
	Phebe delivers Paul's letter to Rome (Rom. 16)
	Christian women in Rome (Rom. 16)
A.D. 56–60	Paul's first imprisonment in Caesarea and Rome (Acts 23–28)
	Drusilla and Bernice hear Paul's testimony of Christ (Acts 24–25)
A.D. 60–64	Paul is freed and continues his ministry in various areas of the empire (1 Tim.; Titus)
A.D. 64–68	Paul's second imprisonment, which ends with his execution (2 Tim. 4)
	Prisca and Aquila in Ephesus (2 Tim. 4:19)

Appendix B

WOMEN OF THE NEW TESTAMENT

The following list of women named or described in the New Testament is not certain because on occasion either the woman or the name is uncertain. Some of the meanings of the names are likewise uncertain.

Anna "Grace"
   Luke 2:36–38
Apphia "That which is fruitful"
   Philem. 1:1–3
Bernice "Victorious"
   Acts 25:13, 23; 26:30
Candace "Foreign origin"
   Acts 8:27
Chloe "Verdant"
   1 Cor. 1:11
Claudia "Belonging to the clan of Claudius"
   2 Tim. 4:21
Damaris "Gentle"
   Acts 17:34
Diana/Artemis (Ephesian goddess)
   Acts 19:24–35
Dorcas (see Tabitha)
Drusilla "Belonging to clan of Livius"
   Acts 24:24
Elisabeth "God is my oath"
   Luke 1:5–25, 36–45, 56–80
   D&C 84:27

Eunice "Happy victory"
   Acts 16:1
   2 Tim. 1:5
Eve "Life"
   Gen. 2:21–25; 3; 4:1, 25
   2 Cor. 11:3
   1 Tim. 2:13–15
   1 Ne. 5:11
   2 Ne. 2:18–21; 9:9
   Alma 12:25–26
   D&C 138:39
   Moses 2:27; 3:22–25; 4:6–30; 5:1–27; 6:2–6, 9
   Abr. 5:16–19
Herodias "Heroic"
   Matt. 14:3–11
   Mark 6:17–28
   Luke 3:19–20
Joanna "Favored of Jehovah"
   Luke 8:2–3; 23:49, 55–56; 24:1–12, 22–24
Jochebed "Jehovah is glory"
   Ex. 2:1–2; 6:20
   Num. 26:59
   Heb. 11:23

Julia "Belonging to the clan of Julius"
    Rom. 16:15
Junia "Belonging to the clan of Julius"
    Rom. 16:7
Lois "Agreeable"
    2 Tim. 1:5
Lydia "Woman from Lydia"
    Acts 16:14–15, 40
Martha "Mistress"
    Luke 10:38–42
    John 11:1–46; 12:2
Mary[1] "Beloved [of God]"
    (Mother of Jesus)
    Isa. 7:14; 2 Ne. 17:14
    Matt. 1:16–25; 2:11–14, 20–23
    Matt. 12:46–50; 13:55–56
    Mark 3:31–35; 6:3
    Luke 1:26–56; 2; 8:19–21
    John 2:1–12; 6:42; 19:25–27
    Acts 1:14
    Gal. 4:4
    1 Ne. 11:13–21
    Mosiah 3:8
    Alma 7:10; 19:13
Mary[2] (Mother of James and Joses)
    Matt. 27:55–56, 61; 28:1–8
    Mark 15:40–41, 47
    Luke 23:49, 55, 56
    Luke 24:1–12, 22–24
Mary[3] (of Bethany)
    Luke 10:38–42
    John 11:1–46; 12:3–9
    Matt. 26:6–13; Mark 14:3–9
Mary[4] (Wife of Cleophas?)
    John 19:25

Mary[5] (Mother of John Mark)
    Acts 12:12
    Col. 4:10
Mary[6] (belonging to the clan of Marius)
    Rom. 16:6
Mary Magdalene
    Matt. 27:55–56, 61; 28:1–8
    Mark 15:40–41, 47; 16:1–11
    Luke 8:1–3; 23:49, 55–56; 24:1–12, 22–24
    John 19:25; 20:1–18
Persis "Persian woman"
    Rom. 16:12
Phebe "Radiant"
    Rom. 16:1–2
Prisca/Priscilla "Venerable"
    Acts 18:2, 18, 26
    Rom. 16:3–5
    1 Cor. 16:19
    2 Tim. 4:19
Rachab/Rahab "Spacious; broad"
    Josh. 2:1–21; 6:17–25
    Heb. 11:31
    Matt. 1:5
    James 2:25–26
Rachel "Ewe"
    Gen. 29–35; 46:19, 22, 25; 48:7
    Ruth 4:11
    1 Sam. 10:2
    Jer. 31:15 (spelled Rahel)
    Matt. 2:18
Rebecca/Rebekah "Ensnarer"
    Gen. 22:23; 24–29; 35:8; 49:31
    Rom. 9:10–13 (spelled Rebecca)
Rhoda "Rose"
    Acts 12:12–15

Ruth "Friend"

    Ruth 1–4

    Matt. 1:5

Salome "Peace of Zion"

    Mark 15:40–41; 16:1–8

    Luke 23:55–24:2, 22–24

Sapphira "Sapphire"

    Acts 5:1–11

Sarah "Princess"

    Gen. 11:29–31; 24:67; 49:31

    Isa. 51:2; 2 Ne. 8:2

    Rom. 4:19; 9:9 (spelled Sara)

    Gal. 4:22–31

    Heb. 11:11

    1 Pet. 3:6

D&C 132:34–37; 137:5–6

    Abr. 2

Susanna "White lily"

    Luke 8:2–3

Tabitha/Dorcas "Gazelle"

    Acts 9:36–42

Thamar/Tamar "Palm tree"

    Gen. 38

    Ruth 4:12

    1 Chr. 2:4

    Matt. 1:3

Tryphena ("Delicate or dainty")

    Rom. 16:12

Tryphosa ("Luscious, or living luxuriously")

    Rom. 16:12

SPECIFIC WOMEN DESCRIBED IN THE NEW TESTAMENT

1. Jesus' sisters (Matt. 13:56; Mark 6:3)
2. Jesus' aunt (John 19:25)
3. Herodias's daughter (Salome) (Matt. 14:6–11; Mark 6:22–28)
4. Jarius's daughter (Matt. 9:18–25; Mark 5:22–24, 35–42; Luke 8:41–42, 49–56)
5. Maid of the high priest (Matt. 26:69–70; Mark 14:66–68; Luke 22:56–57; John 18:16–17)
6. Maid (Matt. 26:71–72; Mark 14:69; Luke 22:58)
7. Peter's mother-in-law (Matt. 8:14–15; Mark 1:30–31; Luke 4:38–39)
8. Pilate's wife (Procla) (Matt. 27:19)
9. Woman taken in adultery (John 8:3–11)
10. Woman of Samaria (John 4:5–42)
11. Woman with an infirmity (Luke 13:11–17)
12. Widow who gave all (Mark 12:42–44; Luke 21:2–4)
13. Woman who loved much (Luke 7:37–50)
14. Woman of the company (Luke 11:27–28)
15. Woman of Syrophonecia (Matt. 15:21–28; Mark 7:24–30)
16. Woman who touched hem of Jesus' garment (Matt. 9:20–22; Mark 5:25–34; Luke 7:11–18)
17. Widow of Nain (Luke 7:11–15)
18. Neglected widows (Acts 6:1)

328 APPENDIX B

19. Widows with Tabitha (Acts 9:39)

20. Women of Antioch (Acts 13:50)

21. Rufus's mother (Rom. 16:13)

22. Women of Philippi (Acts 16:13)

23. Nereus's sister (Rom. 16:15)

24. Slave-girl soothsayer (Acts 16:16–18)

25. Women of Thessalonica (Acts 17:4, 12)

26. Women of Berea (Acts 17:12)

27. Philip's daughters (Acts 21:8–9)

28. Paul's sister (Acts 23:16)

29. Elect lady (2 John)

30. Sister of elect lady (2 John 1:13)

31. Widow of Zarephath/Sarepta (1 Kgs. 17:8–24; Luke 4:25–26)

WOMEN IN JESUS' PARABLES

1. Ten virgins (Matt. 25:1–13; D&C 63:54)

2. Widow and unjust judge (Luke 18:3–8; D&C 101:83–84)

3. Woman with lost coin (Luke 15:8–9)

4. Woman who hid leaven (Matt. 13:33; Luke 13:20–21)

5. Two women grinding (Matt. 24:41; Luke 17:35)

6. Wife and children who were sold (Matt. 18:25)

NOTES

INTRODUCTION

1. Kraemer, "Women in the Religions of the Greco-Roman World," 128.
2. *Theological Dictionary,* 3:786–89.
3. Willard, *Women in the Pulpit,* 21–22.
4. Grimké, *Letters,* 16.
5. Grimké, *Letters,* 16–17, 4.

MARY, THE MOTHER OF JESUS

1. Fitzmyer, *Gospel according to Luke,* 344.
2. Stephen D. Ricks first shared with me the possibility of an Egyptian origin for the name; see Gardiner, "Egyptian Origin of Some English Personal Names," 194–97; *New Bible Dictionary,* s.v. "Mary," 746; Bromily, *International Standard Bible Encyclopedia,* s.v. "Miriam," 3:382.
3. Streete, "Women as Sources of Redemption and Knowledge," 348.
4. *Protevangelium of James,* in Schneemelcher, *New Testament Apocrypha,* 1:421–38.
5. Brown, *Birth of the Messiah,* 34–35; Fitzmyer, *Gospel according to Luke,* 307.
6. *Anchor Bible Dictionary,* s.v. "Nazareth," 4:1050; Reed, *Archaeology and the Galilean Jesus,* 82–83.
7. Philo viewed unmarried daughters as a constant danger to a family's reputation should they be found unchaste when they married (*Spec Leg* 3.31).
8. Jeremias, *Jerusalem in the Time of Jesus,* 362–63.

9. Cohick, *Women in the World of the Earliest Christians,* 232.
10. *Joseph and Asenath,* 14.12–17, in Charlesworth, *Old Testament Pseudepigrapha,* 2:225. Although Joseph and Asenath lived around the seventeenth century B.C., this document was a Jewish work of the time period ranging from the first century B.C. to the second century A.D. It is therefore descriptive of customs of the New Testament era. See *Anchor Bible Dictionary,* s.v. "Dress and Ornamentation," 2:237.
11. Lachs, "Studies in the Semitic Background," 195–97.
12. Jeremias, *Jerusalem in the Time of Jesus,* 368.
13. Brown, *Mary and Elisabeth,* 48.
14. Huntsman, *Good Tidings,* 33.
15. In *Jesus the Virgin-Born,* 90–110, 284, Nutt reviews the evidence and strongly concludes that Jesus' own use of the passage in Isaiah underscores that it is to be interpreted to mean that Jesus was born of a virgin.
16. Peterson, Roper, and Hamblin, "On Alma 7:10 and the Birthplace of Jesus Christ."
17. Nutt, *Jesus the Virgin-Born,* 60–63. Ignatius, bishop of Antioch (A.D. 100–118), asserts that Mary was of the lineage of David (*Eph* 20; *Smyrn* 1) and two pseudepigraphal gospels, *GBir* and *Prot Jas,* identify Mary as a descendant of "the royal race and family of David."
18. Dahl and Cannon, *Teachings of Joseph Smith,* 19.
19. Gaventa, *Mary,* 53.

20. Nutt, *Jesus the Virgin-Born*, 264–65.

21. Nutt, *Jesus the Virgin-Born*, 245.

22. Talmage, *Jesus the Christ*, 77.

23. Brown, *Mary and Elisabeth*, 48.

24. Brown et al., *Mary in the New Testament*, 128.

25. Brown, *Mary and Elisabeth*, 39.

26. "O Little Town of Bethlehem," *Hymns,* no. 208.

27. Brown, *Birth of the Messiah*, 314.

28. Brown, *Birth of the Messiah*, 333.

29. Brown, *Birth of the Messiah*, 334–35, 340–41; Huntsman, *Good Tidings*, 58–59.

30. Brown, *Birth of the Messiah*, 334–35, 340–41.

31. Brown, *Birth of the Messiah*, 338.

32. *New Smith's Bible Dictionary*, s.v. "Inn," 157. See also Edersheim, *Life and Times of Jesus the Messiah*, 130; Nelson, "Christ the Savior Is Born," *Speeches*, 146–47; Huntsman, *Good Tidings*, 71–72; an inn, translated "habitation," is described in Jer. 41:17.

33. Young, in *Journal of Discourses*, 3:366.

34. Osiek and Balch, *Families in the New Testament World*, 66.

35. Osiek and Balch, *Families in the New Testament World*, 66n99.

36. See LDS Bible Dictionary, s.v. "Watches," 788.

37. "O Little Town of Bethlehem," *Hymns,* no. 208.

38. Fitzmyer, *Gospel according to Luke*, 407.

39. Brown et al., *Mary in the New Testament*, 153–54.

40. Brown, *Birth of the Messiah*, 460–66.

41. Brown et al., *Mary in the New Testament*, 155–56.

42. See Justin Martyr, *Dial* 78.

43. Brown, *Mary and Elisabeth*, 60.

44. Brown, *Birth of the Messiah*, 204.

45. Brown, *Birth of the Messiah*, 226.

46. Huntsman, *Good Tidings*, 109.

47. Smith, *Doctrines of Salvation*, 1:32.

48. Dahl and Cannon, *Teachings of Joseph Smith*, 350.

49. Ogden and Skinner, *Four Gospels*, 109–10.

50. "There Is a Green Hill Far Away," *Hymns,* no. 194; emphasis added.

51. For a discussion of the various arguments concerning the "brothers of Jesus," see Nutt, *Jesus the Virgin-Born*, 156–88.

52. Swidler, *Biblical Affirmations of Women*, 177–78.

53. Brown and Comfort translate the word as "family," *New Greek Interlinear New Testament*, 129.

54. McConkie, *Doctrinal New Testament Commentary*, 1:461.

EARLIER WOMEN IN THE LINEAGE OF JESUS

1. Brown, *Birth of the Messiah*, 68.

2. Nutt, *Jesus the Virgin-Born*, 45–46; Jeremias, *Jerusalem in the Time of Jesus*, 275.

3. Nutt, *Jesus the Virgin-Born*, 47–48.

4. Brown, *Birth of the Messiah*, 74–75.

5. Nutt, *Jesus the Virgin-Born*, 49.

6. Brown, *Birth of the Messiah*, 65.

7. Scheck, *St. Jerome*, 59; emphasis added. In *Private Women, Public Meals*, 147–52, Corley concludes they were morally suspect with a reputation for promiscuity.

8. Brown et al., *Mary in the New Testament*, 80–81.

9. *Gospel of Nicodemus,* in Roberts and Donaldson, *Ante-Nicene Fathers*, 8:416–58; Origen, *Cels* 4:395–669, and *Gospel of Thomas,* in *Nag Hammadi Library*, 124–38.

10. Schaberg, *Illegitimacy of Jesus*, 32–34, 109–10.

11. Brown et al., *Mary in the New Testament*, 82.

12. Spencer, *Dancing Girls*, 35–41.

13. Bauckham, *Gospel Women*, 26–27.

14. Cundall and Morris, *Judges [and] Ruth*, 318.

15. Brown, *Birth of the Messiah*, 73–74; Nutt, *Jesus the Virgin-Born*, 54.

16. Ginzberg, *Legends of the Jews*, 5:258.

TAMAR

1. In Pritchard, *Ancient Near Eastern Texts*, 182, 196.

2. See Niditch, "Wronged Woman Righted," 143–49; Frymer-Kensky, *Reading the Women of the Bible*, 264–77; Schneider, *Mothers of Promise*, 151–60;

Wassen, "Story of Judah and Tamar," 354–66; Wray, *Good Girls, Bad Girls,* 101–11.

3. Ginzberg, *Legends of the Jews,* 1:332.

4. See Olson, *Women of the Old Testament,* 14–15, 60–61.

5. Waltke, *Genesis,* 509.

6. Ginzberg, *Legends of the Jews,* 2:32.

7. *Jubilees,* in Charlesworth, *Old Testament Pseudepigrapha,* 2:35–142.

8. *Testaments of the Twelve Patriarchs,* in Charlesworth, *Old Testament Pseudepigrapha,* 1:797.

9. Ginzberg, *Legends of the Jews,* 2:32.

10. In Pritchard, *Ancient Near Eastern Texts,* 184.

11. Ginzberg, *Legends of the Jews,* 2:33.

12. Ginzberg, *Legends of the Jews,* 2:33–34.

13. In Pritchard, *Ancient Near Eastern Texts,* 183.

14. Hamilton, "Book of Genesis Chapters 18–50," 2:442–43.

15. Falk, *Hebrew Law,* 94.

16. Frymer-Kensky, "Tamar 1," 162.

17. Speiser, *Genesis,* 296.

18. For a discussion of another word used for "harlot" when Judah attempted payment, see Westenholz, "Tamar," 245–65.

19. For examples of related laws, see *Code of Hammurabi* #129 and *Middle Assyrian Law* #14, in Pritchard, *Ancient Near Eastern Texts,* 181.

20. Ginzberg, *Legends of the Jews,* 2:35.

21. Ginzberg, *Legends of the Jews,* 2:35–36.

22. See Brown, Driver, and Briggs, *Hebrew and English Lexicon,* s.v. "tsadeq," 842.

23. Ginzberg, *Legends of the Jews,* 2:34–35.

RAHAB

1. Ginzberg, *Legends of the Jews,* 4:117.

2. Ginzberg, *Legends of the Jews,* 5:258.

3. McKenzie, *World of the Judges,* 47–48.

4. Kenyon, *Bible and Recent Archaeology,* 42.

5. In Pritchard, *Ancient Near Eastern Texts,* 528.

6. Ginzberg, *Legends of the Jews,* 6:171.

7. Ginzberg, *Legends of the Jews,* 4:5.

8. Frymer-Kensky, "Rahab," 140.

9. Hoerth, *Archaeology,* 205–6.

10. Boling, *Joshua,* 146.

11. Unger, *New Unger's Bible Dictionary,* s.v. "Canaan, Canaanites," 203.

12. Ginzberg, *Legends of the Jews,* 2:36–37.

13. Ginzberg, *Legends of the Jews,* 4:5.

14. Ginzberg, *Legends of the Jews,* 6:171.

15. Ginzberg, *Legends of the Jews,* 6:171.

16. Madvig, "Joshua," 292.

17. Borowski, *Daily Life in Biblical Times,* 22–24.

18. In Pritchard, *Ancient Near Eastern Texts,* 170.

19. Kautzsch and Cowley, *Gesenius' Hebrew Grammar,* 212–13.

20. Borowski, *Daily Life in Biblical Times,* 37–39.

21. Bowen, "'According to All That You Demanded.'"

22. Brown, Driver, and Briggs, *Hebrew and English Lexicon,* 338–39.

23. Meyers, "Roots of Restriction," 97–100.

24. Frymer-Kensky, *Reading the Women of the Bible,* 42–43.

25. Bauckham, *Gospel Women,* 36.

26. Ginzberg, *Legends of the Jews,* 4:5.

27. Ginzberg, *Legends of the Jews,* 6:173.

28. Brown, Driver, and Briggs, *Hebrew and English Lexicon,* 876.

RUTH

1. Fischer, "Book of Ruth," in Brenner, *Ruth and Esther,* 24.

2. Meyers, "Returning Home," 88–91.

3. Bal, *Lethal Love,* 73–77.

4. See Hamlin, *Surely There Is a Future,* 40–41, 56–59, 60; Ricks, "Ruth," 249; Cundall and Morris, *Judges [and] Ruth,* 238–39.

5. Campbell, *Ruth,* 50–51.

6. *Anchor Bible Dictionary,* s.v. "Moab," 4:891–92.

7. Ginzberg, *Legends of the Jews,* 4:85.

8. Trible, "Two Women in a Man's World," 251–79.

9. Brown, Driver, and Briggs, *Hebrew and English Lexicon,* 298–99, 791c, 1093.

10. Ginzberg, *Legends of the Jews,* 4:85.

11. Campbell, *Ruth,* 78, 82.

12. Frymer-Kensky, *Reading the Women of the Bible,* 241; see also Cundall and Morris, *Judges [and] Ruth,* 261.

13. Laffey, "Ruth," 554–55.

14. For a discussion of women's informal networks in the book of Ruth, see Meyers, "Women of the Neighborhood," 116–24.

15. Campbell, *Ruth,* 67.

16. Muhlestein, "Ruth, Redemption, and Covenant," 189.

17. Matthews, *Manners and Customs,* 54.

18. Campbell, *Ruth,* 108; Matthews, *Manners and Customs,* 50–51.

19. Campbell, *Ruth,* 85.

20. For an argument that Boaz's servant showed prejudice against the Moabitess, see Grossman, "Gleaning among the Ears," 703–16.

21. Shepherd, "Violence in the Fields?" 447, 450.

22. Campbell, *Ruth,* 104; Ricks, "Ruth," 251; Hamlin, *Surely There Is a Future,* 35.

23. Laffey, "Ruth," 556.

24. Shepherd, "Violence in the Fields?" 453.

25. Campbell, *Ruth,* 88–89; Atkinson, *Message of Ruth,* 86, 97.

26. For a discussion of Naomi's lack of a plan before this time, see Trible, *God and Rhetoric,* 179.

27. Cundall and Morris, *Judges [and] Ruth,* 286.

28. DeWaard and Nida, *Translator's Handbook,* 54.

29. Ginzberg, *Legends of the Jews,* 4:33–34.

30. Niditch, "Wronged Woman Righted," 148.

31. Campbell, *Ruth,* 131.

32. Phillips, "Book of Ruth," 1–17.

33. Ginzberg, *Legends of the Jews,* 6:188.

34. Campbell, *Ruth,* 127–28.

35. Hamlin, *Surely There Is a Future,* 56.

36. Ricks, "Ruth," 253.

37. Laffey, "Ruth," 556; Gaskill, "'Ceremony of the Shoe,'" 133–50; Beattie, "Evidence for Israelite Legal Practice," 251–67; Falk, *Hebrew Law,*

138–39. Mace argues in *Hebrew Marriage,* 99, that if this were a levirate marriage, Naomi, not Ruth, would have married the redeemer.

38. See Beattie, "Evidence for Israelite Legal Practice," 264–67; Ricks, "Ruth," 255; Gaskill, "'Ceremony of the Shoe,'" 133–50.

39. Beattie, "Evidence for Israelite Legal Practice," 263.

40. Beattie, "Evidence for Israelite Legal Practice," 262–66.

41. Beattie, "Evidence for Israelite Legal Practice," 264.

42. Thompson and Thompson, "Legal Problems," 90–94; Baker, *Women's Rights,* 157.

43. For a full discussion of the literary motif contrasting themes of emptiness and fulnes in the book of Ruth, see Rauber, "Book of Ruth," 163–76.

44. Cundall and Morris, *Judges [and] Ruth,* 318.

45. Campbell, *Ruth,* 80.

BATHSHEBA

1. Berlin, "Characterization in Biblical Narrative," 73.

2. Ginzberg, *Legends of the Jews,* 5:258; see also 6:281.

3. Ginzberg, *Legends of the Jews,* 4:103.

4. Levenson, "1 Samuel 25," 27; Levenson and Halpern, "Political Import," 507, 513.

5. Ginzberg, *Legends of the Jews,* 4:94.

6. McCarter, *II Samuel,* 285–86.

7. Bailey, *David in Love and War,* 88.

8. Hafen and Hafen, *Belonging Heart,* 280.

9. Frymer-Kensky, *Reading the Women of the Bible,* 143–56.

10. For an insightful discussion of the literary style used to relate the story of Bathsheba and David, see Yee, "Fraught with Background," 240–55.

11. Pritchard, *Ancient Near Eastern Texts,* 181,196.

12. Bailey, *David in Love and War,* 88–89.

13. McCarter, *II Samuel,* 286.

14. Bailey, *David in Love and War,* 86–87.

15. Ginzberg, *Legends of the Jews,* 4:103.

16. Ginzberg, *Legends of the Jews,* 4:103.

17. Ginzberg, *Legends of the Jews,* 4:129.

18. Cogan, *1 Kings,* 156.

19. Ginzberg, *Legends of the Jews,* 6:277.

20. Ginzberg, *Legends of the Jews,* 6:277.

21. Berlin, "Characterization in Biblical Narrative," 75.

22. Cross, *From Epic to Canon,* 94.

23. Wharton, "Plausible Tale," 349.

WOMEN IN JEWISH SOCIETY

1. Swidler, *Biblical Affirmations of Women,* 161; Jeremias, *Jerusalem in the Time of Jesus,* 1969 ed., 205.

2. Jeremias, *Jerusalem in the Time of Jesus,* 1969 ed., 83–84; Vamosh, *Daily Life at the Time of Jesus,* 22.

3. *Anchor Bible Dictionary,* s.v. "Nazareth," 4:1050; Reed, *Archaeology and the Galilean Jesus,* 82–83; Borg, "Palestinian Background," 41.

4. Schürer, *History of the Jewish People,* 2:74–80.

5. Simmons, *Peoples of the New Testament World,* 178.

6. Simmons, *Peoples of the New Testament World,* 115.

7. Ilan, *Jewish Women in Greco-Roman Palestine,* 134.

8. Ilan, *Jewish Women in Greco-Roman Palestine,* 113.

9. Witherington, *Week in the Life of Corinth,* 37.

10. Hanson and Oakman, *Palestine in the Time of Jesus,* 130–31.

11. Hanson and Oakman, *Palestine in the Time of Jesus,* 140.

12. Jeremias, *Jerusalem in the Time of Jesus,* 1969 ed., 56; Hanson and Oakman, *Palestine in the Time of Jesus,* 141.

13. Rabbis tried to formulate a general rule to clarify which commandments applied to men only and which also included women: "The observance of all positive ordinances that depend on the time of the year is incumbent on men but not on women, and the observance of all positive ordinances that do not depend on the time of the year is incumbent both on men and on women. The observance of all the negative ordinances, whether they depend on the time of year or not, is incumbent both on men and on women" (*mQidd* 1.7). See also Cameron and Kuhrt, *Images of Women in Antiquity,* 283.

14. Schottroff, *Lydia's Impatient Sisters,* 111–12.

15. Ilan, *Jewish Women in Greco-Roman Palestine,* 147.

16. Ilan, *Jewish Women in Greco-Roman Palestine,* 188.

17. Ilan, *Jewish Women in Greco-Roman Palestine,* 189–90.

18. Harris, *Ancient Literacy,* 330; Patterson, "Sources for a Life of Jesus," 19–20.

19. Ilan, *Jewish Women in Greco-Roman Palestine,* 204.

20. D'Angelo, "Women in Luke-Acts," 441–61.

ELISABETH

1. Getty-Sullivan, *Women in the New Testament,* 11; Reid, *Choosing the Better Part?* 58.

2. Cohick, *Earliest Christians,* 152.

3. Jeremias, *Jerusalem in the Time of Jesus,* 207.

4. Schürer, *History of the Jewish People,* 2:245–50; Brown, *Birth of the Messiah,* 258.

5. Jeremias, *Jerusalem in the Time of Jesus,* 199.

6. Jeremias, *Jerusalem in the Time of Jesus,* 201; Daniel-Rops, *Daily Life in Palestine,* 377–81.

7. Jeremias, *Jerusalem in the Time of Jesus,* 200–203; Daniel-Rops, *Daily Life in Palestine,* 377, cites an estimate of 20,000 men of the priesthood at any given time.

8. *Letter of Aristeas,* in Charlesworth, *Old Testament Pseudipigrapha,* 2:19. For a detailed description of the hierarchy and assignments for each group, see Hanson and Oakman, *Palestine in the Time of Jesus,* 130–37.

9. Bruce, *New Testament History,* 141.

10. Jeremias, *Jerusalem in the Time of Jesus,* 206.

11. Jackson, *Joseph Smith's Commentary on the Bible,* 119.

12. Reid, *Choosing the Better Part?* 74.

13. S. Kent Brown, in *Mary and Elisabeth,* 23–24, surmised that they communicated through hand gestures or a trusted friend who was literate.

14. Reid, *Choosing the Better Part?* 79.

15. Limberis, "Elizabeth," 74.

ANNA

1. Grossman, "Women and the Jerusalem Temple," 15–37.
2. Grossman, "Women and the Jerusalem Temple," 27.
3. Jeremias, *Jerusalem in the Time of Jesus,* 164.
4. See Hanson and Oakman, *Palestine in the Time of Jesus,* 122, 131. See also Schürer, *History of the Jewish People,* 285; Finegan, *Archaeology of the New Testament,* 197.
5. Reid, *Choosing the Better Part?* 86.
6. Elliot, "Anna's Age," 102.
7. For evidence that Hannah was a prophetess, see Olson, *Women of the Old Testament,* 137–38.
8. Getty-Sullivan, *Women in the New Testament,* 39.

THE WIDOWS

1. Reid, *Choosing the Better Part?* 93.
2. Limberis, "Widow of Nain," 439–40.

THE WIDOW WHO GAVE ALL

1. Malbon, "Poor Widow in Mark," 119.

THE WOMAN HEALED IN THE SYNAGOGUE

1. Cohick, *Earliest Christians,* 218.

TABITHA AND THE WIDOWS IN JOPPA

1. Getty-Sullivan, *Women in the New Testament,* 238.
2. Reimer, *Women in the Acts of the Apostles,* 37.
3. For discussion of how the chamber that the Shunammite made for Elisha "on the wall" was likely an upper room, see Olson, *Women of the Old Testament,* 241–42.
4. Getty-Sullivan, *Women in the New Testament,* 238.
5. Fitzmyer, *Acts of the Apostles,* 445; Belnap, "Clothed with Salvation," 68.
6. Reimer, *Women in the Acts of the Apostles,* 43.

7. Osiek and Balch, *Families in the New Testament World,* 139.
8. Belnap, "Clothed with Salvation," 43–69.

MARTHA AND MARY

1. Reinhartz, "From Narrative to History," 171.
2. Haskins, *Mary Magdalen,* 20.
3. Esler and Piper, *Lazarus, Mary and Martha,* 59–60.
4. Matthews, *Manners and Customs,* 239; see also Brown, *Gospel according to John,* 1:424.
5. See Gen. 25:8; 49:29; Num. 20:24; Deut. 32:49–50; 2 Chron. 24:28.
6. Parvey, "Theology and Leadership of Women," 141.
7. Corley, *Private Women, Public Meals,* 145.
8. Reinhartz, "From Narrative to History," 184.
9. D'Angelo, "Women in Luke–Acts," 454.
10. For a discussion of dangers associated with being "cumbered about" in our service, see Olson, *Mary, Martha, and Me,* 31–49.
11. O'Rahilly, "Two Sisters," 69; Olson, *Mary, Martha, and Me,* 51–67.
12. Esler and Piper, *Lazarus, Mary and Martha,* 124.
13. McConkie, *Doctrinal New Testament Commentary,* 1:532.
14. Esler and Piper, *Lazarus, Mary and Martha,* 114–16.
15. See Olson, *Mary, Martha, and Me,* 69–81.
16. McConkie, *Doctrinal New Testament Commentary,* 1:700.
17. Brown, *Gospel according to John,* 1:448.
18. Bruce, *New Testament History,* 88.
19. Esler and Piper, *Lazarus, Mary and Martha,* 64–65.
20. Esler and Piper, *Lazarus, Mary and Martha,* 66–67.
21. Brown, *Gospel according to John,* 1:454.
22. Farrar, *Life of Christ,* 496.
23. Malbon, "Poor Widow in Mark," 122.
24. Esler and Piper, *Lazarus, Mary and Martha,* 70–74.

THE WOMAN TAKEN IN ADULTERY

1. Hanson and Oakman, *Palestine in the Time of Jesus,* 41. See also Gench, *Back to the Well,* 150–57,

for other implications for divorced Jewish women at the time.

2. Getty-Sullivan, *Women in the New Testament,* 103.
3. Gench, *Back to the Well,* 139.
4. I am indebted to Stephen E. Robinson for this insight. At least one of the witnesses had to have been involved in this adulterous encounter for the Savior's condition to have relevance and for the witnesses to be "pricked in their conscience" according to the law.
5. Schottroff, *Lydia's Impatient Sisters,* 182–84.
6. Haskins, *Mary Magdalen,* 28.
7. Getty-Sullivan, *Women in the New Testament,* 104.
8. Holzapfel and Holzapfel, *Sisters at the Well,* 94.

RHODA

1. Spencer, "Out of Mind, Out of Voice," 143–44n.
2. Schottroff, *Lydia's Impatient Sisters,* 125.
3. Spencer, "Out of Mind, Out of Voice," 142–45.

WOMEN OF GALILEE

1. Reid, *Choosing the Better Part?* 126.
2. Luke may apply the term differently when referring to women as compared to men in order to avoid considering women in leadership roles. In the Gospel of Luke and in Acts, women perform table service whereas men are leaders; see Corley, *Private Women, Public Meals,* 121.
3. Reid, *Choosing the Better Part?* 98–100. In *Families in the New Testament World,* 135, Osiek and Balch review the continuing debate over the core meaning of the word: one who serves at table or who ministers.
4. *Theological Dictionary,* 2:84.
5. Bruce, *Gospel of John,* 124.
6. Brock, *Mary Magdalene,* 11.
7. Robinson, *Nag Hammadi Library,* 145.

PETER'S MOTHER-IN-LAW

1. For a discussion of the significant differences between Mark's account and Luke's, see Corley, *Private Women, Public Meals,* 87–88, 119–21.

THE MOTHER OF JAMES AND JOHN

1. Schottroff, *Lydia's Impatient Sisters,* 204.

THE WOMAN WHO LOVED MUCH

1. Reid, *Choosing the Better Part?* 113.
2. Corley, *Private Women, Public Meals,* 125.
3. Kilgallen, "John the Baptist," 675–79.
4. Fitzmyer, *Gospel according to Luke,* 689.
5. Simmons, *Peoples of the New Testament World,* 110.
6. Cosgrove, "Woman's Unbound Hair," 675–92.
7. Cosgrove, "Woman's Unbound Hair," 679.
8. Marshall, *Commentary on Luke,* 308–9.
9. Marshall, *Commentary on Luke,* 309.
10. Fitzmyer, *Gospel according to Luke,* 690n42; Kilgallen, "John the Baptist," 675.
11. Reid, *Choosing the Better Part?* 107–23.

THE WOMAN WHO TOUCHED THE HEM OF HIS GARMENT

1. Reid, *Choosing the Better Part?* 139.
2. Ogden and Skinner, *Four Gospels,* 252; LDS Bible Dictionary, s.v. "Hem of Garment," 700.
3. Cotter, "Mark's Hero," 59.
4. Cotter, "Mark's Hero," 60.

THE DAUGHTER OF JAIRUS

1. Fitzmyer, *Gospel according to Luke,* 745.

JOANNA

1. Corley, "Slaves, Servants and Prostitutes," 196–97.

MARY OF MAGDALA

1. Reed, *Archaeology and the Galilean Jesus,* 82–83.
2. *Anchor Bible Dictionary,* s.v. "Magdala," 4:463–64; Nun, "Ports of Galilee," 27–29.

3. Schottroff, *Lydia's Impatient Sisters*, 83–84; Corley, "Slaves, Servants and Prostitutes," 200.

4. Corley, *Women and the Historical Jesus*, 34–35.

5. Ricci, *Mary Magdalene*, 133.

6. Haskins, *Mary Magdalen*, 14.

7. Ricci, *Mary Magdalene*, 138.

8. Bruce, *Gospel of John*, 126.

9. Fitzmyer, *Gospel according to Luke*, 1521.

10. Bruce, *Gospel of John*, 379.

11. See Matt. 28:1–6; Mark 16:1–6; and Luke 23:55–24:10. See also Brown, *Gospel according to John*, 2:977–78, 1001. Rather than suggesting that the women returned to anoint the body with fragrances, the apocryphal *Gospel of Peter* posits that their purpose was to appropriately "weep and lament" for the loss of a loved one, as "women are wont to do for those beloved of them who die" (vv. 50–52), in Schneemelcher, *New Testament Apocrypha*, 1:225.

12. Brock, *Mary Magdalene*, 57–59.

13. Haskins, *Mary Magdalen*, 9.

14. Huntsman, "Mary Magdalene," 8.

15. Getty-Sullivan, *Women in the New Testament*, 189.

16. Ricci, *Mary Magdalene*, 143.

17. Swidler, *Biblical Affirmations of Women*, 204.

18. Brown, *Gospel according to John*, 2:992; Bruce, *Gospel of John*, 389–90.

19. Marion G. Romney, quoted by Maxwell, "Called to Serve," 137.

20. King, *Gospel of Mary of Magdala*, 153.

21. Ehrman, *Peter, Paul, and Mary Magdalene*, 253.

22. Robinson, *Nag Hammadi Library*, 222, 243.

23. Robinson, *Nag Hammadi Library*, 252.

24. Robinson, *Nag Hammadi Library*, 252.

25. Robinson, *Nag Hammadi Library*, 138.

26. Robinson, *Nag Hammadi Library*, 525.

27. Robinson, *Nag Hammadi Library*, 526–27.

28. King, *Gospel of Mary of Magdala*, 150; Schaberg, "How Mary Magdalene Became a Whore," 31–52.

29. Ambrose, *Fid* 4.2.

30. Gregory, *Hom* 33.

31. Cohick, *Earliest Christians*, 318–19; Haskins, *Mary Magdalen*, 25–27.

32. King, *Gospel of Mary of Magdala*, 149, 152.

WOMEN OF SAMARIA

1. Simmons, *Peoples of the New Testament World*, 122.

2. Simmons, *Peoples of the New Testament World*, 128–30; Bruce, *New Testament History*, 37–38; Ricks, "No Prophet," 205.

THE WOMAN AT THE WELL

1. This Jewish regulation from A.D. 65–66 is cited in Brown, *Gospel according to John*, 1:170.

2. Joseph Smith taught that "no man can *know* that Jesus is the Lord, but by the Holy Ghost" is a better translation of the phrase in 1 Cor. 12:3, in Dahl and Cannon, *Teachings of Joseph Smith*, 346.

3. See, for example, John 8:58–59; 10:7, 11; 11:25; 14:6.

WOMEN AMONG THE ARISTOCRACY

1. Alföldy, *Social History of Rome*, 100.

2. Alföldy, *Social History of Rome*, 115–21.

3. Alföldy, *Social History of Rome*, 122–26.

4. See Matt. 27:2, 11–26, 58, 62–65; Mark 15:1–15, 43–45; Luke 3:1; 13:1; 23:1–25, 52; John 18:28–19:22, 31, 38.

5. See Acts 24:22–27.

6. See Acts 25–26.

7. Jeffers, *Greco-Roman World*, 181–87; Alföldy, *Social History of Rome*, 127–30.

8. Arlandson, *Women, Class, and Society*, 38.

9. Goodman, *Ruling Class of Judaea*, 49.

10. Prayer to Isis from Oxyrhynchus Papyrus, 2nd century A.D.; P. Oxy. XI 1380.214–16, in Massey, *Women in Ancient Greece and Rome*, 28.

11. Massey, *Women in Ancient Greece and Rome*, 28–29.

12. For New Testament examples, see Luke 7:36; 11:37; 17:7; John 13:12.

13. Witherington, "Anti-Feminist Tendencies," 82–84.

14. Arlandson, *Women, Class, and Society,* 30–33, 44–45.

15. Thompson, "Hairstyles, Head-Coverings, and St. Paul," 99–115, especially 109.

16. Thompson, "Hairstyles, Head-Coverings, and St. Paul," 106–8.

17. Vamosh, *Daily Life at the Time of Jesus,* 84.

18. Vamosh, *Daily Life at the Time of Jesus,* 68.

PROCLA, WIFE OF PONTIUS PILATE

1. "Paradosis Pilati," in Elliot, *Apocryphal New Testament,* 210–11.

THE HERODIAN WOMEN

1. Arlandson, *Women, Class, and Society,* 38–39.

2. Macurdy, *Vassal-Queens,* 63.

3. See Luke 7:24, in which Jesus used the phrase to describe what John the Baptist was not.

HERODIAS

1. See Matt. 14:3–11; Mark 6:17–18; Luke 3:19–20 for the teachings of John the Baptist against the marriage of Herod Antipas and Herodias.

SALOME, DAUGHTER OF HERODIAS

1. Macurdy, *Vassal-Queens,* 84.

BERNICE

1. It is unclear from the Greek manuscripts whether this is a statement (as rendered in the King James Version) or a question, "Do you think that in such a short time you can persuade me to be a Christian?" (New International Version), or the more neutral question, "Are you so quickly persuading me to become a Christian?" (New Revised Standard Version).

2. Maxwell, *Men and Women of Christ,* 81.

WOMEN IN GRECO-ROMAN SOCIETY

1. Osiek and Balch, *Families in the New Testament World,* 37; Parkin, *Demography and Roman Society,* 5.

2. Leon, *Jews of Ancient Rome,* 77–78.

3. Leon, *Jews of Ancient Rome,* 118–21.

4. Leon, *Jews of Ancient Rome,* 257.

5. Osiek and Balch, *Families in the New Testament World,* 67; in *Demography and Roman Society,* 135, Parkin estimates an infant mortality rate of 300 per 1,000 births in the Roman empire; he further estimates that 30 to 60 individuals per 100,000 would on average would live to be 90 years old.

6. Gardner, *Women in Roman Law,* 40.

7. Rowlandson, *Women and Society,* 84–85.

8. Leon, *Jews of Ancient Rome,* 250–51.

9. Leon, *Jews of Ancient Rome,* 9.

10. Leon, *Jews of Ancient Rome,* 15–17; Schottroff, *Lydia's Impatient Sisters,* 146–47.

11. Jeffers, *Greco-Roman World,* 101.

12. Alföldy, *Social History of Rome,* 146–56.

13. Cohick, *Earliest Christians,* 320.

14. Alföldy, *Social History of Rome,* 131–32.

15. Jeffers, *Greco-Roman World,* 20.

16. Simmons, *Peoples of the New Testament World,* 284; Wilken, *Christians as the Romans Saw Them,* 35–37.

17. Jeffers, *Greco-Roman World,* 197.

18. Alföldy, *Social History of Rome,* 104.

19. Jeffers, *Greco-Roman World,* 198.

20. Jeffers, *Greco-Roman World,* 201.

21. Osiek and Balch, *Families in the New Testament World,* 31.

22. Gardner, *Women in Roman Law,* 248.

23. Bradley, *Slavery and Society,* 127.

24. Massey, *Women in Ancient Greece and Rome,* 21.
25. Osiek and Balch, *Families in the New Testament World,* 83n202.
26. Osiek and Balch, *Families in the New Testament World,* 66n93.
27. Cohick, *Earliest Christians,* 156–67.
28. Gardner, *Women in Roman Law,* 40; Kraemer, "Jewish Mothers and Daughters," 104.
29. Rowlandson, *Women and Society,* 84–85.
30. Osiek and Balch, *Families in the New Testament World,* 83n198.
31. Cameron and Kuhrt, *Images of Women in Antiquity,* 81–82.
32. Osiek and Balch, *Families in the New Testament World,* 57.
33. Harris, *Ancient Literacy,* 245.
34. Harris, *Ancient Literacy,* 176.
35. Parvey, "Theology and Leadership of Women," 118.
36. Ketter, *Christ and Womankind,* 21–24.
37. Harris, *Ancient Literacy,* 275.
38. Cohick, *Earliest Christians,* 46.
39. See also Harris, *Ancient Literacy,* 252.
40. Herzenberg et al., "Women Scientists and Physicians," 102.
41. Rowlandson, *Women and Society,* 72–73.

THE SYROPHOENICIAN WOMAN

1. Fiorenza, *But She Said,* 12.
2. Jeffers, *Greco-Roman World,* 286–91.
3. Jeffers, *Greco-Roman World,* 287, 291.
4. Ogden and Skinner, *Four Gospels,* 219, 322; Getty-Sullivan, *Women in the New Testament,* 87.
5. Corley, *Private Women, Public Meals,* 168.
6. Bauckham, *Gospel Women,* 44–45.

EUNICE AND LOIS

1. Cohen, "Was Timothy Jewish?" 266. See Lev. 24:10; 1 Chr. 2:17.
2. Cohen, "Was Timothy Jewish?" 254–58.
3. Kraemer, "Jewish Mothers and Daughters," 104–6.

4. Cohick, *Earliest Christians,* 44–46.
5. Rowlandson, *Women and Society,* 118–24.

LYDIA

1. Abrahamsen, "Women at Philippi," 29.
2. Jeffers, *Greco-Roman World,* 26.
3. Gardner, *Women in Roman Law,* 238.
4. Jeffers, *Greco-Roman World,* 26.
5. Cohick, *Earliest Christians,* 188–89.
6. Leon, *Jews of Ancient Rome,* 256.
7. Cohick, *Earliest Christians,* 188.
8. D'Angelo, "Women Partners in the New Testament," 75–76.
9. Cohick, *Earliest Christians,* 189.
10. Getty-Sullivan, *Women in the New Testament,* 251.
11. Wayment and Gee, "Did Paul Address His Wife in Philippi?" 71–73; Bruce, *Philippians,* 140.

THE SLAVE-GIRL SOOTHSAYER

1. Spencer, "Out of Mind, Out of Voice," 146.
2. Lampe, *From Paul to Valentinus,* 172.
3. Jeffers, *Greco-Roman World,* 221.
4. Bradley, *Slavery and Society,* 87.
5. Bradley, *Slavery and Society,* 88.
6. Simmons, *Peoples of the New Testament World,* 196.

PHEBE

1. Cranfield, *Epistle to the Romans,* 2:780.
2. See Word Study discussion of *diakonos* in "Women of Galilee," page 179 of this volume.
3. Jeffers, *Greco-Roman World,* 195.
4. Fiorenza, "'Quilting' of Women's History," 47.
5. Cranfield, *Epistle to the Romans,* 783.
6. Jewett, "Paul, Phebe, and the Spanish Mission," 149.
7. Jewett, "Paul, Phebe, and the Spanish Mission," 145.
8. Lampe, *From Paul to Valentinus,* 155–56; Jewett, *Romans,* 947–48.
9. Jewett, "Paul, Phebe, and the Spanish Mission," 151.
10. Jewett, "Paul, Phebe, and the Spanish Mission," 154–55.

PRISCA

1. Everett, *Rome's First Emperor;* D'Angelo, "Women in Luke-Acts," 450.
2. Lampe, *From Paul to Valentinus,* 181, 183; Ilan, *Jewish Names in Late Antiquity,* 3:607.
3. Hoppin, *Priscilla's Letter,* 89–104; Jewett, *Romans,* 954–57.
4. Jewett, *Romans,* 955.
5. Jewett, *Romans,* 955.
6. Hoppin, *Priscilla's Letter,* 111.
7. Jewett, *Romans,* 956.
8. Lampe, *From Paul to Valentinus,* 190–95. Working in the same profession as Aquila, Paul often observed his humble living conditions (1 Cor. 4:11–13; 1 Thess. 2:9).
9. Cranfield, *Epistle to the Romans,* 2:784; Lampe, *From Paul to Valentinus,* 167.
10. Jewett, *Romans,* 955.
11. Cranfield, *Epistle to the Romans,* 784.
12. Jeffers, *Greco-Roman World,* 195.
13. Hoppin, *Priscilla's Letter,* 110–13.
14. Jewett, *Romans,* 956.
15. Gardner, *Women in Roman Law,* 239.
16. Simmons, *Peoples of the New Testament World,* 198.
17. Hock, *Social Context,* 21.
18. Lampe, *From Paul to Valentinus,* 187–89; Pliny (*Nat hist* 19.24) wrote of linen sun roofs that covered atriums of private homes, and Cicero (*Verr* 2.5.29–31, 80–82) mentioned linen "tents."
19. Simmons, *Peoples of the New Testament World,* 196–98.
20. Hock, *Social Context,* 33.
21. Hock, *Social Context,* 33.
22. Gruen, *Diaspora,* 38; Leon, *Jews of Ancient Rome,* 25.
23. Blumell, *Lettered Christians,* 37–38; Leon, *Jews of Ancient Rome,* 23–27; Lampe, *From Paul to Valentinus,* 12–13.
24. Leon, *Jews of Ancient Rome,* 26–27.
25. Jewett, *Romans,* 954.
26. Gritz, *Paul, Women Teachers,* 12.
27. Witherington observes in "Anti-Feminist Tendencies," 82, that "there is a definite effort [in the Western text of Acts] to reduce the prominence of Priscilla, probably because she appears to the editors to be assuming her husband's first place and also because she was a well-known teacher of a male Christian leader, Apollos."
28. In *Priscilla's Letter,* Hoppin argues for Prisca as the anonymous author of the Epistle to the Hebrews in the New Testament, based on evidence of her intellect, Roman education, and grasp of Jewish scripture.
29. Schaff, *Nicene and Post-Nicene Fathers,* 11:245n2.
30. Paul consistently referred to her as Prisca in the earliest Greek manuscripts. The King James translators used the informal diminutive Priscilla in 1 Cor. 16:19 and Rom. 16:3 but accurately preserved her name as Prisca in 2 Tim. 4:19.
31. Jeffers, *Greco-Roman World,* 62.
32. Jewett, *Romans,* 957.

CHRISTIAN WOMEN IN ROME

1. Jeffers, *Greco-Roman World,* 85.
2. Lampe, *From Paul to Valentinus,* 172.
3. Jewett, *Romans,* 961.
4. Massey, *Women in Ancient Greece and Rome,* 18.
5. Lampe, *From Paul to Valentinus,* 175–76; Jewett, *Romans,* 960.
6. Leon, *Jews of Ancient Rome,* 105.
7. D'Angelo, "Women Partners in the New Testament," 67; Bauckman in *Gospel Women,* 178, argues that they were not apostles but were well known and beloved by the apostles.
8. Jewett, *Romans,* 961; Lampe, *From Paul to Valentinus,* 175.
9. Cohick, *Earliest Christians,* 216–17.
10. Jewett, *Romans,* 962.
11. Bauckham, *Gospel Women,* 165–85; Cohick, *Earliest Christians,* 315.
12. Jewett, *Romans,* 968.

13. D'Angelo, "Women Partners in the New Testament," 73–75.

14. Lampe, *From Paul to Valentinus,* 179–80.

15. Lampe, *From Paul to Valentinus,* 175.

16. Jewett, *Romans,* 969.

17. Olympas is a shortened form of Olympiodorus or Olympianus, a masculine name; see Jewett, *Romans,* 972.

18. Jewett, *Romans,* 972.

19. Jewett, *Romans,* 972.

20. Lampe, *From Paul to Valentinus,* 175; Jewett, *Romans,* 971–72.

21. Lampe, *From Paul to Valentinus,* 174.

22. Arnold, *Early Christians,* 9–14.

23. Arnold, *Early Christians,* 13.

24. Jewett, "Paul, Phebe, and the Spanish Mission," 145.

25. Jewett, *Romans,* 952–53.

CONCLUSION

1. Stowe, *Women in Sacred History,* 222.

2. Maxwell, *That My Family Should Partake,* 86.

3. For specific examples, see Schottroff, *Lydia's Impatient Sisters,* 209–23.

NEW TESTAMENT CHRONOLOGIES

1. Finegan gives impressive evidence for 2 B.C. in *Handbook of Biblical Chronology,* 288–324; Blumell and Wayment argue for a date closer to 7–6 B.C. in "When Was Jesus Born?" 53–81.

2. Schürer, *History of the Jewish People,* 1:464–67.

3. Schürer, *History of the Jewish People,* 1:465.

4. Schürer, *History of the Jewish People,* 1:465.

5. Finegan, *Handbook of Biblical Chronology,* 299–301.

6. Schürer, *History of the Jewish People,* 1:351–54, 357.

7. Schürer, *History of the Jewish People,* 1:350–51.

8. Rist, "Luke 2:2," 489–91.

9. Finegan, *Handbook of Biblical Chronology,* 302–6.

10. Schürer, *History of the Jewish People,* 1:351–58; Finegan, *Handbook of Biblical Chronology,* 302.

11. Finegan, *Handbook of Biblical Chronology,* 304.

12. Everitt, *Augustus,* 310–14.

13. Finegan, *Handbook of Biblical Chronology,* 345, 367.

14. Adapted from tables in Finegan, *Handbook of Biblical Chronology,* 389, 402.

ANCIENT SOURCES
AND ABBREVIATIONS

No source exceeds the value of canonized scripture to bring the women of the New Testament vividly to life, and yet close examination of the numerous histories, reports, and other documents surviving from the first century A.D. and shortly thereafter is instrumental in augmenting truths found in scripture. Jewish, Greco-Roman, and early Christian sources all add dimension to daily life in Jewish and Hellenistic societies during the New Testament era.

Writings from early Jewish historians, philosophers, and other writers contribute insight to everyday life in New Testament times. Observations from the Jewish historian Josephus (A.D. 37–100) are invaluable for visualizing religious ritual and history. Josephus's genealogical pedigree—a mother of royal Davidic descent and a father of priestly descent—adds credibility to his perspective. Similarly, the Hellenistic Jewish philosopher Philo (20 B.C.–A.D. 50), hailing from a highly respected and wealthy family in Alexandria, Egypt, provides an authentic elite viewpoint on Jewish life. Finally, Joshua son of Sira (Ben Sira), a Jewish scribe in Jerusalem, wrote a collection of ethical teachings around 180–175 B.C. that increase our ability to understand Jewish thinking about women's place in society.

Jewish literary works cited include apocryphal and pseudepigraphal works written during the intertestamental period and the early Christian era. Rabbinic literature, especially the Mishnah and Tosefta, a compilation of sayings taught as the oral law before A.D. 200, provide essential context. Varied and sometimes contradictory views on the roles and privileges of men and women are highlighted in Jewish Midrashim, written traditions that evolved for applying Jewish law.

This volume also references Roman and Greek works describing society, domestic environments, and aristocratic life. A sampling of those cited includes several prominent historians and politicians. Tacitus (A.D. 56–117) wrote of events throughout the first-century empire that sometimes reference women and family. Suetonius (A.D. 69–ca. 122) gives perspectives on life in densely populated cities of the time, including the Jewish community in Rome. Dio Cassius (ca. A.D. 155–235) wrote an eighty-volume Roman history. And though the writings of the Roman poet Juvenal (ca. A.D. 60–138) cannot be taken as a literal description of Roman life, his satirical view of early imperial Rome contributes occasional hints on attitudes about women in general. Because these authors overwhelmingly focused on aristocratic life, observations about other social classes are incidental inclusions.

Early Christian theologians and historians are a third important category of primary sources describing New Testament women. Although Clement of Alexandria (ca. 150–215), Tertullian (160–225), and Origen (184–253) were not contemporaries with these women, these Christian fathers and many others knew their stories and spoke of them. They and other early Christians offered viewpoints that give an indication of how early Christian women were remembered in the decades and centuries after their death.

Because the references for these ancient sources are abbreviated in the text, the following key to the various works and their abbreviations is helpful.

OLD TESTAMENT PSEUDEPIGRAPHA AND APOCRYPHA

JosAsen	*Joseph and Asenath*
Jub	*Jubilees*
T Reu	*Testament of Reuben*
T Levi	*Testament of Levi*
T Jud	*Testament of Judah*
Aris	*Letter of Aristeas*
2 Macc	*2 Maccabees*
Jdt	*Judith*
Ben Sira	*Wisdom of Ben Sira/Ecclesiasticus*

ANCIENT JUDEAN SOURCES

Josephus (A.D. 37–100)

Apion	*Against Apion*
Ant	*The Antiquities of the Jews*
War	*The Jewish War*
Life	*Life*

Philo (20 B.C.–A.D. 50)

Leg All	*Allegorical Interpretation*
Embassy	*On the Embassy to Gaius*
Prelim Stud	*On the Preliminary Studies*
Spec Leg	*On the Special Laws*

MISHNAH, TALMUD, AND RELATED RABBINIC LITERATURE

The prefixes in the references refer to the specific Talmudic tractate from which the passage is cited: y=Jerusalem Talmud; b=Babylonian Talmud; t=Tosefta; and m=Mishnah.

Aboth	Aboth	Mid	Middoth
BQ	Bava Qamma	MQ	Mo'ed Qatan
Ber	Berakoth	Naz	Nazir
Dem	Demai	Ned	Nedarim
Erub	Erubin	Nid	Niddah
Gen Rab	Genesis Rabbah	Pes	Pesahim
Gitt	Gittin	Qidd	Qiddushin
Hag	Hagigah	Shabb	Shabbath
Hal	Hallah	Sheb	Shebi'ith
Hull	Hullin	Shek	Shekalim
Kel	Kelim	Sot	Sotah
Ker	Keritoth	Toh	Tohoroth
Ket	Ketuboth	Yeb	Yebamoth
Meg	Megillah	Yoma	Yoma
Men	Menahoth		

NEW TESTAMENT APOCRYPHA, PSEUDEPIGRAPHA, AND GNOSTIC TEXTS

Assum Vir	Assumption of the Virgin	GPhil	Gospel of Philip
DSav	Dialogue of the Savior	GThom	Gospel of Thomas
GBir	Gospel of the Birth of Mary	Prot Jas	Protevangelium of James
GMary	Gospel of Mary	SophJesChr	Sophia of Jesus Christ
GNic	Gospel of Nicodemus (includes Acts of Pilate)		

EARLY CHRISTIAN AND GRECO-ROMAN SOURCES

Ambrose (ca. A.D. 340–397)

    Fid   *On the Christian Faith/De Fide*

Apuleius (ca. A.D. 125–180)

    Met   *The Golden Ass/Metamorphoses*

Arius Didymus (1st century B.C.)

    Ethics   *Epitome of Peripatetic Ethics*

Aristotle (384–322 B.C.)

    Pol   *Politics*

Augustine (A.D. 354–430)

    Catech   *Catechizing the Uninstructed*

Cicero (106–43 B.C.)

    Verr   *In Verrem*

Clement of Alexandria (ca. A.D. 150–215)

    Misc   *Miscellanies/Stromata*

Cyprian (3rd cent A.D.)

    Don   *To Donatus*

    Dig   *Roman Law/Digest*

Dio Cassius (ca. A.D. 155–235)

    Hist Rom   *Roman History*

Eusebius (A.D. 263–340)

    Hist Eccl   *Ecclesiastical History*

Gregory the Great (ca. A.D. 540–604)

    Hom   *Homilies*

Horace (65–8 B.C.)

    Sat   *Satires*

Ignatius (bishop of Antioch A.D. 100–118)

    Eph   *To the Ephesians*

    Smyrn   *To the Smyrnaeans*

Iraneaus (A.D. 120–202)

    HaerAgainst   *Heresies/Aversus Haereses*

Jerome (ca. A.D. 347–420)

    Comm Matt   *Commentary on Matthew*

John Chrysostom (A.D. 337–407)

    HomActs   *Homilies on Acts*

Justin Martyr (A.D. 110–165)

    Dial   *Dialogue with Trypho*

Juvenal (ca. A.D. 60–138)

    Sat   *Satires*

Marcarius Magnes (early 4th century A.D.)

    Apoc   *Apocriticus*

Martial (A.D. 40–103)

    Epig   *Epigrams*

Origen [A.D. 185–254]

    Cels   *Against Celsus*

Orosius (A.D. 385–420)

    Pag   *Against the Pagans*

Ovid (43 B.C.–A.D. 18)

    Fast   *The Festivals/Fasti*

Pliny the Elder (A.D. 23–79)

    Nat His   *Natural History*

Pliny the Younger (A.D. 61–112)

    Ep   *Letters/Epistulae*

    Pan   *Panegyricus*

    LXX   Old Testament in Greek/Septuagint

Soranus (A.D. 100–138)

    Gyn   *Gynaecology*

Strabo (64 B.C.–A.D.24)

    Geogr   *Geography*

Suetonius (A.D. 69–ca. 122)

    Gramm   *On Grammarians/De Grammaticis*

    Claud   *Claudius*

    Tit   *Titus*

Tacitus (A.D. 56–117)

    Ann   *Annals*

    Hist   *Histories*

Tertullian (A.D. 160–225)

    Marc   *Against Marcion*

    Prax   *Against Praxeas*

    Virg   *The Veiling of Virgins*

    Nat   *To the Heathens/Ad Nationes*

Valerius Maximus (early first century A.D.)

    Memo   *Memorable Doings and Sayings*

MODERN SOURCES

Abrahamsen, Valerie. "Women at Philippi: The Pagan and Christian Evidence." *Journal of Feminist Studies in Religion* 3, no. 2 (1987), 17–30.

Alföldy, Géza. *The Social History of Rome.* David Braund and Frank Pollock, trans. Baltimore, Md.: Johns Hopkins University Press, 1988.

The Anchor Bible Dictionary. Edited by David Noel Freedman et al. 6 vols. New York: Doubleday, 1992.

Arlandson, James Malcolm. *Women, Class, and Society in Early Christianity: Models from Luke–Acts.* Peabody, Mass.: Hendrickson, 1997.

Arnold, Eberhard, ed. *The Early Christians: In Their Own Words.* Farmington, Pa.: Plough, 1997.

Atkinson, David. *The Message of Ruth: The Wings of Refuge.* Downers Grove, Ill.: Inter-Varsity, 1983.

Bailey, Randall C. *David in Love and War: The Pursuit of Power in 2 Samuel 10–12.* Journal for the Study of the Old Testament, Supplement Series 75. Sheffield, England: Sheffield Academic, 1990.

Baker, James R. *Women's Rights in Old Testament Times.* Salt Lake City: Signature Books, 1992.

Bal, Mieke. *Lethal Love: Feminist Literary Readings of Biblical Love Stories.* Bloomington, Ind.: Indiana University Press, 1987.

Bauckham, Richard. *Gospel Women: Studies of the Named Women in the Gospels.* Grand Rapids, Mich.: Eerdmans, 2002.

Beattie, D. R. G. "The Book of Ruth as Evidence for Israelite Legal Practice." *Vetus Testamentum* 24, no. 3 (July 1974): 251–67.

Belnap, Daniel. "Clothed with Salvation: The Garden, the Veil, Tabitha, and Christ." *Studies in the Bible and Antiquity* 4 (2012): 43–69.

Berlin, Adele. "Characterization in Biblical Narrative: David's Wives." *Journal of the Study of the Old Testament* 23 (1982): 69–85.

Blumell, Lincoln H. *Lettered Christians.* Boston: Brill, 2012.

Blumell, Lincoln H., and Thomas A. Wayment. "When Was Jesus Born? A Response to a Recent Proposal." *BYU Studies* 51, no. 3 (2012): 53–81.

Boling, Robert G. *Joshua.* Anchor Bible 6. Garden City, N.Y.: Doubleday, 1982.

Borg, Marcus J. "The Palestinian Background for a Life of Jesus." In Shanks, *Search for Jesus,* 37–57.

Borowski, Obed. *Daily Life in Biblical Times.* Atlanta, Ga.: Society of Biblical Literature, 2003.

Bowen, Matthew. "'According to All That You Demanded' (Deut 18:16): The Literary Use of Names and *Leitworte* as Antimonarchic Polemic in the Deuteronomistic History." Doctoral dissertation, Catholic University of America, forthcoming.

Bradley, Keith R. *Discovering the Roman Family: Studies in Roman Social History.* New York: Oxford Press, 1991.

————. *Slavery and Society at Rome.* Cambridge: Cambridge University Press, 1994.

Brenner, Athalya, ed. *Ruth and Esther: A Feminist Companion to the Bible.* Sheffield, England: Sheffield Academic, 1999.

Bright, John. *A History of Israel.* 4th ed. Louisville, Ky.: Westminster John Knox, 2000.

Brock, Ann Graham. *Mary Magdalene, the First Apostle: The Struggle for Authority.* Cambridge, Mass.: Harvard University Press, 2003.

Bromily, Geoffrey W., ed. *The International Standard Bible Encyclopedia.* 4 vols. Grand Rapids, Mich.: Eerdmans, 1986.

Brown, Francis, S. R. Driver, and Charles A. Briggs. *A Hebrew and English Lexicon of the Old Testament.* Oxford: Clarendon, 1951.

Brown, Raymond E. *The Birth of the Messiah: A Commentary of the Infancy Narratives in Matthew and Luke.* Garden City, N.Y.: Doubleday, 1977.

Brown, Raymond E., Karl P. Donfried, Joseph A. Fitzmyer, and John Reumann, eds. *The Gospel according to John.* 2 vols. Anchor Bible 29–29A. Garden City, N.Y.: Doubleday, 1966–70.

————. *Mary in the New Testament.* Philadelphia: Fortress Press, 1978.

Brown, Robert K., and Philip W. Comfort, trans. *The New Greek Interlinear New Testament.* Wheaton, Ill.: Tyndale House, 1900.

Brown, S. Kent. "Family and Home in the Savior's Life and Ministry." In *To Save the Lost: An Easter Celebration,* edited by Richard Neitzel Holzapfel and Kent P. Jackson. Provo, Utah: BYU Religious Studies Center, 2009.

————. *Mary and Elisabeth: Noble Daughters of God.* American Fork, Utah: Covenant Communications, 2002.

Bruce, F. F. *The Gospel of John.* Grand Rapids, Mich.: Eerdmans, 1989.

————. *New Testament History.* Garden City, N.Y.: Doubleday, 1972.

————. *Philippians.* Peabody, Mass.: Hendrickson, 1983.

Cameron, Averil, and Amélie Kuhrt. *Images of Women in Antiquity.* Detroit: Wayne State University Press, 1993.

Campbell, Edward. *Ruth.* Anchor Bible 7. Garden City, N.Y.: Doubleday, 1975.

Charlesworth, J. H., ed. *The Old Testament Pseudepigrapha.* 2 vols. Garden City, N.Y.: Doubleday, 1983–85.

Cogan, Mordechai. *1 Kings.* Anchor Bible 10. New York: Doubleday, 2001.

Cohen, Shaye J. D. "Was Timothy Jewish (Acts 16:1–3)? Patristic Exegesis, Rabbinic Law, and Matrilineal Descent." *Journal of Biblical Literature* 105, no. 2 (1986): 251–68.

Cohick, Lynn H. *Women in the World of the Earliest Christians.* Grand Rapids, Mich.: Baker Academic, 2009.

Corley, Kathleen E. *Private Women, Public Meals: Social Conflict in the Synoptic Tradition.* Peabody, Mass.: Hendrickson, 1993.

———. "Slaves, Servants and Prostitutes: Gender and Social Class in Mark." In Levine, *Feminist Companion to Mark*, 196–97.

———. *Women and the Historical Jesus: Feminist Myths of Christian Origins.* Santa Rosa, Calif.: Polebridge, 2002.

Cosgrove, Charles H. "A Woman's Unbound Hair in the Greco-Roman World, with Special Reference to the Story of the 'Sinful Woman' in Luke 7:36–50." *Journal of Biblical Literature* 124, no. 4 (2005): 675–92.

Cotter, Wendy. "Mark's Hero of the Twelfth-Year Miracles: The Healing of the Woman with the Hemorrhage and the Raising of Jairus's Daughter (Mark 5:21–43)." In Levine, *Feminist Companion to Mark*, 59–78.

Cranfield, C. E. B. *A Critical and Exegetical Commentary on the Epistle to the Romans.* 2 vols. International Critical Commentary. Edinburgh: T. & T. Clark, 1975–79.

Cross, Frank Moore. *From Epic to Canon: History and Literature in Ancient Israel.* Baltimore, Md.: Johns Hopkins University Press, 1998.

Cundall, Arthur E., and Leon Morris. *Judges [and] Ruth.* Tyndale Old Testament Commentaries. Chicago: Inter-Varsity, 1968.

Dahl, Larry E., and Donald Q. Cannon, eds. *Teachings of Joseph Smith.* Salt Lake City: Bookcraft, 1997.

Danby, H., trans. *The Mishnah.* Oxford: Oxford University Press, 1933.

D'Angelo, Mary Rose. "Women in Luke-Acts: A Redactional View." *Journal of Biblical Literature* 109, no. 3 (1990): 441–61.

———. "Women Partners in the New Testament." *Journal of Feminist Studies in Religion,* 6, no. 1 (Spring 1990): 65–86.

Daniel-Rops, Henri. *Daily Life in Palestine at the Time of Christ.* London: Phoenix Press, 1979.

DeWaard, Jan, and Eugene A. Nida. *A Translator's Handbook on the Book of Ruth.* New York: United Bible Societies, 1973.

Edersheim, Alfred. *The Life and Times of Jesus the Messiah.* Peabody, Mass.: Hendrickson, 1993.

Ehrman, Bart D. *Peter, Paul, and Mary Magdalene: The Followers of Jesus in History and Legend.* Oxford: Oxford University Press, 2006.

Elliot, J. K. "Anna's Age." *Novum Testamentum* 30, no. 2 (April 1988): 100–102.

———, ed. *The Apocryphal New Testament.* Oxford: Oxford University Press, 1999.

Esler, Philip F., and Ronald Piper. *Lazarus, Mary and Martha.* Minneapolis: Fortress, 2006.

Everitt, Anthony. *Augustus: The Life of Rome's First Emperor.* New York: Random House, 2006.

Falk, Ze'ev W. *Hebrew Law in Biblical Times.* 2nd ed. Provo, Utah: Brigham Young University Press, 2001.

Farrar, Frederic W. *The Life of Christ.* 1874. Reprint, Salt Lake City: Bookcraft, 1994.

Finegan, Jack. *The Archaeology of the New Testament: The Life of Jesus and the Beginning of the Early Church.* Rev. ed. Princeton: Princeton University Press, 1992.

———. *Handbook of Biblical Chronology: Principles of Time Reckoning in the Ancient World and Problems of Chronology in the Bible.* Rev. ed. Peabody, Mass.: Hendrickson, 1998.

Fiorenza, Elisabeth Schüssler. *But She Said.* Boston: Beacon, 1992.

———. "The 'Quilting' of Women's History: Phebe of Cenchreae." In *Embodied Love: Sensuality and Relationship as Feminist Values,* edited by Paula M. Cooey, Sharon A. Farmer, and Mary Ellen Ross, 35–49. San Francisco: Harper and Row, 1987.

Fischer, Irmtraud. "The Book of Ruth: A 'Feminist' Commentary to the Torah?" In Brenner, *Ruth and Esther,* 24–49.

Fitzmyer, Joseph A. *The Acts of the Apostles.* Anchor Bible 31. New York: Doubleday, 1998.

———. *The Gospel according to Luke.* Anchor Bible 28–28A. Garden City, N.Y.: Doubleday, 1981–85.

Friedman, Mordechai A. "Tamar, a Symbol of Life: The 'Killer Wife' Superstition in the Bible and Jewish Tradition." *AJS Review* 15, no. 1 (Spring 1990): 23–61.

Frymer-Kensky, Tikva. "Rahab." In Meyers, *Women in Scripture,* 140–41.

———. *Reading the Women of the Bible: A New Interpretation of Their Stories.* New York: Schocken Books, 2002.

———. "Tamar 1." In Meyers, *Women in Scripture,* 161–63.

Gardiner, Alan H. "The Egyptian Origin of Some English Personal Names." *Journal of the American Oriental Society* 56, no. 2 (June 1936): 189–97.

Gardner, Jane F. *Women in Roman Law and Society.* London: Croom Helm, 1986.

Gaskill, Alonzo. "'The Ceremony of the Shoe': A Ritual of God's Ancient Covenant People." In *By Our Rites of Worship: Latter-day Saint Views on Ritual in Scripture, History, and Practice,* edited by Daniel Belnap, 133–50. Provo, Utah: BYU Religious Studies Center, 2013.

Gaventa, Beverly R. *Mary: Glimpses of the Mother of Jesus.* Columbia, S.C.: University of South Carolina Press, 1995.

Gench, Francis Taylor. *Back to the Well: Women's Encounters with Jesus in the Gospels.* Louisville, Ky.: Westminster John Knox, 2004.

Getty-Sullivan, Mary Ann. *Women in the New Testament.* Collegeville, Minn.: Liturgical Press, 2001.

Ginzberg, Louis. *The Legends of the Jews.* 7 vols. Baltimore, Md.: Johns Hopkins University Press, 1998.

Goodman, Martin. *The Ruling Class of Judaea: The Origins of the Jewish Revolt against Rome A.D. 66–70.* Cambridge: Cambridge University Press, 1987.

Grey, Matthew J., and Jodi Magness. "Finding Samson in Byzantine Galilee: The 2011–2012 Archaeological Excavations at Huqoq." *Studies in the Bible and Antiquity* 5 (2013): 1–30.

Grimké, Sarah Moore. *Letters on the Equality of the Sexes and the Condition of Woman, Addressed to Mary S. Parker.* 1838. Reprint, New York: Burt Franklin, 1970.

Gritz, Sharon Hodgin. *Paul, Women Teachers, and the Mother Goddess at Ephesus.* Lanham, Md.: University Press of America, 1991.

Grossman, Jonathan. "Gleaning among the Ears—Gathering among the Sheaves: Characterizing the Image of the Supervising Boy (Ruth 2)." *Journal of Biblical Literature* 126 (2007): 703–16.

Grossman, Susan. "Women and the Jerusalem Temple." In *Daughters of the King: Women and the Synagogue,* edited by Susan Grossman and Rivka Haut, 15–37. Philadelphia: Jewish Publications Society, 1992.

Gruen, Erich S. *Diaspora: Jews amidst Greeks and Romans.* Cambridge, Mass.: Harvard University Press, 2002.

Hafen, Bruce C., and Marie K. Hafen. *The Belonging Heart: The Atonement and Relationships with God and Family.* Salt Lake City: Deseret Book, 1994.

Hamilton, Victor P. "The Book of Genesis Chapters 18–50." In *The New International Commentary on the Old Testament,* edited by R. K. Harrison and Robert L. Hubbard Jr. 24 vols. Grand Rapids, Mich.: Eerdmans, 1995.

Hamlin, E. John. *Surely There Is a Future: A Commentary on the Book of Ruth.* Grand Rapids, Mich.: Eerdmans, 1996.

Hanson, K. C., and Douglas E. Oakman. *Palestine in the Time of Jesus: Social Structures and Social Conflicts.* 2nd ed. Minneapolis: Fortress, 1998.

Harris, William V. *Ancient Literacy.* Cambridge, Mass.: Harvard University Press, 1989.

Haskins, Susan. *Mary Magdalen: Myth and Metaphor.* New York: Harcourt Brace, 1993.

Herzenberg, Caroline L., Susan V. Meschel, and James A. Altena. "Women Scientists and Physicians of Antiquity and the Middle Ages." *Journal of Chemical Education* 68, no. 2 (February 1991): 101–5.

Hock, Ronald F. *The Social Context of Paul's Ministry: Tentmaking and Apostleship.* Philadelphia: Fortress, 1980.

Hoerth, Alfred J. *Archaeology and the Old Testament.* Grand Rapids, Mich.: Baker Books, 1998.

Holzapfel, Jeni Broberg, and Richard Neitzel Holzapfel. *Sisters at the Well: Women and the Life and Teachings of Jesus.* Salt Lake City: Bookcraft, 1993.

Hoppin, Ruth. *Priscilla's Letter: Finding the Author of the Epistle to the Hebrews.* Fort Bragg, Calif.: Lost Cost, 2009.

Huntsman, Eric D. *God So Loved the World.* Salt Lake City: Deseret Book, 2011.

———. *Good Tidings of Great Joy: An Advent Celebration of the Savior's Birth.* Salt Lake City: Deseret Book, 2011.

———. "Mary Magdalene: Biblical Enigma." Lecture presented at the BYU Museum of Art lecture series, "Mystery, Metaphor, and Meaning: LDS Perspectives on *The Da Vinci Code,*" Provo, Utah, February 25, 2004.

Hymns of The Church of Jesus Christ of Latter-day Saints. Salt Lake City: The Church of Jesus Christ of Latter-day Saints, 1985.

Ilan, Tal. *Jewish Women in Greco-Roman Palestine: An Inquiry into Image and Status.* Tübingen, Ger.: J. C. B. Mohr, 1995.

———. *Lexicon of Jewish Names in Late Antiquity.* 4 vols. Tübingen, Germany: Mohr Siebeck, 2008.

Jackson, Kent P., comp. and ed. *Joseph Smith's Commentary on the Bible.* Salt Lake City: Deseret Book, 1994.

Jeffers, James S. *The Greco-Roman World of the New Testament Era: Exploring the Background of Early Christianity.* Downers Grove, Ill.: InterVarsity, 1999.

Jeremias, Joachim. *Jerusalem in the Time of Jesus.* Philadelphia: Fortress, 1969, 1975.

Jewett, Robert. "Paul, Phoebe, and the Spanish Mission." In *The Social World of Formative Christianity and Judaism,* edited by Jacob Neusner et al., 142–61. Philadelphia: Fortress, 1988.

———. *Romans: A Commentary.* With Roy David Kotansky. Edited by Eldon Jay Epp. Minneapolis: Fortress, 2007.

Josephus, Flavius. *The Complete Works of Josephus.* Translated by William Whiston. Peabody, Mass.: Hendrickson, 1987.

Journal of Discourses. 26 vols. Liverpool: Latter-day Saints Book Depot, 1854–86.

Kautzsch, E., and A. E. Cowley. *Gesenius' Hebrew Grammar.* Oxford: Clarendon, 1970.

Keil, C. F., and F. Delitzsch. *Commentary on the Old Testament.* 10 vols. Peabody, Mass.: Hendrickson, 1996.

Kenyon, Kathleen M. *The Bible and Recent Archaeology.* London: British Museum Publications, 1978.

Ketter, Peter. *Christ and Womankind.* Westminster, Md.: Newman, 1952.

Kilgallen, John J. "John the Baptist, the Sinful Woman, and the Pharisee." *Journal of Biblical Literature* 104, no. 4 (1985): 675–79.

King, Karen L. *The Gospel of Mary of Magdala: Jesus and the First Woman Apostle.* Santa Rosa, Calif.: Polebridge, 2003.

Kraemer, Ross S. "Jewish Mothers and Daughters in the Greco-Roman World." In *The Jewish Family in Antiquity,* edited by S. J. D. Cohen, 89–112. Atlanta, Ga.: Scholars, 1993.

———. "Women in the Religions of the Greco-Roman World." *Religious Studies Review* 9, no. 2 (April 1983): 127–39.

———. *Women's Religions in the Greco-Roman World: A Sourcebook.* Oxford: Oxford University Press, 2004.

Lachs, Samuel Tobias. "Studies in the Semitic Background to the Gospel of Matthew." *Jewish Quarterly Review,* New Series 67, no. 4 (April 1977): 195–217.

Laffey, Alice L. "Ruth." In *The New Jerome Biblical Commentary,* edited by Raymond E. Brown, Joseph A. Fitzmyer, and Roland E. Murphy, 553–57. Upper Saddle River, N.J.: Prentice Hall, 1990.

Lampe, Peter. *From Paul to Valentinus: Christians at Rome in the First Two Centuries.* Minneapolis: Fortress, 2003.

Leon, Harry J. *The Jews of Ancient Rome.* Peabody, Mass.: Hendrickson, 1960.

Levenson, Jon D. "1 Samuel 25 as Literature and as History." *Catholic Biblical Quarterly* 40 (1978): 11–28.

Levenson, Jon D., and Baruch Halpern. "The Political Import of David's Marriages." *Journal of Biblical Literature* 99, no. 4 (1980): 507–18.

Levine, Amy-Jill, ed. *Feminist Companion to Mark.* With Marianne Blickenstaff. Sheffield, England: Sheffield Academic, 2001.

Limberis, Vasiliki. "Elizabeth." In Meyers, *Women in Scripture,* 73–74.

———. "Widow of Nain." In Meyers, *Women in Scripture,* 439–40.

Mace, David R. *Hebrew Marriage: A Sociological Study.* New York: Philosophical Library, 1953.

Macurdy, Grace Harriet. *Vassal-Queens and Some Contemporary Women in the Roman Empire.* Baltimore, Md.: Johns Hopkins, 1937.

Madvig, Donald H. "Joshua." In *The Expositor's Bible Commentary: Old Testament,* edited by Kenneth L. Barker and John R. Kohlenberger III, 289–327. Grand Rapids, Mich.: Zondervan, 1994.

Malbon, Elizabeth Struthers. "The Poor Widow in Mark and Her Poor Rich Readers." In Levine, *Feminist Companion to Mark,* 111–28.

Marshall, I. Howard. *Commentary on Luke: New International Greek Testament Commentary.* Grand Rapids, Mich.: Eerdmans, 1978.

Massey, Michael. *Women in Ancient Greece and Rome.* Cambridge: Cambridge University Press, 1988.

Matthews, Victor H. *Manners and Customs in the Bible.* Peabody, Mass.: Hendrickson, 1991.

Maxwell, Neal A. "Called to Serve." In *BYU 1993–94 Devotional and Fireside Speeches,* 127–38. Provo, Utah: Brigham Young University Press, 1994.

———. *Men and Women of Christ.* Salt Lake City: Bookcraft, 1991.

———. *That My Family Should Partake.* Salt Lake City: Deseret Book, 1974.

McCarter, P. Kyle. *II Samuel.* Anchor Bible 9. Garden City, N.Y.: Doubleday, 1984.

McConkie, Bruce R. *Doctrinal New Testament Commentary.* 3 vols. Salt Lake City: Bookcraft, 1965–73.

McGinn, Thomas A. J. *Prostitution, Sexuality, and the Law of Ancient Rome.* New York: Oxford University Press, 1998.

McKenzie, John L. *The World of the Judges.* Englewood Cliffs, N.J.: Prentice-Hall, 1966.

Meyers, Carol. "Returning Home: Ruth 1:8 and the Gendering of the Book of Ruth." In *Feminist Companion to Ruth*, edited by Athalya Brenner, 85–114. Sheffield, England: Sheffield Academic, 1993.

———. "The Roots of Restriction: Women in Early Israel." *Biblical Archaeologist* 41 (September 1978): 91–103.

———. "Women of the Neighborhood: Informal Female Networks in Ancient Israel." In Brenner, *Ruth and Esther*, 110–27.

———, ed. *Women in Scripture: A Dictionary of Named and Unnamed Women in the Hebrew Bible, the Apocryphal/ Deuterocanonical Books, and the New Testament.* Grand Rapids, Mich.: Eerdmans, 2000.

Muhlestein, Kerry M. "Ruth, Redemption, and Covenant." In *The Gospel of Jesus Christ in the Old Testament: The 38th Annual BYU Sidney B. Sperry Symposium*, edited by D. Kelly Ogden, Kerry M. Muhlestein, and Jared Ludlow, 189–208. Provo, Utah: BYU Religious Studies Center, 2009.

Nelson, Russell M. "Christ the Savior Is Born." In *BYU Speeches of the Year, 2002*, 145–49. Provo, Utah: Brigham Young University Press, 2002.

New Bible Dictionary. Edited by J. D. Douglas et al. 2nd ed. Leicester, England: Inter-Varsity, 1982.

The New Smith's Bible Dictionary. Edited by Reuel G. Lemmons. New York: Doubleday, 1996.

Niditch, Susan. "The Wronged Woman Righted: An Analysis of Genesis 38." *The Harvard Theological Review* 72, no. 1–2 (January–April 1979): 143–49.

Nun, Mendel. "Ports of Galilee: Modern Drought Reveals Harbors from Jesus' Time." *Biblical Archaeology Review* 25, no. 4 (July/August 1999): 18–31, 64.

Nutt, Edgar Alan. *Jesus the Virgin-Born.* N.p.: Xulon, 2007.

Ogden, D. Kelly, and Andrew C. Skinner. *The Four Gospels.* A volume in the Verse by Verse series. Salt Lake City: Deseret Book, 2006.

Olson, Camille Fronk. *In the Hands of the Potter.* Salt Lake City: Deseret Book, 2003.

———. *Mary, Martha, and Me.* Salt Lake City: Deseret Book, 2006.

———. *Women of the Old Testament.* Salt Lake City: Deseret Book, 2009.

O'Rahilly, A. "The Two Sisters." *Scripture* 4, no. 3 (July 1949): 68–76.

Osiek, Carolyn, and David L. Balch. *Families in the New Testament World: Households and House Churches.* Louisville, Ky.: Westminster John Knox, 1997.

Parkin, Tim G. *Demography and Roman Society.* Baltimore, Md.: Johns Hopkins University Press, 1992.

Parvey, Constance F. "The Theology and Leadership of Women in the New Testament." In *Religion and Sexism:*

Images of Women in the Jewish and Christian Traditions, edited by Rosemary Radford Ruether, 117–49. New York: Simon and Schuster, 1974.

Patterson, Stephen J. "Sources for a Life of Jesus." In Shanks, *Search for Jesus*, 9–34.

Paul, Shalom M., and William G. Dever. *Biblical Archaeology.* New York: Quadrangle/New York Times Book, 1974.

Peterson, Daniel C., Matthew Roper, and William J. Hamblin. "On Alma 7:10 and the Birthplace of Jesus Christ," 1995. Available at http://publications.maxwellinstitute.byu.edu/transcript/on-alma-7-10-and-the-birthplace-of -jesus-christ/.

Phillips, Anthony. "The Book of Ruth—Deception and Shame." *Journal of Jewish Studies* 37, no. 1 (Spring 1986): 1–17.

Pritchard, James B., ed. *Ancient Near Eastern Texts Relating to the Old Testament.* 3rd ed. Princeton: Princeton University Press, 1969.

Rauber, D. F. "The Book of Ruth." In *Literary Interpretations of Biblical Narratives*, edited by Kenneth R. R. Gros Louis, James S. Ackerman, and Thayer S. Warshaw, 163–76. Nashville, Tenn.: Abingdon, 1974.

Reed, Jonathan L. *Archaeology and the Galilean Jesus: A Re-examination of the Evidence.* Harrisburg, Pa.: Trinity Press International, 2002.

Reid, Barbara. *Choosing the Better Part? Women in the Gospel of Luke.* Collegeville, Minn.: Liturgical Press, 1996.

Reimer, Ivoni Richter. *Women in the Acts of the Apostles.* Minneapolis: Fortress, 1995.

Reinhartz, Adele. "From Narrative to History: The Resurrection of Mary and Martha." In *Women like This: New Perspectives on Jewish Women in the Greco-Roman World*, edited by Amy-Jill Levine, 161–84. Atlanta: Scholars, 1991.

Ricci, Carla. *Mary Magdalene and Many Others: Women Who Followed Jesus.* Minneapolis, Minn.: Fortress, 1994.

Ricks, Stephen D. "No Prophet Is Accepted in His Own Country." In *The Gospels*, vol. 5 of Studies in Scripture series, edited by Kent P. Jackson and Robert L. Millet, 201–12. Salt Lake City: Deseret Book, 1986.

———. "Ruth." In *Genesis to 2 Samuel*, vol. 3 of Studies in Scripture series, edited by Kent P. Jackson and Robert L. Millet, 249–57. Salt Lake City: Deseret Book, 1989.

Rist, John M. "Luke 2:2: Making Sense of the Date of Jesus' Birth." *Journal of Theological Studies* ns 56, no. 2 (October 2005): 489–91.

Roberts, A., and J. Donaldson, eds. *Ante-Nicene Fathers: The Writings of the Fathers Down to A.D. 325.* 10 vols. Peabody, Mass.: Hendrickson, 1999.

Robinson, James M., ed. *The Nag Hammadi Library.* San Francisco: HarperCollins, 1990.

Rowlandson, Jane, ed. *Women and Society in Greek and Roman Egypt: A Sourcebook.* Cambridge: Cambridge University Press, 1998.

Schaberg, Jane. "How Mary Magdalene Became a Whore." *Bible Review* 8, no. 5 (October 1992): 31–37, 51–52.

———. *The Illegitimacy of Jesus: A Feminist Theological Interpretation of the Infancy Narratives.* San Francisco: Harper and Row, 1987.

Scheck, Thomas P., trans. *St. Jerome: Commentary on Matthew.* Washington, D.C.: Catholic University of America Press, 2008.

Schneemelcher, Wilhelm, ed. *New Testament Apocrypha.* Vol. 1, *Gospels and Related Writings.* English translation edited by R. McL. Wilson. Rev. ed. Cambridge, England: James Clark, 1991.

Schneider, Tammi J. *Mothers of Promise: Women in the Book of Genesis.* Grand Rapids, Mich.: Baker, 2008.

Schottroff, Luise. *Lydia's Impatient Sisters: A Feminist Social History of Early Christianity.* Louisville, Ky.: Westminster John Knox, 1995.

Schürer, Emil. *A History of the Jewish People in the Age of Jesus Christ.* Revised and edited by Géza Vermès et al. 4 vols. Edinburgh: T. & T. Clark, 1973–87.

Shanks, Hershel, ed. *The Search for Jesus: Modern Scholarship Looks at the Gospels.* Washington, D.C.: Biblical Archaeology Society, 1994.

Shepherd, David. "Violence in the Fields? Translating, Reading, and Revising in Ruth 2." *Catholic Biblical Quarterly* 63, no. 3 (July 2001): 444–63.

Simmons, William A. *Peoples of the New Testament World.* Peabody, Mass.: Hendrickson, 2008.

Smith, Joseph Fielding. *Doctrines of Salvation.* Compiled by Bruce R. McConkie. 3 vols. Salt Lake City: Bookcraft, 1954–56.

Speiser, E. A. *Genesis: A New Translation with Introduction and Commentary.* Anchor Bible 1. New York: Doubleday, 1962.

Spencer, F. Scott. *Dancing Girls, Loose Ladies, and Women of the Cloth: The Women in Jesus' Life.* New York: Continuum, 2004.

———. "Out of Mind, Out of Voice: Slave-Girls and Prophetic Daughters in Luke-Acts." *Biblical Interpretation* 7, no. 2 (1999): 133–55.

Stowe, Harriet Beecher. *Women in Sacred History.* Rev. ed. New York: Portland House, 1990. First published 1893 by Fords, Howard, and Hulbert.

Streete, Gail Corrington. "Women as Sources of Redemption and Knowledge in Early Christian Traditions." In *Women and Christian Origins,* edited by R. S. Kraemer and M. R. D'Angelo, 330–54. New York: Oxford University Press, 1999.

Swanson, Reuben J., ed. *New Testament Greek Manuscripts: Luke.* Sheffield, England: Sheffield Academic, 1995.

Swidler, Leonard. *Biblical Affirmations of Women.* Philadelphia: Westminster, 1979.

Talmage, James E. *Jesus the Christ: A Study of the Messiah and His Mission according to Holy Scriptures Both Ancient and Modern.* Classics in Mormon Literature series. Salt Lake City: Deseret Book, 1983.

Talmon, Shemaryahu. "The Gezer Calendar and the Seasonal Cycle of Ancient Canaan." *Journal of the American Oriental Society* 83, no. 2 (April–June 1963): 177–87.

Theological Dictionary of the New Testament. Edited by Gerhard Kittel and G. Friedrich. Translated by G. W. Bromiley. 10 vols. Grand Rapids, Mich.: Eerdmans, 1964–76.

Thompson, Cynthia L. "Hairstyles, Head-Coverings, and St. Paul: Portraits from Roman Corinth." *Biblical Archaeologist* 51, no. 2 (June 1988): 99–115.

Thompson, Thomas, and Dorothy Thompson. "Some Legal Problems in the Book of Ruth." *Vetus Testamentum* 18 (1968): 79–99.

Trible, Phyllis. *God and the Rhetoric of Sexuality.* Philadelphia: Fortress, 1978.

———. "Two Women in a Man's World: A Reading of the Book of Ruth." *Soundings* 59, no. 3 (Fall 1976): 251–79.

Unger, Merrill F. *The New Unger's Bible Dictionary.* Edited by R. K. Harrison, Howard F. Vos, and Cyril J. Barber. Chicago, Ill.: Moody, 1988.

Vamosh, Miriam Feinberg. *Daily Life at the Time of Jesus.* Herzlia, Israel: Palphot, 2004.

Waltke, Bruce K. *Genesis.* Grand Rapids, Mich.: Zondervan, 2001.

Wassen, Cecilia. "The Story of Judah and Tamar in the Eyes of the Earliest Interpreters." *Literature and Theology* 8, no. 4 (December 1994): 354–66.

Wayment, Thomas A., and John Gee. "Did Paul Address His Wife in Philippi?" *Studies in the Bible and Antiquity* 4 (2012): 71–93.

Westenholz, Joan Goodnick. "Tamar, Qĕdēšā, Qadištu, and Sacred Prostitution in Mesopotamia." *The Harvard Theological Review* 82, no. 3 (July 1989): 245–65.

Wharton, J. A. "A Plausible Tale: Story and Theology in II Samuel 9–20, I Kings 1–2." *Interpretation* 35 (1981): 341–54.

Wilken, Robert L. *The Christians as the Romans Saw Them.* New Haven, Conn.: Yale University Press, 1984.

Willard, Francis E. *Women in the Pulpit.* Boston, Mass.: D. Lothrop, 1888.

Witherington, Ben, III. "Anti-Feminist Tendencies of the 'Western' Text of Acts." *Journal of Biblical Literature* 103, no. 1 (March 1984): 82–84.

———. *A Week in the Life of Corinth.* Downers Grove, Ill.: Inter-Varsity, 2012.

———. *Women in the Earliest Churches.* Society for New Testament Studies Monograph Series 59. Cambridge: Cambridge University Press, 1988.

Wray, T. J. *Good Girls, Bad Girls: The Enduring Lessons of Twelve Women of the Old Testament.* Lanham, Md.: Rowman and Littlefield, 2008.

Yee, Gale A. "Fraught with Background: Literary Ambiguity in 2 Samuel 11." *Interpretation: A Journal of Bible and Theology* 42, no. 3 (July 1988): 240–53.

Zertal, Adam. "Israel Enters Canaan: Following the Pottery Trail." *Biblical Archaeology Review* (September/October 1991): 29–47.

SUBJECT INDEX

Page numbers in italics indicate paintings and other visual images.

ABOUT THE ILLUSTRATORS

Al Young Studios is an internationally recognized family of artists whose original oil paintings and drawings have appeared in invitational exhibitions and received awards in international competitions. Their works are also regularly featured in national and international publications. Founded in 1998 by Al and his wife, Nancy, the Studios is organized after the pattern of the Renaissance workshops of the old masters. Each artist works as a peer in the Studios' intensely creative community, employing techniques reaching as far back as the sixteenth century.

Artworks created by the artists of Al Young Studios are part of six ongoing creative projects featured at www.alyoung.com: *Women of the Bible, Heroes of the Book of Mormon, The Messiah, Pioneers of the American West, High Valley,* and *Limited Editions.* In addition to original artworks and fine art prints, the Studios publishes *The Storybook Home Journal* (published bimonthly since 2000), *My Father's Captivity* (a true story of hope and endurance), *The Papers of Seymore Wainscott* (novellas featuring a story of creative genius, home, family, and endurance), and the photographic prints of Tanner Young. All Studios products are available exclusively at www.alyoung.com. In addition to its commercial portfolio, the Studios has a history of consulting in areas of specialization ranging from artwork commissions and illustration to interior design, installation art, stained glass, and furniture.

Al R. Young (BA, MA, BYU). Al has been a professional artist, author, and craftsman for more than thirty-five years. Following postgraduate studies at the University of Virginia, he worked in various occupations for eighteen years: freelance writer and editor; part-time faculty member at Brigham Young University and Utah Technical College; partner in a consulting firm with contracts in the western United States and the Middle East; senior researcher and advanced product designer, senior engineer, and head of corporate communications and documentation.

Elspeth Young (BA in visual arts, BYU). Since graduating magna cum laude from BYU in 2003, Elspeth has worked full-time as an artist of Al Young Studios, where she also plays a major role in the creation and publication of *The Storybook Home Journal.* A diverse range of commissions has given her experience in various media as well as working with project teams. Portraiture and religious subjects continue to be her primary focus, with an increasing amount of time devoted to the Special Projects Department of The Church of Jesus Christ of Latter-day Saints.

Ashton Young (BA in history, BYU). Following his graduation from BYU with a degree in history, Ashton has had diverse experience in oil painting, pen and ink, pencil, stained glass, ceramics, lithography, block printing, working with vinyl, furniture construction, documentary editing of original historical sources, museum-quality custom framing, and exhibit fabrication. The earliest publication of his artwork appeared in *Victoria Magazine* (published by the Hearst Corporation) in 1997 as part of a series accompanying excerpts from *The Country of the Pointed Firs,* by Sarah Orne Jewett.

Tanner Young (BA in art history and curatorial studies, BYU). Tanner is a professional landscape photographer and web systems engineer. He composes and produces music to accompany his photography and videography and has published a variety of piano, choral, and orchestral arrangements and original compositions.